Bleeding Kansas

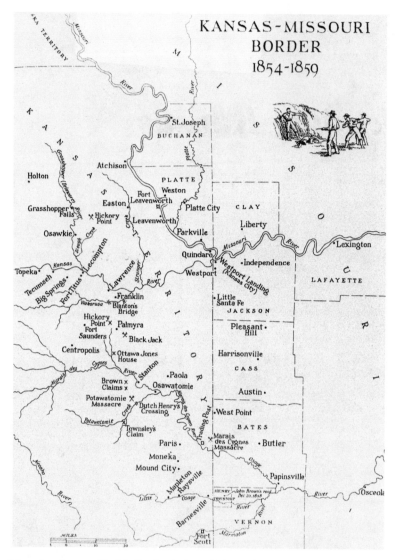

KANSAS-MISSOURI BORDER 1854-1859

NEBRASKA TERRITORY

MISSOURI River

St.Joseph
BUCHANAN

Atchison

Holton

PLATTE
Weston
Fort Leavenworth
Easton
Platte City
CLAY

Grasshopper Falls
Hickory Point
Leavenworth
Parkville
Liberty

Osawkie

Quindaro
Independence
Lexington

Topeka
Kansas
Lecompton
Westport Landing (Kansas City)
Westport

Tecumseh
Big Springs
Fort Titus
Lawrence
LAFAYETTE

Franklin
Blanton's Bridge
Little Santa Fe
JACKSON

Hickory Point
Fort Saunders
Palmyra
Black Jack
Pleasant Hill

Centropolis
Ottawa Jones House
Stanton
Harrisonville
CASS

Brown x Claims x
Paola
Osawatomie
Austin

Potawatomie Massacre
Dutch Henry's Crossing
West Point
BATES

Townsley's Claim
Paris
Marais des Cygnes Massacre
Butler

Moneka

Mound City
Papinsville

Mapleton
Raysville
HENRY TOWNSHIP
John Brown's raid Dec 20, 1858
Osceola

Barnesville
VERNON

Fort Scott

Neosho River

Marais des Cygnes River
Pottawatomie Creek

MILES

Map by James C. Malin in Atlas of American History, *ed. James Truslow Adams (New York: Charles Scribner's Sons, 1943), plate 121. Reprinted by permission of the Gale Group.*

Bleeding Kansas

CONTESTED LIBERTY IN THE CIVIL WAR ERA

Nicole Etcheson

UNIVERSITY PRESS OF KANSAS

Published by the University Press of Kansas (Lawrence, Kansas 66045),
which was organized by the Kansas Board of Regents and is operated and
funded by Emporia State University, Fort Hays State University, Kansas
State University, Pittsburg State University, the University of Kansas, and
Wichita State University

Library of Congress Cataloging-in-Publication Data

Etcheson, Nicole.
  Bleeding Kansas : contested liberty in the Civil War era / Nicole
Etcheson.
        p. cm.
Includes bibliographical references and index.
  ISBN 978-0-7006-1287-1 (cloth : alk. paper)
  ISBN 978-0-7006-1492-9 (paper : alk. paper)
  1. Kansas-Nebraska bill.   2. United States—History—Civil War,
1861–1865—Causes.   3. Kansas—Politics and government—1854–
1861.   4. United States—Politics and government—1849–1861.
5. Slavery—Political aspects—Kansas—History—19th century.
6. African Americans—Civil rights—Kansas—History—19th century.
7. Violence—Kansas—History—19th century.   8. Kansas—Race
relations.   9. United States—Race relations.   I. Title.
  E433.E83 2004
  973.7'113—dc21   2003010980

British Library Cataloguing-in-Publication Data is available.

Printed in the United States of America

10 9 8

The paper used in this publication meets the minimum requirements of
the American National Standard for Permanence of Paper for Printed
Library Materials z39.48-1984.

For my son

CONTENTS

ILLUSTRATIONS

In graduate school, I became interested in the Southerners who settled in the Ohio Valley between the American Revolution and the Civil War. As I studied their political culture for what eventually became a dissertation and later a book, I noticed that references to Kansas occurred over and over again. After that project drew to completion, I began to read about Kansas and discovered a fascinating story that had not been told for a while.

What had struck me during the research for my earlier project was the omnipresence of the Kansas issue throughout the 1850s. It appeared in letter after letter written by Midwesterners. Why, I wondered, was Kansas so important in the minds of people who had not been there, knew no one personally who was there, and had no intention of going to the territory? Eventually I was to find that Kansas meant something not just to Midwesterners but also to New Englanders, Southerners, and African Americans.

But it turned out that Kansas meant different things to all these groups. The literature was fraught with paradoxes. If the Kansas struggle was rooted in slavery, why did so many free-state Kansans seem to care not a whit about the slaves and why did so many proslavery Kansans not own any? If Bleeding Kansas was about racism, then how does one explain the eventual embrace of black rights by someone so fiercely racist as free-state leader Jim Lane? And if it was about economics, then why did so many people venture into guerrilla activities that surely hurt their economic interests? Certainly, slavery, race, and economics played their parts, but I found all the discussions about Kansas contained another element: a concern for the fate of white men's liberty in the republic.

There is sometimes a temptation to treat Kansas as a rather comic-opera sideshow in the great national drama of the 1850s. There is no doubt that Kansas Territory possessed more than its fair share of memorable characters: the aloof, keenly intelligent Charles Robinson; the reckless, rabble-rousing Jim Lane; John Brown, zealous in God's righteous cause; David Atchison, who defended southern rights; Sheriff Sam Jones, who repeatedly tried to enforce "law and order" in Kansas; the frustrated John Calhoun struggling with an intransigent constitutional convention; and an array of governors of varying talents, ranging from the tippling Wilson Shannon to the firm, unswerving John Geary. While I have tried to preserve those qualities that make their stories interesting, I have also tried to take them and their stories seriously, as they deserve. For after all, their stories are about what it means to be free.

The temptation after completing a long project such as this is to selfishly claim all the credit. After all, no one but the author read all that microfilm or all those faded letters. But the truth is that the author has a lot of help from people who make reading microfilm possible, or at least share the author's conviction that reading it is a worthwhile pursuit.

My work on this book began while I was at the University of South Dakota. Alton Lee, Bob Hilderbrand, and Jerry Wolff supported the project in its early stages. Jerry later read the entire manuscript for me and did it with amazing rapidity. Clayton Lehmann helped translate a German poem written by citizens of St. Louis. Judy Sebesta provided a little help with Latin and lots of tea and friendly conversation. The interlibrary loan staff kept me supplied with books and the all-important microfilm. The university's research office provided fellowships that made work in Kansas and Missouri archives possible. Moreover, I thank the members of the history and classics departments at USD for their friendship and collegial support. The weather in South Dakota can be brutally cold, but the people are not.

At the University of Texas at El Paso, Bob Righter and Sherry Smith provided critiques of early drafts. They, along with Charles Martin and other members of the UTEP history department, have heard a great deal about Kansas in the last few years and have never suggested that they are tired of the subject. In fact, they have even provided helpful comments. I thank them for their patience and their friendship. Ken Shover, my predecessor as the expert on the nineteenth-century United

States, has generously given me the benefit of his experience. He slaved over early drafts of chapters and set an unsurpassed example of graciousness to a junior colleague. Gracie Galvez, Olga Narvaez, and the rest of the interlibrary loan staff unflaggingly procured miles of microfilm and untold numbers of books. UTEP granted me a fellowship for work at the Library of Congress.

The staffs of the Illinois State Historical Library, Kansas State Historical Society, University of Kansas Library, Missouri Historical Society in St. Louis, Western Historical Manuscript Collection at the University of Missouri, and Library of Congress were of great help in finding documents and other research materials. I particularly thank Debbie Greeson at the Kansas State Historical Society for facilitating a particularly urgent microfilm request. A number of other archives photocopied and mailed parts of their collections too small to justify a visit but often containing very significant information. They include the Albany Institute of History and Art, Boston University Special Collections, Connecticut Historical Society, Duke University Special Collections Library, Colorado Historical Society, University of Kentucky Library, University of Maine Library, Michigan State University Archives, Minnesota Historical Society, Mississippi Department of Archives and History, New-York Historical Society, Ohio Historical Society, Western History Collections at the University of Oklahoma Libraries, Rutherford B. Hayes Presidential Center, West Virginia and Regional History Collection at West Virginia University, Western Reserve Historical Society, Wichita State University Special Collections, State Historical Society of Wisconsin, and Yale University Library.

Help with photographs and permissions came from Nancy Sherbert of the Kansas State Historical Society, Jackie Jones and Jacqueline Key of the Gale Group, Kim Bauer and Mary Michals of the Illinois State Historical Library, Susan Sutton of the Indiana Historical Society, and Christine Montgomery of the State Historical Society of Missouri.

In addition, I thank Michael Fellman for reading the entire manuscript and for providing uncharacteristically gentle criticism. Ken Winkle provided extensive and very helpful comments that have done much to make this a better book. An anonymous reader for University Press of Kansas also pushed for changes that improved the manuscript. Virgil

Dean has been a friendly supporter of this project for many years. As the Kansas work evolved, Virgil published some of my ideas in *Kansas History,* answered many questions, and only asked an occasional manuscript review in return. Fred Woodward had faith in this project when it was no more than an outline. He and his staff at the University Press of Kansas are models of patience and professionalism. I would particularly like to thank Melinda Wirkus, Susan Schott, and Doris Maxfield for their help.

The support of Drew Cayton, Jim Madison, and Randy Roth has been crucial not just to this project but to my historical career. Randy Roth's class at Grinnell College on the Jacksonian era first stimulated my interest in that period. Jim Madison became my dissertation adviser in graduate school and has been a good-natured supporter ever since. Drew Cayton's work has been an inspiration for many years. I agree with the phrase oft heard at professional conferences, I "admire their work," and their stamina.

As large as are my scholarly debts, they cannot match the personal ones. When we first met, Robert J. Williams asked me, "Do you only read history? Or do you ever read anything interesting?" Over a decade and a half later, I am still not reading anything Robert considers interesting, but he seems resigned to it. He's even learned a few things about Sheriff Jones and Jim Lane along the way. He has not complained, or at least not much, about research trips or conferences that took me away from home. And he did read and painstakingly copyedit the entire manuscript, as well as doing two of the photographs. Our son, Robert, has literally grown up with this book. I was just beginning work on it when he was born. He is now old enough to be excited about having it dedicated to him and exasperated that making a book takes so long. This book is for Robert G. Williams, because he is my son and I love him.

INTRODUCTION: SLAVES *OURSELVES*

On July 4, 1855, Dr. Charles Robinson, a physician from Massachusetts who had settled in Kansas Territory, gave the holiday oration in a grove outside Lawrence. In front of picnicking families, Robinson solemnly condemned the territorial government: "We must not only see black slavery . . . planted in our midst, and against our wishes, but we must become slaves *ourselves.*"[1]

Contemporaries called the summer of 1856, the summer of the Kansas Civil War, Bleeding Kansas, but the conflict extended well before and after that short season. It began with the Kansas-Nebraska Act of 1854 and continued into the bloody border conflict of the national Civil War. Many historical treatments of the Kansas Civil War have focused on the first issue Robinson raised, black slavery. These accounts have assumed that the settlers of Kansas cared deeply about slavery, whether for or against it. Numerous works on the 1850s have treated Kansas as one of the many heated slavery-related issues that widened the breach between North and South and brought on the Civil War. Other discussions, however, have stressed the absence of slaves in the territory and the antiblack sentiments of the settlers and have argued that the settlers' real concerns during the period were economic.[2]

This book concentrates on Robinson's second concern, the political liberties of whites, as crucial to understanding the meaning of Bleeding Kansas. Though the terms *liberty* and *freedom* have been much used in the United States, they are susceptible to varied definitions which are not always universally applied. The struggle to balance personal liberty with communal order, and the rights of individuals and states against the power of the federal government, has led Americans to give the term *liberty* many meanings. Nineteenth-century Americans shared a belief in republicanism, with its emphasis on representative government as the bulwark of the people's rights and liberties, and its fears of potential subversion of those liberties. In a republic, however, liberty's definition always encompassed the right to decide political institutions at the ballot box.[3] It was the denial of that choice at the ballot box that prompted Robinson's attack on the territorial government. It was bad enough, Robinson warned, that "black slavery" was to exist in Kansas. It was worse, however, that slavery's establishment was to be accomplished by disregarding the "wishes" of the majority of white settlers, thereby enslaving voters to the proslavery agenda.

The 1854 Kansas-Nebraska Act sought to expand the political liberties of the territory's white men by giving them the power at the local level to pronounce on the most contentious issue of the time, black slavery. Popular sovereignty, the principle of the Kansas bill, built on the belief that the balance between personal freedom and government power ought to tilt toward the former. Stephen A. Douglas, the chief architect of popular sovereignty in the 1850s, made the slavery issue, once the province of congressional mandate, subject to popular vote. In doing so, Douglas claimed to be fulfilling the philosophy of the American Revolution and the U.S. Constitution. But instead of expanding freedom, what occurred in Kansas constituted the greatest attack on political liberties that nineteenth-century Americans had experienced. Fraud occurred in election after election, with the federal government or its officers frequently upholding the obviously illegitimate results. The territorial legislature, elected in the first instance of fraud, passed draconian proslavery legislation in defiance of the sentiments of most settlers. When settlers resisted this rule, the military suppressed them as rebels and the federal government charged their leaders with treason. These events united free-state settlers in the conviction that their political rights and liberties were being trampled by a government determined to impose slavery upon them. In defying the authority of the territorial government, they declared themselves to be the true protectors of the meaning of liberty bequeathed by the men and women who secured United States independence from British tyranny.

The free-state movement had wide appeal among Northerners. Northern supporters saw the attack on the political rights of settlers in Kansas as a wider attack on liberty. Many Northerners, sympathetic to the abolitionist argument for liberty's moral dimension, nonetheless tolerated the existence of slavery in the name of order and condemned abolitionism as lawless. But Northerners drew the line at protecting slaveowners' rights at the expense of the rights of northern citizens.[4] Not until white Northerners saw how slavery threatened them were they drawn into alliance with abolitionism. When northern settlers found their political rights under attack in Kansas, many Northerners had their eyes opened to the threat slavery posed to their rights.

For proslavery Southerners, white liberty depended on black slavery. Convinced of the ineradicable nature of class division, Southerners believed they had constructed an ideal social order that allowed equality among all whites by suppressing the rights of blacks. To interfere with a white man's control of his slaves was to threaten his liberties. Nor did white Southerners feel enslaving blacks violated republican principles. In addition to finding biblical justifications for slavery, and Lockean justifications of the importance of property rights, their belief in the inherent inferiority of blacks convinced white Southerners that blacks were unfit to enjoy the same liberty as whites. Thus racism reconciled black slavery with republican liberty.

But while Northerners emphasized choice at the ballot box as essential to republican freedom, Southerners did not accept the primacy of majority rule if it threatened established rights to hold slaves or the order that kept the much feared black insurrections at bay. Southerners justified suppression of dissent against slavery, which occurred widely, as necessary and reconciled it with majority rule by arguing that it reflected the wishes of most white Southerners to preserve slave society.[5] Even when Northerners avowed their willingness to support Southerners' rights to their slaves, northern tolerance of abolitionism and emphasis on the right to speak and vote against slavery seemed threatening to both southern life and liberty. White Southerners felt their liberty endangered by an abolitionist movement that imperiled property rights in slaves and by a federal government too weak-willed to defend those rights. Many Missourians opposed making Kansas free because freedom in Kansas would undermine slavery in Missouri. As the fight over Kansas intensified, Southerners felt that to acquiesce to northern rule over Kansas would be a step closer to northern rule over the South. Although the proslavery party protected a vested economic interest, it too had an argument to make about liberty. Paradoxically, when Southerners spoke of liberty, they spoke of the liberty to hold slaves. It was a right guaranteed by the Constitution of 1787, as well as the Revolution of 1776, a war fought and won by slaveholders. Northerners had "perverted" the meaning of the Revolution and the Constitution.[6]

But while Southerners suppressed dissent against slavery to protect liberty, problems with liberty arose in Kansas from the flawed implementation of popular sovereignty. Nineteenth-century politics lacked firm standards about residency and voting and tolerated high levels of electoral fraud. This laxness led to massive voting irregularities. Election outcomes often were disputed. Missourians would claim to have legitimately won power under popular sovereignty and to be defending "law and order" by upholding the territorial government; northern settlers would deny the election's legitimacy and establish their own, extralegal government, which they claimed more truly fulfilled popular sovereignty's mandate because it more accurately represented the numerical majority of settlers. The political standoff that became Bleeding Kansas challenged nineteenth-century Americans' claim to have established majority rule among whites. The proslavery/free-state division broke into violence not just because of slavery, but because each side feared the loss of political liberties threatened in the struggle over slavery. In the nineteenth century, few whites cared about the suffering of slaves, but they did care about their own political rights.

A growing literature examines the importance of "whiteness" to nineteenth-century Americans, especially the working class. Drawing on W. E. B. Du Bois's insight that being white paid "wages" in the form of social status and political privilege, historians have elaborated how nineteenth-century Americans came to emphasize race over class. Immigrant groups such as the Irish found that they could improve their status in the eyes of Anglo-descended Protestant Americans by emphasizing their common white skin.[7] While whiteness has chiefly been the province of labor history, the concept also offers insight into the politics of the nineteenth century. As Du Bois noted, whiteness brought political rights such as the vote and the ability to participate in the political life of the nation. Settlers in Kansas accepted the premise that white voters should decide the status of black men and women. Conflict arose when the rights of white settlers to make that decision were threatened.

To argue for the importance of white liberty to understanding Bleeding Kansas is not to ignore the role of either slavery or economics. Many settlers cared deeply about establishing southern rights to own slaves, and others cared just as sincerely about abolishing such rights. Only a minority of the free-state movement, however, can be considered abolitionist. While John Brown, who sincerely believed slavery to be a sin, played a crucial role in turning the struggle in Kansas toward violence, most settlers were unwilling to turn moral objections against slavery into action. Most settlers, southern and northern, viewed the territories as a place for economic advancement. What caused settlers interested in a good farm to ally themselves with avowedly proslavery or antislavery men—to fight, and sometimes to die, in Kansas? The answer: popular sovereignty. This political formula designed to widen the democratic rights of white voters unexpectedly produced turmoil and conflict rather than consensus and resolution on the slavery issue. Popular sovereignty, in fact, was intended to allow white settlers to choose an economic system: slave or free labor. But popular sovereignty privileged white liberty by subjecting the morality of slavery and the choice of an economic system to a vote at the ballot box.

From the concrete historical event of the Revolution, Americans constructed their national identity. A reverence for that founding moment remained powerful for people of both the North and the South.[8] Ironically, Bleeding Kansas made it clear that Northerners and Southerners had drawn very different conclusions about the meaning of that historical event, and thus about the nature of U.S. nationalism. If a nation is indeed "an imagined political community" in which people who do not know each other nonetheless believe they share a commonality,[9] then North and South had imagined different communities based on Revolutionary principles. The conflict in Kansas served to make painfully clear the differences between those communities. In declaring themselves the heirs of the Revolution, free-state and proslavery men contested the meaning of liberty in a slave-holding republic. Free staters envisioned a republic of white men; proslavery men, a republic of slaveowners. As each side held itself to be the true repository of the

Revolution's purpose, each could only look on its adversary as hostile to the republican government created by that conflict. Free staters saw the proslavery party as part of the Slave Power which sought to strip all Americans of their political liberties in order to spread slavery. Southerners saw the free-state movement as part of the advancing hordes of abolitionists intending to deprive them of their property and their equal place within the Union. Popular sovereignty and the resulting struggle in Kansas Territory brought these positions into focus. That no such elaborate conspiracies existed on either the proslavery or free-soil side to deprive the other's rights did not prevent people in the 1850s from believing in them.[10]

Bleeding Kansas would seem to be an absurdity. Why was blood shed over slavery in a place where few thought the institution could go and where so few slaves actually went? Why did the free-state movement, which felt little compassion for the suffering of the slaves, so ardently oppose slavery expansion? Paradoxically, the two adversaries fought about a people who would not go to Kansas and whom they did not want to come.

What, then, did the free staters fight for? Liberty, by which they meant the right of whites not only to elect leaders and ratify constitutions but also to choose their political institutions, including slavery. If for most of them liberty's definition was limited to the white race, they were in that respect no more shortsighted than their often invoked ancestors of 1776. But when they took up the struggle to secure their political rights from the proslavery party, they allied themselves with those who sincerely detested chattel slavery thereby joining the moral crusade against slavery. As free-state Kansans increasingly championed black rights, that debate was shaped by white settlers' fears of what black rights meant for whites. And just as their revolutionary ancestors had sown the seeds for an expansion of liberty's definition, so too would the free staters in Kansas make their contribution to expanding human freedom in a way that would eventually come to include all men, white and black.

Whenever free-state and proslavery men debated the meaning of liberty, the intrinsic issue was slavery. The language with which white political rights were discussed was permeated with the imagery of slavery, illustrative of the arrogance of slaveholders and the degradation of slaves. Many Northerners understood the Revolution's emphasis on liberty to be antithetical to holding other humans in bondage. Slavery and freedom were contradictory. But many Northerners felt constrained against opposing slavery by the Constitution's acceptance of a slaveowning Union. What empowered abolitionists, however, was a profound conviction that slavery was a sin on the nation's soul, intolerable by any sincere Christian.[11] The political discussion of slavery challenged whites to reconcile politics and morality. Were some political issues exempt from the will of the majority? Some Northerners believed that as a moral issue slavery should be treated differently from ordinary legislation; hence, they resisted the Kansas-Nebraska Act which equated slavery with all other political issues as subject to majority rule. Some Southerners also believed slavery to have a special political status. They claimed an exemption from popular rule for their property rights in slaves. If Southerners were right in their contention that the Constitution prohibited interference with slavery, must a government which tolerated, indeed fostered, a great evil be obeyed by those who abhorred that evil? And did the United States possess a form of government that could reconcile democracy with morality? How was a moral issue such as slavery to be resolved in a way consonant with the rights of the majority? In 1858, these questions became central to Stephen A. Douglas's great debates with his rival in the Illinois senatorial race, Abraham Lincoln. Douglas argued that no issue stood outside the realm of politics. Although Lincoln denied the legitimacy of defying the law in the name of a higher moral purpose, he articulated the view that some issues, such as slavery, were morally different and should be treated as such.[12]

Bleeding Kansas did not resolve the tension between morality and majority rule. In fact, the inability (some have said the impossibility) of resolving it led to the Civil War. Bleeding Kansas did, however, shape the debate over political liberty and the place of slavery in a nation which held freedom as a core value. The Kansas-Nebraska Act sought, in part, to widen white men's political rights through popular sovereignty. But the implementation of such decentralized democratic control was marred by fraudulent elections and the subsequent refusal of substantial numbers of settlers to participate in a flawed process. Further, politicians repeatedly failed to find a solution that would both satisfy Southerners' claims for equal treatment in the territories while guaranteeing political rights to free staters. Consequently, the political conflict degenerated into violence. Only with the absence of Southerners from the national debate after 1861 could Kansas Territory, at long last, become a state. The underlying issue of slavery raised during the territorial period still remained powerful during the Civil War, though. When Missouri bushwhackers under William Clarke Quantrill raided Lawrence in 1863, killing almost two hundred men and boys, they were enacting one of the last episodes of the 1850s border warfare. When Kansans became the first to recruit black soldiers during the Civil War, they demonstrated how the struggle of the 1850s over white men's political rights had widened the meaning of liberty for blacks as well. Bleeding Kansas began as a struggle to secure the political liberties of whites and ended by broadening the definition of freedom to include blacks.

1

The Triumph of Squatter Sovereignty
The Kansas-Nebraska Act

Stephen A. Douglas, the powerful chairman of the Senate Committee on Territories, wanted to organize a territory. In the 1850s, Douglas was at the height of his powers. Diminutive in inches, he was still "broad-shouldered and big-chested," with "piercing eyes" and long hair which "he shook and tossed defiantly like a lion's mane" when excited.[1] Westward expansion had been in Douglas's blood ever since he had left his native Vermont in his youth for the Illinois prairies. With his New England birth, western home, and southern marriage, Douglas "was Young America personified,"[2] embodying the political movement which favored westward expansion in the name of spreading the blessings of political freedom to ever-larger areas of the continent. "The tide of emigration and civilization must be permitted to roll onward," Douglas proclaimed, bringing "our institutions" of "christianity, civilization and Democracy" to the West.[3] Douglas's commitment to expanding freedom had become, as one Kentucky senator commented, a "mania" for creating territories.[4]

But in 1854 Douglas was frustrated. To the west of Iowa and Missouri lay vast stretches of unorganized land, the northern remnants of the Louisiana Purchase, which Congress had yet to form into territories and place on the road to statehood. Residents of Iowa and Missouri shared Douglas's frustration. Wyandot Indians took the first steps by repeatedly petitioning Congress to organize a territory. In October 1852, the

Illinois senator Stephen A. Douglas in the late 1850s. (Courtesy of the Illinois State Historical Library, Springfield)

Wyandot elected Abelard Guthrie, a white man with a Wyandot wife, as territorial delegate. Guthrie lobbied congressmen on territorial status for the area west of Missouri. Nonetheless, a territorial bill failed in March 1853. Iowa too had an interest in the development of the western territory and, like Missouri, had even sent a delegate to lobby for organization. Finally, on December 14, 1853, Senator Augustus C. Dodge of Iowa introduced a bill to organize Nebraska territory between

30°30' and 43°30' north latitude. The Dodge bill was reported to Douglas's Committee on Territories.[5]

Not all westerners were so eager to gain territorial status for the unorganized region. In the winter of 1852–1853, Missouri senator David Atchison told Guthrie he opposed organizing the territory because the 1820 Missouri Compromise forbade slavery there. Atchison made the same point again in congressional debates.[6] Some may have dismissed the senator's clout. In the opinion of one congressional observer, Atchison was "a man of very little talent" and "less education," who was out of place in the distinguished ranks of the Senate, yet well liked for his "witty good humored" nature.[7] But Atchison associated with more talented, and equally proslavery, politicians. The Missourian lived at a boarding house on F Street—the so-called F Street Mess—with other powerful defenders of southern rights: Andrew P. Butler of South Carolina and James M. Mason and Robert M. T. Hunter of Virginia. In December 1853, Atchison hinted to Douglas that southern votes were needed to pass a bill organizing Nebraska territory. Atchison himself needed an issue to keep alive his political rivalry in Missouri with Thomas Hart Benton, a supporter of the Missouri Compromise.[8] As Benton's followers put it, Atchison was willing to renew slavery agitation in order "to get up a breeze upon which he can ride." They blamed both Atchison and Douglas for creating unnecessary controversy about slavery expansion.[9]

But Atchison spoke for Southerners reluctant to create a free territory that would produce more free states hostile to southern interests. Claiborne F. Jackson, a Missouri politician, wrote David Atchison that he hoped Congress would establish Nebraska territory without "any infernal restrictions." "If we can't all go there on the same [s]tring, with all our property of every kind, I say let the Indians have it *forever*. They are better neighbors than the abolitionists, *by a damn sight*."[10] For Missourians such as Jackson, the ability to take slaves into the territory was an essential right belonging to free white Southerners.

In contrast to the "Little Giant" Douglas, Atchison towered over six feet tall and, despite being a Presbyterian, cultivated the frontiersman's talents in liquor and profanity. Like Douglas, Atchison had long been an expansionist. In the 1840s, Atchison pushed for Texas annexation and all of Oregon including the region later awarded to the British.

But Atchison's determination to protect and extend slavery outweighed his zeal for expansion. Efforts to keep slavery out of the Mexican Cession alerted Atchison to the abolitionist threat to southern rights in the territories.[11]

In 1820, the Missouri Compromise had divided the Louisiana Purchase at 36°30'. North of that boundary, except for the state of Missouri, slavery was prohibited. The issue of slavery in the territories was thus settled until the wave of expansionism that occurred in the 1840s. The annexation of slaveowning Texas in 1845 was balanced by the acquisition of free Oregon the following year. Then the expansionist administration of James K. Polk went to war with Mexico, a war that all expected would bring new lands to the United States. During that war, Pennsylvania congressman David Wilmot proposed that slavery be prohibited in territories acquired from Mexico. Although never enacted into law, the Wilmot Proviso became the basis of a free-soil position opposed to slavery extension. When the U.S.-Mexican War ended in 1848, no provision had been made concerning slavery in the Mexican Cession. The California Gold Rush, and rapidly being settled California's desire for admittance to the Union, brought the issue before Congress in early 1850. Southerners, fearful of being shut out of territories—they repeatedly pointed out—acquired with southern blood and treasure, blocked California's admission. The stalemate, which threatened the secession of the southern states, was resolved in a compromise drafted by elderly Whig statesman Henry Clay and steered through the divided Congress by Douglas. The Compromise of 1850 admitted California as a free state but organized the rest of the Mexican Cession as Utah and New Mexico territories without restrictions on slavery.[12] The 1850 struggle left Atchison determined to assert southern rights in the organization of any new territories.

Atchison told Douglas that the Dodge bill would not get southern support unless slaveowners could go into the Nebraska territory with their property. Douglas strengthened the bill. On January 4, 1854, Douglas reported back from the Committee on Territories with important changes to the Dodge bill. By altering the northern boundary, the Missouri Compromise restriction regarding slavery implicit in Dodge's bill was now removed.[13] Commentators immediately perceived

Senator David Rice Atchison, proslavery leader from Missouri. (Used by permission, State Historical Society of Missouri, Columbia)

that the revised bill was a "reopening of slavery agitation," "severely test[ing]" the "finality" of the Compromise of 1850 which had been Congress's last legislative deal on slavery.[14]

Still, the legislation was not explicit enough for Southerners. Atchison arranged a meeting with Douglas to discuss whether the bill repealed the Missouri Compromise. Other senators attempted to alter the bill either to expressly repeal or expressly protect the Missouri Compromise.[15] In the confusion of proposed alterations, Massachusetts congressman Nathaniel P. Banks declared, "The Nebraska Bill met terrific opposition & will fail."[16]

President Franklin Pierce preferred language which evaded the issue of repealing the Missouri Compromise, but Douglas could not get southern support without direct repeal. Atchison, Douglas, and others consulted with Pierce in late January and persuaded him to endorse direct repeal. Pierce was largely unprepared for such an issue. The president still grieved over the tragic death of his only child, who had been killed in a railroad accident. The first lady linked the boy's death to his father's recent election. God, she declared, had removed their son so as not to distract his father from his important duties. Psychologically scarred, Pierce embarked on an administration he expected to be dominated by foreign policy. For that the president needed Senate backing, and with Senate confirmation still pending on a number of his appointments, the president could not refuse the powerful senators who requested his support for the bill.[17]

With presidential support secured, Douglas now offered a substitute bill. Presented on January 23, the Kansas-Nebraska bill created two territories: Kansas (from latitude 37° to 40°) and Nebraska (40° to 49°). It declared the eighth section of the Missouri enabling act superseded by the compromise measures of 1850, and also redefined the principles of the 1850 compromise such "that all questions pertaining to Slavery in the territories and in the new States to be formed, are to be left to the decision of the people residing therein, through their appropriate representatives."[18] A Boston newspaper objected to Douglas's substitution, complaining that he sought to "shuffle" the Missouri Compromise out of existence by declaring it superseded.[19]

Although the charge was later made that the territories had been divided in order to increase the chances that one would admit slavery, at the time the bill was drafted both the Iowa and Missouri delegations favored the division. Two territories would allow both states to influence their neighboring territory's selection of territorial delegates. But the division of the territory was a minor matter compared to the removal of the Missouri Compromise's prohibition of slavery and the substitution of the Compromise of 1850's no restriction formula. Douglas hailed no restriction as the democratic principle of popular sovereignty.[20]

In its broadest sense, popular sovereignty meant local self-government. With origins that could be traced to the founding principles of the republic, it recently had been championed by former Michigan territorial governor and now senator Lewis Cass. Cass, as a presidential candidate in 1848, had proposed popular sovereignty as the solution to slavery in the newly acquired Mexican Cession. Cass's doctrine proposed allowing the people of the territory, rather than Congress, to decide whether or not to have slavery. Northerners argued that the organization of the New Mexico and Utah territories in 1850 without restrictions on slavery had been on popular sovereignty principles. Douglas, like Cass a westerner, adopted popular sovereignty as a creed that fit his beliefs in democracy, local self-rule, and expansion. Like Cass also, Douglas had no qualms about applying popular sovereignty to slavery, for he did not consider slavery a moral issue. Popular sovereignty had the added benefit of ambiguity: it left open both the issue of who would gain in the territories, North or South, antislavery or proslavery, and at what point in the territory's settlement that decision would be made.[21]

Southerners found popular sovereignty easy to accept. After all, its inclusion in the Kansas-Nebraska bill opened to them territories that had been formerly closed. Some Southerners fretted that if pro-northern elements of former compromises could be repealed, so too could pro-southern ones. Most, however, knew a good thing when they saw it. Georgia congressman Alexander Stephens found the possibility of introducing slavery preferable to an absolute prohibition against its introduction into the territory.[22] Southerners also reasoned that northern violations of previous compromises invalidated the Missouri Compromise. Senator Robert Toombs of Georgia argued that repealing the Missouri Compromise was proper because the North had already violated it by refusing to apply it to the Mexican Cession.[23] Earlier, during the U.S.-Mexican War, John C. Calhoun, the foremost southern rights thinker, had proposed the principle that Congress had no right to interfere with slavery in the territories as they were the "common property" of all the states. Douglas's formulation seemed merely to confirm southern belief that slavery had a right to go into all the territories.[24]

Southerners further asserted that the Constitution guaranteed equal rights for citizens of all states. Presumably, those rights legitimized popular sovereignty's placing of slavery and freedom on equal footing in the territories.[25] But the notion was not universally shared. When North Carolina senator George E. Badger waxed nostalgic about the inequality of southern and northern rights in the territory, lamenting that he could not bring into the territory the elderly female slave who had nursed him as a child, Ohio senator Benjamin Wade replied, "The only difficulty that the Senator would meet was, that *he couldn't sell her when he got her there.*"[26] Wade's retort demonstrated both northern contempt for avowed slaveowning paternalism and for Southerners' rights to their slaves. Southerners who held that the territories were the "common property" of the states resented the discrimination against slavery in the Missouri Compromise and felt that popular sovereignty alleviated that discrimination. Other Southerners merely held that the Missouri Compromise restriction was a "stigma" upon the South, indicating the nation's disapproval of their institutions. The *Richmond Enquirer* saw the Kansas-Nebraska Act as a step toward fulfilling the southern interpretation of Congress's "duty" to ensure the South's constitutional rights by "throw[ing] open the territory to the equal participation of all the States." For Southerners, Kansas-Nebraska was a "symbolic victory" in which Northerners conceded slavery's equal right to go into the territories. The cost of the victory, however, was great. Southerners willingly squandered political capital to force northern acknowledgment of the South's equal rights in the territories.[27]

Many Northerners found it difficult to accept Douglas's substitution of popular sovereignty for slavery prohibition not only because they had more to lose but also because of moral objections to slavery. Senator Salmon P. Chase of Ohio published "The Appeal of the Independent Democrats," an indictment of Douglas's territorial bill. Chase had long been active in abolitionist and free-soil politics and had served as a lawyer for blacks fleeing the Fugitive Slave Law. His temporizing for political gain would become legendary, but he could speak for principle, as he did now. "The Appeal," coauthored with other antislavery Democrats, condemned the Kansas-Nebraska bill as a plot to extend slavery at the expense of freedom.[28] The authors, self-proclaimed "independent" Democrats, asserted it their "duty to warn our constituents whenever imminent danger menaces the freedom of our institutions or the permanency of our Union," arguing that Douglas's bill posed just such a threat. In addition, "The Appeal" condemned the Kansas-Nebraska Act as part "of an atrocious plot to exclude from a vast unoccupied region immigrants from the Old World, and free laborers from our own States, and convert it into a dreary region of despotism, inhabited by masters and slaves." By the "solemn compact" of the Missouri Compromise, the region had been "consecrated to freedom." To emphasize the immorality of slavery's extension, they called on Christian ministers to intervene and closed "The Appeal" thus: "The cause of human freedom is the cause of God."[29]

Chase repeated these themes in a Senate address when he argued for his amendment to Douglas's bill. The chamber was so crowded that women squeezed into the reporters' gallery to hear the antislavery orator. Chase denied that the Compromise of 1850 had envisioned the 1820 compromise's repeal. No one had so thought at the time, not even Stephen Douglas. He argued that the Founders had intended to limit slavery and had made the Constitution a document for "human liberty." He reviewed the history of the Missouri Compromise, calling it a solemn compact, not just a piece of legislation. The South, having drawn all it could from the compact, now discarded it. Despite his appeal, Chase's amendment, which sought to protect the Missouri Compromise from repeal by Douglas's bill, was decisively defeated.[30]

Senator Charles Sumner of Massachusetts also arraigned the Kansas-Nebraska Act as a breach of faith with the "compact" of the Missouri Compromise. Like Chase's speech and those of other northern senators, Sumner accused the bill of breaking with the antislavery tradition of the revolutionary generation. He hoped for the day when both North and South "will unite . . . in declaring Freedom and not Slavery *national,* while Slavery and not Freedom shall be *sectional.*"[31] Chase and Sumner gave voice to powerful northern sentiments about the sacredness of freedom and the immorality of slavery.

Douglas's opposition to linking morality and democracy became apparent when Edward Everett presented a memorial, bearing three thousand signatures, from clergymen opposed to the Kansas-Nebraska bill. The petition protested against the bill as a "great moral wrong," a "breach of faith . . . subversive of all confidence in national engagements," and a threat "to the peace and even existence of our beloved Union." In addition, Congress threatened to subject the country "to the righteous judgments of the Almighty."[32] Douglas reacted with fury, dismissing the ministers as "political preachers" uttering "calumny." In a later, more polished response, he argued that interference by men of God threatened the people's right to self-government. While he qualified his initial rage by conceding the clergy's right to object as citizens to a public policy, he denied that they possessed a "power from the Almighty, to direct and control the civil authorities of this country." Insofar as they made such a claim, they threatened the Constitution, the "principles of free government," and the "guarantees of civil and religious liberty." He hinted further that the clergy disliked the bill's emphasis on self-government because the policy could undo the power they seemed to claim.[33]

The ministers' petition was ultimately tabled. They had nonetheless raised the issue of how legislation would grapple with a fundamentally moral issue. While the clergymen took the position that legislation should follow God's law, Douglas countered that the people, as they made their laws, determined morality. The debate reached to the heart of popular sovereignty's dilemma. The ministers affirmed, as had other opponents such as Chase and the Anti-Nebraska Democrats, that some issues were fundamentally moral and thus outside the scope of ordinary politics. They were "sacred compacts" apart from the rough and tumble of democracy. Douglas, however, sought to make the rights of the people sacred and all political issues subject to popular rule.[34]

Facing such opposition, Douglas was unable to move the bill through as quickly as he had planned.[35] "Douglas is driving the Nebraska Bill like a locomotive," a correspondent of diplomat James Buchanan reported, "but I rather apprehend, in rail road parlance, that he will before long, have *to switch* off, to let another train pass."[36] The administration desired a quick end to the political controversy which was creating a "good deal of excitement," in the president's words, but the debate dragged on as new controversies arose.[37] The most important of these concerned alien suffrage. Many western states allowed unnaturalized immigrants to vote, but the Senate's Clayton amendment denied that right in Kansas territory.[38]

After a stormy all-night session, the Senate passed the bill 37 to 14 in the early morning hours of March 4. Lewis Cass, the father of popular sovereignty, took the floor. "I congratulate the Senate on the triumph of squatter sovereignty," Cass pronounced.[39] At the time, his felicitations might have seemed premature. Public sentiment was rapidly mobilizing against the bill and passage in the House was by no means assured.[40]

When the bill reached the House of Representatives in late March, it seemed nearly dead on arrival. By a vote of 110 to 95, Kansas-Nebraska was referred to the Committee of the Whole and placed at the bottom of a lengthy calendar of bills under consideration. Its proponents despaired and its opponents gloated. A southern paper predicted the result would be "months of slumber on the table" and an uncertain final passage.[41] William A. Richardson, Douglas's ally in the House, tried to have the bill referred to the Committee on Territories, where it could receive speedier consideration. While Richardson maneuvered, Douglas haunted the House debates.[42] Heated exchanges on the House floor kept Washington alive with rumors of duels.[43]

By early May, a Virginia congressman reported, "The Nebraska bill is in great danger."[44] Then on May 8, Kansas-Nebraska's friends in the House succeeded in laying aside eighteen other bills so that the act could be considered. Three days later, the House went into late night session. Congressmen brought in pillows and lay on sofas while servants delivered food. The session dragged into the early morning hours of the next day as the bill's opponents defeated votes to adjourn. They hoped to delay until it was time to take up the Pacific railroad bill and thus avoid a vote on Kansas-Nebraska altogether. The strategy failed when the House voted to postpone consideration of the railroad bill and to end debate on Kansas-Nebraska. Richardson, called a "slave driver" by the northern press, proposed both measures. Meanwhile, more rumors of duels circulated.[45]

On May 22, Richardson's strategy prevailed and the House took up the Kansas-Nebraska Act without the Clayton amendment regarding alien voting. Opponents attempted to filibuster by making repeated motions to adjourn. They failed. Richardson led the defeat of any amendments. Kansas-Nebraska's proponents feared an amended version would not survive another journey through the Senate. That same day the House passed the bill by 113 to 100. Two days later, the Senate took up the House bill and passed it the next day. President Pierce signed the bill on May 30, 1854.[46]

The final votes on the Kansas-Nebraska bill clearly revealed the sectional divisions it created. In the House, the northern Democrats split evenly, forty-four in support and forty-four opposed. Southern Democrats overwhelmingly supported the bill, with only two exceptions. While no northern Whigs supported the bill, southern Whigs split; fourteen favored it, seven opposed. In the Senate, there was more solidarity among northern Democrats, with fifteen supporting the bill as opposed to five in opposition. Voting in favor of the bill were all but one southern Democrat, the Texan Sam Houston, who believed the South was needlessly agitating antislavery passions. No northern Whigs supported it, while eleven of thirteen southern Whigs did so. The bill badly divided the northern Democrats. The Whigs, who had no party agenda at stake, split cleanly along sectional lines. Southern Democrats embraced the measure, emphasizing that popular sovereignty at least gave slavery an equal chance in the territories. While less certain than a guarantee to protect property in slaves, a chance was nevertheless preferable to the Missouri Compromise's exclusion.[47]

Douglas championed the principle of popular sovereignty as the bill's great contribution to freedom, but he invented the details as he went along. In order to preempt amendments offered by the bill's opponents altering the structure of the territorial government, Douglas introduced such amendments himself. Under Douglas's revisions, territorial legislation did not have to be approved by Congress, and the territorial legislature could override the governor's veto with a two-thirds vote. The Kansas territorial legislature thus possessed far more self-government than was normal for a territory. Douglas correctly judged that few could assail the democratic assumptions behind these changes. Settlers of the territories had hitherto been presumed children; until they reached their majority, a wise Congress would govern them paternalistically. Only isolated voices protested the reversal of this presumption. When the measure passed to the House, that body demanded further changes. Congressmen wanted to remove the Senate's Clayton amendment, which forbade voting by unnaturalized settlers. The House thus broadened the meaning of democracy further.[48] In any case, the provisions for expanded self-government in the territories were added piecemeal, not as part of a consistent program of promoting self-government.

Once committed to popular sovereignty as the principle of the Kansas-Nebraska Act, Douglas defended it with a passion born from more than political expediency. After all, the expansionist Young America movement was rooted in the belief that the United States best spread liberty by spreading its own borders. For Douglas, expansion and liberty were indistinguishable. Popular sovereignty, which made western expansion possible, was also irrefutably democratic in form. As Douglas reiterated ceaselessly, through elections the western settlers would themselves decide any issue, including slavery. What could be more democratic? Douglas could not understand the opposition to popular sovereignty. He asserted the simple right of the people to choose, without himself expressing a preference as to their decision.[49] Failing to understand why others objected to slavery, Douglas also failed to anticipate the dangers of undermining the "finality" of the Compromise of 1850, which had done so much to delegitimize slavery agitation. Douglas's tragic mistake was in thinking that, although the Kansas-Nebraska Act reopened the slavery issue, popular sovereignty was a sufficiently flexible formula to quell any agitation.

Perhaps Douglas committed this error because the supremacy of the Democratic party encouraged him to believe it could weather any storm. During the height of the second-party system of the 1830s and 1840s, the Whig party had vigorously challenged Democratic policies and ideology. Whigs advocated government stimulation of the economy through such measures as protective tariffs, government funding of internal improvements, and a national bank. Democrats cautioned such government intervention might aid the rich and well-connected at the expense of the common, white man. Whigs often embraced more government regulation of private morality through temperance legislation, sabbatarianism, and a preference for antislavery measures. Democrats felt that such regulation of private behavior violated basic rights to personal freedom. By 1852, economic issues possessed less salience for Whig voters. The nomination of the victorious general of the U.S.-Mexican War, Winfield Scott, as Whig candidate for president did not prevent the defection of Whig voters alienated by a party too friendly to immigrants and too antislavery at a time when the Compromise of 1850 had promised an end to agitation of that question. The election of 1852 was a solid defeat for the Whigs. As a result, Douglas put forward the Kansas-Nebraska Act at a time of potential political realignment, when old political issues such as economic policy had lost the power to move voters and new political issues such as nativism and slavery had yet to seize a commanding hold on voters' allegiance. The Kansas-Nebraska Act would do much to determine the shape of the new political order.[50]

Douglas succeeded in making the issues of the Kansas-Nebraska bill those of the Democratic party. As one politician reported, "There has been a division on our ranks upon the expedience of rescinding the Missouri restriction line. But that has been done by a democratic Congress & a democratic President. It is now a past question."[51] In order to ensure backing for Kansas-Nebraska, the administration held up appointments, thereby making it possible to reward the bill's supporters and punish its opponents. Rumors circulated that the president had made it clear to Cabinet members that they were to persuade their friends to support the bill. The administration did indeed possess potent weapons in the form of party loyalty and patronage. The weakness of the moribund Whig party was deluding the Democrats into introducing discord into their own party.[52]

Instead of producing the "peace, union and good feeling" expected by one observer,[53] an Ohio Democrat was much closer to the truth when he wrote, "I fear for my country! If Mr Douglass's bill passes there will be an alarming aspect presented throughout the entire North."[54] Political observers at the time openly speculated that Douglas had backed Kansas-Nebraska to build southern support for future presidential bids. Instead, Douglas found himself rebuilding his political base in Illinois. One politician in that state argued that only demands for party loyalty kept Illinois Democrats in favor of repealing the Missouri Compromise. The Illinois legislature pushed through resolutions supporting Douglas.

Intended as a vote of confidence, the resolutions succeeded only because of heavy political pressure. Without such pressure, support for Douglas and his bill faltered. On his return to the west, Douglas was unable to make himself heard among his own constituents. For two hours, hecklers in a Chicago crowd shouted him down as he attempted to speak. He finally gave up.[55] Douglas himself noted, "I could travel from Boston to Chicago by the light of my own effigy."[56]

The groundswell of protest against the bill threatened the Democratic party's integrity. Reports of Anti-Nebraska meetings testified that citizens had signed petitions without respect to party differences. Among the petitioners were Democrats in opposition to their own party. Kansas-Nebraska was indeed a major blow to the party. In 1852, Democrats had won all but two of the northern states, but just two years later, they lost all but two northern states and the Whigs gained control of the House. Indeed, only seven of the forty-four northern Democrats who had voted for Kansas-Nebraska were reelected in 1854. Even worse, Anti-Nebraska Democrats such as Chase joined forces with refugees from the dying Whig party, with nativist Know-Nothings, and with veterans of antislavery politics in the Liberty and Free Soil parties, to create a new party—the Republicans. The Republican party specifically opposed slavery's expansion into the territories.[57]

As befitted such a varied coalition, the Republican party reflected a multifaceted northern response to the Kansas-Nebraska bill. Republicans drew on northern outrage at the breaking of the Missouri Compromise. They contended "a bargain is a bargain" and the South, having gotten its share of that bargain, should not now be able to scrap it.[58] This pragmatic view was soon enhanced by an ennoblement of the 1820 compromise as more than a bargain, more than ordinary legislation, a "solemn compact between the North and South."[59] The compact theme, initially proposed in the "Appeal of the Independent Democrats," was quickly adopted by Anti-Nebraska speakers.[60] Northerners suspected southern motives in breaking the "compact." During the Senate debates, William Henry Seward had pointed out that the stakes were greater than just Kansas. "Nebraska is not all that is to be saved or lost." He pointed to probable southern designs on other free territories.[61] One congressman avowed that the only purpose behind the bill was to introduce slavery into territories once free. A Columbus, Ohio, meeting concluded the act was a thinly disguised attempt to extend slavery.[62]

The threat to free territory was implicitly a threat to northern freedom. An Anti-Nebraska orator articulated such fears when he remarked that the bill would reduce the laborers of the north to "white niggers."[63] Senator Wade, speaking during the debates over the bill, had avowed that allowing slavery into the territories would make it impossible for free men to go there.[64] A New York City workingmen's meeting accused the bill of depriving Northerners of homesteads in Kansas and forcing them to work alongside slaves. John P. Hale argued Northerners sought a place "where the honest laborer may labor in the dignity of his own manhood," not next to slaves. Kansas-Nebraska marked the "encroachment by the Slave Power on the rights of free labor,"[65] an encroachment made all the more bitter by northern complicity in bringing it about. At a large Anti-Nebraska meeting in New York City, Benjamin Butler pointed out that the bill was the work of Northerners and would pass with northern votes. The South merely stood ready to accept what was to be offered.[66] David Davis lamented, "The Southern Senators are not so much to blame as these Scoundrels at the North."[67]

Still another view reconciled the idea of a conspiratorial South exploiting a weak North by considering Douglas a northern tool of the South. "As usual, when any great outrage is to be committed on the North, a Northern man has been selected to lead it," O. B. Matteson pointed out.[68] Senator Truman Smith of Connecticut regretted that if the North was to be "sold out," it would not be by a "high-toned Southern gentleman," but by a northern "demagogue."[69] Summarizing prevailing sentiment, the *New York Times* argued that most Northerners felt the bill to be "an outrage upon their rights and an insult to their sentiments," all the more objectionable because it was promoted by one of their own in the North.[70]

The Anti-Nebraska movement coincided with the period of nativism. Also rooted in a conspiratorial view, nativists reacted to perceived immigrant and Catholic designs against the integrity of U.S. republican institutions. Antislavery expansion, however, came to eclipse the anti-immigrant Know-Nothing party, and many nativists who possessed antislavery views moved into the Republican party. They concluded the so-called Slave Power conspiracy was fundamentally a greater threat than foreign influences.[71] As one nativist wrote, "Neither the Pope nor the foreigners ever can govern the country or endanger its liberties, but the slavebreeders and slavetraders *do* govern it, and threaten to put an end to all government but theirs."[72] The northern conviction was that with passage of the Kansas-Nebraska Act and the eventual political struggle in Kansas Territory, the "slave power had gone too far" and would overwhelm competing issues such as nativism.[73]

Despite the fact that many Anti-Nebraska men were more "anti-southern" than antislavery, the Republican party expressed also a moral objection to slavery. Republicans inherited both the Whiggish tendency to believe morality could be enforced by law and the abolitionist conviction that slavery was a sin on the United States' conscience. Viewing popular sovereignty as merely a veil to disguise the expansion of slavery, Whig politician Abraham Lincoln condemned the Kansas-Nebraska Act for replacing the moral condemnation of slavery with the people's "right to choose wrong."[74] In a speech at Peoria, Lincoln admitted his willingness to accept slavery's existence as a "necessity" but nonetheless condemned slavery's expansion, and slavery itself, as a "monstrous injustice" at odds with republican institutions and the Declaration of Independence. "In our greedy chase to make profit of the negro," Lincoln warned, "let us beware, lest we cancel and tear to pieces even the white man's charter of freedom."[75] Northern protesters against the bill argued that popular sovereignty created an offensive presumption of equality between freedom and slavery.[76] The bill legitimized abolition sentiment outside traditionally antislavery circles. In the preface to its report on a speech by abolitionist Theodore Parker, the *New York Times* acknowledged that Parker was a fanatic but explained that such fanaticism resonated in the North because of the Kansas-Nebraska Act, which the South had forced on the nation.[77]

If Kansas-Nebraska precipitated a dangerous state of northern public opinion, it created a similarly precarious situation in the South. The *Richmond Enquirer* praised Kansas-Nebraska as "a measure so just in regard to the rights of the South."[78] Aware of northern opposition to the bill, Southerners nonetheless expected the tumult to cease and respect for southern rights to triumph. Georgian Alexander Stephens predicted, incorrectly, that "The excitement has nearly all passed away. Nobody says anything now against [Kansas-Nebraska] but the abolitionists. Let them howl on—"[79] Stephens felt that the practical effect of the bill would be limited but argued that "the moral effect of the victory on our side will have a permanent effect upon the public-mind, whether any positive advantages accrue by way of the actual extension of slavery or not."[80] A Georgia paper expected *"patriotic, conservative men of all parties at the North"* to support the bill. Failure to do so would betray southern faith in the North.[81] Kansas-Nebraska thus raised expectations in the South that its rights would be respected, expectations the North would do little to fulfill.

Indeed, the Kansas-Nebraska Act had raised expectations along the border that would not be fulfilled either. To Missourians, Kansas-Nebraska was a "gift," a special treat like a "Christmas goose." Missourians preserved that sense of delighted receipt of an unexpected present in the term they used for the Kansas issue, "the Goose Question."[82] A St. Louis newspaper endorsed popular sovereignty and condemned the "Appeal of the Independent Democrats" by asking, "Is it true, that a portion of American citizens have been ostracized and denied rights and privileges accorded to others, even foreigners, merely because their opinions and 'property' do not fraternize with the Abolition notions of another portion of the Union?" The editorial then dismissed the abolition threat. "We do not intend to argue the rights of the citizens of Missouri: they are competent to form their own opinions and to defend them."[83] When the bill passed, a meeting of Missourians resolved, "That we congratulate the country upon the passage of the Nebraska bill, and the recognition of the old Revolutionary principle that the people of the Great West are capable of self-government, and of managing their domestic affairs with as much and perhaps more skill than our Abolition sympathizers."[84] Only much later, and with dismay, would Missourians realize their inability to control the new territory.

Senator William Henry Seward, the slim New Yorker with the "oracular tone," proved more insightful. Speaking in the debate over the

Clayton amendment, Seward boasted of the large immigration from abroad into the free states. These immigrants, "good, loyal, liberty loving, slavery-fearing citizens," made New York City only a waystation on their trip westward. "Come on then, gentlemen of the Slave States. Since there is no escaping your challenge, I accept it in behalf of the cause of freedom. We will engage in competition for the virgin soil of Kansas, and God give the victory to the side which is stronger in numbers as it is in right."[85] As Seward recognized, popular sovereignty made numbers at the ballot box more important than sacred compacts.

Popular sovereignty's appeal lay in its assumption that the people could best govern themselves. On its face, it widened liberty in the United States by overruling both the free-soil assertion that Congress decided the fate of the territories and should exclude the moral taint of slavery and the slave-state claim that the territories belonged to all the states and hence could not exclude slavery. Under popular sovereignty, the people of the territories would decide the issue of slavery for themselves. With the passage of Kansas-Nebraska, the principles of popular sovereignty had triumphed, only its "practical application" remained to be worked out by the migrants who now headed west for Kansas territory.[86] Therein lay the rub. A grief-worn President Pierce would later confide "that this Kansas matter had given him more harassing anxiety than anything that had happened since the loss of his son; that it haunted him day and night, and was the great overshadowing trouble of his administration."[87] The open-endedness of the "practical application" of popular sovereignty's democratic principles came to trouble not only the president but also the country. Dissension was inevitable because migrants from different sections brought different assumptions about popular sovereignty's meaning and because popular sovereignty's promise of perfect democratic choice ill fit with the imperfect institutions of balloting in the nineteenth century. But in 1854 western Missourians had no forebodings. They greeted the triumph of squatter sovereignty with the frontiersmen's enthusiasm for new homes in a new country.

2

Freedom in the Scale
The Migration to Kansas Territory

After the passage of the Kansas-Nebraska Act, the economic promise of the new Kansas Territory beckoned to Missourians. Like westerners on many a previous frontier, Missourians anticipated greater prosperity for themselves and their families by settling on, or perhaps just speculating in, Kansas lands. Frederick Starr, a northern minister living in western Missouri, observed town promoters peddling sketches of non-existent settlements, from which would supposedly arise prosperous and bustling metropolises: "Hurrah for the future Emporium of Kansas!"[1] Land seekers registered hundreds of claims, paying fifty cents to join associations to protect them. Soon the country for fifteen miles into Kansas was claimed but not settled. Future residents would remain in Missouri "until the harvesting is all over & cold weather begins to come on, when the persons from this side who have made claims and secured them by laying up a few stores or four logs for a foundation, will go over to make ready for taking possession next spring." Starr himself succumbed to the land fever and joined a squatter association.[2] With few initial settlers coming from other regions, Missourians expected to dominate Kansas Territory. However, migration from the free states would shock Missourians into fearing for their property rights in the territory, and even at home. The situation would also politicize the economic aspirations of migration.

Settlers en route to Kansas in the 1850s. (Kansas State Historical Society, Topeka)

In May 1854, fewer than 800 white settlers lived in Kansas Territory. In the nine months after the territory was opened, that number would increase tenfold until, by the first territorial census, there were over 8,000 white settlers with 192 slaves in Kansas. Almost fifty percent of those settlers came from Missouri and another seven percent from other southern states. Northern states provided almost a third of the settlers, with the majority coming from the midwestern or mid-Atlantic states. New England migrants constituted only four percent of the total population in 1855. Missourian John H. DeWint and his family were representative settlers. A farmer in his thirties, DeWint brought a wife and seven children, all under twenty-one, to Kansas. Accompanying the family was an elderly woman in her sixties the census taker labeled an "old maid." Missourians were slightly more likely to bring bigger, extended families with more children than Northerners. New Hampshire farmer John E. Stewart brought only his wife and daughter to Kansas. Whatever their regional origin, however, farm families dominated the migration.[3] The census bore out initial reports from the border that spoke of "Emigrants . . . now pouring into Kansas from Missouri and Arkansas by thousands."[4]

That observer went on to claim, "These emigrants are all either slave owners of [sic] the friends of the Institution of Slavery."[5] Slaveowners viewed western expansion as essential to prosperity and economic mobility. In this view, slavery promoted equality. Generations of southern migrants started out on the frontier with a few slaves and moderate acreage and acquired more slaves and land as those holdings prospered.[6] Of those slaves in the new territory for whom information is available, half were children, with the remainder divided between adult men and women. Unlike the white settlers, the slaves often possessed no last names. Although occasional mother and child pairings can be discerned in the census records, the small numbers of slaves owned by individual Kansas settlers indicates that chances of forming or preserving a family must have been small for these slaves. In fact, migration to Kansas doubtless meant separation from relatives in Missouri. For these black migrants, popular sovereignty's promise of expanded liberty was meaningless.

The predominance of Missourians in the territory certainly gave reason to expect popular sovereignty would bring slavery to Kansas, especially when the institution was being promoted at home. A St. Louis newspaper predicted that eastern Kansas's climate and soil were suited to plantation agriculture.[7] Missourian Benjamin F. Stringfellow stated, "Its climate [is] peculiarly healthy to the negro. Nature intended it for a slaveholding State."[8] Still Missouri settlers were not ready to risk their property. Seventeen thousand of Missouri's 87,000 slaves lived in the state's hemp- and tobacco-growing counties bordering Kansas, but few were taken into the territory.[9] James B. O'Toole, a Missouri farmer in his forties, brought a family of four to Kansas. Accompanying the white O'Tooles were four slaves, making O'Toole a relatively large slaveowner for the territory. Almost half of Kansas slaveowners had only one slave, although the average slaveholding was two slaves in Kansas, compared to an average of six slaves per slaveowner in Missouri's slaveholding Little Dixie region. Since most Kansas slaves were women and children, and the average slaveowner owned only one or two, many probably worked in the house as servants rather than as field hands.[10]

Missouri's initial advantages in the race to settle Kansas concealed its disadvantages. The state's low population density, ten people per square mile, meant the state lacked the surplus population for western migration. There was still plenty of cheap land inside Missouri for slaveowners who wished to expand.[11] In addition, those Missourians interested in moving likely did not want to take slaves into a territory that, as yet, had no guarantees for their property. An observer elaborated on the difficulties of establishing slavery in Kansas, where there existed both the chance that slavery would not be officially established and the uncertainty of legal title in slaves before slavery was established: "[I]t is clear that Slaveholders will risk far more than free men in colonizing Nebraska. And we apprehend that the owners of slaves in Missouri and elsewhere, will think at least twice before they embark their property in the proposed crusade."[12]

Not all Missourians who migrated were proslavery.[13] As migration from the upper South into the lower Midwest had shown in an earlier period, many whites left the slave states to flee the economic competition of slavery. A free-soil Missourian declared, "I came to Kansas to help make it a free State because I did not want, when I was dead, slaves a-tramping round my grave."[14] A Northerner found the vast majority of the Missouri settlers to be "honest Southerners, who are coming, as they say, to get rid of slavery."[15]

In spite of considerable enthusiasm in the border towns of Missouri for the Kansas-Nebraska Act, few people seriously intended to migrate. Those who did cross were stigmatized as "Border Ruffians," Missourians who freely crossed the border to vote or participate sporadically in Kansas affairs, but who did not settle there permanently. Kansas settlers also referred to western Missourians as "pukes," a term of obscure origin. According to one account, Gold Rush Californians had so dubbed migrants from Missouri, "declaring that they had been vomited forth from that prolific State."[16] An eastern journalist's physical description of the typical western Missourian was equally unflattering. He described how the Missouri ruffian had tobacco juice trickling from his mouth, wore a bowie knife tucked in his boottop, and outfitted himself in jean pants, a "sky-blue blanket overcoat," and a six-shooter.[17] Border Ruffians claimed exciting adventures on the Great Plains, in the war with Mexico, or down in Texas. Behind the Border Ruffians were organizations called Blue Lodges or Self-Defensives, which acted as secret societies to extend slavery to Kansas. The latter name indicated the society's concern with protecting slavery in Missouri by ensuring its expansion into Kansas.[18] Wearing lapel badges of hemp and using "sound on the goose" as their password, the Blue Lodges promised Missourians who would vote in Kansas "free ferry, a dollar a day, & liquor."[19] The most famous of these organizations, the Platte County Self-Defensive Association, was led by B. F. Stringfellow, a middle-aged lawyer and follower of David Atchison. Formed in the summer of 1854, the Platte County Self-Defensives expressed hostility toward free blacks, slaves who hired their own time, blacks and whites who mingled too freely, and abolitionists. Although the organization's members resolved to cross into Kansas to drive out abolitionists, they were as obsessed with preserving slavery in Missouri as with extending it. For if slave-owning secured economic opportunity for whites, opposition to slavery threatened white upward economic mobility. Stringfellow himself emphasized that the organization was "self-defensive," or intended to protect slavery in Missouri.[20] Although a Lecompton man found Stringfellow "good-natured," "gentlemanly," and "not half so violent" in his politics as "you might suppose," Stringfellow's numerous enemies thought otherwise.[21]

Among Stringfellow's enemies was the Reverend Frederick Starr, the Presbyterian minister of Weston, Missouri, whose involvement in Kansas land speculations angered the Missouri lawyer. Stringfellow warned that Starr, a Northerner of dubious allegiance to slavery, might use his participation in founding towns in the territory to create abolition settlements. Stringfellow was already campaigning against "felonious philanthropists," whom he accused of luring away slaves. Over the summer of 1854, the Self-Defensives accused a local man of forging passes for runaways. Convicted of abolitionism, they shaved half his head and gave him forty-eight hours to leave the county.[22] In July 1854, the Platte County Self-Defensives publicly tried a Massachusetts man, who was waiting to move to Kansas, for abolitionism. Sentenced to twenty-four lashes, the man was ultimately escorted to Iowa. Self-Defensives did not distinguish among the varied types of antislavery sentiment, dubbing all abolitionists. When the association established a night patrol for the purpose of suppressing abolitionists, Starr believed they really wanted an excuse to prey on women in the black neighborhoods. The Self-Defensives made membership in their association a test of allegiance to slavery. One man signed, "fearing for his bread & dreading the wrath of the *big 'uns,*" according to Starr.[23] Like other suspected abolitionists, Starr was called before the Self-Defensives to account for himself.[24]

The Self-Defensives charged Starr with teaching blacks to read, helping a black man buy his freedom, and taking a buggy ride in broad daylight with a black woman. The last charge caused a predictable stir, especially among the women in the audience. Starr pleaded that he had never encouraged black resistance to slavery, and that he had only taught blacks with their owners' permission. He dismissed the charge of interracial mixing by pointing out that many Southerners rode in close company with their servants. Starr's remarks were more temperate than his feelings, for he had promised his wife not to call Stringfellow names. According to one observer, Starr defended himself "nobly." Still, when asked his opinion of slavery, he said it was wrong. That was enough for the Self-Defensives. Although the charges were dismissed, Starr was asked to leave Weston. He later returned to New York.[25]

The Platte County Self-Defensive Association rejected Starr's principled denial of slavery's morality. Stringfellow entitled a Self-Defensive manifesto "Negro-Slavery, No Evil." He called on Southerners to stop making excuses for slavery and defend it as "a blessing to the white race and to the negro," who did better under slavery than as impoverished free blacks or heathen, uncivilized Africans. Beyond threatening slave property directly, abolition brought general economic and social problems. According to Stringfellow, crimes (including property crimes such as arson) increased and land values dropped in areas where abolitionists were active. It was in the best economic interest of all Missourians, even nonslaveowners, to defend slavery.[26]

Not all western Missourians endorsed the Association. Weston, Missouri, citizens met on September 1, 1854, and condemned "mob law." One hundred and seventy-four people signed the resolution rejecting the Self-Defensives' call to block northern emigration to Kansas. The citizens of Weston affirmed the equal rights of all men in the territories according to the Kansas-Nebraska Act. They avowed their love not only of the South but also of the Union and made clear their dislike of the Self-Defensives, who had disrupted their peace, quiet, good order, and business.[27] Nonetheless, a Hoosier, who moved to Missouri in the mid-1850s, noted that the Border Ruffians were not "rabble," but some of the "*best men* in *Mo* were engaged *personally* in the *movement*." Those protests that were made against the course set by the Self-Defensives were "*swept away . . .* in the fierce *whirl-wind of popular sentiment*."[28]

Despite the Weston resolution, principled dissent against slavery would not be tolerated along the border. Most Missourians agreed with Stringfellow's ideas, if not his methods. "Are you 'sound on the Goose Question?' may be a query at which an Eastern or Northern man would smile," pointed out William Phillips, himself the victim of a Missouri mob, "but it has a fearful significance applied in Western Missouri." Businessmen and politicians must either adhere to the proslavery position, conceal their doubts, or suffer for them. "Did you ever feel a glow of indignation as you read of the slavery of opinion, of the press, and of speech, in France and Austria?" Phillips queried. "I tell you the veriest tyrant in Europe *dare* not exercise so fearful and despotic control over opinion as the Blue Lodge of Missouri has done."[29] Stringfellow admitted as much. The Self-Defensives stood for free speech but not abolition speech: "In a slaveholding community, the expression of such sentiments is a positive act, more criminal, more dangerous, than kindling the torch of the incendiary, mixing the poison of the assassin."[30] Organizations such as the Self-Defensives were typical of the vigilance committees by which Southerners suppressed dissent against slavery. Such committees investigated and drove out those whose antislavery views and attacks on southern property rights made them subversive to the slaveowning community's good order.[31]

The Self-Defensives might police the subversive sentiments of Missourians and attempt to turn back antislavery migrants, but how far could their influence carry into the territory itself? As on other frontiers, squatters' associations quickly formed to protect the settlers' claims. The first of the squatters' associations seems to have been founded in June 1854, in the Salt Creek Valley near Fort Leavenworth, by settlers and Missourians planning to settle in Kansas.[32] The Salt Creek resolutions recognized the claims of anyone who intended to settle in Kansas. Other squatters would defend a claim "so long as the *bona fide* intention of occupying it is apparent." This intention was signified by clearly marking the claim and erecting a shelter within two weeks.[33]

The Salt Creek resolutions recognized slavery and denied protection to abolitionists, and also distinguished between "actual" settlers and nonresident claimants. Increasingly, actual settlers resented Missourian attendance at claim association meetings. Disputes with Missouri claimholders disrupted meetings of settlers living in the territory in August 1854.[34] The difference between actual settlers and potential ones became important because a surprisingly strong northern migration challenged Missouri control of the territory and Missourians' assumptions about the primacy of slavery to their economic well-being and political rights.

In the fall of 1854, H. Miles Moore of Leavenworth recorded: "The people from the East are beginning to crowd into Kansas. Agents of Eastern Companies are now in town."[35] The eastern companies were the New England Emigrant Aid Company (NEEAC) and other settler organizations. Eli Thayer presented the plan for an emigrant aid organization to the Massachusetts legislature even as the Kansas-Nebraska Act was under consideration in Congress. A descendant of Pilgrims, Thayer had been born poor in 1819. During the 1840s, he had worked as an educator, originally as a teacher, then a principal, and finally founder of his own school for women. By 1854, Thayer's parallel political career had landed him in the lower house of the Massachusetts legislature. Beginning in March 1854, Thayer sought charters, first from the Massachusetts legislature and then from Connecticut, for an emigrant aid company to help New Englanders and foreigners settle in the west. In July, at a meeting in Boston, the NEEAC was finally organized as a joint-stock enterprise capitalized at $200,000. The Massachusetts legislature granted a charter in February 1855, with a capitalization of $1 million. Thayer's model inspired a German organization in Cincinnati, a vegetarian settlement, a proposed free black colony, and believers in the power of the octagon to establish similar organizations. Suspicious Missourians and other observers found it difficult to distinguish these groups from the original NEEAC, so they lumped them all together as "emigrant aid societies."[36]

Despite its impressive appearance on paper, the emigrant aid society's finances were often precarious. In struggles over money and a charter, control of NEEAC passed from Thayer to "stable men of affairs" such as Amos A. Lawrence. Lawrence, a wealthy Massachusetts philanthropist from an old New England family, was reputed to have given away four times the fortune he inherited. He had made his money as a commission agent selling cotton cloth. His southern business connections tempered his dislike of slavery. Like other conservative Northerners, he viewed free-soil politicians as dangerous to the Union, but was likewise repelled by the Kansas-Nebraska Act. Although he served as treasurer of NEEAC, Lawrence seems to have viewed it not as a business venture, but as a rather expensive charity. He always paid the company's overdrafts, sometimes as great as six thousand dollars, himself. Thayer, who talked the most about NEEAC as a money-making venture, himself only bought twenty of the four hundred shares to which he subscribed. Most shareholders held only one to five shares. Stock purchases tended to rise and fall with the significance of Kansas in the national news. Stock buyers responded to pleas to save Kansas for freedom, and probably viewed their stock purchases in Bleeding Kansas's affairs much as Lawrence did, as a philanthropic and political statement rather than as a sensible business investment.[37] Thayer would later write of NEEAC as the power of "ORGANIZED, SELF-SACRIFICING EMIGRATION" in opposition to the "Slave Power."[38] As a financial investment, NEEAC certainly involved considerable self-sacrifice.

For the emigrant, NEEAC offered both opportunity for economic advancement on the frontier and the satisfaction of participating in the holy cause of saving Kansas for freedom. NEEAC assisted with travel, offering cheaper passage through mass purchasing of tickets. A St. Louis merchant reported that NEEAC emigrants paid a substantial 25 percent less in fare than other travelers. The false rumor that the Democratic-appointed territorial governor and his secretary bought their tickets through NEEAC illustrated the company's reputation for providing cheaper rates. Steamboat passage from St. Louis to Kansas City, normally twelve dollars, cost the NEEAC emigrant only ten dollars. A steady stream of parties, from as small as 8 people to as large as 389, made their way westward. During the busy embarkation season of late spring and early summer, parties left Boston weekly. Samuel Johnson estimates the NEEAC emigration to Kansas in 1855 as 1,000 people.[39] According to the 1855 census, New Englanders made up only 4.3 percent of the territorial population. That census was taken before the NEEAC migration became substantial. But by 1860, although the New England-born population in Kansas had increased more than tenfold, New Englanders still accounted for only 4 percent of the population.[40]

In addition to bringing numerous settlers to Kansas, NEEAC provided resources needed to develop the territory. At Lawrence, named after NEEAC benefactor Amos Lawrence, NEEAC agent S. C. Pomeroy detailed plans for a mill, made arrangements with the Delaware Indians to get wood, and set lumber prices. NEEAC also built hotels, sawmills, and gristmills; financed newspapers; and was about to lend money for a steamboat line when the national civil war broke out. One NEEAC guidebook felt obliged to disavow stories that the company provided work or money to emigrants in Kansas.[41] NEEAC, not as rich as its critics feared or its supporters hoped, still supplied resources for non-slaveowners to succeed in Kansas.

Most controversially, NEEAC armed its settlers. Land disputes precipitated the first resort to weapons. In October 1854, Missourians and Northerners camped around the new settlement of Lawrence nearly came to blows. When New Englanders platted Lawrence, they bought out a rival claimant to the site. Other claimants quickly appeared. In the winter of 1854–1855, a compromise distribution of land shares was reached, yet quarrels over the land settlement continued.[42] Because of a claim dispute, Missourians removed tents and burned cabins, uttering sectional imprecations that "the d——d Yankees were taking everything they could get." The Northerners soon formed a military company and posted guards to defend their claims.[43] One settler, a veteran of Gold Rush California, bluffed Missourians off his claim. When he began stripping off his coat and vest, most Missourians took the hint and left. On one occasion, when the Missourians seemed determined to stay and fight, the braggart loudly called on his friends to hold him back.[44]

In April 1855, NEEAC agent Charles Robinson wrote to Thayer that free-state settlers were forming militia companies and needed weapons.[45] Robinson, a Massachusetts doctor who had joined the California Gold Rush after the death of his first wife and their children, had led squatters' riots in Sacramento. Upon his return to his native Fitchburg, Robinson remarried to one of his patients, Sara T. D. Lawrence, a relative of Amos Lawrence. Sara Robinson became a propagandist in the cause of free Kansas, and better known to many readers in the east than her husband. Opponents found Charles Robinson cold and forbidding with a "shrewd" intelligence; his letters reveal an acid wit. Robinson's western travels led NEEAC to recruit him, and he arrived in the territory in the summer of 1854. Although more level-headed than many other free-soil settlers, Robinson appreciated the deterrent value of weapons.[46] Officially, NEEAC decided not to send rifles directly to settlers, but instead offered to facilitate their purchase. Settlers ordered guns through NEEAC, which also handled fundraising for their purchase and distribution. The accounts of the New York State Kansas Committee, an affiliate of NEEAC, show that New Yorkers made direct payments to NEEAC, in addition to paying for newspaper advertisements and tickets; financed free-state political rallies in the East; and reimbursed emigrants for money used to purchase rifles. In early April 1856, before fighting broke out in Kansas, the committee purchased arms from the Sharps Rifle company: twenty-five carbines— as well as primers, percussion caps, and cartridges—were obtained at a cost of $750, excluding the ten percent discount for large orders. The committee's accounts included two other, much smaller, purchases of individual weapons.[47] Eli Thayer himself, in a speech to an amused and appreciative New York City audience, advised, "As to the preparations for going there, seeing that threats had been made, it might be well for the Emigrant to be furnished with his Bible and his rifle; and if he were not protected in his rights according to the principles of the first, let him rely upon the execution of the latter."[48] Though northern settlers would later present themselves as unoffending victims of Missouri violence and intimidation, they were themselves heavily armed long before violence had occurred. One elderly Kansan later recalled that in 1855 he had joined a party of Illinois men headed for Kansas armed with Sharps rifles. "It was a military company that could be changed to a colony or a colony ready for military service."[49]

Initially, proslavery observers were less upset by NEEAC's arming the settlers than by the fear that northern states were dumping their "paupers" into the territory as hired and transient voters. Proslavery men in Douglas, Kansas Territory, condemned the emigrant aid society for buying white slaves to send to the territory. A clerk on a Missouri River steamboat observed that eastern emigrants carried little baggage, much less farming gear, were unencumbered by women or children, talked freely of voting when they got to the territory—and that many returned east. Such reports fueled Missourians' fears that Easterners were importing a transient population of voters that threatened their rights to introduce slavery into Kansas.[50]

Missouri reaction to the eastern migrants reveals the complex interplay between economic and political motives for settlement. Proslavery and free-soil migrants both saw the territory as opening economic opportunity, but they deeply suspected the other side's motives for migration. Eastern migrants would add their own complaint to that of actual settlers who groused Missourians did not take up permanent residence in the territory. Already inclined to believe in and to interpret the Kansas-Nebraska Act in terms of a malign Slave Power, they complained poor white Southerners were being manipulated to serve the interest of slaveowners.[51] Missourians used their belief in the transience of eastern migrants, as well as the language of slavery and classical republicanism, to accuse free-soil settlers of being the tool of abolitionists. Missourians did not object to the so-called "pauper" emigrants because their poverty would render them an economic burden, but rather because, being economically dependent, they would be politically dependent on the northern interests who allegedly financed their migration.

Free-soil proponents scoffed at these charges: "Many of these New England paupers can buy out half a dozen of the largest Missouri slaveholders in the morning and sell them again at night, and then not brag of having down [sic] a big day's business."[52] But the attrition rate among eastern settlers was higher than many cared to admit. Many who planned to settle permanently in Kansas were ill-prepared and quickly grew disillusioned with the territory. Isaac Goodnow, one of the original settlers of Manhattan, estimated that two-thirds of his original party "failed in the hour of *trial*" and returned home.[53]

Despite the efforts of the emigrant aid societies, the journey to Kansas was still long and difficult. Migrants complained of constant overcharging by hotel keepers, or by steamboat captains who sometimes changed fares en route in response to the vagaries of the river. Once there, the migrant found costs high, work scarce, and NEEAC resources skimpy. A disappointed emigrant felt NEEAC had deceived him by representing Lawrence as a finished city.[54] Goodnow recalled early Lawrence as "a rude town of some 30 or 40 log & rough board cabins, with a conservansary for emigrants, built of sod walls, cloth roof, & prairy grass for a carpet."[55] In the spring of 1855, the town's best hotel was a sod-walled, sawdust-floored, thatch-roofed dwelling. A table ran down the middle of the room for diners. Overnight guests slept on boards nailed to posts in the ground. Migrants encountered further problems when they came too late in the year, arriving in Kansas with the onset of winter and without provisions or housing.[56] Elijah Porter left the territory in May 1855, declaring, "Kansas is a *humbug*." Porter complained of the lack of wood, water, food, and rain. Sickness, however, abounded.[57] An unsympathetic proslavery source described northern settlers as "cold and hungry."[58]

While settlers frequently praised the soil, the honest admitted that life in a grass-roofed, sixteen-foot-square log cabin left much to be desired. George Spivey described for his father the fine soil and good prospects in Kansas but warned that his mother would not like the rough life of a log cabin. Of Kansas Territory, Spivey wrote, "The soil is good and also the pasture, and it is the prettiest Co., in the world.

But it is 'sickly'—fevers and ague is the worst there. It will be warm enough to go naked in the bed, and the next hour it will be cold enough to freeze the tail off the dogs, and that is the fault of this country."[59] Kansas was bound to disappoint cultivated easterners, as it did a friend of the Goodnows, who sought "a farm where I could obtain the necessities of life easily."[60] Kansas might be fertile, but economic advancement would not come easily.

New England pioneers later recollected they had endured these hardships for a great cause. Isaac Goodnow remembered that he had been teaching at a Methodist school in Rhode Island when he heard Eli Thayer speak. "Fully believing that the *rule* of Slavery or Freedom would be settled upon the prairies of Kansas for the whole nation, it occurred to me that every Friend of Freedom should throw himself into the scale." Goodnow even recalled one settler who was known for the long hair and beard that he had vowed not to cut until Kansas became a free state.[61]

To validate their vows to work for the cause of freedom, New England settlers, as Goodnow recounted, sang songs of liberty on their passage. By the time Goodnow made his trip, two of the most noteworthy songs had been composed: John Greenleaf Whittier's "Song of the Kansas Emigrant" (to the tune of "Auld Lang Syne"), and Lucy Larcom's "Call to Kansas." The latter was the prize winner in a NEEAC-sponsored contest.[62] Whittier and Larcom spoke of Kansas as the site of freedom. Whittier's song predicted that the eastern migrants would make Kansas "the homestead of the free!" Larcom called on Kansas migrants to "sing, upon the Kansas plains,/The song of liberty." Neither spoke of the slave. In fact, these poets most distinctly connected liberty to the northern migrants' right to earn a living through, as Larcom wrote, "The true man's toil." Only one of several songs celebrating eastern migration explicitly linked the "Freedom's legions" of migrants to the antislavery cause, calling "Death to Slavery!"[63]

The settlers themselves linked economic advancement to a noble cause. William Goodnow, Isaac's brother, could not understand his wife's opposition to migrating as "it would place you in a condition to be above *want* & *care* which is now the chief burden of your life."[64] Goodnow concluded, "If any pioneers deserve prosperity it is the Kansas emigrants that left good homes, kind friends, & very desirable religious & social privilege, to establish the same to *all* the inhabitants of this rich land."[65]

The Kansas migrants were not so pure that they never calculated earning a profit, and so they were not pure enough for many in the abolitionist movement. Often, Thayer acknowledged, northern settlers possessed unenlightened views on race issues.[66] Still, settlers undoubtedly felt both inspired by a crusade for freedom and by the desire to better themselves on the frontier. Proslavery men on the border, however, saw the influx of Northerners as a threat to their freedom to establish their economic and political institutions.

Southerners organized emigration to defend slavery. In November 1855, Major Jefferson Buford, a Eufala, Alabama, lawyer and veteran of the Second Creek War, issued a call for Kansas emigrants. Buford offered more generous terms than NEEAC: free passage, support for a year, and forty acres of land. He sold forty of his own slaves to raise the money and solicited donations, promising a settler for every $50 contribution. Buford promised "bona fide settlers, able and willing to vote and fight." Speakers, including prominent Southerners such as William L. Yancey, canvassed the lower South to raise support. One southern state legislature debated, but did not enact, a bill to appropriate $25,000 for Kansas emigrants. The *Charleston Mercury* proposed the formation of a Kansas Land Company to buy lands in Kansas, with the intention of preventing the expansion of free-soil settlement, but nothing came of the effort.[67] The *Richmond Enquirer* urged Virginians, white and black, to move to Kansas and preserve the "honor and interests of the South."[68] According to one account, a southern planter, somewhat inebriated, gave $1,000 to the proslavery cause in Kansas, saying, "I've just sold a nigger for that, and I reckon it's about my share towards cleaning out the dog-gauned Yankees."[69] Like the planter's gesture, southern support was erratic.

On April 7, 1856, Buford's party of four hundred men, mostly from Alabama, South Carolina, and Georgia, left Montgomery for Kansas Territory. A farewell speech urged them to save Kansas for slavery and advised gentlemanly behavior, good citizenship, and temperance. They arrived in the territory on May 2, just before guerrilla war broke out. Many fought on the proslavery side—some in the territorial militia which attacked Lawrence that month. But the fighting made ordinary settlement impossible; many left Kansas by late 1856. In order to appeal for aid, Buford made trips all summer to the South; he calculated his own losses at over $10,000. He is believed to have returned to Alabama in the spring of 1857.[70]

Although Southerners felt their interests were at stake and that economic opportunity awaited in Kansas, they were unable to send large numbers of migrants. Young southern men sought economic independence from their fathers on frontiers already clearly marked for slavery. Mississippi, Arkansas, and eastern Texas were prime destinations for slaveowning migrants in the 1850s. Population densities were significantly lower in the Deep South than in the Northeast. Ohio, Pennsylvania, and New York averaged over 50 people per square mile, while in New England population was even denser: 77 people per square mile in Connecticut and 124 in Massachusetts. With an average of only about 15 people per square mile in Georgia, Alabama, and Mississippi, 4 people per square mile in Arkansas, and less than a person per mile in Texas, the Deep South possessed plenty of unoccupied land for ambitious young planters.[71]

While NEEAC drew attention to migration from New England, substantial migration also came into Kansas from western states such as Ohio, Indiana, Illinois, and Iowa. Most settlers from those states had no association or familiarity with NEEAC. In the 1855 census, twenty-two percent of settlers came from the Midwest. By 1860, that percentage grew to thirty-five percent. Moving to Kansas in small family parties, these westerners left fewer accounts of their migration than the New Englanders. By 1855, James W. Houser, an Ohio farmer in his twenties, settled with his wife and two sons in the same voting district as Samuel Houser, possibly an older brother, who had a wife and four sons.[72] Many Midwestern settlers like the Housers possessed an agnostic position on slavery in the territories: they disliked competition with slave labor and blacks about as much as they did abolitionist moralizing. James H. Lane, who migrated from Indiana in April 1855, best expressed the prejudices of the Westerners. On first arriving in Kansas, Lane was reputed to have said that he would as soon buy a

Midwest settler and free-state political and
military leader James H. Lane. (Kansas State
Historical Society, Topeka)

black as a mule. In fact, there were rumors that Lane, estranged from
the wife and three children he had abandoned in Indiana, had tried
to purchase a female slave in Missouri.[73] Although western migrants
did not vaunt their special attachment to liberty as New Englanders
did, they nonetheless shared a fundamental commitment to self-
government for whites as the bedrock of the republic. Here, too, Lane,

a former Democratic politician, reflected their sentiments. As a congressman from Indiana he had avowed in the House of Representatives his commitment to "legislate for the whole people" and praised his constituents' independence and lack of obligation to vested economic interests such as slavery, which he described with racist epithets.[74]

Southerners failed to distinguish between New Englanders and Midwesterners, or the varied motives of the migrants. All easterners were abolitionists, a New York reporter found, whether raised on New England "Johnny-cake" or "Ohio corn."[75] Both groups of migrants came to fear Missouri opposition to their settlement. While camping on the prairies, a group of six northern migrants were awakened by the sounds of another traveler, a Missourian. When a migrant who had lived in Kentucky greeted the newcomer, the Missourian was so happy to encounter a group of supposed Southerners that he exclaimed, "Too many infernal abolitionists are getting into the country, and for my part, I am for tarring and feathering and gutting and hanging and drowning the scoundrels until not an abolition thief shall be found in Kansas!"[76]

Traveling through Missouri became fraught with peril. When the clerk of a Missouri River steamboat failed to modify "abolition" with the customary oath, a voice ordered him to "Shut up," and "respect the wishes of the sovereign people."[77] Rewards of two hundred dollars were posted along the border for the arrest of Eli Thayer.[78] A St. Louis man stated that northern emigrants would be safe unless they provoked opposition by "wanton imprudence on their own part."[79] What troubled northern migrants was their unfamiliarity with what Missourians considered to be "wanton imprudence." Northerners considered the right to dissent a basic freedom. Yet Southerners emphasized majority approval for slavery and viewed antislavery speech as subversive of the popular will. Increasingly, migrating Northerners faced the challenges to free speech that Frederick Starr and other residents of the border were familiar with. New England and western migrants' allegiance to an abstract principle of liberty, defined and exalted in New England migrants' songs, was dangerous in proslavery states, which had a very different interpretation of liberty.

Although popular sovereignty had enshrined political majorities as the determinant of Kansas's fate, proslavery men did not always view slavery as subject to democratic processes. Whatever the free-soil migration might total, one Missourian asserted, Kansas would be slave because, where no law prohibited it, slavery existed by default. Kansas "was intended for a Slave State, [and] . . . will be so unless the South sleeps on its rights, and neglects its duty."[80] A Virginian agreed. If either Congress or northern migrants to Kansas prohibited slavery there, "the Constitution is violated."[81] Shortly after the Kansas-Nebraska Act passed, Abraham Lincoln noted the different expectations for popular sovereignty possessed by northern and southern migrants. New Englanders, Lincoln noted, were sending migrants in the expectation that "the question [of slavery is] to be decided by voting." Missourians in their public meetings, however, "resolve that slavery already exists in the territory," but without ever referring to a decision at the "ballot-box."[82]

Nonetheless, astute Southerners recognized the political menace of northern migration. In 1855, from the wharf at Kansas City, David Atchison saw a riverboat carrying a NEEAC-purchased steam engine. Atchison asked his companions what the machine was. When he was told "a steam-engine and a steam-boiler," he replied angrily, "You are all a pack of —— fools; that is a Yankee city going to Kansas, and by ——! in six months it will cast one hundred Abolition votes!"[83] News of the formation of northern emigrant aid societies caused especial "excitement" in Missouri. Their formation "was looked upon as an intermeddling with our own business by foreigners," Amos Rees asserted. Missourians "always acted under the idea that slavery existed in the Territory since the passage of the [Kansas-Nebraska] bill. Any movement by societies or organizations connected with foreign influence would have heated the same excitement if it tended to lead to the prohibition of slavery. The people of Missouri felt a deep interest in establishing slavery in Kansas, and regarded it as necessary for their safety."[84] A Missouri judge also resented the New England migration. "Let Massachusetts govern itself, I say; and we'll govern ourselves. That's so. . . . That's right and fair; and they've no right to interfere."[85]

But Missouri's claims to a special right to Kansas were under attack. Easterners did not agree that "Massachusetts men have not a right to emigrate into territories into which Missouri men may move."[86] Even one Missourian claimed puzzlement at the objection to northern settlement in Kansas. Northerners had the perfect right to settle there; it was the essence of popular sovereignty.[87]

Atchison argued that Kansas was too important for the South to lose. Echoing Stringfellow's arguments that undermining slave property threatened all of southern society, Atchison complained that Missouri was acting without help from the rest of the South, even though "the prosperity or the ruin of the whole South depends on the Kansas struggle." If Kansas became free, so would Missouri.[88] A proslavery convention at Lexington, Missouri, agreed with Atchison: "[L]arge monied associations" intended "to abolitionize Kansas, and through Kansas, to operate upon the contiguous states of Missouri, Arkansas and Texas." The $25 million worth of slave property in the border counties of Missouri "is not merely unsafe but valueless, if Kansas is made the abode of an army of hired fanatics, recruited, transported, armed and paid for the special and sole purpose of abolitionizing Kansas and Missouri."[89] The Platte County Self-Defensive Association had been publicizing the nature of this abolitionist conspiracy since early 1855 when it tried Frederick Starr.[90] Now a larger northern migration intensified the conflict between Northerners' belief in a right to condemn slavery and Southerners' belief that such condemnation threatened their property rights.

Both proslavery and free-soil men recognized that popular sovereignty had made elections crucial to deciding Kansas's fate. Missourians justified their involvement in Kansas elections by their geographic proximity to Kansas, and by their belief that the continued health of slavery in Missouri depended on its extension to Kansas.[91] Voting in Kansas elections seemed a legitimate reaction by nonresidents to the dangerous and "unfair encroachments of the north."[92] In a November 1854 speech, Atchison warned that controlling the ballot box was the only way to prevent Kansas from becoming a base for abolitionizing the entire South. He maintained if a "set of fanatics and demagogues" can send people from a thousand miles, then "when you reside in one day's journey of the Territory, *and when your peace, your quiet and your property depend upon your action, you can, without an exertion, send five hundred of your young men who will vote in favor of your institutions.*" Atchison urged Southerners "*to go peaceably and inhabit the territory, and peaceable to vote and settle the question.*"[93]

Northerners also recognized that the first elections would be crucial. Samuel Pomeroy reported, "The *roads* are lined with teams from the border states, and in about every *fifth* or *eighth* wagon you will see a sprinkling of negro slaves. Don't make yourselves believe the slave holders have given up Kansas! A terrible *struggle* is before us at this very *first Election.* They are determined to have a law recognizing slavery at the very *first meeting* of the *Legislature.* If [they] do *not* get it at the *first* legislature they *never* will!!"[94]

As Kansas filled with settlers and prepared for the first elections, free-soil and proslavery migrants did more than establish their communities and overcome early hardships. They refined the meaning of popular sovereignty. Missourians, who had eagerly supported popular sovereignty, had assumed that proximity to the territory legitimized and ensured their political dominance. Yet Missourians did not define democracy as including the right to question or undermine slavery. In a slaveowning society, the people accepted slavery as vital to the economic well-being and opportunity of slaveowners and nonslaveowners alike. To oppose slavery was to oppose the people and subvert the good order of the community. Missourians denigrated the voters from the East as temporary residents, hirelings of NEEAC who lacked the long-term interest in Kansas that neighboring Missourians possessed. Free-soil settlers, many of whom had not wanted the Missouri Compromise replaced by popular sovereignty, maintained they came to Kansas because they had faith in the principle of popular sovereignty. They had come to Kansas to settle and to vote. If many of their number failed in the hour of trial, that did not invalidate the claims of those who stayed, or of the newly arrived who intended to become actual residents of the territory. They did not acknowledge neighboring Missourians' special political rights in the territory. While some New Englanders linked their migration to a crusade for liberty, only a minority of northern settlers came to Kansas with strong moral positions against slavery; most sought better homes in the west. But both New England and western settlers did share a commitment to the political rights of white settlers. When proslavery forces closed ranks to defend slavery, free-soil settlers felt forced to define what they meant by liberty and to defend their own political rights.

3

All Right on the Hemp
The Territorial Legislature

While settlers constructed shelter against the coming cold weather, proslavery men approached the new territorial governor, Andrew H. Reeder, about moving up the date of the elections for the legislature. An early election would secure a strong proslavery vote before northern migrants arrived. When Reeder quizzed the delegation's leader, F. Gwinner, about his place of residence, Gwinner claimed to live on Salt Creek in Kansas Territory. "Do you live in a house?" Reeder asked. No, Gwinner demurred, he had no house but had located a claim. "I believe I have your residence in my pocket-book," Reeder replied, pulling from his wallet a playing card marked "Gwinner's Claim–Oct. 21, 1854." Like many other Missourians, Gwinner had marked his claim by nailing the card to a tree while continuing to live in Missouri. Reeder's secretary had found the card while hunting. When Gwinner admitted owning the card, a three of diamonds, Reeder teased him, "Why your card was rather low—some fellow might have come along with the four of diamonds, and jumped your claim." The governor and his guests enjoyed a good laugh and parted amicably.[1] In his official reply, the governor maintained the polite, if not jocular, tone of the interview. However, he informed the committee that while Missourians were welcome to visit or settle in the territory, Kansas settlers must rule themselves.[2]

Popular sovereignty intimately bound migration to politics in a way unprecedented for the United States. Through the

A. H. Reeder, Democratic politician and first territorial governor of Kansas. (Kansas State Historical Society, Topeka)

ballot box, Kansas settlers were to decide the contested issue of slavery. But faith in the ballot box presupposed general agreement on electoral practices that did not exist in the nineteenth-century United States. Actual procedures varied greatly from locale to locale. In most parts of the country by 1855, voters deposited colored paper ballots, often printed by the political parties, into the ballot box. Although less public than the oral casting of votes still favored in parts of the South, bystanders could often know a man's vote by the color of his ballot.

Whether voting orally or by ballot, voters' names were recorded in a poll book. In the eastern states, advance registration of voters was often required. Registration was intended to limit the movement of voters from poll to poll on election day. Residency requirements also varied in different states. Massachusetts, Missouri, Ohio, and Illinois all required for state and federal elections a year's residency in the state. For local elections, Massachusetts required six months' residence in a town or district, Missouri only three, but the western states six months to a year's residence. Widespread internal migration in the United States, however, had undermined the idea that voting was tied exclusively to residence. If an individual intended to settle in that locale, the community accepted his right to vote even if he did not yet physically reside there. In practice, though, a slate of election judges, respected local men who would know the voters, determined the validity of the ballots cast. Whenever a judge or bystander challenged the right of a voter to cast his ballot, the judges voted on whether or not to accept the ballot. Sometimes judges and voters were required to swear an oath to administer the election or vote fairly. In both the territorial delegate election in the fall of 1854 and the election of a territorial legislature in March 1855, Governor Reeder's proclamation specified that the voter must actually reside and intend to continue residing in Kansas Territory. Voters would swear an oath as to their residency in the territory. Despite Reeder's provisions, voting was both highly public and dependent on local norms. There was no one standard of popular sovereignty to be implemented in Kansas.[3] Missourians' proprietorial interest in Kansas, including the conviction that Kansas must have slavery if Missouri's economic interests were to be safe, made actual settlement less important to their defintion of popular sovereignty than intent to eventually settle in the territory. Fluid residence and voting requirements reinforced their belief. But the Missourians voting in Kansas came in such numbers and flaunted their presence so openly they offended free-soil voters who felt intimidated, overwhelmed, and denied the choice offered by popular sovereignty. The tumult of the first elections left both proslavery and free-soil voters complaining about violations of their political rights and brought the proslavery men into conflict with their neighbors and the governor.

Nothing in Reeder's undistinguished career indicated his future course in Kansas. A Pennsylvania lawyer and popular-sovereignty Democrat, Reeder was appointed by the Pierce administration in order to strengthen the party in that state. When he arrived in the territory in October 1854, Reeder was forty-seven years old, of a "ruddy" complexion, and inclined to put on weight. He had never held office before.[4] H. Miles Moore described him as "rather thick set, stout built & commanding appearance, looks like a man of a strong & determined will of his own, although, mild, affable to all." As eager to make money in Kansas as any other settler, Reeder bought one thousand dollars worth of shares in Moore's land company.[5]

Reeder's first official action was to order an election of delegate to Congress on November 29, 1854. Reeder's pre-election proclamation clearly defined "residence" as "the actual dwelling or inhabiting in the Territory to the exclusion of any other present domicil or home, coupled with the present *bona fide* intention of remaining permanently for the same purpose."[6] Missourians took a large interest in J. W. Whitfield, the "Southern Rights candidate."[7] A Leavenworth meeting, consisting mostly of nonresident Missourians, nominated Whitfield for delegate to Congress.[8]

Whitfield won easily. A Leavenworth man described how "The whole country was overrun on the day of the election by hordes of ruffians from Missouri, who took entire possession of the polls in almost every district, brow-beat and intimidated the Judges, forced their own votes into the ballot-box for WHITFIELD, and crowded out and drove off all who were suspected of being in favor of any other candidate."[9] Frederick Starr called the delegate election "the greatest outrage on the ballot box ever perpetrated on American Soil." In the new towns near Leavenworth, Starr reported, "Some 1200 or 1400 Missourians armed with bowie knives & revolvers took the polls . . . more than 40 free soilers were unable to come to the polls at all."[10]

Those who made it to the polls at Leavenworth encountered a throng that made it hard for free-state men to vote. "When I would try to get in, they would pull me by the coat, crowd me, and I could not succeed to get through the crowd," John A. Lindsay recalled. "I then went round and hurrahed for General Whitfield, and some of them who did not know me said, 'There is a good proslavery man,' and lifted me up over their heads, and I crawled along over the heads, and put in my vote. Then some one who saw my ticket cried out, 'He is a damned abolitionist, let him down!' and they dropped me."[11]

Several disgruntled voters testified to the voters' organization. Near the polling place, a Hoosier settler found a large camp of armed men, some drunk, who departed in wagons an hour or so after voting. "I heard them say they had as good right to come from Missouri and vote there as others who were there and had come from other States," William Moore said.[12] H. Miles Moore, who came over to Leavenworth with a large party from Platte County, reported that messengers recruited voters in Missouri and gave parties destinations in the territory. Another observer noted that a judge from Jackson County, Missouri, was supervising imported voters.[13] Intimidation was part and parcel of the commotion. One Missourian made it bluntly clear to John A. Wakefield, the free-soil candidate, what to expect if he challenged voters: "You will be badly abused, and probably killed." To underscore that threat, proslavery men who voted were armed and drinking, and cursed both Yankees and abolitionists.[14] Another observer at Douglas remarked, "The men seemed to be very noisy, and hurrahed for Whitfield, and some for hell, and some for Whitfield and hell both."[15]

In early December 1854, Reeder received the results of the November election. Whitfield was elected territorial delegate with 2,258 votes, having received a majority of the votes in every district except the NEEAC town of Lawrence. Whitfield's vote greatly exceeded that of the next leading candidates, Wakefield with 248 votes and Robert Flenneken with 305. A congressional investigation later concluded that over 1,700 votes cast in the election were fraudulent.[16]

While this investigation cast some shadow on the election, whatever fraud existed did not materially change the election's result. The proslavery side, which Whitfield represented, simply had more people in Kansas in November 1854. In any case, Reeder apparently felt that grounds did not exist to contest the results. He let them stand.[17] Although the territorial secretary, Daniel Woodson, reported to his wife that Whitfield's election had been a "great triumph of our friends,"[18] proslavery men worried that the election of the territorial legislature, which Reeder had set for March 30, gave northern migration time to endanger proslavery dominance.[19]

In January 1855, David Atchison wrote, "The Abolitionists will make great efforts in the Spring to send into Kansas their battalions & Regts. for the *holy* purpose of excluding Slaveholders. They should be met by corresponding efforts on our part. *We can and must defeat them,* and nothing that is fair and honourable should be left undone."[20] Atchison himself planned to visit South Carolina and Georgia, to raise interest in the cause of slavery in Kansas: "Money, time, private interest and all other things are but as dust, compared to this question in its consequences; the Abolitionists are most energetically at work, we must meet and conquer them 'peaceably if we can forcibly if we must.'"[21]

Residents of Lawrence feared giving Missourians any excuse for an election-day invasion. When three Missourians demanded the return of a young black woman, who they claimed was a runaway, Lawrence men initially believed the woman instead of her white accusers. However, they soon worried that she and the three men were conspiring to create "a pretext for an invasion of our legal rights" on election day, which was only three weeks away. Despite her pleas that she "would rather go to hell than with them men,"[22] they gave the woman to the Missourians.

As Northern settlers suspected, Missourians were preparing for the election. J. W. Reid struggled to turn out the proslavery vote, bemoaning the difficulties of getting voters to the necessary polling places. But he took heart because, "I learn that a larger portion of the Judges are friendly to us, *unknown to Reeder.*"[23]

A month before the election, preparations were being made at the western Missouri Masonic Lodge, where H. Miles Moore noted a "secret meeting . . . of Slaveholders." They intended, Moore thought, "to plan for Kansas election to come off before long." Three weeks later, in early March, B. F. Stringfellow spoke at a "large & enthusiastic" proslavery meeting in Missouri, whose purpose was to raise money for sending men to Kansas. Stringfellow urged voters to cross over and hold Kansas until sufficient slave-state migration arrived. Two weeks before the election, Moore met with Atchison and recorded in his diary that proslavery men would indeed make a strong effort to carry the Kansas election.[24]

The day of the election proved tumultuous. Frederick Starr reported that Missouri River ferries carried eight hundred men a day, for three days prior to the election, across the river. Organized in companies, some of these men went as far inland as Pawnee, some 120 miles into the territory. At the Leavenworth election, there appeared five times the number of voters recorded in the census. When the free-soil judge of election resigned, he was replaced by one sympathetic to slavery. Some judges refused to take the governor's oath, while others decided that voters did not have to take their oath. Intimidated, most free-soil supporters simply did not vote.[25] A Missourian who had lived in Kansas since the fall of 1854 saw no violence at the Leavenworth election, although he reported an open display of bowie knives and guns. He himself did not vote, he explained, "because [he] considered squatters directly insulted by Missouri, by taking our rights in voting away from us."[26]

Similar irregularities occurred at other polling places: voters from outside the territory cast ballots, judges of election refused to follow procedures set by the governor, and free-soil candidates, judges, and voters withdrew from the polling places.[27] A report from Lawrence estimated that from seven hundred to three thousand Missourians had come to vote, forcing the judge of election to hand over the poll book. Free soilers were so intimidated that they did not even try to vote. With banners flying, the Missourians had marched in to a drumbeat. Provisioned with two fieldpieces, wagons, tents, and food, they wore pieces of white or blue ribbon—or hemp—in their buttonholes, from which arose their password, "all right on the hemp." So many Missourians turned out that, according to one Lawrence resident, having a surplus for the Lawrence polls, a camp on the Wakarusa was able to spare extra voters for another polling place.[28]

Although reports from Lawrence indicated no violence, free soilers blamed their loss on the threat of violence. Election judge N. B. Blanton failed to appear at the Lawrence polls, he said, after Missourians threatened to hang him if he insisted on enforcing the governor's oath.[29] One of Blanton's fellow judges, James B. Abbott, did show up but quickly became frustrated when the other two judges outvoted him each time on the acceptability of ballots. Seeing himself outnumbered, he too resigned and was replaced.[30]

More flagrant intimidation occurred at Bloomington. Missourians broke in the windows of the log house that served as a polling place and picked it up by one corner, letting it fall. Samuel J. Jones entered the house with a half-dozen Missourians. One of the election judges ran out of the house carrying the ballot box and hurrahing for Missouri. Pointedly looking at his watch, Jones gave the remaining judges five minutes to resign or be killed. They resigned.[31]

Free-soil sources provided other dramatic accounts of organized nonresident voting and intimidation. Missourians verified them. Moore recorded that a "great crowd," presumably including himself, went over to Kansas on election day and that "all voted that pleased, no objections, no swearing in voters."[32] A Doniphan man was unnerved by the Missourians' behavior. He noted that armed men, who were "cutting up," were "pretty well corned [drunk], and were noisy and boisterous."[33] A Missourian later recalled that he had voted at the March 1855 election while still residing in Missouri. He intended to move to Kansas and, in fact, did so not long after the election. Because he was "naturally anxious to have a voice in moulding the institutions" where he intended to reside, he did not regard his vote as ethically wrong.[34]

That view was widely accepted among the proslavery party. In an editorial three days before the election, the Atchison *Squatter Sovereign* insisted that residency was unnecessary for voting. "By the Kansas act, every man in the Territory on the day of the election is a legal voter, if he have not fixed a day for his return to some other home."[35] On election day, many Missourians told a Lawrence man that they had a legal right to vote because residents could vote and "they were residents while they were here."[36] One Missourian explained, "By the Nebraska Bill every man who happened to inhabit the territory at the time of the election was a qualified voter. No man was ever sworn *that he would not go away*."[37]

Missourians also rationalized their actions by asserting that the threat to Missouri was so severe that it justified measures that seemingly violated democratic processes.[38] A Missouri lawyer wrote in his diary of the proslavery victory in Kansas, "It is certain th[a]t the Missourians regard this as a simple question whether they shall leave here—or those abolitionists shall leave Kansas."[39] Fearing that free Kansas would harbor fugitive slaves and endanger the safety of slave property in their state, Missourians asked, "If Kansas be settled by Abolitionists, can Missouri remain a slave state?" Many Missourians thought not. In fact, if abolition should spread to Missouri, one southern state after another would be endangered, until slavery everywhere was under siege.[40]

In the aftermath of the election, Missourians closed ranks to defend slavery. When the *Parkville Luminary,* published in Missouri, objected to election fraud and lawlessness in Kansas, a crowd of two hundred threw the printing press into the river. The publisher and editor were ordered out of the state.[41] When settler Pardee Butler publicly announced his intention to vote to make Kansas free, proslavery editor Robert S. Kelley and his followers seized him, dragged him to the river, and "tried" him for two hours before a crowd, debating whether to hang him. They finally set Butler adrift on a raft with a sign reading "Eastern Emigrant Aid Express. The Rev. Mr. Butler's Agent for the Underground Railroad." Butler tore down the flag and used its staff to paddle ashore.[42] When William Phillips, a Leavenworth lawyer with abolitionist sympathies, filed a formal protest about the election in his district, a committee of a dozen men took Phillips into custody in Weston, Missouri. They shaved one side of his head, stripped him of his clothing, tarred and feathered him, and rode him on a rail for a mile and a half. As a final touch, they carried out a mock auction with a black auctioneer and sold Phillips for one dollar.[43]

Missourians also wanted to counter the transient vote that they believed NEEAC and other northern agencies were importing. John H. Stringfellow, Benjamin's brother, later insisted that Missourians came to Kansas on March 30 "to prevent or counteract illegal voting on the part of hired voters from the east and other free States."[44] A Lawrence man recalled hearing Missourians say that "they had as good a right to vote as men who came from other States. I heard them say there were men here from the east and north who came here to vote. They said that these men had come here for no other purpose, and that they had as much right to come here and vote as the others had; and that was the reason they gave for coming here."[45] In fact, Charles Robinson had arrived in Lawrence on election day with between sixty and a hundred emigrants from the east who voted.[46]

The importing of voters and other types of ballot fraud Missourians practiced were, in fact, staples of U.S. elections at the time. In a period of rampant political corruption and lax residency requirements, violence and threats at the polling places were nothing to shock Westerners. A Weston, Missouri, man found the delegate election perfectly ordinary: "There was some excitement during the election, but nothing very serious—but a little knock-down—some of our old Kentucky election fights."[47] Free-soil voters, however, may have been genuinely shocked. Many came from New England where such election irregularities were rare compared to the western states. The righteous indignation of free-soil voters also served as valuable propaganda against the proslavery party. Free-soil voters liked to recall that they had taken refuge behind the U.S. flag when their right to vote was infringed. Tecumseh voter Charles Jordan told the proslavery men, "The flag was floating over us just about where we were standing. . . . I had defended my country; that that was our true flag, the stars and stripes, and under that flag I never intend to vote while it floats over a seditious mob."[48] Free-soil flag-waving caused Missourians to find themselves on the defensive after the election. Voter fraud may have been common but it still violated the sanctity of the democratic process. A Pennsylvania newspaper contended that even defenders of the South "would not extenuate, much less sanction, so gross a violation of every principle of Republican Government."[49] The sheer numbers voting seemed flagrant evidence to the contrary. The territorial census earlier that month had found 2,905 voters in the territory, but over 6,000 men voted on March 30. Proslavery votes totaled 5,427. The Missourians had simply gone too far.[50]

In a memorial presented to Congress, the free-soil settlers protested that the disruption of the March 30 election was "a well matured and settled plan" to "enslave" them. The memorial rehearsed complaints about the massive invasion of the polls, intimidation of judges and voters, and Atchison's role in encouraging Missouri voting. "Foreign oppression" threatened to destroy popular sovereignty's promise of majority rule.[51] Unless the provisions of the Kansas-Nebraska Act were enforced, Kansas was destined to become "a vassal province" of Missouri.[52]

The free-soil citizens of Kansas were not the only ones whom the election appalled. Some Southerners recoiled from the Border Ruffians' actions. A Kentuckian wrote, "How any virtuous and patriotic man can justify the lawless and armed mob of Missourians who went to Kansas to control the elections, is marvellous to me."[53] Another Southerner wondered "how the Missourians can expect to be sustained by any persons who have the slightest pretentions to fairness, or even to civilization."[54] Missouri state legislator George R. Smith publicly declared, "Important as I consider it to my own interest in slaves that Kansas should be a slave state, I would not violate the laws of my country to make it so, nor would I advise others to do so."[55]

Even Atchison felt some qualms. He did not lead a company of illegal voters, armed with bowie knife and revolver, as antislavery sources claimed.[56] "I did not vote, nor did I go to the place of the election," Atchison wrote, "but I was on hands, I know that it was a matter of doubtful policy to go into the territory on the day of the election but I could not reconcile it to myself to persuade men to do what I would not do myself, and it was great encouragement to the boys, we have carried everything I suppose in the territory." Atchison praised the actions of the western Missourians who had ensured that Missouri would be "represented" in the territory: "What a glorious thing it was to carry the Sebastopol of Abolitionism in the gallant style in which it was done." Not content to rest with this victory, he intended to "purge" Kansas.[57]

Atchison hinted that a "purge" would need to include Governor Reeder, who had the power to set aside election returns. Barely two weeks after the election, a proslavery newspaper called for Reeder's removal. But outrage over incidents at the polls created more of a stir. The governor's official records show a flood of complaints, many from election judges. The reports confirmed that large numbers of men had appeared at polls, had threatened violence, had taken poll books and certificates of election from the authorized judges. Again and again, the petitioners complained that intimidated actual residents of Kansas had simply opted not to vote.[58]

On April 6, Reeder set aside the results in six of the disputed districts. A congressional investigation would later hold that only 1,410 of the votes had been cast legally, thus throwing out far more of the vote than did Reeder.[59] To fill the disputed seats of the March 30 election, Governor Reeder ordered a special election for May 22, which occurred with minimal disturbance.[60] Despite Reeder's intervention, the result was an overwhelmingly proslavery territorial legislature. Yet interference opened him to the charge of partiality in counting the returns. Proslavery men now felt their rights had been infringed. They threatened "Revolution," quoting Patrick Henry to denounce Reeder's "despotism."[61]

The turmoil in Kansas caused Reeder to return east seeking presidential approval of his authority. He requested a new election for the legislature—with sufficient military force to ensure fairness—and threatened to resign unless his request was granted. Some prominent Democrats thought Reeder right in resisting illegal voting, but the Pierce administration was skittish. An unhappy Pierce allowed Reeder to return to Kansas in June. Reeder later recalled that the president had approved his course, even though much of their conversation had dwelt on how to arrange Reeder's resignation. A more astute politician than Reeder would have realized that the president's support was weak.[62]

Reeder returned to confront a territorial legislature that many Kansas settlers felt did not represent them. Free soilers claimed that when a friend of one of the newly elected legislators looked for his political acquaintance at the territorial capital, "he was asked 'if he enquired for the member from Fort Scott [Kansas Territory]?' His reply was 'Fort H——ll!—I wish to see the member from Lafayette Co., Mo.'"[63]

Confronting free soilers was a serious question: how should they respond to a territorial legislature whose legitimacy they denied? On June 8, 1855, citizens of Lawrence called a convention to discuss "the relation the people of this Territory bear to the Legislature about to convene." Free soilers who had been legally elected to the body were urged to resign their seats.[64] As Sara Robinson explained, "The question is, shall the laws, whatever they may be, be boldly repudiated as no laws for us, the makers being not of us; or shall the matter be delayed until the so-called Legislature meets?"[65] Free-soil settlers were moving toward an outright rejection of the territorial legislature.

Territorial legislators encouraged this estrangement by their own unwillingness to compromise. The legislative committees on credentials found against the winners of the May special elections, favoring instead the candidates elected in the original March polling. Denying that Governor Reeder possessed the authority to overturn the election results, they asserted the territorial legislature's role as final judge of its members. A minority report by free-soil legislators, many of whose seats were in question, protested against the frauds of the March election, but most members of the territorial legislature adamantly refused to accept the governor's readjustment of the election results.[66] In the face of this pressure, the free-soil legislators resigned. Martin F. Conway summarized their position when he wrote Governor Reeder explaining that he could no longer lend legitimacy to a legislature which had been elected by Missourians in order to suppress the liberties of Kansans. To remain in the legislature, he said, would be "derogatory to the respectability of popular government." He hinted at the conflict to come when he said that, as a private citizen, he would refuse to obey the authority of a foreign government.[67]

Conway resigned before the legislature convened, but he was quickly followed by frustrated free-soil legislators. Samuel D. Houston complained of a systematic effort to drive out free-soil members, about one-quarter of the body, and of the open admission by his fellow legislators that they were not now and had never been residents of the territory. "I cannot but feel," Houston wrote the governor, "that their position is utterly subversive of the dearest rights of American citizens."[68] Houston was the only free-soil legislator whose right to his seat was not contested. John Hutchinson claimed that he took his seat despite the misgivings of his constituents, and then found his right to it disputed by his fellow legislators. He, like Conway, resigned saying that he would not acknowledge the authority of the legislature. In a speech to the territorial House before he resigned, Hutchinson warned that if the legislature sided with the other claimant to his seat and endorsed election fraud, it would not be a "legal legislature."[69] A free-soil settler wrote his wife, "It is the unanimous disposition of the settlers to resist any, every, and all laws that the present Assembly may pass. What the result will be, God knows, I do not. They think here, however, that everything will go off peaceably. I earnestly hope so."[70]

The mottoes of territorial legislators revealed their prosouthern leaning. Mixed in with the partisan, mostly Democratic slogans, and the sentiments in favor of justice and union, were those that signaled a prosouthern and proslavery sentiment: "Hemp for Negro-stealers," "The South and her institutions," "Negro Slavery for Kansas," "The South—her rights and interests," "Kansas with Southern Institutions," "Union first—South all the time," and "Kansas for the South, now and forever." In a newspaper report mottoes with a prosouthern tilt constituted one-quarter of the total listed, being surpassed in number only by mottoes of a general nature such as "Justice to all."[71] Members of the territorial legislature further clarified their allegiances when, on August 30, 1855, they rejected the formation of a Democratic party, fearing that it would divide proslavery forces in the territory. They resolved instead, "That it is the duty of the Pro-Slavery Party, the Union-loving men of Kansas Territory, to know but one issue, Slavery; and that any party making or attempting to make any other, is, and should be held, as an ally of Abolitionism and Disunionism."[72] Under the aegis of Atchison and the self-defensive associations, the devotion to slavery that ruled western Missouri would triumph in Kansas.

All acknowledged that the legislature's principal business would be slavery. At the legislature's opening, Governor Reeder argued that, while the people would ultimately decide the matter, the legislature would need in the interim to "temporarily prohibit, tolerate or regulate Slavery in the Territory."[73] The legislature acted by giving the territory a slave code.

In the "act to punish offences against slave property," the legislature provided two years at hard labor for writing or circulating antislavery material, death or imprisonment at hard labor for stealing or aiding in the theft of slaves, and the death penalty for instigating a slave rebellion. In cases tried under this act, no one who opposed slavery might sit as a juror. At John Stringfellow's urging, the legislators adopted viva voce voting instead of ballots. Stringfellow argued that the former method was less "cowardly" than the latter; it also meant that free-soil voters would have to publicly advertise their political loyalties and risk proslavery retaliation.[74]

The Kansas territorial slave code, Benjamin Stringfellow boasted to an Alabama newspaper, provided "laws more efficient to protect slave property than any State in the Union. These laws . . . have already silenced the Abolitionists."[75] A Missouri newspaper applauded the territorial legislature's work, saying it was common sense to have laws against stealing slaves just as there were laws against horse theft. "Kansas has set the example of justice and good faith to her neighbors."[76] A Kansas resident called abolitionism "defunct" in the territory after passage of the legislature's code.[77]

The implementation of this code, however, was not as stringent as Stringfellow and others claimed. Because the law now prohibited the circulation of antislavery material, the Atchison postmaster returned copies of the *Herald of Freedom* to its editor, George Brown. "You will confer a favor," the postmaster wrote, "by keeping your rotten and corrupt effusions from tainting the pure air of this portion of the Territory."[78] Yet there seems to have been no effort to prosecute Brown under the statute. Further, there is some indication that even the proslavery party was divided over laws that, in the view of some prominent men, infringed freedom of speech.[79] The poem "Kansas Laws" predicted: "If any Yankee, in this Territory/Shall circulate an abolition story/. . . . Then brave STRINGFELLOW, or the gallant JONES,/Or ATCHISON, or any man of note,/May cut his cursed antislavery throat."[80] But in fact, no such executions took place.

Even Benjamin Stringfellow seemed unsure whether the proslavery party could hold its gains. As he bragged about the work of the territorial legislature, he informed Alabamians, "We are on the outposts, fighting your battles. We will hold the port, while we have a man left—and if you will give us a little help, we will not only gain a victory, but place you and all your friends 'out of danger' in the future."[81] The image was not one of proslavery victory but of slavery under siege.

Free-soil opposition, in fact, was just consolidating. The March election, and the actions of the territorial legislature it elected, radicalized the free soilers. In a letter to David Atchison at the time of the March election, Amos Lawrence had denied that the eastern migrants were

abolitionists. But he had also warned "oppression may make them abolitionists of the most dangerous kind."[82] As the territorial legislature
began its session, residents of Lawrence seized upon the Fourth of July
celebration as an opportunity to proclaim "a new Declaration of Independence," one that made clear Kansans' plight. "We in Kansas already feel the iron heel of the oppressor, making us truly white slaves,"
wrote Sara Robinson.[83] During the day's ceremony, a Massachusetts
woman presented the U.S. flag to the Lawrence militia, and a procession moved down Massachusetts street to a grove outside town. Once
there, a crowd estimated at from one to two thousand listened to prayer,
the reading of the Declaration, songs, and orations by Sara's husband,
Dr. Charles Robinson, and others.[84] Charles Robinson recollected that
he was chosen to speak because he was best able to detail the situation of Kansans as "subjects of Missouri."[85]

But as Robinson remembered, the plight of the antislavery party after
the March election was difficult. How could the free-soil men contest
the legal authority of the legislature, which had the power to set territorial laws and to control the selection of constitutional conventions
that would write a state constitution?[86] The answer to Robinson's question lay, in part, in the free soilers' sudden love of the Kansas-Nebraska
Act. The memorial to Congress protesting fraud in the March election
had now elevated that legislation to the status of a "solemn covenant"
violated by the proslavery party:

That bill is made to mean popular sovereignty for them, serfdom for
us. The doctrine of self-government is to be trampled under foot here,
of all other places in the world, on the very spot which had been hal-
lowed and consecrated. . . . The compact is to be basely broken, and
the ballot of the freeman (in effect) torn from our hands, almost before the ink of the covenant is dry. . . . The question of *negro* slavery
is to sink into insignificance, and the greater portentious issue is to
loom up in its stead, whether or not *we* shall be the slaves, and fanatics who disgrace the honorable and chivalric men of the south shall be
our masters to rule us at their pleasure.[87]

On that July 4, surrounded by many who felt their political rights
under the Kansas-Nebraska Act had been trampled, Robinson voiced
the free soilers' dilemma: "We must not only see black slavery . . . in

Dr. Charles Robinson, governor of Kansas under the extralegal Topeka movement, in 1857. (Kansas State Historical Society, Topeka)

our midst, and against our wishes, but we must become slaves *ourselves.*"[88] He articulated the issue that would unite northern settlers, whether from New England or the Midwest, and even bring a few Missourians into the cause of free Kansas. The proslavery struggle to claim Kansas had attacked the rights of white men; popular sovereignty had promised them a choice they were not being allowed to make.

But the legislators were less concerned with the free soilers' opposition than with the governor's. Reeder, after all, possessed the power to veto their work. However, Reeder had concerns of his own. His land speculations, although not unusual for a politician in his position, troubled the Pierce administration and opened the governor to attack.[89] Besides possibly being guilty of land fraud, he clearly attempted to profit from his position as governor by forcing the legislature to convene on land that he owned.[90] Reeder had called the legislature to meet at Pawnee, on land he had invested in—land that would increase in value if it became the territorial capital. Both free-soil and proslavery men criticized the site for its lack of adequate housing. The legislative building lacked windows or doors, so the legislature had to conduct business under the trees of a nearby grove. The members camped in wagons and tents. Legislators voted to meet at Shawnee Mission but the governor vetoed the motion. Overriding his veto, they adjourned to the mission. Pawnee was territorial capital for only four days.[91]

The conflict over the legislature's location quickly led to an impasse in the territorial government. Reeder vetoed all the legislature's bills, claiming the body's removal from Pawnee meant the legislars were not in legal session.[92] Cyrus K. Holliday reported, "The Governor and the Assembly are at perfect loggerheads. The Gov. does not recognize them as a legal body, vetoes all their bills, and pays no respect whatever to them." Dramatically, Reeder warned his wife that "she might never see him again."[93]

Benjamin Stringfellow did in fact become so exasperated with the governor's stubbornness about the slave code and the legislature's location that he picked a fight with Reeder. Stringfellow challenged Reeder to a duel because the governor admitted calling Stringfellow a "border ruffian." When the governor declined to duel, Stringfellow leapt on him, knocking him from his chair. Reeder went down with Stringfellow on top, but managed to free himself. Both men drew pistols. Hearing the fight, other territorial officials entered the room and restrained Stringfellow.[94]

Infuriated by Reeder's intransigence, legislators petitioned the president for the governor's removal.[95] The territorial legislature's attack on Reeder merely joined that of Atchison and proslavery leaders.[96] On August 15, 1855, Reeder received notice of his dismissal for unethical land speculations. Southern Democrats would have preferred that the administration condemn Reeder's support of the free-soil side as grounds for his dismissal. Still they could comfort themselves with the removal of an increasingly open enemy.[97]

If the administration missed an opportunity to make political capital out of his removal, A. H. Reeder did not. He now openly advocated the free-soil side. In a speech at Lawrence, he attacked the territorial legislature as representing the proslavery party of Missouri. Shortly after his removal, the eastern press anticipated he would receive a hero's welcome on his return journey to the East, with receptions, dinners, speeches, and perhaps even a nomination for the governorship of Pennsylvania.[98] Prominent Democrats considered Reeder a potent force to be contended with. "The Reeder & Kansas questions," a friend cautioned presidential aspirant James Buchanan, "will be difficult matters to settle."[99]

Reeder was to be the first of a long series of failed territorial governors. Missourians had welcomed popular sovereignty in the confident expectation it meant a slave Kansas. Free-soil settlers thought popular sovereignty offered a fair opportunity to exclude slavery. The election made the divergent understandings of popular sovereignty apparent. Missourians argued that they had won the election and that attempts to revise the election returns were illegitimate violations of popular sovereignty. The free soilers feared popular sovereignty was a "farce and a fiction," leaving majority rule with little chance of resolving the slavery issue. A Leavenworth man assessed the plight of free-soil Kansans in language that echoed Charles Robinson:

Here in Kansas, this modern Canaan, flowing with milk and the Missouri river, we have been made to bear and wear the brand and earmarks of that great absurdity 'squatter sovereignty,' while we are the veriest slaves and serfs. . . . Without a vestige of those natural and inalienable rights asserted in the Declaration of Independence, as the heritage and birthright of every American citizen, we exist . . . as sovereign squatters without a single attribute of sovereignty, governed by officers appointed from abroad to rule over us. . . . The laws of Missouri have been legislatively extended over us . . . by the Legislature, a Legislature who have attempted to deprive us of the freedom of speech. Was there ever such sovereignty known to a civilized world?[100]

Rather than be "enslaved" by Missourians, Kansas settlers chose to defend their political rights and resist the territorial legislature.

4

We Are But Slaves
The Free-State Movement

By conferring martyrdom on Reeder, the administration elevated him into the free-soil leadership. "He is a brave and noble-hearted man," one Lawrence settler wrote.[1] Succeeding him was a mediocre Ohio politician, Wilson Shannon. Shannon's ineptitude for any post of delicacy should have been apparent from his disastrous term as minister to Mexico in the mid-1840s. Formerly governor of Ohio, he later served only one term in Congress, declining to run for reelection because his support of the Kansas-Nebraska Act had alienated his constituents.[2] H. Miles Moore summed up the new territorial governor as a man "of medium talents" and "a good deal of an old fogy."[3] Another observer said Shannon was "a stoutly built, elderly gentleman" who "looked dignified. . . . But good-natured withal."[4] Shannon's good nature did not extend to the free soilers. He arrived in Kansas convinced that the territorial legislature was legal, its opposition plainly not. While traveling through Missouri en route to his new job, he had injudiciously remarked that Missouri and Kansas institutions should "harmonize." To many in his audience, this remark suggested that he favored introducing slavery into Kansas.[5] Shannon found a free-soil movement determined to implement popular sovereignty by creating their own government and a proslavery response that would deem such an extralegal government a violation of "law and order."

To protest the March election and the actions of the legislature, free soilers met at Lawrence on August 14 and 15, 1855.

Wilson Shannon, governor of Kansas Territory, whose ineptitude precipitated many of the problems in the territory. (Kansas State Historical Society, Topeka)

Comparing themselves to the revolutionaries of 1776, they denied the legality of the territorial legislature and recommended electing delegates to a convention that would write a state constitution and apply for admission. They called for the convention to meet at Big Springs on September 5.[6] By so doing, the New Englanders joined forces with westerners who, in what they called the Sand Bank convention, had called for the convention at Big Springs. On a sand bank of the Kansas River, some Lawrence men had held an impromptu gathering on July 17, 1855. Worried that Charles Robinson's July 4 oration had been too extreme, they chose Big Springs, the site of a four-cabin trading post on the emigrant road to California, as the convention site. Fifteen miles west of Lawrence, it was a convenient distance from the extremists there. Robinson initially opposed the Big Springs movement, but eventually he joined forces with the westerners and easterners at the Lawrence convention in August, and called for a large turnout at Big Springs that September.[7]

The evolving political views of James H. Lane, a recent immigrant from Indiana, showed the rapid solidification of free-soil sentiment against the territorial legislature. A Democrat, Lane had presided over a meeting in June 1855 to organize the Democratic party in Kansas. The assembled Democrats had endorsed both the Democratic platform of 1852 and the Kansas-Nebraska Act. Exaggerating his influence, Lane hinted that he was privy to President Pierce and Senator Douglas's wishes on Kansas policy.[8] Lane's true power lay in what a fledgling poet described as his "oratory capped with fire" that "swayed/The crowds that listen and admire."[9]

Lane quickly abandoned his efforts to secure settlers' loyalty to the territorial government. By October, Lane, with a chameleon-like change of political principle, was making speeches against the territorial legislature and in favor of an independent movement to statehood.[10] By scenting the shifting political winds and changing loyalties accordingly, Lane soon challenged Robinson for leadership of the settler movement. Lane's transformation demonstrates that the free-soil movement in Kansas was becoming the dominant political force.

Both easterners and westerners now agreed on the need for resistance, possibly by force, to the territorial legislature. Lane and his followers "said they had a new code of laws called Sharps Revised Statutes,"[11] referring to their Sharps rifles. Delegates to Big Springs arrived so heavily armed that the landlady refused to retrieve one man's coat, saying, "Go in and get it. I would not touch that armory for all the property in the room."[12] Vowing to resist peaceably but to go "to a bloody issue as we ascertain that peaceable remedies shall fail," the convention recommended the formation of military companies.[13]

Lane and the westerners still objected to Robinson's condemnation of black slavery, as well as the attempted enslavement of whites he broached in his Fourth of July address. At Big Springs, the Lane faction pressed for and got a black law to prohibit black emigration into the territory. One Kansan reminisced that the Big Springs delegates' "hatred to slavery was not as strong as their hatred to Negroes." But disagreements over race did not deter the delegates from their main purpose.[14]

The Big Springs convention formally transformed free-soil resistance into the Free State party. Open to men from any of the established parties, the Free State party was not abolitionist, its organizers avowed, nor did it intend interference with slavery where it currently existed. It was united by its opposition to nonresident voting, its belief that Kansas should be a free state, and its conviction that the "crisis" obliged them to save "the guarantees of Republican institutions by the Constitution." Although delegates hotly debated whether to set up a territorial government in opposition to the federally recognized one, the Free State party ultimately accepted A. H. Reeder's resolutions to ignore the territorial legislature and create its own, and to elect its own delegate to Congress, for which post they nominated Reeder.[15] Lane's faction opposed Reeder's candidacy, ironically, on the grounds that he was not a resident of the territory. Reeder had never brought his family to Kansas, and some free staters believed he intended to leave the territory unless he got the Free State party nomination. Despite Lane's opposition, Reeder was nominated by acclamation.[16] He was, as free staters had to acknowledge, "much the strongest man and will have by far the most influence in Washington of any man that could have been nominated."[17] Rather than surrender "our great American birthright—the election franchise" to fraud, the Big Springs delegates vowed to boycott the next election. The delegates also called for another convention to be held in Topeka, on September 19.[18]

Condemnations of the March 30 election and nonresident voting intensified at the Topeka meeting. Concluding that "the people were left without any legal government," the convention determined that settlers "are compelled to resort to the only remedy left—that of forming a government for themselves." Free soilers called for another constitutional convention to be held in that town in October, intending to organize a state government and apply for immediate admission.[19] Jim Lane, as chairman of the executive committee to oversee the election of delegates to the constitutional convention, adopted a suitably Jeffersonian tone, enumerating the grievances suffered and invoking the right of the people to make new governments.[20]

From the first, free-soil men recognized that the movement toward statehood was dangerously radical. The Big Springs delegates had deliberately avoided the issue, some deeming it "untimely and inexpedient."[21] H. Miles Moore acknowledged independent actions were "a desperate and strong" move, but concluded that the legislature's "outrageous laws" made "extreme but pure & conservative steps" necessary.[22] It was not contradictory to deem the statehood movement both "extreme" and yet "conservative." The free-soil settlers knew flouting the territorial government was not a light measure. "We had a big meeting last Sat.," settler Edward P. Fitch wrote his father from Lawrence, "and we spoke our sentiments against the infamous laws and their makers. We all committed a State Prison offence."[23] However, they could and did cite a number of precedents in which states had skipped or somehow abbreviated the territorial period.[24] Free-state sympathizers claimed, "The people of Kanzas . . . have done, what half the Western States did while territories—called their constitutional conventions."[25] Their efforts to minimize the radicalism of their actions were in vain. The Missouri press quickly dubbed the free staters "revolutionists" and the label stuck.[26]

Selecting a territorial delegate was the free-state movement's first test. The territorial legislature had called for that election to be held the first Monday in October, but the Big Springs convention ostentatiously preferred the second Tuesday. Free staters had many reasons for avoiding this election: they repudiated the authority of the territorial legislature, evaded taking the proscribed oath, and did not have to compete or fight with illegal voters from Missouri.[27] By ignoring, rather than confronting, the territorial government, free staters hoped to maintain northern public support.[28] They held their election for delegate on the date they had chosen.

The candidates were J. W. Whitfield, then the current delegate, ex-governor Reeder, and a Democrat, George W. Perkins.[29] When Perkins became ill and could not campaign, H. Miles Moore reported that "the National Democratic Party has *Busted*."[30] Northern Democrats would have to choose between open avowals or open repudiation of slavery. Such a choice, an eastern newspaper wrote, directly posed the question for Congress: "Shall Kanzas be governed by Missouri, or by her own people?"[31]

In Kansas, the free-soil decision to boycott the territorial election and hold their own escalated tension. From Lawrence, Fitch reported bands of armed Missourians near town who threatened "to burn this town and kill all the Yankees and . . . not take more than ten minutes!"[32] The Missourians Fitch heard about may have only been a party that had crossed the border to vote in the election the next day. Free staters also reported seeing an unusually large number of Missourians around Leavenworth and Kansas City.[33] Lawrence residents were in just as belligerent a mood as Fitch claimed the Missourians were: "There have been large numbers of cartridges made today. The company have cleaned up all their rifles and put new caps in all of them and are preparing to give the Missourians 'Jesse' if they come here."[34]

Whitfield won the October 1 balloting and was issued the official certificate of election. Equally unsurprising, Reeder won the following week's free-state election. For some of his backers, it sufficed that Whitfield had won the legally sanctioned first election; but others sought further legitimacy by insisting that their candidate had actually received more total votes than had Reeder in the following election, despite accusations that fraud had contributed to Whitfield's total. Free staters claimed that Reeder had polled more votes than Whitfield and would have received a larger number if it were not for the haste with which they were obliged to act, the nearness of winter, and the distance required for voters to travel, which had depressed the free-state vote. Reeder contested Whitfield's seat, to which Whitfield replied that Reeder's actions threatened anarchy.[35] The administration's position was simple: Whitfield possessed the governor's certificate of election. Reeder's election denied the legality of the law under which Whitfield had been chosen, and the legitimacy of the territorial legislature that had passed it.[36]

Even as free staters defended Reeder's claim to the delegate's seat as the choice of "the Sovereign People,"[37] the constitutional convention that brought thirty-seven free-state delegates to Topeka from October 23 to November 11, 1855 echoed the rhetoric of the American Revolution.[38] Using Jeffersonian language, the Topeka constitution invoked the rights of the people to "life, liberty, and property, and the free pursuits of happiness." As "all political power is inherent in the PEOPLE," they have the right to "alter, reform, or abolish governments."

Settlers merely exercised those rights in creating the "free and independent . . . STATE OF KANSAS."[39]

Throughout the constitutional convention, fissures within the free-state movement became evident. A discussion of banking briefly exacerbated differences between Democrats and Whigs. Race provoked deeper disagreement. A small number of members, including Robinson, proposed black suffrage and the omission of the word "male." Lane, by contrast, hoped for "a fair and liberal course" toward slaveowners inside and outside Kansas and suggested excluding free blacks. The convention partially accepted Lane's suggestion; a resolution on free blacks was to be submitted to the voters along with the constitution itself. Although Robinson opposed the exclusion, others argued that it was vital to the success of the Free State party. The final document prohibited slavery, but the Topeka constitution clearly compromised the varied attitudes on race possessed by different groups of free-soil migrants. Robinson, who possessed sincere abolitionist convictions, abandoned advocacy of black rights to appease the more numerous and more antiblack westerners led by Lane.[40]

With the Topeka constitution, the Free State party achieved the strategy it would follow throughout its existence. While many free staters possessed antislavery convictions, many did not. Antislavery could not be the party's unifying tie. Thus, as Charles Robinson wrote, "The invasion of their own civil and political rights" became the issue, and the Topeka constitution its forum.[41] Only the cry of self-government could bind the free-state factions into a cohesive party, granting their cause legitimacy in the nation's eyes. Loss of self-government was in fact what most Kansas settlers feared. As one Kansan wrote Senator Charles Sumner in November 1855, "Admit us not and we are but slaves."[42]

In a ratification vote on December 15, the Topeka constitution received 1,731 votes in favor and 46 opposed; the exclusion of free blacks passed by 1,287 to 453. Proslavery interference with the election was minor, although Charles Dunn, an Irish immigrant, led twenty men to the polls at Leavenworth. They seized the ballot box and knocked down the clerk of the election who had intervened to save it.[43] On December 27, 1855, Lane proclaimed that the Topeka constitution, having been ratified by the voters, was now in force and called an election of state officers for January 15. Free-state factions maneuvered for those offices. Nineteen different tickets, by one man's count, circulated for legislative candidates in the Lawrence district.[44] The free-state ticket for these offices nicely balanced the party's competing factions. While Charles Robinson received the nomination for governor, he was the only New England candidate. Of the six offices, nominations for three went to Southerners, one of whom was the former slaveowner Mark W. Delahay. Three of the candidates were also Democrats.[45]

Political action was not free staters' only reaction to poslavery shenanigans. Always close to the resort to arms, free staters gradually intensified their military activities. As Amos Lawrence wrote, "That a revolution must take place in Kansas is certain. . . . When farmers turn soldiers they must have *arms.*"[46] In February 1855, over a month before the controversial March 30 election, free-soil men had formed the Kansas Legion: "First, to secure to Kansas the blessing and prosperity of being a free State; and, secondly, to protect the ballot-box from the LEPROUS TOUCH OF UNPRINCIPLED MEN." The Legion was a combination of fraternal order, with oaths of secrecy, and free-state army.[47]

An Irish immigrant named Patrick Laughlin entered the Legion in the summer of 1855. Initially a proslavery man, he joined the free-state party out of disgust with proslavery actions in the March 30 election but soon became repelled by free-state tactics. As part of the Kansas Legion, Laughlin saw shipments marked as dry goods that contained rifles, listened to discussions of arming free-state settlers, and heard George W. Brown, editor of the *Herald of Freedom,* discourse about soliciting arms money from Easterners. The Kansas Legion employed the codes used by secret societies, such as the anti-immigrant Know-Nothings. Members wore black ribbons on their shirt bosoms and signalled to one another by secret signs (such as rubbing the corner of the eye with the left little finger), passwords, and handshakes. Disillusioned, Laughlin reverted to the proslavery party. To the Legion's chagrin, he exposed their operations to the proslavery side and later killed a free-state Missourian who argued with him over his change of political loyalties.[48]

The Kansas Legion was not the only free-state military organization. Shipments of Sharps rifles and other munitions began arriving in Kansas by May 1855 and continued to arm the free-state militias through the fall of 1856. James Abbott, Frederick Olmsted, Eli Thayer, Henry Ward Beecher, T. W. Higginson, and others subscribed large sums of money, raised by themselves or by organizations they headed, in order to buy rifles, ammunition, several cannon, and a howitzer. Additional funding was provided by NEEAC, the New York Kansas Committee, the National Kansas Committee, the Massachusetts Committee, and even the state of Iowa. Students at the small college in Grinnell, Iowa, raised funds to buy fifteen rifles for Kansas, as befitted a college founded by antislavery New Englanders, and perhaps thereby began its long tradition of supporting radical causes. All sources combined, sympathizers raised over $43,000 to buy arms for free-state Kansans.[49]

Publicly, the New England Emigrant Aid Company disavowed its role in arming the settlers. Eli Thayer informed one potential donor that "The E.A. Co. do nothing of this." Nevertheless, NEEAC officials lent considerable aid to the fundraising. Thayer himself solicited aid to arm emigrants.[50] The executive committee of NEEAC provided the means for one hundred Sharps rifles to be shipped to Kansas in boxes marked "books." Thayer's dissimulation is particularly egregious as he himself had been the single greatest donor toward arms purchases, having given $4,500.[51]

Free-state settler J. B. Abbott traveled east to buy munitions with a letter of introduction from Amos Lawrence that made clear his warlike mission. Among Abbott's purchases were a mountain howitzer, fifty rounds of canister and shells with time fuses, five hand grenades, fifty rockets, and a half dozen swords.[52] Upon his return to the territory, he boasted of the weapons' impact: "These R.[ifles] are having precisely the effect we anticipated. The some 250 or 300 guns we have rec. have been already magnified into over 15000 as you may see by the Mo Papers and the distance they will kill is enormous. It has killed the courage at least of some six families a few miles south of us, and they have left the county for its good posably, saying (or swaring) that they will not live in a Free State. The fact is our neighbors are *right smartly* sick *we* were never better[.]"[53] Abbott and other free-state leaders professed the arms were defensive and would help secure the rights of Kansans without ever being used. But clearly the free-soil movement now sought to do exactly what free staters condemned the proslavery party for doing: achieve its ends by the threat of violence.[54]

Upon occasion, free staters used their weapons to protect the rights of blacks. In Lawrence, Edward Fitch wrote of a free black neighbor threatened with kidnapping by proslavery men who insisted he was a runaway slave. "Last Sun. The news came in that there had been a party gone to take him," Fitch wrote his parents. "A lot of us armed with Sharps rifles went out under the command of our Orderly Sargent to protect him but the slave holders backed out and dared not try anything. If they had we should have pitched in to them with our rifles."[55] Despite isolated confrontations, free-state violence remained constrained throughout 1855; it was understood that excessive violence risked suppression by the federal government, which considered the Topeka movement illegitimate.[56]

As free staters organized themselves politically and armed themselves to protect their rights, proslavery men seized the banner of "law and order." At a Leavenworth meeting on October 3, 1855, they accused free staters of denying the legal authority of the territorial legislature, and of thereby leading to "anarchy and confusion." These law and order men labeled free-state actions as *"Treason."*[57] When the Law and Order party met again at Leavenworth in mid-November, Governor Shannon presided. Territorial officials and proslavery men made up the party's core. Present at the party's organizational meeting were John H. Stringfellow, a member of the legislature; John Calhoun, territorial surveyor general; Daniel H. Woodson, the territorial secretary; and territorial judge Samuel Lecompte. Resolving that the Topeka movement was treasonable and rebellious, the convention endorsed the Kansas-Nebraska Act.[58] In addition, proslavery men now invoked the same rhetoric of enslavement that free staters had used. Calhoun attacked abolitionism as at odds with popular sovereignty and asked the meeting:

Shall abolitionists rule you? (No! Never! &c.) Give them all the demands, and abolitionism becomes the law of the Government. You yield, and you will have the most infernal Government that ever cursed a land. I would rather be a painted slave over in the State of Missouri, or a serf to the Czar of Russia, than have the abolitionists in power. (Deafening Cheers.) . . . If the laws are unconstitutional they must be repealed at the proper tribunal. Until they are repealed they are the law of the land, and should be enforced.[59]

Before when free-soil men invoked the right of revolution in defense of their political rights, proslavery men condemned them for defying the legitimate government. But proslavery men feared the loss of their right to own slaves as much as free soilers feared the loss of the right to exclude slavery.

At Hickory Point, a squabble over land claims ignited these political quarrels. A settler named Franklin M. Coleman had been squatting on land abandoned by some Hoosiers, who subsequently sold the claim to Jacob Branson, another Hoosier. In late 1854, when Branson informed Coleman of his legal claim and attempted to move into Coleman's house, Coleman held him off with a gun. A group of arbitrators later awarded part of the claim to Branson, but the boundaries between his land and Coleman's were not determined. Branson invited in other men, including a young Ohioan named Charles W. Dow. Branson belonged to the free-state militia, a connection he used to intimidate Coleman, although Branson later testified that there had been no problems between Dow and Coleman—until the day of Dow's murder.[60]

On the morning of November 21, 1855, Dow went to the blacksmith shop at Hickory Point to have a wagon skein and lynchpin mended. While there he argued with one of Coleman's friends, but left unharmed. As he walked away, he passed Coleman on the road. Coleman snapped a cap at him. When Dow turned around, he received a charge of buck-shot in the chest and died immediately. His body lay in the road until Branson recovered it four hours later. Coleman claimed that Dow had threateningly raised the wagon skein (a two-foot piece of iron) as they argued over their claim dispute, forcing him to act in self-defense. Fearing that he could not get fair treatment at the free-state settlement of Hickory Point, Coleman and his family fled to Missouri.[61]

Up to this point, the conflict was more about confused land titles than free-state or proslavery animosities. Despite long-standing rumors of Missouri efforts to drive out free staters, there was no clear-cut political division over the claim dispute or the quarrels between Coleman and his neighbors. Some free-staters had favored the Missourian Coleman's claim to the disputed land. Some proslavery men had sided with Branson.[62] The political divisions at Hickory Point did not solidify until Dow's death became a political issue.

On the afternoon of November 26, a meeting convened at Branson's house in Hickory Point. Predominantly comprising members of a local military company, the group appointed a committee of vigilance to punish Dow's murderers. Some free-state men had already been intimidating witnesses to the murder. Armed men had burned the houses of two proslavery men and ordered several women to leave their homes. After the meeting broke up in the early evening, some of the appointed vigilantes burned down Coleman's empty house. A few hours later, Sheriff Samuel J. Jones arrived with a posse and arrested Branson, then in bed, for disturbing the peace. Jones had warrants sworn out by victims of the free-state militia.[63]

Jones was "tall, muscular, athletic . . . clad in the Border Ruffian costume—blue military overcoat, large boots, skull cap and cigar in mouth."[64] When he arrested Branson, Jones said he was sorry to have missed the others. But he did not have those regrets long. The posse soon ran into a free-state party of fifteen—Jones claimed thirty to forty— from the military company. Having heard of Branson's arrest, the party had gathered at Major Abbott's house and was debating what to do next when they heard the approaching posse. The free-state men blocked the road, forcing the posse to stop. Tensions rose when a free-state man accidentally discharged his gun.[65] Finding Branson with the posse, the free staters urged Branson to join them, but he feared that his captors would shoot. Lawyer S. N. Wood called out, "Let them shoot, and be d——d; we can shoot too." Branson then rode over to the free-state men, followed by Jones. Jones asserted he had a warrant for Branson's arrest, but refused to show it to Wood, who had suddenly announced Branson was his client. After an inconclusive hour of bickering, the posse withdrew. Jones acted with restraint, telling the free staters that there would be no fighting and "gently" reprimanding one of them for threatening to shoot him.[66] Faced with the excited and well-armed free-state force, Jones chose not to provoke violence even though he considered the men who took his prisoner as violators of territorial law and the authority of territorial officers such as himself.[67]

*Samuel Jones, sheriff of Douglas County, Kansas
Territory, and proslavery leader. (Kansas State
Historical Society, Topeka)*

Branson's rescuers escorted him safely into Lawrence, reaching
Charles Robinson's house around 4 A.M. Citizens of Lawrence then
organized a committee of safety and, according to Robinson's account,
seemed almost as worried about the threat to the town as to Branson.
Their fear was well-founded. Jones immediately notified the governor
that a large body of armed vigilantes had taken a prisoner from his
custody. In response to the sheriff's plea, Shannon called out the territorial militia.[68]

Governor Shannon fully concurred with fears of a "secret military
organization," containing between one and two thousand men, that
defied territorial laws. Unsure of how much force was required to
subdue the rebellious free staters, Shannon later called unsuccessfully
on Col. Edwin Sumner, the local army commander, for help.[69] Shannon's
report to the president was a ringing call for law and order: "The time
has come when this armed band of men, who are seeking to subvert

and render powerless the existing government, have to be met and the laws enforced against them, or submit to their lawless dominion."[70] Shannon astutely recognized there was a danger that the situation might provoke "civil war" along the border. He avowed his fierce commitment to surmounting that danger—which he then proceeded to exacerbate. A day later, Shannon called on the people of the territory, urging them to help Sheriff Jones overcome "this armed band" of lawless men.[71] He got far more than he bargained for.

Missourians rallied to the governor's call. As many as a thousand men, from as far away as St. Joseph, Boonville, and Lexington, assembled in Kansas Territory. One Missourian could not believe reports that Jones had only three hundred men because his county alone had sent that many, including a dozen local college students—some as young as sixteen years old.[72] H. Miles Moore described the flood of Missourians over the border as "all armed & determined to burn Lawrence."[73] An elderly Missouri man was said to have brought not only his son and grandson, but also "an antiquated flint-lock." He announced to the men camped on the Wakarusa, "Gentleman, this hyar old firelock war carried by my father through thar dark days of thar Revolution." With an oath and thump of the gun's butt on the ground, he continued, "Yes, I'll be derned, gentelman, *ef she war ever carried in a better cause than this.*"[74]

While Missouri forces massed on the Wakarusa River, military companies in Lawrence kept guard. Parties of free-state men swarmed into the town, having responded to calls for aid. Writing to his wife from "Head Quarters Army of Defense," C. K. Holliday estimated that there were two thousand defenders in Lawrence and an equal number of Missourians outside the town. Melodramatically, he warned that he might never see his wife or young daughter again.[75] Edward Fitch wrote a similar farewell letter to his parents and reported that his company "slept under arms," fearing attack at any moment.[76] Every house served as a barracks. At night, free-state "officers" held lanterns so that men could continue digging the earthworks. Built in circles, those fortifications stood seven feet high and one hundred feet in diameter. Four or five were constructed and connected by entrenchments and rifle pits. While Lawrence men entrenched themselves across Massachusetts

Street, fortified their circular redoubts, and prepared for a siege, the women gathered to make cartridges and even practiced shooting with revolvers. Free-state patrols guarded the town at night.[77]

Residents of Lawrence were not grateful for the trouble Branson had brought them. A meeting voted down resolutions praising Branson's rescuers, and within forty-eight hours of his triumphant entrance into the town, Branson and his party left Lawrence. Residents tempered their military preparations with efforts to avert violence from the mob that gathered outside town. While Lane drilled the troops, free-state leaders, from their headquarters in the town's hotel, opened negotiations with Shannon and petitioned the president.[78]

Aid to the beleaguered town had to pass a Missouri blockade. One man claimed, "Nothing is allowed to pass the Wakarusa everything is stopped or destroyed,"[79] including a shipment of arms intended for free-state men.[80] But the Missouri blockade was not impermeable. A free-state man smuggled a howitzer out of Kansas City, Missouri. When a suspicious Missouri merchant asked questions, the free stater replied that it was a buggy, opening the package just enough to show the wheels. Later, when his wagon became stuck on the muddy roads, he hailed a passing group of Missourians who helped pull it out.[81]

In the most daring ruse of all, two Lawrence women, Lois Brown and Margaret Wood, brought ammunition and kegs of gunpowder past the Missourians. Early one morning, they drove their buggy to a location on the Santa Fe road where munitions were hidden. Clad in several layers of dresses and petticoats, they concealed Sharps rifle caps in their stockings and quilted cartridges into their petticoats. Unable to carry more, they gave the remaining cartridges and caps, which had been hidden at a second location, to a nine-year-old boy who was driving an ox team into Lawrence, trusting his youth to protect him. Too overburdened to outrun the patrol, the women were stopped on their return, but the Missourians merely apologized for disturbing the ladies and let them pass. The boy too was stopped and searched, but he succeeded in hiding the cartridges in his trousers. When the ladies reached Lawrence, a free-state man commented that bustles had returned to fashion, "for they were swelled out *awful!*" Indeed, the women were so burdened with contraband that they could not climb out of their buggy and instead had to be lifted.[82] If anything, the incident proved that the Missourians were not the barbarians depicted by free-state propaganda, which portrayed them as a degenerate rabble that would ride into Lawrence *"killing every man and ravishing every woman."*[83] The Missourians did not make war on women and children, even when women and children were preparing to make war on them.

Men were not so fortunate in passing through the Missouri patrols. On the early afternoon of December 6, a party including territorial militia and government officers intercepted three free-state settlers on their way home from Lawrence. The settlers had excited suspicion by turning off the main road onto a shortcut that led to their cabins. Major George Clarke and Col. Burns intercepted the men while, a few hundred yards away, the main party waited on the road. A heavyset Missourian on a gray horse, Clarke questioned the three settlers, asking where they were from and what was happening in Lawrence. Thomas Barber, one of the three, answered the questions and asked what law they had broken. Clarke answered by ordering the men to accompany him, but Thomas Barber refused. Clarke drew his gun. Barber's brother, Robert, who had brought a revolver from Lawrence despite Thomas's objections, now struggled to draw his weapon, getting it caught in its holster. Meanwhile, Clarke fired at Thomas, who was unarmed. Having finally freed his gun, Robert exchanged several shots with the two Missourians. "Boys, let us be off," Thomas shouted, and the three men rode away. After a hundred yards, Thomas announced that he had been hit but seemed unconcerned. Wounded in the abdomen, he soon fell from his horse. At that point, Thomas M. Pierson, the Barbers' brother-in-law, wanted to surrender to the Missourians, but Robert Barber said the proslavery men would kill them and, as Thomas was dead, they could do him no good by staying with him. When they saw the Missourians in pursuit, the two kinsmen fled, leaving the body. In fact, Thomas Barber was still alive and lived for forty minutes, in much pain, unable to speak or drink the water a woman brought him from her nearby house.[84]

When Robinson first learned of Barber's death, he ordered the news kept secret, fearing a rash reaction from the free-state men, including Lane. Despite such precautions, word quickly spread.[85] But the very fear that men on both sides were rapidly slipping out of the control of their leaders was hastening a resolution to the conflict between free-state and proslavery factions.

Governor Shannon increasingly worried that the territorial militia, which had swelled from the addition of "irregulars," could not be controlled.[86] Uneasy about the forces under his own command, Shannon searched for a way to resolve the standoff. On December 4, he received members of the Lawrence Committee of Safety and heard their fears that Missourians would destroy Lawrence. Two days later, Col. Albert Boone of Westport, grandson of Daniel, accompanied Atchison and Shannon to the Wakarusa camp. From 8 P.M. to midnight on the day of Barber's death, Shannon talked with the Missouri leaders. On December 7, the governor and Boone went into Lawrence, the same day Barber's body arrived.[87] As the two men entered the room at the Free State Hotel where they would negotiate with free-state leaders, they saw the body of Thomas Barber laid out in the room across the hall. Clearly shocked, Boone "expressed surprise and regret."[88] Shannon spent the day in Lawrence, dined at Robinson's house, and expressed the appropriate regrets as to Barber's death and the Missourians' aggressiveness. That night a committee in Lawrence drafted a document outlining the points agreed upon with the governor. Shannon had already returned to Franklin to discuss the plan with the proslavery leadership. Yet before retiring that night, the governor stopped members of the territorial militia from a planned attack on Lawrence.[89]

Negotiations continued the next day, a Saturday, with Boone and Atchison representing the territorial government and Lane and Robinson the free staters. After five hours of discussions, both sides signed a written statement. The settlement excused the citizens of Lawrence from complicity in the Branson rescue, affirmed their willingness to aid in any legal action against a criminal, but evaded the question of their definition of legality. Nothing in the document, free-state sources maintained, could be construed as an agreement to the validity of the territorial legislature's laws.[90] Free staters bowed to the reality of the territorial militia's threat without conceding the legitimacy of the militia force or the illegitimacy of the free-state movement.

Lawrence residents feared that if Missouri forces were released from their officers' control, they would mob the town. Shannon shared this fear. Although his trip to the scene had convinced him of the threat to Lawrence, he did not know how to disband the forces around Lawrence, now grown to two thousand men. Many of the men yearned to destroy the town, newspapers included, and to confiscate its Sharps rifles.[91] Even Atchison hoped "not to excite but to control and keep within proper bounds the over excited."[92] Because of the peace agreement, Atchison felt the propaganda advantage had shifted to the proslavery side. An attack now would only make the Missourians look bad. Weather aided those who wanted peace. The cold and wind of a fierce winter storm pierced troops on both sides.[93] On December 8, Governor Shannon ordered the military forces around Lawrence to disband, informing the militia leaders that he had made "satisfactory arrangements" to ensure that the law would be enforced. He cautioned the militia generals to "repress all demonstrations of a disorderly character" and to turn back any movement on Lawrence.[94]

The governor, having successfully averted a bloodbath, now stumbled again. Unsure of his ability to control the disappointed men surrounding Lawrence, Shannon authorized Lane and Robinson to raise a militia force to repel invaders.[95] During the celebrations ending the conflict, Robinson came to Shannon and, saying that the force outside town threatened it, asked for written authorization to repel the force. Without considering its implications, and slightly tipsy, Shannon signed the paper Robinson thrust in front of him. Only later did he learn there was no threatened attack.[96] Lane joyfully told his men they were now "United States dragoons."[97] Shannon insisted the "commission" he gave Robinson only authorized the free-state men to repel this one attack. However, he apparently genuinely believed that, without U.S. troops to preserve order, Lawrence remained in danger. He thus felt justified in encouraging Lawrence citizens to remain organized for self-protection. But by being oblivious to the difficulty that free-state leaders were having in restraining their own men, many of whom wanted to attack the Missouri camp, he was potentially increasing tensions.[98] Shannon also failed to anticipate that free staters would use the governor's commission to legitimize their revolutionary military force. Edward Fitch reassured his parents, "The Gov has come round to our side and all is right."[99] Shannon was not so sure. In his report to the president, he confided his "forebodings as to the future." The militia and volunteers obviously could not be relied upon to preserve the peace. Only U.S. troops, Shannon advised, could do that job, and the governor should have the authority to call on them. Pierce disregarded the advice; in his annual message, he reported that while there had been events "prejudicial to good order" in Kansas Territory, none had required his intervention.[100]

To celebrate the dispersal of the Missourians and the cessation of hostilities, the ladies of Lawrence held a ball at the Free State Hotel. Among the eight hundred people in attendance was Sheriff Jones, who impressed the women with his courtliness.[101] Even Jones's social grace and proslavery boasts about the Missourians' "magnanimous" withdrawal from Lawrence could not hide their embarrassment.[102] Isaac Goodnow, who lived far from Lawrence, read in the newspapers "the History of the 1st War in Kansas. Freedom victorious!"[103] The "free and gallant bearing" of the Lawrence free staters also earned free-state men a sympathetic audience in the North. Free-state resistance satisfied a northern desire to finally show "backbone" to the South.[104] In Illinois, the "unparalelled outrages committed . . . upon the natural rights of the People" and upon the Kansas-Nebraska bill's principles brought support for free-state demands.[105] An Ohioan argued that, without men and arms, Kansas would be lost to freedom, endangering freedom in the entire country.[106] The free staters fought not just for their political rights, but those of all Northerners. The free staters asserted that the Wakarusa War had shown the mettle of their people, entitling them to the protection of Congress and admission as a state. Not all northern politicians were convinced. The governor of Minnesota responded icily that he knew of no such officers as Lane and Robinson claimed to be.[107] But free-state propaganda did have an effect. Congressman Nathaniel P. Banks, soon to be selected speaker of the house, was in regular correspondence with NEEAC functionaries.[108]

Southerners viewed the Wakarusa War as the triumph of lawlessness. A border resident thought the Missourians had been "consummate fools" for the citizens of Lawrence had "without a struggle, reaped all the glory."[109] The "*washout* of the border ruffians!" and the triumph of "the outlaws of the border" was an "indelible disgrace upon Missouri."[110] By overreacting, Missourians forfeited some of the high ground, belying their claim of acting on behalf of legitimate authority. Conservatives in Leavenworth had hoped to steer the law and order movement out of the hands of proslavery radicals such as Stringfellow, but their convention, scheduled for December 7, was overtaken by the Wakarusa War. As a result, the convention retained a proslavery version of law and order. During the Wakarusa War, a law and order convention in Calhoun County called on Governor Shannon to suppress the "nullifiers" of territorial laws. They spoke darkly of eastern arms shipments to the Kansas Legion, and of the murder of proslavery women and children.[111] But in fact, free-state men had not committed murder. Even Missourians sensed they had gone too far with their seige of Lawrence. In the days after the Wakarusa War, Atchison assured a supporter that "the border Ruffians will do nothing but what he can easily vindicate."[112]

Indeed, the Border Ruffians had already committed the indefensible. Thomas Barber, temporarily interred during the conflict, was buried with all due solemnity on December 16. Robinson gave the oration, calling Barber a "martyr to principle," and the military companies discharged three volleys.[113] In "The Burial of Barber," John Greenleaf Whittier counseled the free-state movement:

> Bear him, comrades, to his grave
> While the flag, with stars bedeck'd,
> Threatens where it should protect,
>   And the Law shakes hands with Crime. . . .
> Plant the Buckeye on his grave,
> For the hunter of the slave
>   In its shadow cannot rest;
> And let martyr mound and tree
> Be your pledge and guarantee
>   Of the freedom of the West![114]

The free-state cause had its first hero, one whose death mocked popular sovereignty's promise of freedom and the law's promise of peace and good order.

5

The War Commences in Earnest
Bleeding Kansas

The winter of 1855–1856 brought heavy storms. One New Englander likened them to "a regular Vermonter." "Such weather," he hoped, "must frighten off *slaveholders* & their *servants*."[1] Garbed in buffalo robes, Lawrence citizens added stoves to their fortifications. They also target practiced, using pictures of David Atchison. With the growing cold, the threat of attack did diminish, and free staters soon wearied of patrols.[2] The weather, however, could not forestall continued conflict. Missourians remained committed to enforcing the rule of the proslavery legislature by coercion if the free staters would not accept that body's legitimacy. Even though leaders such as Charles Robinson viewed nonviolent resistance as the free-state movement's best hope of success, some settlers thought force necessary to advance their cause. Bleeding Kansas resulted when proslavery and free-state men turned to violence to achieve their political ends.

Border Missourians, embarrassed by the Wakarusa War's failure to destroy the free-state movement, saw in the free-state elections another opportunity to restore the flouted authority of the territorial legislature. On January 15, free staters were to vote for state officers under the Topeka Constitution. But as in the Wakarusa War, proslavery efforts to establish law and order served instead to create free-state martyrs.

Since the mayor of Leavenworth had forbidden polling, voters met in their own homes, postponing the vote three days to prevent violence.³ Despite this precaution, thirty to fifty proslavery men interfered with the polling by disarming voters and threatening to take the ballot box. In the ensuing scuffle, free staters managed to drive them off, but the incident did not end there. At 2 A.M., Stephen Sparks, his son, Moses, and his nephew started home from the polls. Their road ran by Dawson's store, where a group of Missourians blocked their path, cursing and threatening them. Stephen Sparks, a free-state man from Platte County, Missouri, unavailingly appealed to the men as former neighbors. Unbeknownst to Sparks, a party of Kickapoo Rangers had that night visited his house. They had held Sparks's twelve-year-old son at gunpoint and had given his wife a paper, warning her husband to leave the community. Sparks thus appealed to the goodwill of a community that had decided to expel him. The Missourians at Dawson's store fired on the Sparks men, but Moses escaped and ran to the polling place to get help.

In order to free Sparks, a free-state military company formed a rescue party of about fifteen men. The leader of the company, Reese Brown, had helped defend Lawrence in the Wakarusa War. Brown and his men had spent the evening drinking until summoned to Sparks's aid. They freed Sparks and his nephew, but both Sparks and a proslavery man named Cook were wounded during a ten-minute exchange of gunfire. The free-state party then returned to Leavenworth and spent the night.

The next day, when Brown and his company started home, they were taken prisoner by a party of Kickapoo men under the command of John W. Martin. Martin arrested Brown and his men for shooting Cook. As Martin escorted his free-state prisoners back to Dawson's store, he was already having trouble controlling his men. One of them, Bob Gibson, attacked a free-state prisoner with a hatchet and continued his assault until proslavery and free-state men restrained him. Although Martin tried to maintain order, the men continued to drink and make threats. If protection from these men was his object in bringing the free staters to the store, as Martin claimed, he failed. In the store building, Cook lay dying, his moans audible to the excited proslavery men.

Martin and proslavery politician D. A. N. Grover wanted to turn the free-state men over to the authorities at Leavenworth, but some objected that Brown would escape. Men twice broke into the room where Brown was being questioned. The second time, Gibson led a dozen others into the room and attacked the prisoner with a hatchet. Martin and other proslavery men were unable to repulse Brown's assailants. Martin left the room, saying he could not bear to stay and watch. Explaining that he had lost control of his men, Martin asked the free-state men to sign their names on a roster and released them. In the next room, Brown was being savagely beaten.

At this point, the Kickapoo men decided that Gibson and Brown should engage in single combat. But when Brown was taken outside for the fight, he broke free from the circle of men, blood spurting from a wound to his head. The proslavery men decided Brown had endured enough. As night fell, they took Brown home and left him on the doorstep, where his wife and two-year-old daughter found him. Neighbors summoned a doctor, but it was too late. Brown was bleeding profusely from a two-inch long, fingerwide gash over the left temple, probably caused by Gibson's hatchet. His last words to his wife were, "They murdered me like cowards."[4]

With the exception of Brown's death, comparative quiet prevailed during the January 15 election. Over seventeen hundred men voted, including proslavery men who feared that the free-state organization would succeed and leave them without representation. Charles Robinson was elected governor by a three-to-one margin.[5] Yet a successful election could not allay the shock of Brown's death, which reminded the free-state movement of the hostility that imperiled the free exercise of their political rights—rights they hoped would be guaranteed by the emerging free-state government.

But that government faced the president's implacable hostility. In a special message on January 24, 1856, Pierce blamed the "propagandist emigration" from New England for attempting to force its views of "social organization" (i.e., abolitionism) on others, thereby provoking the Missouri counteraction. Although there had been "irregularities" in forming the territorial government, the president called it "legitimate"; he condemned the Topeka constitution as "revolutionary" and the Topeka movement as potentially "treasonable." Pierce threatened the free-state movement with military intervention and asked Congress to make the necessary appropriations to pay for keeping order in Kansas.[6]

The timing of this special message so long after the Wakarusa disturbance still mystifies observers. Pierce may have used the message to attack Reeder—whose tardiness in arriving in the territory, slowness to hold elections, and improper speculations in lands Pierce enumerated—before the former governor could defend his right to the territorial delegate's seat in Congress.[7] But the message hardened free-state resistance by making it clear that free staters could not get an impartial hearing from the federal government.[8] From Kansas Territory, settler E. P. Fitch warned his parents, "Pierce says we are traitors so of course the Missourians are to put us down but if they try it we shall have a bloody time out here."[9]

Pierce backed his message with force. In February, he issued another proclamation, calling on irregular bands of armed men to disperse. He put federal troops at Fort Leavenworth at Governor Shannon's disposal. While the president ostensibly condemned both Missourian and New England troublemaking alike, he especially denounced those "engaged in unlawful combinations" against the territory's legitimate authorities, placing the onus on the free-state side.[10]

The newly elected free-state government might not even be allowed to meet. A proslavery newspaper called the free-state legislators "outlaw leaders," deeming Robinson and Lane "paid disturbers of the peace and good order of Kansas."[11] The proslavery press thundered that the organization of an extralegal government was an "act of revolt" and of "actual, overt and consummate treason."[12]

When the free-state government assembled in Topeka, Sheriff Jones was present, taking down the names of the officers as they took their oaths. It was expected that the participants would be arrested for treason.[13] Robinson's inaugural discussed the usual subjects for such speeches: schools, charities, public lands, and the regulation of alcohol. Had he merely urged defense against the Indians, and not "the assassin on the east," his call for an organized militia would have been similarly mundane. Clothing the free-state movement in the mantle of popular sovereignty, Robinson called for suspending the territorial government and admitting Kansas, citing the precedents of other states.

The president, by opposing them and threatening force, misunderstood the true nature of both popular sovereignty and of the Topeka movement. Robinson avowed that the free staters would be justified in revolution, but asserted it would not be necessary as he expected the president to draw back first. Robinson's penultimate paragraph outlined the essential strategy of the free-state movement:

We should be unworthy the constituency we represent did we shrink from martyrdom on the scaffold or at the stake should duty require it. Should the blood of Collins and Dow, of Barber and Brown, be insufficient to quench the thirst of the President and his accomplices in the hollow mockery of "Squatter Sovereignty" they are practicing upon the people of Kansas, then more victims must be furnished. Let what will come, not a finger should be raised against the Federal authority until there shall be no hope of relief but in revolution.[14]

To justify their resistance, the free staters claimed the moral authority of revolution and the political legitimacy of acting as true popular sovereigns. They would accept violence as the cost of resistance, but they would not incite violence by actually resisting the federal government.

The new attorney general, H. Miles Moore, recorded in his journal on March 4, 1856, "To day has a new era dawned upon us today have the new State of Kansas been ushered into existence, & now having taken upon ourselves the oath to support that constitution in the mind of that ninney Frank Pierce we have committed the overt act of treason, and in the language of another, 'if we do not all hang together we shall hang separate,' so mote it be."[15] Although Moore was attorney general, neither he nor anyone else seemed sure of the legality of their actions. Both houses of the Topeka legislature passed resolutions deferring any enactment of laws they passed until after Congress's acceptance of statehood. This deferment was done to avert the charges of treason for which they expected to be arrested.[16]

Cautiously though the free staters moved, to the proslavery party their actions betokened a radical assault on slavery that would have to be countered. Certainly, Robinson's rhetoric could not conceal that the Topeka movement still failed to acknowledge the legitimacy of the territorial government. Settlers at Manhattan and Osawatomie resolved not to pay taxes assessed by the "Bogus Legislature."[17] More fundamentally, David Atchison warned Amos Lawrence that "you and your people are the aggressors upon our rights. You come to drive us and our 'peculiar' institution from Kansas. We do not intend, cost what it may, to be driven or deprived of any of our rights."[18] Atchison's pronouncement indicated that Missourians considered migration a political statement hostile to southern rights.

To protect their rights, Missourians harassed northern emigrants. Travel on the Missouri River became increasingly dangerous. Bible study embroiled William C. Clark in conflict with fellow passengers on the *Polar Star*. Clark argued the biblical account of creation implied a common origin of all races—white, black, and Indian. Clark's fellow passengers muttered that he was an abolitionist. He confessed favoring freedom in Kansas. Although fellow travelers seemed to take his position in stride, he considered it prudent to spend much of his time reading in his stateroom. Despite this precaution, the mood soon turned ugly. Another passenger struck him with a chair at breakfast. The captain determined to let him off at the next town, but he got off when the boat stopped for wood, afraid that the cry of "abolition Yankee" might follow him into any settlement.[19]

Even cargo incurred suspicion. Residents of Lawrence had to pay for private mails because St. Louis stagecoach drivers abandoned "abolition" mail at the side of the road. Missourians also expressed suspicion about a crate marked "piano" and informed the hapless merchant to whom it had been consigned that they would inspect it, but they found no guns—only a musical instrument. In fact, not all packages were so innocent. In early March, Missourians discovered a shipment of nine boxes of rifles aboard a Missouri River steamboat. Upon confiscating the weapons, a committee of passengers scrupulously presented the courier with a receipt. Unbeknownst to the Missourians, the rifles lacked slides, rendering them useless; these had gone by land and successfully reached Lawrence on March 12, along with ammunition, rifle primers, musket percussion caps, break pins for a cannon, and cannon molds.[20]

In addition to impeding free-state migration, Missouri's secret lodges were said to be forming land companies and raising money by selling shares. When the weather improved, a large migration would move to

Kansas from the South.[21] Organizations "to *forward, encourage and assist, actual pro-slavery emigration to the Territory of Kansas*" formed in Jackson and Howard counties and in Lexington, Missouri. In order to send settlers, support them while in Kansas, and enable them to buy land, these associations promised to raise money.[22] Late in the summer of 1856, a southern settler reported a rumor that Missourians would send three hundred cows to Kansas: "Every Proslavery man who is keeping house and has no cow is entitled to one."[23] Like Atchison, the Missouri Kansas Association warned Southerners that the success of the free-soil cause meant a "war upon the institutions of the South, which will continue until Slavery shall cease to exist in any of the States, or the Union is dissolved." So that the rich lands of Kansas might not fall into the hands of "Abolition enemies," they asked for tens of thousands of men to come from the South. If proslavery men settled there, "Kansas would be a slave State, and the slavery agitation would cease."[24]

Missourians did receive help from other Southerners. Atchison's allies in the U.S. Senate prepared to "vindicate the Border Ruffians" and tar the "Abolitionists" with "treason +c."[25] In due course, Senator A. P. Butler delivered what he termed an "Atchisoniad," praising Atchison and the Missourians.[26] With their purpose to raise funds and settlers for the territory, Kansas associations were formed as far away as Gainesville, Mississippi; Scott County, Kentucky; Charleston, South Carolina; and Macon and Atlanta, Georgia. The Alabama and Georgia legislatures considered special taxes on slave property to fund sending men to Kansas.[27]

Yet the southern efforts were limited. The southern states did not legislate funds to pay for migration, and aside from the Buford party, few organized parties of immigrants came from the Deep South.[28] The Orangeburg, South Carolina, chairman of the Kansas committee sent only four young men, promising two more, with a request that Atchison "instruct them where to settle, how to vote, and, if necessary, when to fight."[29] A settler at Fort Leavenworth promised to write a family member "such an account of Kansas that he'll stay away from it—Missouri will do to live in on a pinch, but Kansas Territory is worse than nowhere and has been greatly overrated." Still even he avowed, "Of course we keep up the cry to get the emigration from the South here—

thousands come—but by some means they continue to find better farms, and better land, and better people in Missouri—and there they stay—"[30] Controversy even surrounded the policy of blockading and examining cargo that passed through Missouri to the free-state settlements in Kansas. Merchants in Kansas City, Missouri published a letter "to the Public" in the *Herald of Freedom,* denying involvement in the raid on the piano and condemning it as "unlawful and sinister." When proslavery political allegiances conflicted with the money to be made from northern migrants, Kansas City merchants chose to make money. They pledged to protect property passing through their town. Because Kansas City proved an easier transport point than Leavenworth, emigrants and cargo began moving through it.[31] However, many considered southern efforts to aid in Kansas settlement to be too little, too late. A Missouri man wrote, "But I fear all this is too late. The Free-soilers and Abolitionists of the North are ready to pour into the Territory the moment the ice breaks up in the rivers."[32]

Missourians were indeed correct to predict continuing emigration from the North. To arm a Connecticut party of one hundred migrating to Kansas, Yale college students and professors donated money for Sharps rifles.[33] One New York man decided against settlement in Illinois and planned to move to Kansas, where he "hope[d] to be able to repay Freedom a little of the debt due from us to her."[34] John Brown, Jr., wrote that such emigrants should "come *thoroughly armed with the most efficient weapons they can obtain and bring plenty of ammunition.* The question here is shall we be freemen or slaves?"[35] Professing his willingness to go to Kansas, a young, but poor, carpenter avowed, "I would not run from a Border Ruffian or two," and advanced as his attributes his possession of a revolver, dagger, and ammunition. He hoped that the New York Kansas Committee would provide him with a rifle.[36] Another desired to emigrate to Kansas both to "improve my circumstances" and to spread "the institutions of political and religious liberty," adding that his "simpathies are with those that favour equal rights without respect to Colour."[37]

Despite the interference with migrants and cargo, Governor Shannon reported that all had been quiet since the Topeka legislature adjourned. He anticipated no invasions from Missouri, but acknowledged that arms were still smuggled into the territory. Although all was yet calm, Shannon possessed "misgivings" about the future.[38] The determination of both Missourians and free staters to possess the territory, and both sides' militance, provided ample grounds for his concern.

Meanwhile Congress moved to provide its own solution to the territorial issue. On March 12, Douglas's Senate Committee on Territories reported on the president's January message and February proclamation. The report condemned NEEAC, blamed Missouri actions on NEEAC provocation, and called the Topeka movement a "revolutionary" attempt to overthrow the territorial government. In order to fulfill the intent of the president's message, the committee proposed calling a constitutional convention to write a state government and additional money to enforce laws in Kansas Territory. Republicans countered with a minority report, defending the Topeka movement and calling for the admission of Kansas under the free-state constitution.[39] This minority report summed up Republican assessments of Democratic policy in Kansas: "the subjugation of white freemen may be necessary, that African slavery may succeed."[40]

In another move to increase the legitimacy of the free-state movement, a week later congressional supporters secured a committee to investigate election fraud in Kansas. This created the investigating committee of William A. Howard (Rep., Michigan), John Sherman (Rep., Ohio), and Mordecai Oliver (Dem., Missouri).[41] The committee members set out for the territory.

Both political parties now competed to organize a government for Kansas. On March 17, Douglas introduced the promised bill for Kansas admission. Three days later, Senator Seward answered by announcing he would introduce a bill to admit Kansas under the free-state constitution. Free-state supporters began to organize a petition campaign in support of admitting Kansas under the Topeka Constitution. In the northern states, convention proceedings favoring Kansas's admission as a free state were forwarded to Congress.[42]

The campaign to admit Kansas as a free state climaxed on April 9, when Seward spoke in the Senate. He condemned the president's record in Kansas, comparing Franklin Pierce to George III. Kansans now resisted tyranny as had their forefathers, but their resistance was both "peaceful" and "constitutional," and the remedy for the oppression of their liberties at presidential hands was quick admission under the Topeka Constitution. To do otherwise, Seward avowed, would be to impose slavery on Kansas at the price of "all the existing liberties of the American people."[43]

For supporters of Kansas admission under the Topeka Constitution, numerous difficulties yet remained. On April 7, Lewis Cass presented to the Senate the memorial of the Topeka legislature asking admission as a free state but withdrew it when Democrats pointed out irregularities: corrections had been written between the lines and the signatures were all in one handwriting. Jim Lane, who had brought the memorial east, explained the interlineations and recopying of the signatures. With his taste for the dramatic, Lane even took an oath, before Justice John McLean of the Supreme Court, that he had submitted the original copy of the memorial, not a forgery.[44] When Douglas still attacked the memorial as a fraud, Lane demanded satisfaction. Douglas refused to meet Lane on the field of honor, citing his privilege in Congress. Lane deferred to that privilege, but not without hinting that Douglas was a coward. Douglas's objections to the memorial, however, went beyond questions of authenticity. To receive it, Douglas wrote, would be to recognize the revolutionary proceedings which had created it. Although the House voted by a majority of two to admit Kansas under the Topeka Constitution, the Senate refused.[45] Seward's powerful appeal that Kansas had the necessary requirements for statehood—"a substantial civil community, and a Republican Government," and had applied in a "peaceful" and "constitutional" manner—failed to move the senators.[46]

Senator Charles Sumner's two-day oration, "The Crime Against Kansas," on May 19 and 20, articulated Republican frustration. In lurid prose, Sumner described how the "Slave Power of our Republic" with its "depraved longing for a new slave State" had used force to acquire Kansas, perpetrating the "rape of a Virgin Territory." To enforce obedience to unjust laws, as proposed by the president and Senator Douglas, was the "remedy of tyranny." Sumner called for Kansas's admission under Seward's plan. Throughout the debate, Sumner's language was unusually offensive. In his reply to Douglas, he compared that senator to a "noisome, squat, and nameless animal."[47] Another victim of Sumner's vitriol was the elderly South Carolina senator, A. P. Butler. Butler was known for his "bubbling good nature," erudition, and fondness for quoting classical authors. None of this prevented Butler from "flar[ing] up fiercely, to assume the haughty air of the representative of a higher class" when slavery was attacked.[48] In his speech, Sumner accused Butler of having taken "a mistress . . . who . . . though polluted in the sight of the world is chaste in his sight—I mean the harlot, slavery."[49]

Douglas responded powerfully to Sumner's speech, condemning the "malignity" of Sumner's "personalities," as well as their "lasciviousness and obscenity." Particularly reprehensible to Douglas was the attack on "the venerable, the courteous, and the distinguished Senator from South Carolina."[50] Above all, Douglas addressed the substance of the free-state claim "that they are carrying out the principles of the Declaration of Independence; . . . inasmuch as our fathers were rebels against England, they have a right to be rebels against the United States of America." But that argument was only valid "provided they prove that the American Constitution is as vile as the English constitution; provided they prove that the American Government is as oppressive as the British Government; but until they prove that this Government is so weak, so corrupt, so unjust, that it is better to destroy it than to live under it, they must abandon this revolutionary right under the Declaration of Independence."[51] Prophetically, Douglas inquired about Sumner's choice of the word "crime" to title his speech. "Is it his object to provoke some of us to kick him as we would a dog in the street, that he may get sympathy upon the just chastisement?"[52]

Three days later, Congressman Preston Brooks strode to the floor of the Senate. Brooks, a South Carolinian and relative of Senator Butler, found the senators scattered about the chamber. Some chatted in the aisles, while others, including Sumner, worked at their desks. Brooks approached the Massachusetts senator and struck him over the head and shoulders with his cane. As Sumner struggled under the rain of blows, he wrenched his desk from its bolts. Several minutes elapsed before astonished congressmen restrained Brooks. Having sustained severe head injuries, Sumner did not return to the Senate for two and a half years. To express outrage at Brooks's attack, Massachusetts re-elected Sumner even though he was physically unable to fill his seat. Brooks resigned his congressional seat but was reelected as a testament of South Carolina's support for his action. In fact, as he had broken his cane over Sumner's head, Southerners sent him replacements, including one engraved, "Hit Him Again."[53]

The news of the attack on Sumner shocked the North. In Boston, a Fanueil Hall meeting condemned the attack as outside the bounds of the usual congressional brawling. Brooks had struck down freedom of speech and debate as well as Sumner. The attack on Sumner seemed much like the assault on northern liberties taking place in Kansas.[54] Some Kansans felt that the country must now understand the iniquities of the proslavery party inside and outside the territory. "Almost too good news to be true! C. Sumner has been knocked down in the Senate Chamber. Slavery must settle for this! She is fast filling up her cup of iniquity! The lord speedily send her downfall!"[55] exulted Kansas settler Isaac Goodnow.

Southerners interpreted the attack differently. They dismissed Sumner as cowardly and accused him of "feigning illness." After all, Brooks had struck "not . . . more than a dozen blows." Brooks, on the other hand, had displayed "coolness and courage" as well as "spirit and delicacy of sentiment."[56] Most of all, Brooks had defended the honor of his family and of the South from Sumner's vicious attack.[57] Violent suppression of dissent against slavery had become common in southern society; now it had come to the Senate floor.

The attack on Sumner coincided with Kansas officials' renewed efforts to suppress free-state defiance of their authority. Just as Brooks struck down Sumner for his assault on southern honor and slavery, so Missourians would strike down the free staters for their defiance of the territorial government's legitimation of slavery. On April 19, Sheriff Jones went to Lawrence, described by a Southerner as "that nasty Abolition town," to arrest S. N. Wood, one of Branson's rescuers. The crowd disarmed the angry Jones and his assistant, and they left town without Wood. Facetiously, a free-state reporter said that when Jones called for help, he didn't specify whom the Lawrence citizens were to help, so they helped Wood.[58]

The next day, Jones returned with a small posse. Again he was thwarted of his prey, and when called upon to aid the sheriff, citizens of Lawrence refused "with threats and curses." When Jones invoked the "laws of Kansas Territory," the crowd shouted "we will never submit" and threatened the sheriff. Jones gave up and left town accompanied by "the groans, hisses and insults of the mob." Lawrence residents certainly expected Jones to return. Edward Fitch wished for "a good Colts revolver" with which to greet the sheriff.[59]

Three days later, Jones, now reinforced with a party of U.S. dragoons, returned. The presence of U.S. troops tested the free staters' resolve not to defy the U.S. government. While the officer who accompanied Jones reported no resistance to his authority, he added that "Mr. Jones and the territorial government [were] freely and bitterly denounced." With the U.S. troops' help, Jones made six arrests. But Lawrence residents seethed at seeing the six prisoners, all men who had refused to help arrest Wood, marched the length of the town between a double file of dragoons.[60]

Having still failed to nab his chief quarry, S. N. Wood, Jones decided to spend the night camped outside Lawrence. Gunfire resounded throughout the evening. Around 10 P.M., someone shot Jones in the back as he sat in his tent. For all their insistence on nonresistance, it was clear that free-state restraint was wearing thin.[61]

The proslavery press immediately seized on this breach of law and order. A proslavery newspaper's headline read, "The Abolitionists in open Rebellion—Sheriff Jones Murdered by the Traitors!!!"[62] The "BRUTAL ASSASSINATION" of Jones, although it had to be downgraded to a mere wounding, seemed proof of "Continued Resistance to Our Laws!!" The editorialist blamed it on "this clan of assassins—this sworn, secret organization, against law, against order, against the true pillar of our government." These midnight assassins were those "who wish to establish independent government," who wished, as the headline screamed, to commit "TREASON!!!"[63] Although Jones quickly recovered, it was reported, "The excitement on the border consequent upon the attempt to kill Jones is great."[64] Had Jones died, a proslavery man reported, general warfare would have commenced.[65]

The free-state leaders in Lawrence, recognizing their peril, instantly repudiated the assault on the sheriff. Reeder called it an "outrage" that violated the free-state party's insistence on peaceful means. A public meeting in Lawrence labeled it the "isolated act" of an "individual." Robinson, in an unusually hotheaded speech, hinted that it was the work not of a free-state man, but rather of the proslavery group seeking to provoke an outrage while the congressional investigating committee, which had arrived the day before Jones's first attempt to make an arrest, was present. Robinson seemed to think that Jones had invited trouble by not posting a guard at his tent.[66]

The shooting temporarily interfered with the work of the congressional investigating committee. Indeed, Congressman Oliver and Delegate Whitfield claimed that witnesses now feared appearing in Lawrence to testify. While the free-state side scoffed at these fears as pretexts for not cooperating, Whitfield withdrew with his witnesses to Leavenworth and rendezvoused there with the committee. Most witnesses insisted on appearing only in locales friendly to their politics: free staters in Lawrence and proslavery men in Lecompton or Leavenworth.[67]

The committee itself continued its work, putting in ten-hour days and then extra hours at night. Howard reported to Speaker of the House Banks that the testimony of election fraud "deeply implicated" Missourians. "Some of the most important facts have been proven by leaders of the invasion & even by candidates elected."[68]

Even the sympathy of the Republican members of the committee could not protect the free staters from a hostile territorial government. On May 5, Judge Lecompte charged his grand jury to indict all free-state officials and to abate Lawrence's free-state newspapers and hotel as nuisances.[69] Many Missourians found the hotel a suspiciously defensible structure. Its walls were two feet thick at the basement and tapered to eighteen inches on the upper three stories. The walls, which rose two to six feet above the roof, had covered portholes. From the roof, these covers could be easily knocked out, allowing the portholes to serve as gunports.[70]

Although the indictments were not made public for several days, free-state leaders and the Republicans learned of them from one of the grand jurors, a Lawrence man. Free-state officials decided that Robinson would travel east to raise help, while Reeder would be the test case, allowing himself to be arrested. That same evening, when an officer arrived with a subpoena for Reeder, the former governor nonetheless ignored it, alleging it was "irregular." Reeder then asked for the congressional committee's protection, claiming privilege as a delegate to Congress. Howard and Sherman were prepared to uphold that privilege; Oliver was not. Still, even the Republicans on the committee did not think it proper for them to intervene. So when Reeder refused to submit to arrest, the marshal left.[71]

Abandoning the possibility of being a test case, two days later, Reeder decided to flee. In a borrowed overcoat and cap, he walked down a ravine and hid in the house of a Lawrence man. Over the next days, traveling at night, Reeder moved to a succession of safe houses. Eventually, free staters smuggled the ex-governor to Kansas City where he was delayed for a week by bright, moonlit nights. To throw possible pursuers off the track, free-state men planted false telegraph reports that Reeder had been seen in Chicago and mailed a letter to him there.[72]

Robinson also attempted to travel eastward. The collaboration between Republicans on the congressional investigating committee and free-state leaders had gone so far that Robinson not only carried a copy of the testimony taken but also was entrusted to give Republican leaders in the east "full particulars of our situation & progress."[73] Robinson and his wife took passage on a Missouri River steamboat. In Lexington, Missouri, a "committee" arrested him for fleeing the grand jury's indictment. Sara Robinson feared for her husband's life, and wanted him to resist, but the committee treated him cordially before forwarding him to Leavenworth. Missourians gawked at the free-state leader, and may have muttered threats of assassination, but Robinson suffered no violence.[74] Captain Martin of the Kickapoo Rangers guarded Robinson at Leavenworth. Although Martin's experiences safeguarding Reese Brown boded ill for Robinson, this time Martin kept his prisoner alive and delivered him to Lecompton.[75] Sara Robinson, who had concealed the papers the congressional committee entrusted to Robinson in her clothing, delivered them to Republican politicians in Washington.[76]

Robinson's arrest did not satisfy all the provisions of the grand jury's order. A federal marshal and posse, aided by the now recovered Sheriff Jones, rode to Lawrence. Citizens of the town requested the U.S. Army's protection from the men gathering near their town. Col. Sumner forwarded the request to the governor, who replied that only the marshal, with a legal posse, was nearby.[77] Clearly the situation was rapidly passing out of the governor's hands. The marshal and sheriff had summoned the posse without Shannon's knowledge. The force from Missouri, estimated at five hundred to seven hundred men, surrounded Lawrence.[78]

"[G]uns are firing in the camps of the different companies of soldiers who are gathering to attack Lawrence," a Southerner living near the town reported. "Sunday as it is, they are shooting in every direction. I expect before you get this Lawrence will be burnt to the ground."[79] Lawrence settler Edward Fitch observed, "We never have been quite so near a war as we now are."[80] In their fright, Lawrence citizens abandoned the free staters' cherished principle of resistance to the unjust territorial government and issued a statement that the town would not resist "the execution of the laws, national or territorial."[81]

A few days later, the uneasy peace broke. It was to be hot that day, over 90 degrees. That morning, one of Marshal I. B. Donaldson's officers made some arrests, lunched at the hotel, and then returned to the proslavery camp. In mid-afternoon, Sheriff Jones, "quite emaciated and pale," arrived at the head of a new posse. He called for Lawrence citizens to turn over their arms. The Committee on Public Safety surrendered the public property, including one howitzer. Jones declared that he would carry out the grand jury's order to remove obnoxious buildings such as the Free State Hotel and the newspapers. The hotel's proprietor was given until 5 P.M. to move the furniture out of the building. Jones's men moved into position, placing four cannon to command Massachusetts Street. Marshal Donaldson, having made his arrests, dismissed his men and Jones enrolled them. Jones's posse bombarded the Free State Hotel for an hour, then tried blowing it up with kegs of gunpowder, which only shattered the windows but left the structure intact. In frustration, the Missourians set it afire. Jones then dismissed his posse and the individual men proceeded to loot nearby houses until after dark. They burned the Robinsons' house, broke up the newspaper presses and dumped them into the river, and burned books and papers in the street. No free staters were killed, but property damage was substantial. The only injury came to a proslavery man, who was killed by a falling piece of masonry. Throughout the day, free staters made no resistance.[82]

The Sack of Lawrence was a moral victory for the free-state side; it shifted public opinion from distaste for free-state defiance of territorial law to admiration for restraint in not responding to the violence.[83] A rabble-rousing speech by David Atchison circulated, encouraging acts of violence on the citizens of Lawrence, even the women. In one version, Atchison urged the men to "Spring like *your bloodhounds at home* upon that d——d abolitionist hole" and to loot the homes of "those infernal *nigger-stealers,*" all in the name of "Southern Rights." In truth, Atchison gave no such speech and tried, unsuccessfully, to restrain Jones and other proslavery leaders.[84]

Circulating false reports of Atchison's intemperance was only part of the free-state propaganda war. To northern governors went a petition warning of proslavery intent, backed by the federal and territorial governments and by the national Democratic party, to "exterminate" free-state residents of Kansas. The settlers asked for help from their home states.[85] Although the first reports in eastern papers that "*the town of Lawrence was destroyed and a number of persons killed*" were considered doubtful, they caused "intense excitement."[86]

The recently escaped Reeder joined the Republican propaganda effort. Still in hiding in Kansas City when Jones's posse sacked Lawrence, Reeder's friends feared for his life. Reeder wrote a will, cut off his beard, darkened his face with cork, and dressed as an Irish laborer. His disguise caused some problems, for, while waiting to catch a steamship, a man tried to hire Reeder to chop some wood. Reeder escaped the chore by haggling over the price. Boarding the steamboat as a tramp laborer, Reeder was given a protective escort arranged by the attaché of the congressional committee. Fearing that he had been spotted, Reeder disembarked at Jefferson City and traveled overland in a thunderstorm

Ruins of the Free State Hotel after the "Sack of Lawrence." (Kansas State Historical Society, Topeka)

toward Alton, Illinois. With his escorts, Reeder crossed the Mississippi in a skiff a little after daybreak on May 27. On the Illinois side, Reeder exclaimed, "For the first time since leaving Lawrence, I feel easy and safe."[87] Within two days, Reeder was making lengthy speeches to enthusiastic crowds. The ex-governor was photographed in his disguise but he was no longer the fugitive. Instead, he was now a fundraising speaker for the free-state cause, and he quickly extended his tour from Chicago to Detroit.[88]

Free-state efforts such as Reeder's to exploit the attacks on Sumner and Lawrence faltered because their allegiance to nonviolence was incomplete. Some chaffed at the free-state restraint demonstrated in the Sack of Lawrence. The Lawrence *Herald of Freedom* defended that town's residents from charges of cowardice. They had followed the policy of nonresistance to federal authorities "however flagrant, wanton, and unjust" the attack. Rather than censure, they deserved praise for their "forebearance."[89] Not all agreed.

From southeastern Kansas, a free-state rifle company captained by John Brown, Jr., mustered in response to the threatened attack on Lawrence. They were en route to defend that town when they learned they were too late. John's father, old John Brown, and some of his brothers parted company with the volunteers.[90] John Brown had followed his older sons to Kansas Territory in late 1855. In southeastern Kansas, the Brown clan had settled among proslavery neighbors, suffering the privations common to Kansas settlers. They endured the winter of 1855–1856 in a three-sided lean-to. At its open end, a fire blunted the cold, consuming a cord of wood a day. Their diet was an unremitting round of "bears + Johny cake & Johny cake + bears with a very little milk," Oliver Brown recorded.[91] Migration was nothing new to the older Brown, buffeted throughout his life by economic striving and failure.[92]

John Brown, a lifelong abolitionist, had become increasingly disillusioned with both nonviolent abolitionism and the ineffectiveness of free-state resistance to the territorial government. Mainstream abolitionism emphasized pacifism both out of religious conviction and fear of violent retaliation. Such restraint was wearing thin among many abolitionists increasingly radicalized by proslavery triumphs such as the Fugitive Slave and Kansas-Nebraska acts. But religious abolitionism itself contained the seeds of violence in its conviction that Christians must *combat* sin and in Old Testament images of a vengeful and bloody God. Still, abolitionists had not acted on such beliefs. Brown had been committed to a violent war against slavery before he came to Kansas, but he too had not yet acted.[93] The elder Brown had raised money in the east to arm his sons in Kansas. Some of that money came from his patron, wealthy abolitionist Gerrit Smith.[94] John Brown's eagerness to engage Missourians in the Wakarusa War had earned him the reputation of a "gun-happy nonconformist."[95]

Despite its rhetoric of revolution and military preparations, Brown did not find in the free-state movement a violent outlet for antislavery beliefs. Although John Brown, Jr., had been involved in the free-state movement, his father remained on its fringes. John Jr. was a candidate for state office under the Topeka government, and he had organized and led a free-state military company, the Pottawatomie Rifles.[96]

Abolitionist settler John Brown in the 1850s.
(Kansas State Historical Society, Topeka)

The elder Brown arrived too late in Kansas to participate in the formation of the Topeka government. He did not vote in free-state elections, although he stood guard at the polls. Brown did attend the
free-state convention which nominated John Jr. for office, and participated in the April 1856 Osawatomie meeting that passed resolutions
condemning the territorial legislature and vowing noncooperation with
its laws. Brown was among those settlers who rallied to the aid of
Lawrence in the Wakarusa War. Although he may have helped construct earthworks to defend the town and drilled with the volunteers,
he was not involved in the leadership, nor was he impressed by it.

John Brown dismissed Charles Robinson as "a perfect old woman" and condemned the free-state leadership as "more talk than cider," consisting solely of "broken-down politicians" who "would rather pass resolutions than act."[97] Vexed by what he deemed inaction, John Brown seethed with frustration. Learning that Lawrence had been attacked, Brown's frustration flared into violence. His actions would profoundly alter the course of the free-state movement.

An hour before midnight on Saturday, May 24, travellers knocked on the door of the Doyle cabin. Originally from Tennessee, the Doyles had lived in Kansas since November 1855, settling along Pottawatomie Creek. When the men outside asked directions to another cabin, James P. Doyle opened the door, intending to show them the path. Several men, armed with guns and "large knives," forced their way into the cabin. More waited outside. Their leader was an angular old man. They announced that they were taking James and his two oldest sons, William, twenty-two, and Drury, twenty, as their "prisoners." They would have taken sixteen-year-old John, but his mother "asked them in tears to spare him." Cowering in the cabin with her four younger children, Mahala Doyle heard two gunshots, moaning, and a "wild whoop."[98] In the morning, John found the bodies of his father and eldest brother on the road near the house. James Doyle had been shot in the forehead and stabbed in the chest. William's head was cut open, and his face and side bore knife wounds. Drury lay apart from the others in the grass near a ravine. His fingers and arm were severed, his head and chest slashed open. All the Pottawatomie victims would bear the marks of death by sword, displaying the gashes and severed fingers, arms, and hands that resulted when victims such as young Drury Doyle threw up their arms to protect themselves.[99]

Shortly after midnight on the night the Doyles died, a barking dog awakened Louisa Wilkinson. She woke her husband, Allen, but he thought it unimportant and went back to sleep. The Wilkinsons also had come from Tennessee, settling on Pottawatomie Creek in November 1854. After a while, someone knocked on the door, asking the way to Dutch Henry Sherman's. Louisa again woke her husband but warned him not to go outside. She thought she heard men whispering in the yard. Then a voice asked if Wilkinson was a "northern armist." He answered yes. His wife was unsure what this exchange meant but thought her husband was signaling his opposition to the free-soil party. The voice from the yard said that he was their prisoner and that he should open the door or they would open it for him. Despite his wife's objections, Wilkinson complied. Four men entered. Their leader, Louisa described, was "in soiled clothes and a straw hat, pulled down over his face. He spoke quick, is a tall, narrow-faced, elderly man." While Wilkinson dressed, the intruders searched the house. Louisa Wilkinson pleaded that she needed her husband with her as she was ill with measles. The old man brushed aside her request. They left with her husband, telling her he would be taken as a prisoner to their camp. The next day, neighbors found Allen Wilkinson's body 150 yards from the house in some brush. His throat had been cut twice, and there were gashes in his head and side. Perhaps because of her precarious health and the body's mutilation, Louisa Wilkinson's friends would not let her see her husband's corpse.[100]

The murderers, calling themselves the Northern Army, next visited the cabin of James Harris. Here they were recognized as "[O]ld man Brown" and his son, Owen. Brown's "army" was looking for "Dutch" Henry Sherman, a German immigrant. Several men were staying with Harris and his family that night. One by one, Brown's men took them outside for questioning. Although Henry was not among them, his brother William was. Unlike the other men, William did not return after being interrogated. Hearing a cap burst, Brown's two guards in the cabin left. In the morning, Harris found William Sherman. His skull was split open in two places, there was a large hole in his chest, and his left hand was almost entirely severed from the arm.[101]

Why did the Doyles, Wilkinson, and William Sherman die? None of the victims owned slaves, but all were connected to the proslavery party: Wilkinson was a member of the territorial legislature; the store run by William Sherman's brother Dutch was a rendezvous for Buford's Georgians and other proslavery settlers; the Doyles, illiterate poor whites, supported the proslavery party. Brown's son-in-law, Henry Thompson, who helped hack the Doyles to death, later recalled a conversation with the senior Doyle back in the fall of 1855. Doyle, Thompson claimed, had pontificated about "nigger" inferiority until Thompson said he knew many blacks smarter than Doyle.[102] Brown's defenders impugned the good character of the victims and praised Brown for a preemptive strike that eliminated the Doyles and Wilkinson before they could attack the free-state settlers. These rationales for the murders, however, circulated after the Pottawatomie killings, not before.[103] Brown never made these arguments. In fact, Brown evaded a direct answer when asked if he had committed the murders: "I did not; but I do not pretend to say that they were not killed by my order, and in doing so I believe I was doing God's service."[104]

Brown's apologists later proclaimed that by means of the Pottawatomie Massacre, Brown put the fear of God into the proslavery side and singlehandedly prevented Kansas from becoming a slave state.[105] Charles Robinson argued differently. Just as the Sack of Lawrence provided "a decisive victory over the Slave-State party," the Browns' actions justified the use of military force against free staters.[106] Robinson correctly observed that the Pottawatomie killings were an aberration from the free-state strategy which hurt, rather than helped, their cause.

That the killings deviated from the free-state emphasis on forebearance was precisely Brown's point. A modern historian describes the philosophy of terrorism thus: "Calculated atrocities . . . restore to the forces of revolution, long stupefied by a policy of concession and compromise, the will to fight." Brown, according to this reading, acted as a modern terrorist with an Old Testament ideology.[107] Whether Brown was a hellfire and brimstone Calvinist bringing the judgments of the Lord down on the unrighteous, or a product of the millennialist Second Great Awakening seeking perfectionism and a society cleansed of sin, the result was to push the free-state movement to use the violent means they had threatened but not yet implemented.[108] Whereas Robinson recognized that free-state use of violence would only legitimize the forceful suppression of the Topeka movement, Brown wanted to wrench the free staters from their half measures, their "policy of concession and compromise," and instill in them "the will to fight."

But the free-state allegiance to nonviolence—given their stockpiling of arms, militia drills, and revolutionary rhetoric—had always been precarious. Brown ignited the latent violence of Kansas Territory. A Kansas settler noted, "The war seems to have commenced in real earnest."[109] People fled the countryside as men gathered in military companies. Citizens appealed to the governor for arms. Chasing through the countryside, U.S. troops disbanded armed groups, only to see them quickly reform.[110]

General violence, however, only endangered the revolutionary cause that Brown served. Governor Robinson was under arrest for usurping office and high treason.[111] Reeder had fled the territory. Even the congressional investigating committee came under threat. The murders on Pottawatomie Creek now justified the federal government in loosing the military on free-state guerrillas.[112] For almost a year, the free-state movement had successfully threatened revolution in defense of their rights without actually coming to blows. Now Brown's actions had catapulted the movement into a guerrilla war for their freedom.

6

We Fight to Free White Men
The Guerrilla War of 1856

The Pottawatomie killings shattered the uneasy peace and inaugurated guerrilla war. Charles Robinson was in jail, unable to restrain the hotheads such as John Brown and Jim Lane and the many free staters for whom forbearance had worn thin. Border Ruffians "should be shot as mad dogs," free-stater D. R. Anthony wrote.[1] Another even hoped for the defeat of the federal troops, "so that we may have a chance at the Ruffians."[2] Similarly, moderate Missourians could not hold back men whose friends and neighbors were under attack in Kansas. John Brown and a growing band of young followers disappeared into the brush. Free-state and proslavery men rallied to other guerrilla leaders. Violence, however, was the continuation of the political struggle. The men on both sides, and their supporters inside and outside the territory, framed their conflict in terms of rights and liberty even as they shot, burned, and terrorized. Now that free-state men openly brandished arms, the federal government could legitimately move to suppress their lawlessness and rebellion. But the federal authorities still faced the difficult task of suppressing the violence without violating the rights of their citizens. One observer called the guerrilla war "three-cornered," with "free-state men on one side, pro-slavery men on the other, and Uncle Sam's men pretending to keep the peace, but not able to do it."[3] In the confusion of Bleeding Kansas, free staters defended their use of revolutionary violence to protect their liberties. Missouri slaves used the confusion to expand the meaning of freedom by seizing theirs. Although many free staters initially denied their movement intended black liberty as well as white, blacks increasingly found allies among the free-state ranks. Missourians once again took up arms against the lawless rebels who committed murder, arson, and slave-stealing.

Proslavery men rallied to protect their settlers from "hired Abolitionists" who wanted "to deprive Southern men of their constitutional rights." In a reference to the Pottawatomie murders, citizens of eastern Kansas condemned the "midnight assassinations" of those, like the Doyles, whose only crimes were "that they believed Southern people had equal rights with Northern, in the Territories."[4] H. C. Pate, captain in the territorial militia and a deputy U.S. marshal, captured Brown's sons, John Jr. and Jason, and turned them over to federal troops. Pate's men also burned John Jr.'s cabin and a store belonging to Theodore Weiner, who was suspected of participating in the Pottawatomie killings. By early June, Pate was camped at Black Jack, near Hickory Point. Brown learned of Pate's location and decided to surprise Pate before the proslavery force could find him. On June 4, two free-state companies—one under a Captain Shore with twenty-five men and the other under John Brown with ten—attacked Pate's camp at breakfast. After a fight lasting two to three hours, Frederick Brown, mounted on horseback, rode around Pate's force shouting that they were outnumbered. As Shore's men had abandoned the battle, Frederick's ruse was a desperate trick to rescue Brown's outnumbered force. It worked. Pate surrendered with twenty-eight of his men as the others fled. Among Brown's wounded were his son-in-law and three of his sons. Pate remembered the Battle of Black Jack: "I went to take Brown—and he took me."[5] Pate's failure to arrest Brown and the Wakarusa War had made clear the territorial militia could not restore order. Too closely linked to the proslavery party, free staters did not acknowledge the territorial militia's authority as an arm of the territorial legislature. Only the U.S. Army's authority was acknowledged by both sides, but even the army was initially ineffective.

In a torrent of orders to military authorities, Governor Shannon moved troops to trouble spots in the territory and ordered illegal military companies to disperse.[6] Soldiers dispersed such groups, but they quickly reassembled. In fact, Brown's company alone was twice dispersed by government troops in the first week of June. U.S. troops investigating guerrilla attacks themselves became targets of violence.[7]

Col. Edwin Sumner, a cousin of the Massachusetts senator, did make a show of force in southeast Kansas, eliciting promises to comply from several free-state companies. Brown even released Pate into Sumner's custody. Sumner admonished Pate and his men to return to Missouri and mind their own business. Then he set them free. Soon after, Sumner disbanded two to three hundred Missourians led by Col. Whitfield, the territorial delegate, and Gen. Coffee of the militia. But even Sumner doubted that this would be "a final dispersion."[8] A free-state guerrilla complained that the troops would corner Missouri guerrilla bands and read the governor's proclamation. The proslavery guerrilla captain would then order his men to disperse and they would scatter into the timber and regroup.[9] The governor's proclamation and its implementation thus proved ineffective at suppressing the guerrilla forces. One free-state settler reported a "heap of fighting going on."[10]

Governor Shannon was at a complete loss to control the worsening conflict. Fear of another Wakarusa War haunted the governor. In ordering one troop movement, Shannon noted that if the army failed to act, "the people will rise in mass to defend themselves and their friends, and Missouri will pour into this Territory her thousands."[11] Not only did Shannon doubt his ability to control the Missourians, he lacked any credibility with free staters. Their newspapers rumored that he was continually drunk, had threatened the wife of free-state Captain Samuel Walker, and had personally led a proslavery posse of South Carolina bushwhackers.[12] A more believable account depicts the governor's state of mind. When a man approached Shannon in Kansas City to complain about the theft of his cattle, Sara Robinson observed on Shannon's face "a look of utter weariness, of inability to do any thing, or incapacity to know what to do."[13] Shannon did seem utterly out of touch: he wrote the president from St. Louis that "there are not at this time, on either side, any armed bodies of men in the Territory, so far as I am advised."[14] By the end of June, when Shannon left for St. Louis on official business, some residents had begun to speak of Colonel Sumner as the true governor of Kansas.[15]

In fact, Shannon's departure left Daniel Woodson, the territorial secretary, as acting governor. Woodson, a Marylander in his early thirties, had been active in the proslavery party and was indifferent to free-state complaints. Shannon also attempted to shift the burden of controlling the crisis to the military. He left Col. Sumner the responsibility for dealing with the meeting of the Topeka legislature on July 4, which he called on Sumner to disperse as an illegal body. Clearly uncomfortable with the leading role in this drama, Sumner asked for a civilian official to accompany the troops. Woodson agreed.[16]

From Lecompton, Robinson and the other free-state prisoners advised against resisting Sumner's authority. If the federal government, which the colonel represented, prevented the legislature from meeting, this would be a "tyranical usurpation of power." Although this made resistance "justifiable self-defense," the free-state prisoners emphasized the need to present an unblemished picture of the "oppressed people of Kansas" to the country and the world.[17]

On the days before the Fourth, Topeka swelled with men arriving for a mass convention and the meeting of the free-state legislature. One observer estimated that there were also about one thousand dragoons, with cannon, surrounding the town. "It is greatly feared there will be difficulty," he noted.[18]

On July 4, after the roll was called, Col. Sumner interrupted the legislative proceedings. Having placed his men before the building in which the legislature met, Sumner took a position on the speaker's platform in the lower house. Armed with proclamations from the president and the territory's acting governor, Sumner announced that it was "the most painful duty of my whole life" to "command you to disperse." A spectator pointedly asked if "the legislature is dispersed at the point of the bayonet?" Sumner replied, "I shall use the whole force under my command to carry out my orders." With that threat extracted from the unhappy officer, the Topeka legislature dissolved.[19] As Sumner left the hall, a spectator told him, "Colonel, you have robbed Oliver Cromwell of his laurels."[20] Others found a symbol of tyranny closer to home. Sumner "wheeled" through the crowd in the Topeka streets "more like a lordly slave holder thru a gang of slaves on his own plantation, than a gentleman among Free Citizens on a highway equally free for all."[21]

Colonel Sumner dispersing the free-state legislature, Topeka, Kansas, July 1856. (Kansas State Historical Society, Topeka)

Although H. Miles Moore had feared trouble due to the "fighting spirit" he observed among the free-staters, the dispersal of the legislature was not resisted. In fact, once again the federal government played into the free-staters' hands: "this being just the position the Legislature desired to occupy to be dispersed at the point of the bayonet."[22] By self-restraint, the free staters had shown the government's intolerance of dissident political movements.

Sumner quickly found that he would be the administration's scapegoat for popular condemnation of the dispersal. In response to his formal report, he received a cold reply from the adjutant general. The secretary of war was dissatisfied that other means had not been used to disperse the Topeka legislature. Further correspondence from Washington, D.C., grew even more curt.[23] Sumner found himself explaining that, since the federal government had arrested the Topeka movement's leaders, it seemed not at all unreasonable to him and Woodson to suppress the Topeka legislature as "insurrectionary" under the terms of the president's proclamation.[24] Eventually the Pierce adminis-

tration removed Sumner from command in Kansas and replaced him
with Persifor Smith, an old friend of Pierce's from the U.S.-Mexican
War.[25]

Sumner's action supported the free-state point that the U.S. Army
was a weapon of tyranny against Kansans. On July 28, John Sherman
offered an amendment to the army appropriations bill to prevent further military support of the territorial government. The House passed
it decisively, 80–47, but it ultimately failed, despite three conferences
between the House and Senate. Congress adjourned on August 18
without passing a bill for the army, forcing Pierce to call Congress into
special session three days later. Sherman again introduced his proviso, but the army appropriations bill narrowly passed without it.[26] The
Republicans wanted to punish Pierce's administration for using troops
against the Topeka legislature, and to take pressure off the free-state
movement by preventing confrontations between it and the army.
They feared such confrontations would dim northern enthusiasm for
the free-state cause. They invoked the dangers of standing armies to
the liberties of a free people. When opponents warned that anarchy
threatened to engulf the territory, Senator William H. Seward asked,
"What measure of anarchy could reconcile, or ought to reconcile,
American citizens to a surrender of constitutional Liberty in any part
of the Republic?"[27]

Kansans, however, were learning a great deal about anarchy. A
proslavery settler described these "exciting times" in Kansas: "I never
lie down without taking the precaution to fasten my door, and fix it in
such a way that if it is forced open, it can be opened only wide enough
for one person to come in at a time. I have my rifle, revolver, and old
home-stocked pistol where I can lay my hand on them in an instant,
besides a hatchet & axe. I take this precaution to guard against the
midnight attacks of the Abolitionists."[28] So far had Kansas come from
the innocent days, not even a month past, in which the Doyles had
admitted strange men to their cabin at night.

Once again proslavery forces closed the emigrant route through
Missouri. Once again Missourians stopped or opened mail and cargo,
and took teamsters prisoner.[29] Travelers excited special suspicion.
Missourians often demanded that a migrant say "cow" "to see if he would

give the Yankee pronunciation & thus decide if he was right on the goose." So New Englanders practiced, "saying KOW right not ceow."[30]

Emigration continued, but it was significantly below normal. The military struggled to distinguish genuine emigrants, often coming armed, from the guerrilla bands they were trying to disperse. A lieutenant confronted just that problem on the border, where he ordered a camp of fifty to sixty men back into Missouri. They claimed to be emigrants but he did not believe them.[31]

Free staters included the disarming of northern parties, and their forced return eastward, among the "outrages" they endured, lamenting that "it has got to be perfectly intolerable when citizens from Ohio, Ills. or Pa. dare not emigrate to Kansas."[32] A New England woman, Mrs. E. P. Cutter, embarked as part of an emigrant company in mid-June. Their only weapons were for defense, she maintained. At Boonville, Missouri, they were told to turn back, but they pressed on. The clerk of their steamboat took charge of their weapons. At Waverly, armed men lined the shore; some boarded and confiscated more weapons. As the party passed through Missouri, they continually saw armed crowds of men on the shore and suffered searches and confiscation of weapons. Mrs. Cutter was particularly indignant when "our masters gave another turn to the slave driver's screw": they searched private staterooms. Mrs. Cutter felt when northern citizens could not travel freely to the territories, northern subjugation to the South was complete.[33]

Despite the fact that Mrs. Cutter's party was obviously heavily armed, stories such as hers had an impact. The governors of Iowa and Wisconsin formally protested the military blockade of emigration. Citizens of Ohio and Illinois petitioned their governors to take action to protect citizens and their rights in the territories. Nonetheless, the military authorities were right: Free staters did come in bands, organized as military companies, and were well armed.[34]

As the river route through Missouri became increasingly perilous, free staters began to explore overland routes through Iowa.[35] Extolling the virtues of the route from Tabor, Iowa, to Nebraska City, a New York man wrote, *"We shall not lose any arms on that road."*[36] A large army under Jim Lane, estimated at 250 to 500 men with a cannon, came through Iowa and Nebraska to reinforce the free-state cause.[37]

At the end of August, Lane's force attacked Missourians two miles from Bull Creek. The proslavery men had a larger force and more cannon. After the attack, both armies fell back, the free-staters exhausted and the Missourians disorganized and surprised. The next day, the free staters found the Missourians retreating. While Lane was a relative latecomer to the fighting, he proved himself indefatigable and demonstrated his legendary common touch. To disguise Lane from prying U.S. troops, free-state guerrillas "tried putting old clothes on him; but the worse clothes we put on, the more like Jim Lane he looked."[38]

What were the free staters fighting for? Marching back to Lawrence in early September, 1856, a slave tried to join Lane's army. Lane ordered him returned to his owner, saying "that we were not fighting to free black men but to free white men."[39] Nonetheless, free staters still used the imagery of black enslavement to illustrate the plight of whites in Kansas. A minister's wife reported that free-state prisoners had been "chained like galley-slaves, and had actually been made slaves of" by their proslavery captors.[40] Free staters still acted in the cause of white liberty, but the slave man's attempt to run away and the lament of southern settlers such as Axalla Hoole, revealed that the fighting in Kansas was reshaping the status of blacks. "One of our neighbors has missed a Negro fellow and supposes he has been carried off by the Abolitionists," Hoole wrote. "He thinks that they had to carry him off by force, as he does not think the Negro would go off willingly. They have tried to induce a good many to run away."[41] Hoole's assurance, common to slaveowners, that blacks would never leave of their own volition could not disguise the fact that disorder in Kansas opened possibilities for freedom that many blacks exploited.

Southerners followed events in Kansas intently. "To much blood has been shed to much time and money spent to give up Kansas now," Atchison lamented, while describing a plan to raise money and provisions to colonize Southerners in the territory. Still, Atchison complained, "The South has placed on my shoulders more than I am willing or able to bear."[42] Virginian James M. Mason agreed that Kansas controlled the "destiny" of the South.[43] A Kentuckian summarized the meaning of Kansas. Southerners did not care, he argued, whether Kansas became slave or free; they merely demanded that the territories acquired at the expense of both sections be open to both. Kansas had descended into turmoil when the North sought to seize for itself that which had been acquired by all.[44] In an August skirmish, free-state guerrillas captured a proslavery band's flag, which bore the motto "Our constitutional rights or death."[45]

The fighting, however, brought danger to proslavery lives as well as abstract rights. A Missouri man wrote eloquently of "the havoc made by the Abolitionists, how they have killed the Settlers, or have driven them from their possessions, burned down their dwellings, and plundered or stolen every thing they could carry off, and that not one pro slavery man is left south of the Kansas river in peaceable possession of his property." Proslavery men called upon Missourians to counter the "war of extermination upon pro-slavery settlers." On August 7, Brown's company had attacked the Georgia colony at Osawatomie—largely populated by women, children, and slaves—burned the houses and farm equipment, and had even stolen the children's clothing.[46] On the night of August 12, free staters attacked Franklin, killing six and capturing "Old Sacramento," the cannon used by Missouri troops in the U.S.-Mexican War. Although the free-state men were outgunned, clouds obscured the moon long enough for them to move a wagon of hay in front of a building in which the proslavery men had taken refuge. The darkness lasted until the free-state men fired the hay. While the burning hay threatened the front of the building, other free staters created a diversion by firing at the rear. Most of the proslavery men escaped through the windows, however, when free staters pulled the haywagon away. Left behind were the wounded, large quantities of arms, and the famous cannon.[47] On August 15, Brown used the cannon in an attack on a small settlement in Douglas County. "The next breath from Kansas," a proslavery appeal warned, "may bring to our ears the death shrieks of our Fathers, brothers, sisters, sons, daughters, neighbors and friends who went there to find a home, but have been butchered by the abolitionist." If Missourians did not rally to defend their right to be in Kansas Territory, "*Kansas is lost to the South forever*—and our slaves in upper Missouri will be useless to us—and our homes must be given up to the abolition enemy."[48]

On August 16, the fighting climaxed with the free-state attack on Titus's fort, nine miles west of Lawrence. Samuel Walker led about forty men, some of whom fired balls cast from the type of the *Herald of Freedom,* which had been destroyed in the Sack of Lawrence. "This is the second edition of 'The Herald of Freedom,'" the free-state men called as they fired. "How do you like it?" Not very well, it seemed, for the proslavery men quickly surrendered, yielding thirty-four prisoners, including Titus himself.[49] Among the wounded free staters was an Indiana man who died the next day with the parting words, "Tell them I freely offer my life in behalf of the freedom of Kansas."[50]

Two weeks later, proslavery guerrillas swept into Osawatomie. A force of four hundred men under John W. Reid had been hunting for Brown. Brown's band had arrived there the night before, exhausted. Brown expected an attack from the east, but Reid circled the town and came in from the west. Twelve-year-old Charles Adair rode to warn the town. Young Adair made it to Brown's camp as the men were making breakfast, and brought news that Frederick Brown had been killed when proslavery forces encountered him on the road. In order to buy time for the women and children to flee, Brown ordered his men to intercept the proslavery band before it reached the town.

Heavily outnumbered, and outgunned by proslavery possession of a cannon, free-state men under Brown and J. B. Cline took refuge in a log house and in the brush along the river. Fortunately, the proslavery band was unable to aim the cannon effectively; but their greater numbers forced the free-state forces to fall back. After a half hour of fighting, Cline's men ran out of ammunition and retreated. Brown's men were forced to follow. They planned to cross the river and re-form at a log house on the other side. Many were wounded and captured while trying to cross the river. Upon reaching the log house, Brown was puzzled that the proslavery men did not pursue them. The enemy did not follow the retreating free-staters because they set the town on fire instead.[51] When the residents of Osawatomie returned, they buried the three free-state dead as "martyrs to the liberty of Kansas."[52]

The escalation of violence caused Acting Governor Woodson to declare the territory in rebellion and call on patriotic citizens to defend the law. His actions prompted the free staters to call the inter-

The capture of proslavery military leader Colonel Henry C. Titus by free-state forces. (Kansas State Historical Society, Topeka)

regnum between Shannon and his replacement "Woodson's Reign of Terror." A territorial governor's call for help was the very situation that had brought Missourians into Kansas in December 1855 and May 1856 and that Shannon had hoped the U.S. Army could prevent.[53] As they had in previous crises, Missourians raised forces. Lexington, Ray, and Boone counties sent almost three hundred men; Cooper County residents donated five thousand dollars and more men; and Boone County citizens asked the county court to raise five thousand dollars to arm and equip a hundred volunteers. Under Atchison's direction, the army gathered at New Santa Fé.[54] In employing these forces, Woodson clearly worried about their ability to distinguish *"peaceable, unoffending citizens"* from guerrillas.[55] Although Woodson enjoined the territorial forces against burning out settlers, army officers worried that his orders would widen the conflict. Relations between Woodson and the military broke down completely when Woodson arrested a free-state man whom the military authorities had referred to the governor. Then Woodson called on the army for forces to disarm the insurrectionists at Topeka and level their forts. He received a curt refusal.[56]

The territorial government's paralysis and the army's ineffectiveness permitted both sides to suffer from what a free-state man described as "drought, robbery, burning, plundering and driving."[57] As one member of a free-state band recorded, life in the summer of 1856 was a continual round of rumors, alarms, and marching to perceived threats. In late August, his band proceeded from Plymouth to Lexington, Topeka, Tecumseh, and Lawrence—all on a diet of fried mush and sugarless coffee. Deserted buildings and half-finished earthen forts littered the countryside. Another free-state man said his band lived on "slapjacks" and bacon. They wrapped coffee in canvas, beat it with a hammer, then boiled and sweetened it. The guerrillas often had much to learn. One free-state man grabbed a gun by the muzzle to lift himself into a wagon and was fatally wounded. A proslavery guerrilla complained that they had to burn houses and destroy crops because the Yankees would not come out and fight.[58]

Journalist James Redpath provided a vivid portrait of John Brown's camp. Searching for it, Redpath first encountered Frederick Brown, who was armed with a half-dozen pistols and a bowie knife. Frederick was unshaven and wore a coarse blue shirt and red-topped boots. A dozen horses were tethered at the camp, and rifles and sabers were stacked. While men lounged on blankets in the grass, a woman picked blackberries. "Old Brown himself stood near the fire, with his shirt-sleeves rolled up, and a large piece of pork in his hand. He was cooking a pig. He was poorly clad, and his toes protruded from his boots." Swearing was not allowed in Brown's camp, morning and evening prayers were said, and all food was blessed.[59]

Such sympathetic portrayals of free-state guerrillas made it difficult for Democratic appeals to law and order to resonate with the public. Law and order were central to the government's case against the free-state prisoners. In June, Robinson, Reeder, and others had been indicted for trying to prevent the execution of the Kansas-Nebraska Act. Testimony taken in the summer of 1856 pinpointed their involvement in free-state military companies, their refusal to pay taxes to the territorial government, and their repudiation of the territorial legislature's authority.[60] In mid-July, a visitor found Robinson "very much dispirited & discouraged" and convinced "that he will be *executed.*"[61] Free-state newspapers emphasized the suffering of the free-state prisoners who, wearing chains, had been made to walk in the heat with little food or water. Such treatment had allegedly driven John Brown, Jr., insane. It was said that his chains were distinguished from the others' by their shininess. They were polished in his ravings to be freed.[62]

In mid-June, Sara Robinson joined her husband at Lecompton— "Uncle Sam's Bastile on the Kansas prairies." But conditions belied the images of dungeons her rhetoric summoned. The prisoners lived with their wives and were free to come and go without guard. During the summer, they received many visitors, curious to see the "traitors." A Southerner who visited Lecompton found a prison without bars; outside, the prisoners pitched quoits unguarded.[63] Their comfortable quarters did not prevent John Greenleaf Whittier from composing a tribute to their righteousness in the antislavery cause.[64] Perhaps because the image of U.S. political prisoners was such effective propaganda, perhaps because he did not trust the excitable Lane, or perhaps because he anticipated the prisoners' imminent release, Robinson refused an offer of rescue from Jim Lane.[65]

Had Robinson, and the others involved in the Topeka movement, committed treason? The word had been much used by both sides, but now Pierce's administration would have to make that charge in a court of law, not the court of public opinion. Under the Constitution, where was the line between political protest and treason? Washington's administration prosecuted the whiskey "rebels" as traitors and won convictions, although the defense argued they were guilty only of riot. Other cases of the early national period did not revise the law's interpretation, yet presidents were reluctant to follow through on convictions. (Before leaving office, Washington pardoned all the whiskey rebels, indicating respect for the legitimacy of political dissent.)[66] In the 1850s, the federal government tried to convict Castner Hanway of treasonable defiance of the Fugitive Slave Law for his role, which was largely that of a bystander, in the murder of a Maryland slaveowner by the slaves he was trying to recover. Despite the federal government's strong desire for a conviction, the jury acquitted Hanway.[67] The closest parallel to the free staters may have been Rhode Island's Dorr rebels, who created an extralegal government in defiance of the state government.[68] Still, charging treason in order to suppress political opposition had traditionally failed. The Pierce administration seemed poised to fly in the face of this venerable tradition.

In Congress, opposition grew to prosecuting the prisoners. Republican congressman Schuyler Colfax attacked the validity of the original indictments. Although resolutions to free the free-state prisoners failed in Congress, that result was only obtained by "executive promises" to drop the case.[69] The Pierce administration was willing to abandon the treason prosecutions in return for Republican cooperation on the army appropriations bill. Judge Lecompte granted a postponement until the next term of court and admitted the prisoners to bail. The president then entered a nolle prosequi in the case and ordered General Smith to provide the prisoners with an escort home.[70] The treason prisoners returned to Lawrence. The Stubbs rifle company met them and escorted them into town, where a cheering crowd greeted them. The evening was filled with speech making by several local dignitaries, including Robinson, Lane, and John Brown.[71]

Yet the release did not solve the problem of providing a legitimate government for Kansas. Congress debated the issue throughout the summer. On June 23, Senator Robert Toombs of Georgia announced that he would introduce a bill for Kansas statehood. A census preparatory to calling a constitutional convention would end the attempt to force more population into Kansas. A constitutional convention would itself possess legitimacy independent of both the territorial legislature and the Topeka government. In addition, the election of delegates would occur on the day of the presidential election, and would thus inhibit nonresident voting and remove Kansas from the issues of the presidential election. Toombs himself thought the free staters had a good chance of winning such an election, but Republicans made clear they would not accept a Democratic bill.[72]

The Republicans countered with the investigating committee's report, which was read on July 1. It "created a sensation" and mobilized Republicans to ask for Kansas admission under the Topeka Constitution.[73] The committee's Republican majority predictably concluded that if the Kansas-Nebraska Act had not been passed, Kansas would have become a free state. Until the bill "agitated" the slavery issue, Missourians had no expectation of extending slavery to Kansas. The committee further concluded that fraudulent voting had rendered the territorial legislature invalid: "A legislature thus imposed upon a people cannot affect their political rights. Such an attempt, if successful, is virtually an overthrow of the organic law, and reduces the people of the Territory to the condition of vassals to a neighboring State." The Topeka movement, being an "expression of popular will," was therefore legitimate.[74] Fair elections were impossible in Kansas, the majority report concluded, without "a new census, a stringent and well-guarded election law, the selection of impartial judges, and the presence of United States troops at every place of election."[75]

After two days of debate, the Senate passed the Toombs bill on July 3 by a vote of 33 to 12, but it died in the House because of Republican opposition. Instead, the House narrowly passed a bill to admit Kansas as a state under the Topeka Constitution. This bill was sent to the Senate, where Douglas succeeded in having the Toombs bill substituted and passed again. Although Pierce lobbied House members to accept the Senate's substitution, the House refused.[76]

Republicans objected that the Toombs bill did not provide for submission of a constitution to the people; that it created a board of commissioners answerable to the president, not to the people, to supervise the election of delegates; and that it would make the enumeration of voters after many free-state men had fled the territory. Congress should instead set aside the territorial legislature and restore to Kansans *the free enjoyment of all their political rights as American citizens.*[77] Some objected that Republican opposition to the Toombs bill arose mainly out of unwillingness to lose an issue in an election year. The charge contained sufficient truth to stick. In requesting campaign material for the upcoming election, Republicans specifically mentioned the congressional committee report, the laws of the "bogus" territorial legislature, and congressional speeches on Kansas issues.[78] But Republicans legitimately feared that Pierce's appointments under the Toombs bill would be no less proslavery than his previous selections for the territory. Even if the presidential appointees were impartial, they would still rely on the proslavery judges and sheriffs in the territory. By the end of the session on August 18, no bill for the admission of Kansas had passed the Congress.[79] Texas senator Louis T. Wigfall, speaking from the extreme proslavery position, had said, "Let Kansas bleed if she has a fancy for it."[80] And Congress now seemed prepared to do so.

Democrats stood to suffer most from "the unhappy state of affairs in Kansas." Political operatives throughout the North reported their apprehensions of a looming "disastrous defeat." Northern voters blamed Democrats for the territorial legislature's repressive actions.[81] "The 'Kansas outrages' had penetrated the popular heart," a Maine Democrat noted, "and made a *deeper impression* than any one anticipated. The people were enraged and ready to believe any representation no matter how absurd."[82]

The troubles in Kansas affected the Democratic party's search for a candidate. As early as 1854, some had puffed James Buchanan. Buchanan's career as a statesman promised the diplomatic ability to reconcile clashing factions that Pierce lacked. More importantly, Buchanan had been out of the country and, lacking personal involvement in Kansas affairs, had made no enemies.[83] Following the advice Buchanan received from other Democrats would have challenged Solomon: the presidential candidate must reassure the South, yet at the same time convince the North that he repudiated the Pierce administration. Buchanan was no Solomon. Pledging himself to the principle of popular sovereignty, he expressed the conviction that the problems of the territories were "rapidly approaching a 'finality.'"[84]

The strange case of A. H. Reeder revealed the divisions within the Democratic party. Reeder still pressed his claim to the congressional delegate's seat. The ex-governor made a powerful plea to the House of Representatives, arguing that his election, although irregular, had greater legitimacy than Whitfield's. Citing Jefferson, Locke, and the *Federalist Papers,* Reeder contended for the right of the people to change their government regardless of the will of government officials, whom Reeder called mere "agents" of the people. Reeder also cited, at length, precedents in which states had been admitted, or congressmen selected, by a popular movement rather than a congressionally sanctioned procedure. Congress chose to leave the seat open.[85] Whitfield blamed the "Black Republicans" for ousting him, and he called on the "independent freemen" of Kansas to resist this attempt to make them the "supple slave" of congressional Republicans.[86] But why was Reeder not arrested? He had been indicted for treason, yet was instead allowed to speak and raise money for the free-state cause, which he likened to the Patriots of 1776. Some answered that President Pierce feared the backlash an arrest would cause in the North, which would hurt the Democrats before the election.[87]

While Democrats hesitated, the Republicans embraced the free-state movement. When Charles Robinson was appointed a member of the Republican National Committee "for the State of Kansas," the Republican convention crowd cheered upon hearing the word "state."[88] The Republican party platform advocated Kansas's admission as a free state under the Topeka Constitution, and urged Congress to use its powers "to prohibit in the territories those twin relics of barbarism—polygamy and slavery." What aroused the party's chief ire was not slavery in Kansas, but rather that, under Democratic rule,

the dearest Constitutional rights of the people of Kansas, have been fraudulently and violently taken from them . . . spurious and pretended legislative, judicial, and executive officers have been set over them, by whose usurped authority, sustained by the military power of the government, tyrannical and unconstitutional laws have been enacted and enforced . . . the freedom of speech and of the press has been abridged— the right to choose their representatives has been made of no effect— murders, robberies, and arsons have been instigated and encouraged, and the offenders have been allowed to go unpunished.[89]

The Republicans determined to fight the election on the Pierce administration's violations of political liberty. "Geo. W. Smith of this County who was arrested and in custody in Kansas all summer, returned home a few days before the election, to rattle the chains of his bondage in the sacred cause of liberty in Kansas, and implore everybody to vote for freedom and Fremont,"[90] a Pennsylvania Democrat reported. Smith, the Pennsylvanian might have noted, was not the only free-state victim of violence dispatched east; others, including the recently released Robinson, had been sent there to spread the free-state word on events in Kansas.[91] For a New York City audience, Robinson not only detailed the outrages committed against Kansans in the already lengthy history of the territory, but also argued that the free staters had been denied the exercise of popular sovereignty in the territory. President Pierce, Robinson alleged, "has endorsed this treason" against the settlers of Kansas, and Buchanan, having endorsed the Pierce program, "is an accessory after the fact."[92] Although the free-state men of Kansas had resorted to violence to defend their political rights, the election offered another means to secure those rights.[93] In Republican candidate John C. Frémont's election "is our only rescue," a Kansas woman wrote, and the only hope to preserve the "Liberty and Democracy" of "our glorious Republic!"[94]

Democrats responded by continuing their condemnation of free-state, and by extension Republican and abolitionist, lawlessness. They endorsed popular sovereignty as the "only sound and safe solution of the slavery question," and opposed "all sectional parties and platforms concerning domestic slavery, which seek to embroil the States and incite to treason and armed resistance to law in the territories." The Democratic party recognized the right of a territory to form a constitution and join the Union, but only "through the legally and fairly expressed will of the majority,"—not, presumably, through the irregular proceedings of the Topeka government.[95] Law and order, the mantle worn by local opponents of the free staters, became the rallying cry of the national party. Speaking at a Democratic rally in New York state, Virginia senator R. M. T. Hunter argued that the Topeka Constitution, which lacked sanction from either Congress or the territorial government, posed the threat that any group might subvert lawful government.[96] "I consider Lane and Robinson Traitors to their country," a New York man wrote presidential candidate Buchanan, and "they ought to be dealt with as such."[97] But Democratic failure to prosecute the treason prisoners or to arrest Reeder demonstrated their weakness as the party of lawful government. Too many northern voters blamed Democratic maladministration and proslavery policies for having driven free staters to a violent defense of their rights.

As Democrats attempted to recoup their political fortunes, they sought yet another governor to bring order to Kansas. Shannon later exclaimed, "Govern Kansas in 1855 and '56! You might as well attempt to govern the devil in hell."[98] But his successor, John W. Geary, was expected to do just that. A commanding presence at well over six feet in height, Geary had served in the U.S.-Mexican War and as Gold Rush mayor of San Francisco.[99] Unlike Shannon, Geary would not be easily frightened. He intended to follow a path of "strict neutrality" on slavery and to establish an "impartial line of policy" for all.[100] Geary set out for Kansas with instructions to "maintain order and quiet" and to bring lawbreakers to justice.[101]

On his way to Kansas, Geary crossed paths with Shannon, who gave him a lurid account of the violence in the territory. All along the way, Geary found signs of the turmoil Shannon described: outside Leavenworth, he observed emigrant wagons drawn in a defensive circle; and at Alexandria, he inspected a ransacked store that had been attacked by a half-dozen men.[102]

Geary arrived at Lecompton the day the treason prisoners were released.[103] In this emotional atmosphere, Geary's inaugural address appealed, "Men of the North—, men of the South—of the East, and of the West, *in Kansas,* you, and you alone, have the remedy in your own hands. Will you not suspend fratricidal strife? Will you not cease to regard each other as enemies, and look upon one another as the children of a common mother, and come and reason together?" Although Geary described the territories as the *"common property"* of the states—a proslavery catchphrase generally meaning slavery could not be prohibited there—throughout the speech, he emphasized Kansas-Nebraska's promise of self-government to the "bona fide" settlers and condemned *"outside influences."*[104] He sincerely intended to implement popular sovereignty's promise of democratic choice. "Impartiality" was Geary's watchword. For him, popular sovereignty meant indifference as to the outcome, free or slave, as long as democratic procedures were followed. The only result Geary cared about was the success of the Democratic party in the fall. He openly acknowledged that quick ac-

John W. Geary, territorial governor during
Bleeding Kansas. (Kansas State Historical
Society, Topeka)

tion in suppressing disorder would provide "the most essential service
in bringing about the triumphant election of Mr. Buchanan."[105]

Crucial to Geary's success would be the trust of the military authorities. Without such trust, his predecessors had been unable to
wield military power effectively. Because of Shannon's incompetence
and Woodson's proslavery bias, army officers in Kansas had lacked
confidence in their judgment. The army, after Sumner's chastisement
for carrying out Woodson's order, was understandably reluctant to
serve as a scapegoat for civilian politicians. With Geary as governor,
Persifor Smith soon decided that military and civil authorities could
work together.[106]

Freed from their uncertainty about the governor's mettle, the military forces took a strong line in warning free staters that "excesses"
on their part in driving out settlers would cause U.S. troops or state
militia to be used against them. Officers warned that the president might

authorize not just disarming or imprisoning the guerrilla forces, but shooting them down.[107] Meanwhile, Geary secured Missouri governor Sterling Price's agreement to help disperse any uncooperative proslavery forces.[108]

Geary quickly faced the nemesis of Kansas governors: a Missouri force surrounding Lawrence. Indeed, the celebration of the treason prisoners' return to Lawrence had been cut short by news that a Missouri army was again marching on that town.[109] Once again, the town was defended by military companies—including one led by a querulous John Brown.[110] During the summer, free staters had built what one described as a "large fort" to protect Lawrence.[111] Professional troops scoffed at these "ridiculous attempts at defences," easily ridden over by cavalry, but their derision failed to dampen the free-state martial spirit.[112] Short on ammunition, a free-state woman recorded that the troops "were told to divide their cartridges with their neighbor till ALL WAS GONE, then take to their bayonets, and those who had none, to use their pitchforks."[113] Such bravado had little effect; Geary had more.

On September 15, Governor Geary arrived at Lawrence with U.S. troops and told the Missourians that if they wanted to attack the town, they would first have to fight the army.[114] In the words of a free-state soldier, "This seemed to stagger them." Faced with Geary's tough stance, the Missourians pulled out, but not before Weston, Missouri, men murdered a Massachusetts settler, David Buffum, while he worked in his fields.[115] Charles Robinson, just released from captivity, was so relieved that Lawrence was spared that the normally teetotaling free stater treated the officers, who had lately imprisoned him, to wine. Geary had demonstrated his willingness to stand up to proslavery as well as free-state men, part of the impartial stance he believed inherent in popular sovereignty. But Buffum's death cast a shadow over Geary's triumph and deeply affected the governor.[116]

Despite the truce at Lawrence, Jim Lane remained in the field. Throughout the summer, Lane's "outlaws" had punished proslavery settlers, and some said even free staters who questioned Lane's methods, by destroying or stealing their property. Lane still limited the purposes of the free-state campaign to securing the liberties of white Kansans, and with proslavery forces also still in the field, Lane saw no reason to halt that campaign. Lane planned to "blot . . . out" the enemy at Hickory Point in retaliation for a proslavery attack on Grasshopper Falls. Hickory Point consisted of a double log house, a blacksmith's shop, and a few sheds and outbuildings. Fifty Kickapoo Rangers were reported to be there. On the morning of September 13, Lane posted his men on a hill to the west. He sent a horseman to demand the Rangers' surrender, but they refused. The initial exchange of fire showed that the Sharps rifles had little effect on the log walls. Lacking artillery, Lane decided to withdraw. During the retreat, however, the Missourians left the cover of the log houses and attacked. Now vulnerable to free-state fire, a half-dozen Missourians were killed. The fire from the free staters drove the Missourians back under cover. Lane then withdrew. Learning that night of Geary's disbanding order, Lane abandoned plans for a follow-up battle. The next day, however, the battle continued under Col. James A. Harvey. Harvey's men fought the Missourians for six hours, while U.S. troops captured over one hundred free-state men who were returning from the fight.[117]

The free-state men taken after Hickory Point signed themselves "political" prisoners, replacing the treason prisoners as fodder for propaganda.[118] At trial, the jury deliberated an hour and a half before acquitting them. The defense had argued that the prosecution could not prove the presence of the defendants at Hickory Point during the fight itself, and that, in any case, the free-state men had been fired upon first and acted in self-defense. Meanwhile, Lane retreated into Nebraska, driven out by the governor's policies.[119] While the newspapers continued exaggerated reports of violence in Kansas, by mid-November, Smith had decided that because the insurrection had been successfully put down, the army could go into winter quarters.[120] Reports of peace, however, did not convey the impact of the civil war's disruption of territorial life.

Throughout the territory, crops had gone unplanted or unharvested when their owners were driven out. Men went into the fields in companies, "armed with the invincible Sharpe's rifle," if they went at all.[121] Large parts of the countryside were deserted. Struggling to live on green corn mush and pumpkins, many settlers faced starvation as winter set in. A veteran of the guerrilla war returned to find his crops ruined, his wife dead, and himself in ill health. This man was at least lucky not to have had his claim jumped in his absence, the fate of other abandoned sites. From the Wakarusa War to the end of 1856, violence in the territory destroyed an estimated $2 million in property and killed perhaps thirty-eight people.[122]

Sympathizers helped the impoverished settlers. A Connecticut committee attempted to raise $42,715 for the "oppressed and destitute Free-State settlers of Kansas."[123] Despite quarrels as to whether relief funds had been mismanaged or embezzled, close to a quarter million dollars was raised in the summer of 1856—in addition to supplies of food, clothing, and ammunition.[124] Lady Byron, widow of the English poet, sent sixty-five pounds sterling for supplies to relieve the suffering in Kansas. The money, Lady Byron wrote, "is . . . intended as an expression of sympathy with those who have resisted oppression at the hazard of life and property."[125] Kansas had become an international cause célèbre to European liberals, testing whether republican government could survive.[126] Others were not so humanitarian as Lady Byron. Minister Henry Ward Beecher took up a collection at his fashionable New York City church, bought two dozen rifles, and shipped them to Kansas in crates marked "Bibles."[127] Unlike Lady Byron, the Reverend Beecher and others did not believe that self-government could be achieved without weapons. In his journal, Theodore Parker called guns, "Sharp's *Rights of the People*."[128]

As free staters solicited help from the East, they phrased it not as alms, but as a debt that friends of freedom owed settlers fighting in Kansas.[129] The relief being raised for the Kansas settlers was "not a mere charity but a contribution of the North toward the support of her free-state [torn], who have been bravely battling for the cause of freedom & in the defense of our common rights against the Slave Oligarchy."[130]

With the guerrillas disarmed or driven out of the territory, aid and rebuilding took precedence. Although a relief to conflict-weary settlers, peace served Democratic political needs more than free-state. When Geary succeeded in pacifying Kansas, the weakness of Republican reliance "almost exclusively on the Kansas question" became apparent.[131] The Democrats won in a highly sectional contest. Frémont had no southern support, and although Democrats carried enough of the free states to secure victory, Frémont won more northern states than Buchanan. Millard Fillmore, candidate of the anti-immigrant American Party won only thirteen percent of the vote in the North as, polarized by the Kansas issue, nativism lost salience for northern voters. The Republicans had positioned themselves as the party that protected the rights of free-state Kansans. Advocating popular sovereignty, Democrats professed indifference to the final outcome and boasted their nationalism in contrast to Republican sectionalism, but many Southerners expected Buchanan to protect southern rights.[132]

The new president now faced the dilemma of managing the hostile forces within his own party. From numerous conversations, a New Hampshire man concluded "that, unless the Policy of the administration is decidedly and effectively in favor of perfect freedom in Kansas—freedom of settlement, and in the conduct of their own affairs—freedom to form their own institutions and to come into the Union with a constitution that suits themselves—there will not be a friend of the Government left, at the north." To coerce Kansas would be not only to condemn the Democratic party to minority status, but to encourage disunion. Plaintively he asked, "Cannot southern gentlemen see this?"[133] Apparently not, for a Virginian wrote that "success in Ks." would enable Southerners to "yet live free men under the Stars and Strips [sic]."[134] Reconciling northern demands for the rights of free-state settlers with southern demands for their rights would prove impossible.

Nor was such a reconciliation possible in Kansas itself. Despite Geary's masterful restoration of peace to Kansas, he failed to provide the lasting framework for that peace. The territorial governor may have felt no preference as to whether Kansas should be a free or slave state, but the free-state and proslavery parties still cared, and were still armed to achieve their goals. Although in some disarray, free staters still maintained their opposition to the territorial government. Some argued against voting in upcoming elections for fear of violence, fraud, and an election law whose residency requirements and test oaths aroused free-state suspicions. Again free staters warned against "the seizure of our political rights by a foreign foe."[135] When free staters did nominate a candidate for the territorial delegate's seat, they picked A. H. Reeder. This attempt to dethrone Whitfield fared no better than the earlier ones. Geary reported that the election went off without incident, thanks to the "moral suasion" of U.S. troops, but still did not reflect the will of the settlers, many of whom may have been too busy rebuilding or too suspicious of the process to participate. Whitfield was elected delegate and the next session of Congress seated him.[136] Free staters may have lost the election, but they still adhered to their political principles and possessed the force to fight for those principles. The army had failed to destroy the free-state military potential. Lane still organized military companies from Iowa, and John Brown had slipped through the soldiers' grasp.

Indeed the proslavery party, as much as the free-state one, remained intact and unrepentant. Geary himself complained at length to the president that without a complete administrative overhaul of territorial officials, including judges, peace would not last. Having taken sides so actively, these men could not command the respect of all Kansans. Geary found the territorial judiciary ineffective at best, biased at worst. The governor publicly quarreled with Judge Lecompte. First the judge obstructed Geary's attempts to make arrests by moving the location and meeting date of his court. The governor and the judge next clashed over the accused killer of David Buffum.[137] In November 1856, Charles Hays, a Kickapoo Ranger, was arrested and indicted by a grand jury. Geary used the arrest to rebut a free-state delegation's argument that the territorial judiciary was biased against them, only to discover that Judge Lecompte had granted Hays bail and Sheriff Jones had supplied the "bail-bond." The free-state men present promptly informed the "astounded" governor that they had told him so. Deciding to ignore Lecompte's action, Geary ordered Hays rearrested. A week later, while Geary was absent at land sales in Leavenworth, Lecompte released Hays on a writ of habeas corpus. Geary, feeling he had reassured free staters of his good faith, did not act again but did request the removal of Lecompte and other territorial officials, considering the latter filled with a "dogged determination to *force* slavery into this Territory" in violation of the Kansas-Nebraska Act.[138] Pierce agreed to the removal, but the Senate refused to confirm Lecompte's successor. Lecompte remained.[139] Geary had failed to dislodge proslavery control of territorial offices. Nor was there a shortage of Missourians who might again resort to arms. One of the principal proslavery guerrillas, Col. Titus, left Kansas in late November with 160 men and joined filibusterers in Nicaragua, but others remained.[140] Geary had suppressed the civil war, but not the ability to fight. The martial spirit persisted. A newspaper advertisement announced a new style in hats: "The Border Ruffians Caps!"[141]

Geary had succeeded in returning the struggle in Kansas to the arena of politics, not war. But he had not solved Kansas's underlying difficulty: the peaceful implementation of popular sovereignty. Popular sovereignty had always contained ambiguity as to which side would benefit; indeed, ambiguity was the heart of its political appeal. Geary restored the pre-civil war situation in which that ambiguity was to be resolved by peaceful, political means, not by violence. He did not resolve the ambiguity, nor could he bring free staters to acknowledge the legitimacy of a proslavery party they believed had trampled on their political rights or cause proslavery men to accept a free-state movement they condemned as lawless bandits and subverters of southern rights to slave property. That was to be Buchanan's job. This indeterminate state of affairs justified the laconic diary entry of a settler in late fall 1856: "Pleasant[,] shucked corn[.] Vandever said Kansas would be a Slave State, we will see."[142]

7

Imposing a Constitution Against Their Will
The Lecompton Constitution

Governor John Geary found Kansans distinctly ungrateful. He had been the savior of Kansas in 1856, but encountered entrenched resistance from proslavery partisans and wary distrust from free-state ones. The proslavery party charted a new course in 1857, opposing the governor's policy of impartiality.[1] Determined free staters also remained suspicious of proslavery intentions and the governor's good faith. In many ways, the situation of 1857 resembled that of two years earlier. Proslavery and free-state men remained convinced that the other side was hostile to their rights. The territorial governors, committed to popular sovereignty, were unable to persuade either side to accept the legitimacy of the other. In 1857, the focus would not be a disputed election for the territorial legislature, but a disputed constitutional convention process and the document, the Lecompton Constitution, it produced.

The proslavery party was convinced that the governor was not impartial, but was "playing a double game—that is favoring the Free State movement."[2] Members of the territorial legislature resented Geary's failure to discriminate between the two parties: the defenders of homes, law, and order, and the "outlaws" who committed "revolutionary deeds."[3] Geary's policy led the governor to appoint Samuel Walker and other free-state guerrilla leaders to militia positions.[4] Proslavery settlers resented that "several Proslavery men who held public offices have been turned out, and it is thought that the Gov. is at the bottom of it." Proslavery men saw such actions as proof that Geary was "a double faced Free-soiler."[5]

Geary enraged many proslavery men when he blocked their favorite, William T. Sherrard, from becoming sheriff of Douglas County, despite a legislative committee report in favor of the appointment. An angry Sherrard confronted Geary and spat on him, but another man pulled Sherrard away. Sherrard appeared at a pro-Geary meeting, verbally attacked a resolution supporting the governor, and fired on one of its defenders. In the ensuing melee, Sherrard was shot in the forehead and another man was wounded. Three days later, Sherrard died, further inflaming sentiment against Geary.[6]

To thwart Geary, the members had secretly caucused before the territorial legislature convened in January 1857 and pledged to override all Geary's vetoes. During the legislative session, some members made no attempt to disguise their personal distaste for the governor. In a serious attempt to embarrass Geary, the legislature gave judges the power to admit any prisoner to bail, even if the offense had not previously been bailable. The day after its enactment, Judge S. G. Cato released several proslavery men on bail, even though there were unserved warrants against them. Thus the territorial legislature condemned Geary's interference in judicial processes.[7]

Geary requested the repeal of the proslavery laws, and the legislature did remove some of the more egregious ones—such as the requirement that voters swear an oath to support the Fugitive Slave Act, and the law making it a felony to deny the legality of slavery in Kansas—to prevent congressional retaliation. However, the legislature snubbed the principal free-state settlements by neglecting to locate branch banks in them and made "rebellion" against the territorial government a capital crime.[8]

The governor and the territorial legislature also disagreed on how to handle the free-state movement. Territorial legislators favored suppression, as allowing the free-state "government" to hold sessions seemed to abdicate their own authority. On January 6, when the free staters met in Topeka to draft a memorial to Congress asking for statehood, a deputy marshal interrupted the proceedings and arrested twelve men for "usurping the government."[9] The arrests were made without the governor's knowledge, for Geary believed and argued that the Topeka movement would die quietly if it were given no provocation.[10]

Although Geary was right to oppose the territorial legislature's heavy-handed treatment of the free staters, his own policy was fundamentally flawed. As a good party man, Geary wanted to strengthen the Democracy. He believed this could be achieved by restoring the Democratic party "to the doctrines of its primitive purity"—reliance on the people—by instituting popular sovereignty.[11] But Geary found that proslavery men viewed slavery as a more fundamental right than "reliance on the people" when those people opposed slavery. When the Law and Order party, the old proslavery vehicle, met in mid-January, the convention began by changing the party's name to the National Democratic party. Behind this movement was the surveyor-general of the land office, John Calhoun, an Illinois migrant. But the convention allowed only proslavery members to vote and refused seats to two free-state men.[12] Geary warned President-elect Buchanan that the proslavery men, although all Democrats, did not have the best interests of the Democratic party at heart. Their first loyalty was to making Kansas a slave state, irrespective of the consequences for the national party and the Union.[13]

The territorial legislature did move toward statehood by passing a bill to provide for a constitutional convention to be held at Lecompton in September. Geary objected that Kansas was not ready for statehood, that local officials handling the elections were biased, and that the plan lacked provisions for popular ratification of the resulting state constitution. Geary tried to bargain with prominent members of the legislature, offering his support so long as the bill provided for submission of the constitution to the voters. They refused and he vetoed it. The legislature overrode Geary's veto.[14]

Wary free staters did not trust Geary any more than did proslavery men. They viewed the "moderation" Geary had shown them as merely a "show," "a political necessity" to carry key states in the presidential election. Now that Buchanan was safely elected, Geary would "throw off the mask and openly show the proslavery colors." More basically, the free staters did not agree that popular sovereignty could bring democracy. Was it not ironic, John Everett wrote his father, that the

General John Calhoun, president of the Lecompton constitutional convention. (Kansas State Historical Society, Topeka)

first implementation of popular sovereignty had resulted in a government in which the people had less power than "in any civilized government on earth"? Such was Kansas with its Missouri-elected legislature and its appointed executive and judicial officers.[15]

The constitutional convention seemed merely another effort to make Kansas a slave state. The legislature had forbidden voting by emigrants who came after March 15, making it more difficult for free-state migrants to get to the territory in time to vote. Nearby Missourians would have less trouble. Hundreds of Missourians crossed into Kansas territory, where they established claims in time for the census of voters. Free staters who were resident by the deadline complained that census takers had missed half the counties, had established no voting precinct in Lawrence, and had left free staters off the voting rolls in Leavenworth.[16]

Geary did not stay to resolve these complaints. Frustration with the Pierce administration, which he felt had not fully supported him, brought him to resign.[17] Like other Kansas governors, he had found the federal administration an unreliable ally. He would not agree, he wrote his brother, to force slavery on Kansas. In just six months in Kansas, he continued, "I have learned more of the depravity of my fellow man than I ever before knew," exceeding what he had observed even during the Gold Rush. "I have thought my California experience was strong, but I believe my Kansas experience cannot be beaten."[18] Geary left the territory in mid-March, just as the new president took office.

In his inaugural address, James Buchanan naively hoped for an end to the agitation on slavery. The new president deferred to the Supreme Court's impending announcement in the case of a Missouri slave, Dred Scott.[19] The *Dred Scott* decision, although it invalidated both the Republican party's belief in Congress's power to exclude slavery from the territories and the Democrats' doctrine of popular sovereignty, did nothing to resolve the agitation on slavery.[20] The Richmond *Enquirer* insisted that *Dred Scott* had affirmed the southern position that the territories were "the common domain of all the United States, and, as such, the people of each and every State have an irrefutable right to transfer themselves and their *property* into it."[21] Northerners dismissed the decision as an obiter dictum, thus denying its power to invalidate congressional prohibitions of slavery in the territories. But *Dred Scott* strengthened the position of proslavery men who had long believed slaveowning to be a fundamental right not subject to legislative restriction.[22] Despite *Dred Scott,* Buchanan still looked for a territorial governor to resolve the issue of slavery in Kansas on the basis of popular sovereignty with its implicit promise that settlers could vote against slavery.

Buchanan sought a man of undisputed prestige as Geary's replacement. He found that man in Robert J. Walker. Born in Pennsylvania in 1801, Walker was the son of a U.S. Supreme Court justice and was married to a descendant of Benjamin Franklin. He had moved to Mississippi and become a power in the Democratic party. Because his support made James K. Polk the Democratic nominee in 1844, Polk appointed him secretary of the treasury. In that position, Walker had fathered the 1846 free-trade Walker tariff. Historian Allan Nevins called Walker "a Northerner by birth, a Southerner by adoption, and a Union man by conviction"—seemingly an ideal combination for the Kansas post. Walker's wife, however, disliked the move, and Walker himself demurred repeatedly on the grounds of ill health. Buchanan even took the unusual step of calling on Mary Bache Walker to get her to withdraw her objections.[23] Although initially reluctant, Walker succumbed to the president's pleas that the "safety of the Union" depended on his service in Kansas.[24] Correspondents warned Walker of the job's difficulties, but Walker confidently asserted that he would have a successful mission: "The slavery question in Kansas, is not so *unsolvable*. . . . It is reduced to the simple issue, of slave or free state, and must be decided by a *full* and *fair* vote of a *majority* of the people of Kansas. The same question has thus been decided peacefully in every other state, and why not in Kansas?"[25] A tiny man, just over five feet tall and weighing a hundred pounds, Walker frequently compared his acceptance of the job to that of a soldier ordered into combat.[26]

The comparison to combat duty was apt. Free staters would not trust a national party that had countenanced political fraud. Proslavery Democrats, who were used to dominating Kansas, would be unwilling to share their power with those they considered outlaws. Walker armed himself with popular sovereignty, securing the administration's consent to full submission of a Kansas constitution.[27] Walker's instructions from Secretary of State Lewis Cass called for fair elections and the "right of voting for or against" any constitution.[28]

Walker did not arrive in Kansas until late May. By then the new territorial secretary of state, Frederick P. Stanton, had made the apportionment of delegates to the constitutional convention. A former Tennessee congressman, Stanton had been practicing law in Washington, D.C., when Walker chose him for the job. Stanton adopted a conciliatory stance toward the free-state side. He visited Lawrence, took tea at Robinson's house, and spoke to a crowd of five hundred in front of the Cincinnati Hotel. In his remarks, Stanton stressed that although territorial laws and taxes would be enforced (the crowd shouted "Never"), slavery would not be forced on an unwilling population. But Stanton refused Robinson's urging to alter the election procedures. He lacked the authority to do so and pointed out that if the registry of voters was inaccurate, free staters bore some blame because they had refused to cooperate with its taking. Rather than call a new census, Stanton based his apportionment on the one that had been

*Robert J. Walker, territorial governor during
the Lecompton constitutional convention.
(Kansas State Historical Society, Topeka)*

authorized by the territorial legislature. That count so heavily favored proslavery counties that free staters called it the "bogus census."[29]

The constitutional convention threat reinvigorated the dormant free-state movement. "The people are alive for the reorganization of the Free State party," wrote editor G.W. Brown.[30] A delegate convention held in Topeka on March 10 reinstated Robinson as governor. The meeting resolved to boycott the delegate election for the Lecompton constitutional convention and asked for immediate admission under the Topeka Constitution.[31]

Northerners who sympathized with the free-state movement warned Robinson that the no voting policy might weaken northern support. Schuyler Colfax of Indiana advised Robinson to give up on the Topeka Constitution; with a hostile Democratic president, it could not pass Congress. Indeed, even Republicans objected to it: the Topeka Constitution had been ratified by a small vote, and too much time had passed since it was written. During that time, Kansas's population had grown. The Topeka Constitution now suffered from being out of date with popular sovereignty.[32] An editorial in the *New York Times* confirmed Colfax's reading of northern public opinion. The newspaper recommended that the free staters participate in the election, because in a fair vote for delegates to the constitutional convention "we have every reason to look for a peaceful and final settlement of this great controversy."[33]

The quarrel over the census boded ill for bringing peace to Kansas, but few perceived it. Enthusiastic crowds received Governor Walker as he traveled by steamboat up the Missouri River.[34] But Walker blundered badly in his inaugural address. The new governor urged Kansans to vote for delegates to the constitutional convention. He pledged fair elections and reminded free staters that important issues, such as boundaries and railroad grants, would need to be settled in the convention. More than that, he urged an end to agitation over slavery, for unless Kansas chose peace and prosperity, the chaos of renewed agitation would threaten not only Kansas but the Union: "What is Kansas, with or without slavery, if she should destroy the rights and Union of the States?" In his discussion of slavery, Walker managed to offend both parties. He spoke of both "the treason and fanaticism of abolition" and the hypocrisy of the Topeka government, which had forbidden free black emigration to the territory. But he deemed Kansas's climate unsuitable to slavery, offending proslavery listeners.[35] Robert Toombs seethed, Walker's "'isothermal' and 'thermometrical' arguments and follies I supposed simply means that Kansas is too cold for 'niggers.'" Walker's "folly" had "raise[d] the devil all over the South."[36] At a proslavery dinner on the border, territorial official L. A. McLean contemptuously referred to the tiny Walker as a "pygmy." McLean went on to say that the proslavery party had "unmade governors" and could do so again.[37]

Having alienated the southern wing of the Democracy, Walker struggled to restore the free staters' trust in the political process. The Topeka government was to meet on June 9 in that town, which a traveler described as "a hamlet of fifteen or twenty houses scattered over a green prairie." Three days earlier, Walker had addressed the Free State party there, urging them to abandon the Topeka movement in favor of voting that fall for a new territorial legislature. He renewed his promises that the constitution would be ratified by the voters. He promised his own opposition, as well as the president's, to any document not so submitted.[38] Walker believed that he had prevented the Topeka legislature from enacting a separate law code, although he acknowledged that the free-state party was already deeply divided between those who wanted to avoid conflict with the territorial legislature and those who wanted to put the Topeka government into full force. The free staters sought to hide their weakness by holding sessions despite the lack of a quorum. Robinson attributed the free-state ennui to Walker's promises of fair elections. Free-state obstinacy against entering the regular political system was eroding.[39]

The free-state boycott of the long-awaited election of delegates to the constitutional convention, however, was still in effect. Election day passed quietly. Few Missourians crossed over to vote. In fact, few men in the territory voted either. An estimated seven thousand registered voters boycotted the election, and perhaps another ten thousand adult males had not been registered. As a result, only about ten percent of the electorate, predominantly from the proslavery areas along the Missouri River, voted for the sixty delegates selected.[40] A settler in southeastern Kansas reported that only sixty-four votes were polled in a county of over a thousand adult men: "You cannot shame a man more who voted than by asking him if he was one of the *noble* 64."[41]

Just as the Buchanan administration had expected *Dred Scott* to resolve the national slavery issue, it now looked to the Lecompton Constitution to solve its Kansas problems—and achieved the same result. Because the free staters had played no role in electing the convention delegates, the legitimacy of the constitution would depend on its ratification by all Kansas voters. To affirm his support for submission, Buchanan wrote the governor in mid-July: "It is the principle of the Kansas-Nebraska bill; the principle of popular sovereignty, and the principle at the foundation of all popular government. . . . Should the convention of Kansas adopt this principle all will be settled harmoniously."[42]

Unfortunately, southern support for submission was uncertain. Some felt Kansas was too important to be allowed to become free. William B. Napton, a Missouri lawyer and politician, confided to his diary:

Will the South acquiesce in a virtual exclusion of her slaves from all new territory? Ought she to do so? Can she do so with safety? . . . Kansas, it is now said, will be a free state. If we cannot carry slavery into Kansas, it is quit[e] obvious that we cannot succeed any where else. The result will be that no more slave states will be created. The majority of the North over the South will in a few years become overwhelming, in both houses of Congress. This majority can mould the Constitution to their own purposes. What will Constitutional guarantees be worth under such circumstances?[43]

The diarist doubted that Missouri could remain slave if Kansas were free.[44] More than that, he saw the future erosion of southern political rights under a growing northern majority. Ever since Walker's ill-advised remarks about Kansas's climate, prominent Southerners had called for the governor's removal. In Virginia, Walker's Kansas policy threatened to become the focus of the senatorial election.[45] Georgian Howell Cobb, Buchanan's treasury secretary, worked hard to stave off southern dissent, but also appeased Southerners by hedging on ratification. Congress needed some way of knowing that the constitution was indeed the will of the people. While ratification was not the sole means to that end, it was the most "satisfactory."[46]

Even Walker's firmness in suppressing yet another free-state "rebellion" did not reassure Southerners. By the summer of 1857, Lawrence had grown into a metropolis with two newspapers, two churches, a half-dozen religious societies, and a "well-furnished" school. The ruins of the Free State Hotel dominated Massachusetts Street, but rows of frame, brick, or stone buildings—interspersed with log cabins—sprouted on each side of the free-state landmark.[47] The town's growth caused business-minded citizens, oblivious or indifferent to the implications, to apply to the territorial legislature for a city charter.

The more politically astute citizens of Lawrence repudiated this action as accepting the bogus legislature's authority. They established a city charter without consulting the territorial legislature. City officers were required to swear an oath to support the constitutions of the United States *and of this State,* meaning the Topeka government. On July 14, Walker called on the military for troops to put down this "rebellion" and himself appeared outside Lawrence at the head of those troops. If the city officers took their oaths, it was in secret, for the governor was ready to suppress open action. Lane gibed that Walker had called out the troops because citizens of Lawrence wanted dead animals removed from the streets, but such derision did not conceal that the free staters had backed down under pressure. Like other Kansas governors, Walker had felt compelled to insist that free staters recognize the authority of the territorial legislature. Having made his point, Walker withdrew the troops.[48] Some members of the administration dismissed Walker's call for troops as aimed at impressing the South.[49]

Perhaps Walker encountered little stubbornness at Lawrence because the free staters were seriously rethinking their strategy of nonparticipation in territorial politics. When free staters spoke of not coming into collision with the federal government, they previously meant maintaining a separate government, whereby they could acknowledge federal authority but deny that of the bogus legislature. By midsummer 1857, however, it was clear that avoiding collision meant abandoning the Topeka Constitution as a lost cause and seeking to capture the territorial government by participating in the October elections.[50] Advocates of participation argued that it was legitimate to participate in the election because federal officials (i.e., Governor Walker) had promised fair access to the ballot box. They acknowledged that they would be "recognizing the 'bogus laws,'" but only "to such an extent as will enable us, in a legal manner, to obtain the power to repeal them."[51]

The strategy reflected the influence of more recent free-state migrants, such as Tom Ewing, Jr., who had little loyalty to the Topeka movement. But Ewing recognized that it "is galling to the extreme men of the [free-state] party" to participate in any election under the aegis of the territorial government. They preferred "to keep up the pretended government of the 'State of Kansas' in form, until in obedience to law they can adopt a constitution and ask to be made a state."[52] Ewing's father, Thomas Ewing, the venerable Ohio politician, warned that even sympathetic Northerners would not tolerate resistance to the federal government. "There is an organized government in the Territory—recognized by the United States, whose appointees—Governor & Judges, represent the power and presence of the General Government. In the presence of these there is an attempt to organize another & independent government. . . . The free state party if successful effect a revolution—if beaten, they are guilty of Treason."[53] The choice between revolution and treason had not bothered free staters a short year earlier. It had seemed the only means to preserve their political liberties. Now free staters perceived an alternative.

A heated free-state meeting at Grasshopper Falls in late August adopted resolutions that favored participation in the October elections for the territorial legislature. Robinson initially opposed, then agreed to vote, comparing voting to capturing, and spiking, a battery. While members insisted that voting did not mean abandoning the Topeka movement, it was the first time since the 1855 election that free staters had risked participating in an election not called by their own party.[54]

Challenging the proslavery party at the ballot box might renew the violence of the previous summer. Jim Lane began organizing free-state military companies—to protect the ballot box. But free-state belligerence might be hard to control.[55] A free-state captain threatened to raid Missourians or proslavery settlers in Kansas for arms.[56] Walker took the threat of free-state military organization seriously as a "pretext" for revolutionary "violence."[57] The governor suspected that free staters intended to interfere militarily with the October elections.[58]

While the free staters were moderating their policy by agreeing to participate in territorial elections, the administration continued to advocate a hard-line policy against the free staters in the name of "making the law supreme." Attorney General Jeremiah S. Black urged Walker to crush the Topeka movement by force or by arresting its leaders.[59] Territorial authorities made isolated arrests for conspiracy (attendance at a free-state meeting) and treason (publicly pledging not to pay "bogus taxes").[60] In the most important case, territorial prosecutors revived the previous summer's charges and tried Charles Robinson for usurping office. Marcus Parrott, Robinson's attorney, entered a plea of not guilty on the grounds that Robinson had never claimed to be governor of Kansas *Territory,* and had therefore usurped nothing. Furthermore, the defense argued that since the court had said there was no *state* of Kansas, it followed that there was no such governorship. One could not usurp that which did not exist. The first witness, a member of the free-state legislature, carefully adhered to this distinction: the Topeka movement had done nothing to interfere with the territorial government and had merely sought admittance to the Union. Throughout the trial, the prosecution repeatedly called Robinson "Governor," hastily changing to "Doctor" as if caught in a slip of the tongue. In closing, the prosecutor accused the defense lawyers of quibbling over names. What mattered was not whether Robinson claimed to be governor of the territory or of the state, but rather that he claimed to be governor. Judge Cato instructed the jury that if they could find that Robinson had claimed to be governor of the *state* of Kansas, which the defense consistently had admitted, he was guilty. On August 20, after nine hours of "animated" deliberation, Robinson was acquitted.[61] The Buchanan administration's effort to kill the Topeka movement in court had failed. The verdict was a victory for the free-state movement and for the tradition of popular political dissent, but it was overshadowed by the constitutional convention and received little attention.

If Robinson's trial was a remnant of a past era, the summer of Bleeding Kansas, the constitutional convention that met at Lecompton was the hoped-for portent of a future Kansas in which popular sovereignty's democratic promise would be fulfilled. Walker had repeatedly promised that the constitution would be submitted to the voters. Now the delegates must write the document and draft the plan of submission.

The delegates were overwhelmingly Democratic and overwhelmingly proslavery. Seven had owned slaves. Despite scurrilous descriptions by the free-state press, they were typical of delegates to other frontier constitutional conventions. Before coming to Kansas Territory, they had lived in the Upper South states of Missouri and Kentucky and the western states of Ohio, Indiana, and Illinois. Farmers constituted the largest occupational group, followed by lawyers, merchants, and news-papermen. Over a third had resided in the territory since 1854, and over half since at least 1855. Most were under forty years of age, with half of these under thirty. A few were deeply involved in territorial politics, but many had little or no political experience. They may have been proslavery, but they were not unlike convention delegates in other western states.[62]

As the convention met, it became clear that a substantial number of delegates opposed submission. The anti-submission party elected John Calhoun presiding officer. Calhoun had emerged from the ranks of the law and order movement to become a prominent opponent of the free staters. Born in New England, Calhoun lived for many years in Illinois. He taught surveying to a young Abraham Lincoln and was friends with Stephen Douglas. Calhoun had been three times mayor of Springfield, served in the state legislature, and ran unsuccessfully for Congress. A man of formidable temper, Calhoun once had to be restrained when he attempted to cane a fellow speaker. At Douglas's request, Pierce appointed Calhoun surveyor general of the territory in 1854.[63] Calhoun privately hoped for submission and was considered moderate in his own opinions, but his alliance with the extremists constrained his ac-tions. In taking the chair, Calhoun advised that the constitution should be "framed in such a manner, and *having such an indorsement* [sic]" that Kansas would be admitted without question. The anti-submission party argued that the *Dred Scott* decision had rendered popular sov-ereignty null and void. The administration, committed to submitting the constitution, fervently hoped the convention would cooperate.[64]

As it grew more likely, however, that free staters would participate in Kansas elections, it became less likely that Lecompton would be submitted to the people. After a session of only five days, the constitu-tional convention adjourned on September 11. It would not reconvene until October 19—after the elections for the new territorial legislature. Some argued that a free-state victory in October, which now seemed inevitable, would force the convention to submit the document, other-wise the constitution would be at odds with the views of the majority of the territory. But others just as adamantly contended that in the case of a free-state victory, the constitution should not be submitted;

instead, Congress should decide whether to accept the constitution.[65] That argument, ironically, put the anti-submissionists in ideological agreement with the Republican party, which believed that Congress would and should legislate on slavery in the territories. Meanwhile, all awaited the results of the election.

On October 5, Kansans went to the polls to elect a territorial legislature. John Everett, who had ridiculed free staters who voted in the election for Lecompton delegates, voted and found the polls peaceful. Election day was rainy and chilly, the roads were muddy, and many people were ill. Despite the difficulties, turnout at Lawrence was so large that an extra day of voting was needed, with preference on the first day being given to voters who came in from the countryside. A Missourian who observed the voting at Lawrence noted that blacks followed the proceedings closely, some even offering to vote. U.S. troops were at the polling places. Walker gave enthusiastic praise to the military men and the "moral influence" of their troops in causing the election to be a quiet one.[66]

The election was marred, however, by rumors that a suspicious number of votes had been polled at Oxford, a small hamlet on the Missouri border. There were no widescale border crossings, yet Oxford was said to have registered sixteen hundred votes. Later investigation proved that someone had copied names from the Cincinnati directory onto the Oxford polling records. In McGee County, where over a thousand votes were polled, citizens protested the returns, saying that no more than fifty voters lived in the district. The McGee returns were made in the same handwriting as those from Oxford and tied in the same kind of red ribbon, perhaps from the same strip of cloth. Stanton, who later noted that the Oxford and McGee frauds opened his eyes to the extent of fraud possible in Kansas, remembered rolling the forty- to fifty-foot piece of paper that constituted the Oxford returns out on the floor.[67]

Walker quickly repudiated the Oxford returns, calling them "extraordinary." To record in just one day some fifteen hundred votes, which were submitted viva voce for over twenty candidates, was physically impossible. Walker's personal inspection of Oxford revealed only six houses and no one who recalled a crowd of over fifteen hundred on

Proslavery men voting in Kansas (Kansas State Historical Society, Topeka)

election day. On these grounds, Walker rejected the returns. As Walker pointed out to Kansans, he had allowed his own party to lose control of the territorial legislature—control which the false returns, if accepted, would have given them. The McGee returns also were quickly dismissed as "simulated & fictitious," having originated from a portion of the Indian reserve that had fewer than one hundred qualified voters. Because of Walker's action both houses of the territorial legislature would have free-state majorities.[68]

Free staters credited their pressure with persuading Walker to repudiate the false returns.[69] From Leavenworth, D. R. Anthony wrote "that Gov Walker would not have thrown out the Oxford returns had he not been laboring under a wholesome fear of his neck. I never saw men more desperate than were the Free state men a few days after the Election."[70] Proslavery men also pressured the governor. Judge Cato issued a writ of mandamus ordering the governor to deliver the certificates of election. Walker ignored the writ, declaring himself willing to go to jail, but no further legal action was taken. Sam Jones and a friend, both armed, cornered Stanton and demanded Jones's certificate of election. Stanton refused. Walker had made fair voting a hallmark of his administration. He could not condone so obvious a fraud. By quickly suppressing the Oxford and McGee frauds, Walker averted the kind of crisis that had paralyzed Reeder two years earlier and that had rendered popular sovereignty unworkable. The issue of election fraud in Kansas, which had long sustained the entire free-state movement, was denied the Republicans, earning the gratitude of many northern Democrats. With the subsidence of the Kansas issue, the Republicans suffered low turnouts in the fall elections. Some Democrats predicted the collapse of the Republican party. Even the *Richmond Enquirer* approved Walker's actions as "morally right."[71]

What would the Lecompton constitutional convention do now that the free staters had won the legislature? A free-state meeting called upon the convention to adjourn, since the results of the October election clearly showed they did not represent Kansas.[72] The administration tried to influence the convention to provide for submission. Howell Cobb recommended to a delegate of the constitutional convention that the constitution be submitted to the "qualified voters": "It presents the only fair mode that I see of making Kansas a slave state, a result most desirable, if it can be brought about upon the recognized principle of carrying out the will of the majority, which is the great doctrine of the Kansas bill."[73]

But the administration clearly felt it was losing control of the convention. Senator William Bigler of Pennsylvania, an administration confidant, leaked information that only the slavery portion of the constitution would be submitted. By mid-September, Walker's tone was far less confident than that of his early pronouncements. He now spoke of having no power over the convention.[74] Even Buchanan moderated his statements about the possible results of the constitutional convention. Although the president believed the constitution should be submitted, he knew that only the convention could decide to do so. The president might deplore what the delegates did, but he had no power to countermand them: "It was the lawful work of a lawful body."[75]

When the constitutional convention reconvened, chairman John Calhoun reminded the delegates of their responsibility not only to Kansas, but to the Union: "*A Constitution wisely framed, and properly, fairly and honestly approved by the true citizens of Kansas,* will settle all the difficulties, and will at once restore harmony to the Union."[76] Although Calhoun urged ratification on the delegates, they voted to send the constitution directly to Congress. Calhoun and the moderate delegates engineered a compromise, submitting the section on slavery. By using Stephen Douglas's name to sway the delegates, even though Douglas had not yet voiced an opinion on the proposal, Calhoun managed to get the compromise passed on November 7. A ratification vote was set for December 21. Voters could choose between the Constitution "with" or "with no" slavery; however, a vote for the latter prohibited only future importations of slaves, not the holding of slaves already in Kansas, and no future amendment could affect the right to existing property in slaves.[77]

Partial submission appalled Walker. While the governor had relied on personal assurances from Buchanan that the constitution would be submitted, the president had allowed Cabinet members to undermine that promise. Calhoun informed a startled Walker that the partial submission had administration backing. An Interior Department clerk, Henry L. Martin, had acted as an emissary from Buchanan's cabinet to the Lecompton constitutional convention. Martin's job was to press the convention to include ratification. When that failed, Martin became the conduit for cabinet approval of the partial submission.[78] Martin's dealings had taken place behind the governor's back. Outraged, Walker now prepared to make the free-state case against the Lecompton Constitution. Robinson warned John Sherman, "That Constitution cannot be forced upon us without the shedding of blood & Gov. W. is aware of this truth."[79] Walker returned east to personally make his argument against the Lecompton Constitution to the president.

Feeling that the "cause is critical," free staters set aside their distaste for Walker and accepted him as an ally in the fight against Lecompton.[80]

Such submission as the Lecompton delegates had provided was unsatisfactory to free staters and their allies. At a free-state meeting in mid-November, Lane spoke for an hour and a half. It was, Henry Miles Moore wrote, "one of the most bitter, inflamatory & personally abusive speeches I ever listened to in my life," condemning Calhoun and others. Despite Moore's dismay, the crowd received Lane's speech enthusiastically.[81] A northern newspaper called the constitutional convention process "fraudulent" from start to finish. In sum, the Lecompton convention intended "wholesale subversion of their [Kansan] rights."[82]

In Walker's absence, the free staters acted. A Leavenworth convention resolved that if Acting Governor Stanton did not call the newly elected territorial legislature into session, they would put the Topeka government back into force. "This of course was bunkum," an observer remarked, "& only intended to frighten Stanton." Nonetheless, the free staters worked hard to intimidate. Jim Lane canvassed the territory, making three speeches a day in favor of a special session.[83] In a Leavenworth speech, Lane used typically extreme language to describe the "slave" constitution and its makers. While disavowing violence, Lane nevertheless riddled his speech with talk of choking, hanging, putting to death, cutting throats, driving out, and shooting down like dogs.[84] The pressure succeeded. Because of "agitation" in the territory, Acting Governor Stanton issued a proclamation calling the territorial legislature into session on December 7.[85]

When the new territorial legislature met, members moved quickly to assert free-state control. At Stanton's suggestion, the legislature set January 4, 1858, as the day for a second ratification vote on the constitution. This time voters would be able to negative the entire constitution, not just its slavery provisions. In addition, the legislature passed a concurrent resolution—which did not require Stanton's signature—that requested immediate admission under the Topeka Constitution.[86]

Stanton wrote the administration on December 9, informing it that he had called the legislature into session. Fearing the threat of violence and convinced that the people's demand for full submission was "only just and proper," he explained, "I thought the peace of the territory would be cheaply maintained at the expense of a short session of the legislative assembly."[87] The next day, Stanton was out of a job.

The administration felt Stanton should not have introduced the complications of another vote. His replacement was James W. Denver, the federal commissioner of Indian affairs in Kansas.[88]

Some in the proslavery party were ready to give up. John H. Stringfellow, one of the original Border Ruffians, opposed admission under Lecompton. For three years, the proslavery party had the advantage in Kansas, but, as Stringfellow admitted, "The Free State men declared they would nullify all our laws, *and they did,* and resisted even to the Shedding of Blood." Stringfellow had made great sacrifices in order to bring slavery to Kansas, but when he found that other Southerners would not migrate and bring their slaves, he decided "that for the sake of Slavery in Kansas as an abstraction I am unwilling to be beggared." Nor would he "play the Dog in the Manger by neither occupying the country myself, or permitting others to do so by imposing a constitution on them against their will." And he dismissed fears of disunion: "Surely no sane man can immagine that they will now cut loose from the Union because a northern Congress will not force a Slave State Constitution upon an *unwilling* people."[89]

But Stringfellow was in the minority. Lecompton had renewed southern hopes of making Kansas slave, the first slave state since 1845 and the only new possibility of extending slavery.[90] From Missouri, a man with free-soil sympathies wrote, "The Kansas excitement is up to a high pick here. . . . They look on Kansas as a Slave State certain."[91] Mississippi congressman John A. Quitman wrote expectantly of Lecompton: "The test struggle is before us. . . . It will soon be seen whether we will maintain our equality, or degrading subserviency to political masters."[92] What good would *Dred Scott's* victory for southern "constitutional rights" be, some wondered, if Kansas did not become a slave state?[93]

Very quickly, Southerners made Lecompton a test case of the president's commitment to southern rights. In a public letter, R. M. T. Hunter made support for Buchanan contingent on the president's acceptance of the Lecompton Constitution.[94] Southerners threatened to secede if Kansas were denied admission as a slave state. South Carolinian James D. Tradewell wrote his senator, James H. Hammond, "Save the Union, if you can. But rather than have Kansas refused admission under the Lecompton Constitution, let it perish in blood and fire."[95] Buchanan was well aware of such sentiments. Alabama called for a state convention to reconsider its place in the Union if Congress denied Kansas admission under Lecompton. Texas, in a more qualified threat, passed a measure to act if other southern states did so.[96]

At a cabinet meeting in late November, Buchanan determined to support the Lecompton Constitution despite Walker's strong objections, objections Walker had made clear in a lengthy personal meeting with his old friend the president the day before.[97] On December 8, in his annual message, the president made public his stand on Lecompton. Again and again, he found reasonable the procedures by which the Lecompton delegates had acted. The law providing for their election had been "fair and just," and the convention had not been required to offer the document to the people but had done so anyway. Referring to the *Dred Scott* decision, Buchanan concluded that the Lecompton provisions retaining slave property, even in the case of a ratification vote for the constitution "without slavery," were "just and reasonable" because confiscation of slave property would be "an act of gross injustice" that violated the Supreme Court's ruling.[98]

In deciding to support the Lecompton version of submission, Buchanan made what has been called "one of the most tragic miscalculations any President has ever made." Like his predecessor, Franklin Pierce, Buchanan was a northern man so used to compromising with Southerners and condemning abolitionists, and so far removed from the egregious abuses of political rights in Kansas, that he could not understand the free-state point. Although informed that Lecompton was unacceptable to Kansans, Buchanan was not deterred. If the free staters did not want Lecompton with slavery, they could vote against it and the president would support their choice.[99] Buchanan's friend Bigler appealed to the free-state leaders to participate in the vote on Lecompton: "If the free state party do not act Kansas will be a slave state."[100] Bigler's appeals failed. The free staters vowed noncooperation even though Buchanan sincerely wanted them to participate in the ratification vote. Free-state stubbornness was not new and could hardly have been unexpected. What was unexpected was the resistance within the Democratic party to Buchanan's position on Lecompton.

In his letter of resignation, Governor Walker repeated that he had taken the job at the insistence of the president, whom he could no more refuse "than the soldier in battle who is ordered to command a forlorn hope." Gone were the assurances that he would succeed. The Kansas venture had become a "forlorn hope," a mission doomed from the start. Walker blamed Buchanan for its failure. The president had known and endorsed Walker's views on submission. Lecompton was not submission.[101] Northern rallies against Lecompton reiterated the free-state themes of liberty and featured former territorial officials such as Stanton and Walker. In a letter to an Indiana anti-Lecompton meeting, Walker accused Buchanan of tyranny and called on Hoosier Democrats to save "the liberties of the country," the right of self-government, and to "proclaim . . . that the spirit of the Revolution is not extinct."[102]

In addition to Governor Walker, Senator Douglas had doubts as to whether the Lecompton Constitution reflected the will of the majority of Kansans. Congress might have to send "the whole matter back to the people," Douglas speculated.[103] Lacking close ties to the Buchanan administration, Douglas did not dare further erode his political base of northern Democrats. The Kansas-Nebraska Act had cost Douglas dearly in 1854, and he could not afford to alienate his constituents further before his upcoming 1858 Senate reelection. Furthermore, Lecompton violated his "great principle" of popular sovereignty.[104] On December 3, Buchanan met with Senator Douglas. The Illinoian told the president that he would oppose Lecompton. Buchanan warned him not to defy the administration, threatening him with the kind of political assassination which a previous Democratic president had carried out so effectively. Douglas dismissed the threat contemptuously, telling Buchanan, "Mr. President, I wish you to remember that General Jackson is dead."[105] Nonetheless, with solid Democratic majorities in both the House and Senate and the patronage weapon at his disposal, the president expected to prevail.[106]

In the Senate, Douglas tried to avoid a confrontation with the president. He endorsed the president's message except for its apparent approval of Lecompton. Again and again, Douglas proposed starting over. Reject Lecompton, reject Topeka, and call a new constitutional convention, he told the Senate. On December 18, he introduced a bill to do just that. Still, the senator denied that Lecompton was an administration measure and told the senators they were free to vote their conscience. But Bigler, known to be close to Buchanan, strongly hinted that Douglas was wrong: Lecompton was an administration measure and Democrats who opposed it faced presidential wrath.[107]

Republicans faced none of the hard choices confronting Democrats. They unanimously condemned Lecompton as a proslavery constitution that made only the shabbiest pretense of offering voters a choice on the issue and looked forward to an internecine battle among the Democrats.[108] In fact, rather than accept Lecompton, some northern Democrats joined these denunciations. As one gloomy Democrat pointed out, it was with "great Glee" that the Republicans welcomed the "Traitors"—one of whom was Douglas.[109] The alliance was not an easy one for many Republicans. He was, after all, the author of the Kansas-Nebraska bill. In Illinois, Lyman Trumbull doubted that Douglas really wanted to join the Republicans, but the Democrats had left him no choice.[110]

Both Douglas's Senate bill and House Republican legislation providing for submission awaited the results of the Kansas election.[111] On December 21, Kansans voted on the Lecompton Constitution. They could vote for Lecompton with or without slavery, but could not reject the entire document. Despite Acting Governor Denver's appeals for a strong turnout, the administration's hope that Kansans would vote for Lecompton without slavery was doomed. Free-staters boycotted the election. There were only six hundred votes for the constitution without slavery, but six thousand for the proslavery version. In another of Kansas's colorful elections, a traveller recalled that voters at Kickapoo had formed a circle which rotated around the polls and the nearby saloon. After each man voted, the circle moved forward into the saloon for a drink, then back to the polls to vote again, and then back to the saloon. A later investigation confirmed widespread illegal voting.[112]

Lecompton's passage "with slavery" was a "bomb-shell" panicking northern politicians and elating Southerners.[113] By the time of Congress's Christmas recess, just two days after the Kansas vote, only half of the northern Democrats were expected to support Lecompton, leaving the administration fifteen to twenty votes short of a majority. Public rallies to support the president had mixed results. In Philadelphia, speakers found it difficult to maintain the administration line that Douglas was a traitor, for cheering erupted at each mention of the Illinois senator's name.[114]

With Lecompton's passage, the free-state delegates met at Lawrence to decide whether to participate in the January 4 elections for state officers under the Lecompton Constitution. Thomas Ewing, Jr., was there with a letter from his father, who predicted that Lecompton would be accepted; free staters should thus try to control the election so that they could call a convention to revise the constitution. Robinson advised the same, along with the election slogan, "The People against Usurpation." The Lane faction resisted, however, arguing that to do so would give legitimacy to the Lecompton Constitution. The convention voted against participating. Some attributed this result to Jim Lane, who disrupted the proceedings and swung the vote by announcing an outbreak of violence in southern Kansas, where proslavery and free-state men had renewed old grudges from 1856.[115] "Lane got up his war in Southern Kansas expressly to operate on the Convention, and to induce it to determine against voting—and couriers from the seat of War rushed into the Convention with news of the slaughter of 8 U.S. soldiers—and Generals armed cap-a-pie, held consultation in the Hall and exhorted the Convention to quit speaking and arm for the rescue of their great Captain, blockaded on Possum Creek by the ruffian soldiery!" a bitter Thomas Ewing, Jr., reported.[116]

Lane's victory, however, was temporary. On Christmas Eve, the conservative delegates met at the Masonic Hall in Lawrence. When that sanctuary was invaded and the lights doused by Lane's supporters, editor George Brown took the delegates to the basement of the *Herald of Freedom,* covered the windows with paper, and, in what the radical free staters called "Brown's Cellar Kitchen Convention," nominated a free-state ticket. The kitchen convention adjourned at 2 A.M. on Christmas morning.[117] A Topeka mass convention also resolved to participate in the election of state officers. With characteristic flexibility, even Lane finally endorsed voting in the January 4 election.[118]

As those elections approached, Acting Governor Denver announced that he would keep peace by stationing troops at the polls.[119] But even

Denver did not expect much from his precautions. He wrote to his wife on election day:

Confound the place, it seems to have been cursed of God and man. Providence gave them no crops last year, scarcely, and now it requires all the powers conferred on me by the President to prevent them from cutting each others throats. . . . Among them there is one continual struggle for the ascendancy, and all means are resorted to, fair or foul, to effect their object. They are ready to cheat, to swindle, to violate their word of honor given in the most solemn manner,—in fact they are in good part a most rascally set.[120]

Election day, January 4, was "mild and balmy."[121] There were two elections being held that day: one, set by the constitutional convention, was to elect state officers under Lecompton; the other, set by the free-state territorial legislature, was a referendum on Lecompton itself. Denver's efforts were not enough to preserve order. In Leavenworth, "serious disturbances" before the New Year had required troops to restore quiet.[122] A Missouri man reported that "some of the boys was put in the calaboose for rioting a mob was raised in the City but a company came down from the fort to keep order no one killed."[123] Free staters stole a brass 12-pound cannon belonging to the Kickapoo Rangers. Embellishing it with a sign, "Election returns from Kickapoo," they bore it home.[124] At Delaware City, where a physician's house was used to store a hundred muskets, the doctor was summoned at night on an ostensible house call, whereupon free-state men stole the guns. But Democrats retaliated by opening the ballots and substituting Democratic ones for free-state ones.[125] In southern Kansas, James Montgomery led a free-state company to the polls at Sugar Mound. Montgomery informed the free-state men who had voted that the party advocated nonparticipation. Thus intimidated, the free staters then asked to retract their votes, but the judges of election refused. Montgomery then made a speech that while the people had the right to express their will through the ballot box, these ballots did not represent the people's wishes. He seized the ballot box, broke it open, and destroyed the contents.[126]

The free-state referendum on Lecompton resoundingly defeated the constitution. Fewer than two hundred votes were cast for the constitution, with or without slavery. More than ten thousand voters rejected it completely.[127] Stanton took pride in having provided a legal means to defeat the Lecompton "fraud." "My head will not have fallen in vain; and your quondam friend, Old Buck, is welcome to all the glory he may have acquired by sacrificing me to appease the southern nullifiers," Stanton wrote Walker.[128] Former Border Ruffian John Stringfellow repeated his calls on the South to give up its fruitless quest for Kansas.[129]

The other election of January 4 had been for officers under the Lecompton Constitution. A Leavenworth newspaperman, Col. John D. Henderson, tampered with the returns from Delaware Crossing, inserting a "5" before the "35" total of proslavery votes. A volunteer posse intercepted his stage and held him several days at Lawrence before finally releasing him. A Shawnee man complained that judges of election had falsified the poll books, recording almost 900 proslavery votes when only about 250 men had voted. It was rumored that the Kickapoo polls contained the names of voters such as Horace Greeley, Don Carlos (the pretender to the Spanish throne), the actor Edwin Forrest, and a number of prominent U.S. politicians, including the president. Amusing though some of these frauds were, the tampered returns, especially Henderson's, would give the proslavery party control of the legislature.[130]

Henderson claimed not to have the returns, having given them to Calhoun as required, but Calhoun denied receiving them.[131] Ewing fretted, "There is much reason to apprehend that Calhoun will cheat us yet. He has gone to Washington and will not give certificates or declare the result finally until we are admitted. If the result then declared be against us, we are ruined, for there will be Civil War—*certain.*"[132] Although Calhoun's party was "composed of those of the Ruffians . . . who have not yet died of delirium tremens," Ewing feared that if they gained power, they could not be removed for several years.[133] Ewing made investigating the election frauds a personal crusade.[134]

Ewing's board of commissioners to investigate election frauds was unable to examine the returns, however, because McLean, Calhoun's chief clerk, swore that he had sent them to Calhoun and that he had no idea of the returns' whereabouts. The other clerks confirmed the story. In early February, Ewing was awakened during the night by a

Lecompton man who claimed to know the location of the missing returns. The man told Ewing that about 2 A.M. on the night of January 27, Calhoun's clerks—John Sherrard and McLean—had buried the returns in a candle box under a woodpile near the surveyor general's office in Lecompton. Ewing and the other commissioners drew up a complaint and procured a warrant. Sheriff Samuel Walker found the box under the woodpile and opened it in Governor Denver's presence. The returns showed the vote at Delaware Crossing to have been 43, rather than the claimed 379.[135] From Washington, Ewing's brother reported the reaction of Calhoun: "The Calhoun Crew have been sculking all day—invisible. The strong presumption is that they have been drinking whiskey in the President's Kitchen."[136]

By then Governor Denver had written the president that if the returns were counted fairly, the free-state party had won the January 4 elections. Denver warned that admission under Lecompton would not resolve the slavery issue in Kansas. If Calhoun's party should be announced as winner of the election, civil war would ensue. To illustrate the contending passions, Denver reported that some free staters were pledged to assassinate any who took the oath of office to serve under the Lecompton Constitution. On the other hand, if the free-state party won, they would only call a new constitutional convention. This, in fact, was Denver's proposed solution: Congress should authorize the governor and territorial legislature to order an election of delegates for a new constitutional convention.[137]

Despite free-state fears, election irregularities did not this time stop free staters from taking office. Henderson was indicted for election fraud. In Washington, over the winter months of 1858, Calhoun's old friend Senator Douglas made clear his disapproval of the spurious returns. Calhoun began to backtrack. Although he would not send the certificates of election giving free staters control of the territorial legislature until mid-July, the proslavery party had given up.[138] The territorial legislature passed into free-state hands not with a bang but a whimper.

Perhaps no one realized it at the time, but the January 4 elections marked the end of the Topeka movement. The next day, the free-state legislature under the Topeka Constitution met in that town. Two days later it adjourned to Lawrence, where the territorial government, now captured by free staters, was in session. Someone proposed that the territorial legislature abdicate in favor of the Topeka government, but the legislators refused, wisely fearing how the national government might react. So the Topeka government adjourned, never to meet again. In fact, the Topeka government had abdicated in favor of the territorial legislature that free staters now controlled. Stanton thought little of this legislature. It lacked "intellect" and good sense, and was too much guided by Lane and others, but it was at least the accepted government of the territory.[139]

The Buchanan administration would take little joy in the demise of the extralegal aspect of the free-state movement. Because the Lecompton controversy absorbed all the president's attention, Buchanan failed to notice, much less enjoy, the end of the Topeka movement. Many informants inside and outside Kansas warned the president of the costs of supporting Lecompton. John B. Haskin, an anti-Lecompton Democrat from New York, and two other congressmen met with the president in late January to plead with him not to insist on Lecompton.[140] At a pro-Lecompton rally in New York City that spring, the speakers defended the president, but not the constitution. All but the first speaker came from outside New York, indicating that sentiment in the city was not as favorable as the administration would like. A Tammany Hall rally did better, summoning the talents of John Van Buren and John A. Dix. Still, as much effort was expended to condemn the "Topeka influence" as to defend Lecompton. The administration was losing the propaganda war over Lecompton.[141] From Buchanan's home state came word that forcing Kansas in under Lecompton would cause the Democratic party in Pennsylvania to "reel like a drunken man," dooming chances in local elections if it was compelled to "carry the odium of John Calhouns frauds in Kansas."[142] But pleas to repudiate Calhoun's work fell on deaf ears. Even though they would have preferred full submission, the president and cabinet were determined to have Lecompton.[143]

Resolved to have a final end to the Kansas troubles, Buchanan fixed upon Lecompton despite its imperfections. But he lacked the votes to pass Lecompton. Northern Democrats balked at forcing a constitution that evaded a choice on slavery on a territory founded on the principle of the right to choose. Instead, Democrats would craft a face-saving compromise to stave off an embarrassing defeat for the administration. Once again, the Democratic party would hide behind a legalistic definition of popular sovereignty which evaded the doctrine's true democratic promises.

The Language of a Freeman
The English Compromise

Three days after officially receiving the Lecompton Constitution, Buchanan sent it to Congress, urging its approval.[1] Denying the legitimacy of the free-state movement, Buchanan
described the dispute in Kansas as between "those who are
loyal to this government and those who have endeavored to
destroy its existence by force and by usurpation." He cited the
legality of the convention and proceedings which had produced
Lecompton, in contrast to the extralegal Topeka movement.
Publicly repudiating Walker, the president maintained that
the referendum on the slavery article met his standards for
submission.[2] Determined to put an end to the agitation in
Kansas and confident of the Democratic party's ability to force
Lecompton through Congress, Buchanan was willing to accept
Lecompton because it followed the form of popular sovereignty. He underestimated the opposition's resistance to a form
which lacked the substance of that doctrine: real choice at the
ballot box. The free-state movement and its northern allies drew
legitimacy from what Republican senator John Sherman called
the free staters' long struggle "to secure our republican institutions against fraud and violence."[3] When Kansas voters overwhelmingly rejected Lecompton in the January 4 referendum,
Republicans in the House of Representatives had solid evidence
that Lecompton did not reflect the will of the territory's people.[4]
More than that, Republican figures such as Abraham Lincoln

would increasingly articulate the philosophy that popular sovereignty was an inherently flawed solution to the slavery issue.

The first sign of the administration's weakness came in the struggle over forming a select committee to consider the president's message on Lecompton. The administration wanted a committee without power to investigate. This would avoid producing Republican propaganda. But the move was defeated. Antiadministration Democrats then tried to sneak through the creation of a committee with investigating powers on a Friday night when the administration men were absent at social functions. Alexander Stephens, the administration floor leader, filibustered while anxious messengers interrupted society dinner parties, calling the congressmen back to the House.[5]

At 2 A.M., tension rose when Congressman Laurence M. Keitt of South Carolina protested that Galusha A. Grow, a Pennsylvania Republican, spoke from the Democratic side of the House. Grow insisted that he had the right to speak from any place on the floor he liked, and that no "nigger-driver" could "crack his lash" at Grow. Keitt assaulted the Republican, who fought back. Other congressmen joined in until it became difficult to distinguish the combatants from those trying to restrain them. In the brawl, Congressman Elihu B. Washburne of Illinois knocked off Mississippian William Barksdale's wig. When the Southerner replaced it backwards, the fight dissolved into gales of laughter. At dawn, the House adjourned.[6] But on Monday, the motion for a select committee with power to investigate narrowly passed the House. Buchanan had overreached in his efforts to control his party. The motion signified northern Democrats' resentment at Lecompton's having become a test of party orthodoxy. Buchanan demanded that northern Democrats submit to *administration or southern dictation*"; if they refused, they would be vilified as "Black republicans, renegades, demagogues."[7]

Despite the rebellion of some northern Democrats, the administration still had formidable resources. Speaker James L. Orr packed the committee with pro-Lecompton members.[8] Furthermore, Buchanan wielded patronage like a club. Cabinet members lobbied representatives; Attorney General Jeremiah S. Black alone spent two hours with a wavering congressman whose father was dependent on administration favor. Administration lobbyist and public printer Cornelius Wendell spent thirty to forty thousand dollars, money he may have gotten from the administration to advance its interests on Lecompton and other issues. Buchanan's use of patronage as a weapon during the Lecompton crisis may not have been as vindictive as antiadministration Democrats claimed, although Douglas felt the administration was determined to "crush" dissent, and a Douglas postmaster in Chicago lost his job. Much as they tried, Republicans could never definitively prove links between the lobbyists, their slush funds, and the president, although later historians would agree with their fundamental conclusion that Buchanan's administration was strikingly corrupt.[9]

In early March, Alexander Stephens reported that the House committee considering the Lecompton Constitution recommended admission, saying that Kansans had acted with "great regularity and strict conformity to law." Although noting that sovereignty indeed rested with the people, the committee pointed out that sovereignty could be delegated, and that the U.S. Constitution had never been submitted to a popular vote. In addition, Kansans who had failed to vote for the constitutional convention delegates had no right to complain about the result. In order to further demonstrate Lecompton's legitimacy, the committee pointed to the balloting in Lecompton's favor and to the participation in the January 4 election of state officers. Frauds in the latter election, the committee report concluded, were not under Congress's jurisdiction. Predictably, the minority report denied Lecompton's validity, citing the fraudulent nature of the territorial legislature, the flaws in the census, the lack of submission, and Calhoun's mishandling of the returns.[10]

In congressional debate over admission, Southerners framed the issue as the administration had: as legal government versus extralegal. In the Senate, Robert A. Toombs said that the question was not whether to admit Kansas, but under which constitution—the legal Lecompton one or the illegal Topeka one.[11] Senator James S. Green of Missouri maintained that the real "people" of Kansas were its law-abiding citizens.[12] While Republicans, and some northern Democrats such as Douglas, pressed the issue of fraud and fair submission, Southerners insisted on the technical legality of Lecompton. The Lecompton constitutional convention had acted in a perfectly legal way, consonant with popular sovereignty, and Congressman L. Q. C. Lamar of Mississippi affected not to understand northern objections.[13]

Southerners discerned an antislavery agenda in the objections to Lecompton. Senator James M. Mason of Virginia avowed that the only difference between Kansas and other states applying for admission was that Kansas had asked to be a slave state. John Slidell of Louisiana agreed that the attack on Lecompton was really an attack on the South. To such arguments, Northerner William S. Groesbeck of Ohio replied that if Northerners objected to Lecompton only because of slavery, Southerners advocated Lecompton only because of slavery.[14] But Southerners linked slavery to their rights. In the House, Georgia Congressman Martin J. Crawford referred to "the enemies of slavery and of self-government."[15] Southerners advocated Lecompton for the same reasons they had embraced the Kansas-Nebraska Act: it promised them a slave Kansas and vindicated their right to expand slavery.

Southerners asserted disunion as a necessary alternative to a loss of their rights within the Union. Congressman Eli S. Shorter warned that Alabama might secede unless Lecompton passed. Fearing an attempt to "crush out southern rights" in Kansas, Shorter vowed, "If we are to be vassals at all, I would for myself prefer, a thousand times, to be a vassal of *Old,* than of *New England.*"[16] Governor Joseph E. Brown of Georgia solemnly informed Congressman Stephens that if Congress rejected Lecompton, he would "call the convention which must determine the *status* of Georgia with reference to the Union. . . . If Kansas is rejected I think self respect will compel the Southern members of Congress and especially the members from Georgia to vacate their seats and return to their constituents to assist them in drawing around themselves new safeguards for the protection of their rights in future."[17] Senator Sam Houston of Texas presented his legislature's resolutions calling for a convention of southern states to meet to protect the "equal rights" of the states.[18]

But many Northerners made light of the call to honor southern rights.[19] First, they dismissed the threat of secession as a bluff. A lawyer noted the southern propensity to threaten "*disunion,* in the event of the rejection of the Lecompton Constitution." "Some *women* and *children* are greatly alarmed" by these thunderings, he added.[20] In

Congress, rather than taking seriously southern defenses of a right to slavery, many northern congressmen exploited the debates over Lecompton to vaunt the superiority of northern society over southern. The North, such speakers insisted, had a greater population, higher property values, and more amenities such as schools and libraries.[21] Senator Henry Wilson of Massachusetts noted, "For four years the distant Territory of Kansas has been the battle-field between freedom and slavery—between free labor which elevates, and that servile labor which degrades."[22] Senator Hammond of South Carolina defended the wealth and society of the South, where slaves constituted the "mud-sill," keeping poor whites off the bottom of society, which "hireling manual laborers" occupied in the North. But his speech evoked only an angry rebuttal, not acknowledgment of southern rights.[23]

Many opposed Lecompton not because it was proslavery but because it violated the political rights of white men in Kansas. Lecompton openly flouted the premise of popular sovereignty as Northerners understood it—open choice at the ballot box—for the submission formula had rigged that choice. Indiana congressman Charles Case, a Republican, compared the language of territorial governors and the president describing the Topeka movement to that of royal governors and the king describing the Patriots.[24] Democratic Senator Charles E. Stuart of Michigan objected to Lecompton not because of slavery, but because Lecompton "overthrows" the people's right to govern themselves.[25] This argument was powerfully put by Republican senator Benjamin Wade of Ohio:

I do not like to hear quite so much about rebellion as we have heard for the last year or two. I know that everybody who did not yield a quiet assent to be trampled under foot by border ruffianism was denounced as a traitor. I know that on the other side of this Chamber, . . . you have sought to steal the liberties of a whole people, and screen yourselves behind the technicalities of what you call law, but which, on closer investigation, turns out to be a bare usurpation, without color of authority.

The country, Wade concluded, seemed headed for "slavery and despotism."[26]

The anti-Lecompton coalition of Republicans and northern Democrats disagreed about popular sovereignty. Northern Democrats insisted that they opposed Lecompton because it violated popular sovereignty. Republicans argued Lecompton invalidated the very doctrine of the Kansas-Nebraska Act. A political confidant of John Sherman pointed out that the real issue was whether slavery could be decided democratically. The Kansas-Nebraska Act, the *Dred Scott* decision, and Lecompton prompted one to ask whether the law was not a "mere fiction." The people, he told Sherman, "are no longer the subjects of law, but its slaves." Any question, such as slavery, which continually "disturbs the peace of the nation" should be decided by majority rule, "Yet there are but few in the slave states who would be willing that the majority should determine *any* question relative to slavery. . . . And these very men, have the effrontery to urge upon us the belief that they are devoted to the principles of Democracy."[27] When Senator William Pitt Fessenden of Maine suggested that the whole purpose of popular sovereignty had been to make Kansas a slave state, Douglas denied it.[28]

Pressured by the administration and uneasy in an alliance with Republicans, some northern Democrats sought compromise. Senator George E. Pugh of Ohio amended a southern bill to admit Kansas under the Lecompton Constitution. Pugh added conditions, among them that the slavery article be submitted to a referendum. Both sides quickly objected. Mississippi senator Albert Gallatin Brown remonstrated that Kansas had asked to be a slave state, a request Congress now sought to evade. Free soilers pointed out that Pugh had submitted to a vote only the slavery issue, not the entire constitution. Pugh's effort failed, earning him only ridicule. But other northern congressmen faced Pugh's dilemma: unwillingness to defy the administration or their anti-Lecompton constituents.[29]

Buffeted by such competing forces, Congressman William English of Indiana made an impassioned plea to Southerners, urging them to understand the position of northern Democrats. He begged Southerners to allow an adjustment that would permit northern congressmen to satisfy their constituents and thus preserve the party in the North.[30]

William English, Indiana congressman who
brokered a compromise to resolve the Lecompton
Constitution controversy. (Indiana Historical
Society, Indianapolis)

A week later, Lecompton supporters pressed for a vote in the Senate, but an all-night session failed to get the bill through. The senators continued their debate several more weeks. Douglas, suffering from illness, summoned the energy to denounce Lecompton for violating the will of the people.[31] John J. Crittenden proposed a substitute bill that called for another ratifying election. Despite receiving support from Northerners such as Douglas and Lyman Trumbull, it was defeated 34 to 24. As spectators applauded, senators voted 33 to 25 to admit Kansas under the Lecompton Constitution. Only two southern senators and four northern Democrats joined the Republicans in opposing the bill.[32]

After the Senate vote, a worried Charles Robinson wrote from Washington that the administration was confident of success and its ability to "fasten slavery upon Kansas, both upon the black & white population."[33] Free-state Kansans threatened to renew the border war rather than submit to an illegitimate state government under Lecompton. A Manhattan, Kansas, man wrote, "The question now is not whether we shall have African slavery, but whether we shall be slaves." If Congress accepted Lecompton, the settlers would have to resist it.[34] A northern supporter agreed. An Ohio man wrote, "Does any one suppose that the people of Kansas are so mean . . . to submit to that constitution? If they do, they are but fit to be slaves themselves."[35] Samuel Walker, a veteran of the 1856 guerrilla war, reported to John Sherman of Ohio that Kansans expected Lecompton to pass: "Every man is getting his Rifle in good order god help the few Proslavery men and women in the Territory for thear wil be no mercy shown them if Buck forces that on us." Of the administration, Walker said, they "have no more loyal subjects than we if they give us our Rights." If not, "it is not only Slavery we hate but that Constitution that we consider we have a right to say whether we will have it or no for my part I have got a Wife and Six Small Children that I think I love as wel and Dearly as any man can do but sooner than submit to that infernal Constitution even with free state officers I would see them dying; dead in one heap and the Wolves Gnawing their Bones."[36] The territorial house, now controlled by free staters, passed a bill that made it a capital offense to take office under the Lecompton Constitution, but the bill failed in the council. The legislators had to content themselves with a resolution condemning the Lecompton Constitution.[37]

In the House of Representatives, opposition to Lecompton stiffened. While the arguments reprised much that had been said before the Senate vote, a new urgency seemed upon the congressmen. John Givan Davis of Indiana pointed out his record of defending the South and expressed his resentment at charges that northern Democrats opposed Lecompton because of slavery.[38] When Congressman William Smith of Virginia rose to speak on March 26, he commented on the members' exhaustion. He then inflamed the House when he criticized Davis for questioning the president's ability to drive anti-Lecompton Democrats out of the party. Smith called Davis's words the "language of rebellion." To cries of "Good!" Davis replied, "It is the language of a freeman, and not the language of a slave." The Davis-Smith exchange caused an uproar. A half-dozen congressmen struggled to be heard while the chairman gaveled for order.[39]

House Democratic caucuses failed to resolve the split in the party. Alexander Stephens stressed the importance of party unity. But anti-

Lecomptonite English suggested the need for an amendment to make Lecompton acceptable to the Democrats who wanted to support the administration but could not accept Lecompton. When the caucus voted a few days later to make Lecompton a party measure, the anti-Lecomptonites walked out.[40] Vowing that he was not a "spaniel" to be whipped into doing another's will, S. S. Marshall of Illinois condemned the attack on the anti-Lecompton Democrats. The South defended slavery out of self-interest, Marshall noted; even though northern Democrats had long defended slavery despite the political costs at home, Lecompton was one sacrifice an ungrateful South could not expect from them.[41]

On April 1, Congressman William Montgomery of Pennsylvania offered an amendment to resubmit Lecompton to the people. Written along the lines of the Crittenden amendment, which had failed in the Senate, the amendment contained extensive provisions for ensuring a fair resubmission election and required another constitutional convention if Lecompton failed. But the key issue was to link Lecompton to the land grant for the new state. Montgomery's amended bill passed 120 to 112 in the House, but the Senate rejected it by a vote of 32 to 23 on April 2. After the House's amended bill failed to pass the Senate, Marcus Parrott, Kansas's delegate to Congress, pronounced Lecompton dead.[42]

Parrott was wrong. The House now split over a call for a conference committee with the Senate. The administration pleaded with Democrats not to let the president be humiliated. In one report, Buchanan had sent for an anti-Lecompton congressman from Pennsylvania and then cried during their conversation, saying that the bill's failure would hurt his administration and his health. English proposed a conference committee as a "courtesy" to the Senate. In mid-April, the House voted 108 to 108 on the bill, but Speaker James L. Orr broke the tie in favor of a conference committee after many objections to the vote and much confusion about parliamentary procedure.[43]

By this time, a strange shift had taken place within the free-state movement. Despite their plans to resist a Lecompton state government if it were forced upon them, some free staters now seemed eager to have that hated government after all. From Washington came rumors that Charles Robinson had abandoned the anti-Lecompton position.[44] Then, in April, a letter from Robinson appeared in northern journals. "The people of Kansas," Robinson wrote, "have been schooled sufficiently to know how to rid themselves of the Lecompton or any other objectionable constitution, should they desire it, without strife or bloodshed, if the power shall be in the hands of the majority." Furthermore, Robinson continued, *"I am not certain but Kansas would be the gainer by being admitted under any conceivable Constitution, if the agitation could thus be ended,* rather than to be left in confusion with three State constitutions and governments, beside the Territorial Government, for another year."[45] Even more surprising, Robinson evidently wrote the letter in response to prodding by the administration.[46] Robinson wrote Thomas Ewing, Jr., that if Congress were to pass Lecompton, the territorial legislature would elect antislavery senators, *"peacably"* [sic] co-opting the constitution from the proslavery party. The free-state object was to "rid ourselves of the infamous document [Lecompton] without wars . . . and this they can do in thirty minutes time and by the dash of a pen."[47]

Perhaps Robinson was influenced by the free staters' successful co-optation of the territorial government. "Kansas is lost to us although Congress does admit it under the Lecompton Constitution," a Missourian wrote. "The free State men number as 3 to 1, and having got the strength they are now getting the bravery to show their teeth."[48] Governor Denver, however, was the first adversary of the "Abolition legislature" that had been elected on January 4.[49] The governor and legislators quarreled over a legislative effort to make Minneola, a paper town in which many legislators had a financial interest, the territorial capital. Comparing this to Governor Reeder's infamous effort to remove the territorial capital to Pawnee, Denver vetoed the change. Although the legislature overrode his veto, Denver refused to move the capital. The legislature passed a bill calling for election of delegates to another constitutional convention, which Denver pocket vetoed. Still, the legislators claimed to have passed it over Denver's veto. On March 9, 1858, delegates were elected to yet another constitutional convention to be held at Minneola.[50]

In late March, that constitutional convention adjourned to Leavenworth. Some suspected that egregious land speculation in Minneola had disrupted the convention, thereby prompting the move.[51] On the last night in Minneola, the delegates with interests in its development threatened to break up the free-state party. Lane addressed them in a late-night speech praising the party's contribution to human liberty: "If in the momentous and supreme hour of the party's struggle they were bound to leave it on account of a few paltry shares in Minneola, then let them go—and go to hell!" The convention then moved to Leavenworth.[52]

One observer dismissed the constitution as "Topeka revamped,"[53] but Leavenworth demonstrated the free-state movement's increasing radicalism on race. The Leavenworth convention gave free blacks a vote in ratifying the constitution and provided for a referendum on black suffrage. A Missouri newspaper thought that free staters had over-reached.[54] The editorialist predicted the defeat of Leavenworth because many free staters would reject the radical attempt to "elevate the blackey a little above the superior race."[55] H. Miles Moore warned, "This Abolitionism or attempted abolitionism . . . will never go down with the people of Kansas."[56] Even D. R. Anthony, a Leavenworth insurance salesman who boasted of telling many who cried "*nigger* nigger *nigger*" that "niggers in New York are better educated—more intelligent & industrious than they themselves are," balked at Leavenworth's provisions. He wrote his reforming sister, Susan, that he wanted "white" in the Republican platform to "deprive" "all the *Whiskey-Ruffians—Irish Catholic & Douglas Democrats*" of "their only rallying cry": "Free *white state* for *white men*."[57] Anthony rightly estimated the reaction to Leavenworth's treatment of race. One observer noted that the "freedom shriekers" of the free-state party had been taken aback by Leavenworth's racial egalitarianism and were dividing over the convention's work: "That August assemblage have virtually said that a white man is as good as a negro, provided he behaves himself, and that Mr. Nigger is as good as a white man any how."[58]

The Leavenworth Constitution, originally an attempt to present Congress with an alternative to Lecompton, had only muddied the situation further. While Lecompton was in Congress, free-state men had decided that the territorial legislature should call another constitutional convention. The document thus produced would have had as much authority as Lecompton. But Governor Denver, having tired of the continual stream of constitutions, had not concurred in the bill. So the Leavenworth convention lacked solid legal credentials. In effect, the Leavenworth convention attempted to usurp both the Lecompton Constitution, which was unacceptable to free staters, and the Topeka Constitution, which lacked legal authority. But the attempt was undercut by rapacious land speculation and progressive views on race that most settlers still found unacceptable.[59] S. N. Wood was at a loss as to whether to abandon the Leavenworth convention in favor of calling another, to try to control the election already called, or to stay out "and let the fools make themselves as ridiculous as possible."[60]

Charles Robinson expected nothing worthwhile from the Leavenworth movement: "Although I do not feel at liberty to oppose Leavenworth I am free to say that I expect no good from it. From certain indications I fear should it be ratified by a large vote some of our progressive friends will attempt to start the government under it. To this I am *decidedly opposed*. We have the Territorial Legislature & there can be no apology for attempting to set up another government in opposition to it."[61] But other free staters pressed forward.

In mid-April, C. A. Woodworth, a member of the Leavenworth convention, arrived in Washington with a copy of that document. Senator Seward now argued that Congress should abandon its discussions of Lecompton and consider instead the Leavenworth Constitution. Indeed, the memorial of the Leavenworth constitutional convention stated their belief that if they organized a government, Congress could be deterred from accepting Lecompton.[62] The attempt to sidetrack Congress failed, although it seemed the conference committee would provide no better alternative.

The initial meetings of the conference committee went badly. The president himself acted as broker between northern Democrats such as English and the Southerners, but the committee nearly reported itself unable to agree. The conference committee's final work grew from a draft by Alexander Stephens which linked resubmission to the land grant Kansas was to receive. All new states requested a grant of lands; public buildings were constructed on those lands or their sale financed state programs such as education. The Lecompton Constitution had asked for twenty-three million acres; Stephens offered four million. The change in the size of the land grant became the pretext for Congress to send the constitution back to Kansas for another vote, ostensibly on that change. Opponents of resubmission could argue that it was the land grant, not the constitution itself, that was being resubmitted. Proponents of resubmission could claim they had achieved their aims. Acceptance of the land grant change would bring admission under Lecompton with slavery; rejection meant Kansas lost admission, lost the land grant, and would wait until its population grew to 93,000, the minimum required for a member of Congress. The population requirement would indefinitely postpone Kansans' attempts to join the Union. The revised bill was named after English. The administration hoped to use English's anti-Lecompton reputation to woo other anti-Lecompton Democrats to support the administration.[63] The English Compromise was thus a face-saving way for Democrats to agree to resubmit the Lecompton Constitution and, as Republicans would point out, a bribe that if Kansans did not accept Lecompton with slavery they would lose the land grant.

When the English bill was submitted on April 21, the Republicans voiced their dissent. Senator Jacob Collamer of Vermont described the resubmission of the land ordinance as "cooked up" to cover the submission of Lecompton. Wade frankly labeled the English Compromise a "bribe." Although Green of Missouri, who introduced the compromise bill into the Senate, insisted that land was the real issue, he could not overcome the disbelief of many senators. Stuart pointed out that the land ordinance had never been a focus of discussion.[64] Wilson called the English Compromise "a conglomeration of bribes, of penalties, and of meditated fraud."[65]

Within a week, Douglas declared his opposition. He had hoped for an acceptable compromise, he said, but this "inducement" to vote one way or another could not be considered popular sovereignty. Douglas challenged Southerners to treat the precedent of setting different admission standards with caution: a free-soil majority in Congress could easily use it to raise the bar against admitting slave states. Douglas also disliked the provisions guaranteeing a fair election, regarding them with suspicion. Douglas's opposition may have solidified southern support for the English Compromise. Southern congressmen initially objected to anything that looked like resubmission, but their hostility to Douglas was now such that they would support any bill he opposed.[66]

The English bill's manipulations of a land grant and admission strengthened free-state resistance. The free staters already viewed the Buchanan administration's handling of land policy as an attempt to punish their party. The "money crisis" created by the panic of 1857 augmented their woes. If land sales were held, a Kansas settler said, "The great majority cannot pay now without ruinous sacrifices or more ruinous interest" at rates of perhaps fifty to one hundred percent.[67] Although some Kansans felt Kansas was too poor to afford statehood, the English bill sought to use the settlers' desire for land to coerce their acceptance of Lecompton.[68] The *New York Times* wrote, "It is a gross invasion of popular rights thus to attempt to influence an election by punishing a community for voting against the wish of a dominant party."[69]

While the English bill had little appeal to Kansans, it was the face-saving alternative to Lecompton many northern Democrats needed. In the House, Republicans fought for a delay, but Stephens objected that a postponement to late in the session would cause personal hardship to the members.[70] The ranks of anti-Lecompton Democrats began to thin. To the dismay of his former allies, Samuel S. Cox of Ohio switched sides to support the compromise, earning condemnation as a Judas from other northern Democrats. Cox had been heavily lobbied by administration officials who promised him patronage and influence over appointments.[71]

With the help of men like Cox, on April 30, the House voted 112 to 103 in favor of the English Compromise. Nine northern Democrats and a southern Know-Nothing had switched from anti-Lecompton positions to support the compromise.[72] News that the House had passed the English bill interrupted Senator Seward's speech against it. Seward continued that the Democrats would now appear before the voters without the pretense of fairness that popular sovereignty had given them. They would no longer be a party that "balances equally between freedom and slavery," but rather "a party intervening for slavery against freedom." That day the Senate also voted 31 to 22 in favor of the bill, with Douglas and two other northern Democrats voting with the Republicans.[73] "Both Houses immediately adjourned, and a general scene of congratulation followed," the *New York Times* reported.[74] The next night, a crowd serenaded the president's house with cannon fire and the music of a marching band. The president and other speakers said that the English bill would bring peace to the Union and the Democratic party.[75]

Republicans mourned their defeat. An Ohio man wrote Congressman John Sherman that the English Compromise had "stained" with a "dark spot" the "nation's escutcheon."[76] Others were not so sure what they had won. From Georgia, Joseph E. Brown wrote Congressman Stephens that the "South has lost nothing of principle" by the English bill.[77] But the *New York Times* reported that anti-Lecompton Democrats were crowing that the administration had capitulated to submission. The administration "saves only the point of honor and surrenders to the minority on the real issue."[78] For its part, the administration professed absolute astonishment at any objection to the English bill.[79]

A Kansas man offered the administration hope that Lecompton would be acceptable. The Leavenworth Constitution was so "tainted" with abolitionism that it would repel the proslavery party and many of the free-state men as well. In Leavenworth, a riot nearly occurred when a large group of Irishmen heckled the speakers—including Lane and Ewing—and abused them for favoring the Leavenworth Constitution. The Irishmen objected to the constitution's pro-black features.[80]

In addition, statehood was a temptation to the senatorial ambitions of many Kansans, including Jim Lane.[81] Long prominent in free-state politics and one of the guerrilla captains of Bleeding Kansas, Lane had become notorious enough to receive special mention in the president's message recommending Lecompton. Lane replied with a long "answer." The penultimate sentence declared, "Let Buchanan howl, and Congress enact!—Kansas is free, and all the powers of the earth cannot enslave her!"[82] But Lane might not benefit from Kansas's freedom, for, after a long dispute with neighbor Gaius Jenkins over the boundary between their claims and ownership of a well, Lane shot Jenkins for trespassing. Lane pleaded self-defense in the ensuing murder trial. Witnesses testified that shots were fired before Lane's, and that Jenkins was

advancing with an upraised axe. After a two-week trial, Lane was acquitted, but he temporarily retired from politics.[83] Lane's defense attorney, Thomas Ewing, Jr., also had senatorial ambitions.[84] Dangling
the senatorial position before ambitious Kansans was merely one form
of the "tempting bribe" the English Compromise offered. It would require "Spartan integrity" for Kansans to resist, a Toledo man wrote
John Sherman, but the choice was between "liberty and Slavery."[85] John
McLean warned Ewing, Jr., that the fate of the English bill was the
fate of "popular government." McLean trusted that Kansans, "knowing their rights as freemen, . . . are determined to maintain them."[86]

Ewing, Jr., reassured supporters that Kansans who were "poor, in
debt, struggling to open their farms, and build their houses, . . . have
neither the numbers nor the wealth to bear the burden of a State
Government."[87] From Kansas, a Lawrence man assured an eastern supporter, "The English LeCompton ordinance will go under deep although
the Devil is here with all his allurements trying to bamboozle the people,
but he can't do it to many! hallelujah."[88] A meeting at Mound City called
the passage of Lecompton an "*insult*" to the people of Kansas and a violation of popular sovereignty, pledging to prevent it from becoming law
despite the "*bribe*" of the land grant.[89] The real bribe, a Kansas settler
reported, was what land officers were telling settlers—that if the English
Compromise were accepted, land sales would be postponed. "This is a
very tempting bribe," he remarked, "as thousands can not now pay up
without ruinous sacrifices, and some not at all."[90]

Perhaps chastened by its failure to bring Kansas voters to the polls
in the initial referendum over Lecompton, the administration actually
did little to urge passage under the resubmission provided by the English
bill. One informant warned the president that a "total revolution" of
opinion would be necessary in Kansas. Another blamed disorganiza-
tion by the Democrats.[91] Even Southerners seemed ready to acquiesce
in Lecompton's final defeat. Howell Cobb wrote, "The slavery excitement appears to be over. The result of the vote in Kansas cannot seriously effect the counts. I regard that vote as very doubtful. Denver
when here so considered it. He tells me, that there is no excitement in
the territory on the slavery question, but that the decision will turn
upon other points, such as their inability to support the State Govern-

ment &c &c."[92] All sides agreed that, for once, the hopes of a fair election were solid. The date set fortuitously coincided with the date of the Missouri state elections, a circumstance that would tend to diminish border crossings.[93]

The submission under the English Compromise took place August 2, 1858, and was rejected 11,300 to 1,788 by Kansas voters. Turnout was low, the *Herald of Freedom* said, because of heavy rains and high waters. In his own settlement, one settler recorded 226 votes against "Lecompton junior" and only 3 in favor. H. Miles Moore noted that there was no real excitement about the issue—Kansans just voted Lecompton down, or "slaughtered" it.[94] The effort to win Lecompton's acceptance by forcing settlers to choose between their economic interests and their political rights had failed. In part, the failure resulted because other compelling economic interests—Kansans' poverty and the potential expense of a state government—reinforced free-state commitment not to be bribed into ceding their rights.

Lecompton's defeat once again delayed Kansas's achievement of statehood, and did nothing to resolve the debate over the settlers' right to have slavery or exclude it from the territory. Proslavery men in Kansas still clung to their right to hold slaves, using the *Dred Scott* decision to bolster their argument that slavery could not be excluded from the territory.[95] The Lecompton controversy helped convince Southerners that nothing but congressional protection of slavery would suffice. Because northern Democrats had proven themselves weak allies, Southerners could no longer rely on them.[96] As Congressman Felix K. Zollicoffer of Tennessee had pleaded at the end of the debates over Lecompton, opponents of Lecompton "are wholly unwilling to give to the institutions of the South a fair and equal chance in the Territories which belong in common to all."[97]

The English Compromise further splintered the Democratic party, splitting the northern Democrats between Buchanan and Douglas, and alienating southern Democrats from both. By breaking with the president, Douglas badly compromised his power within the party. In summer 1858, Douglas's friends attempted a reconciliation between the senator and the president. But Douglas, up for reelection in Illinois, had found anti-Lecompton feeling there so strong that he threw away his chance for détente with Buchanan by denouncing Lecompton as a fraud.[98] Douglas was engaged in a struggle not only to retain office but to reassert the badly damaged doctrine that popular majorities could resolve the political conundrum of slavery. Buchanan now ordered, "Judge Douglas ought to be stopped of his pretension to be the great champion of popular sovereignty."[99]

Anxious Democrats feared that Douglas had made a bargain with the Republicans in order to secure his Senate reelection. Some Republicans feared the possibility. Douglas's sudden popularity with Republicans worried Abraham Lincoln, the successful Springfield lawyer who intended to challenge Douglas for his seat. Fortunately for Lincoln, the flirtation was brief.[100] A letter to Republican congressman Elihu B. Washburne urged, "Beat Douglass & beat him as badly as possible. I always considered him the *worst* man, politically prominent in the Union."[101] Douglas would not repudiate popular sovereignty, and popular sovereignty was simply too much for a Republican party—born out of the trauma of the Kansas-Nebraska Act—to accept.

From August through October, Douglas and his challenger engaged in a series of debates throughout Illinois. The issues involved in the Lincoln-Douglas debates were wide-ranging. Could popular sovereignty resolve the political turmoil over slavery? Indeed, how could Democrats still insist on popular sovereignty, the people's right to choose, after *Dred Scott* had denied the possibility of prohibition? More than that, slavery's place in a republican government was at stake, for was it "not destructive of their own rights for any people to vote in favor of establishing slavery as one of their domestic institutions"?[102] The Lincoln-Douglas debates concerned the ability of popular governments to resolve a moral dilemma. Since the Revolution, political thinkers had debated the necessity of moral values as well as republican principles to maintaining free government. Douglas had always rejected morality's interference in politics; Lincoln did not.[103]

Douglas sought to return to popular sovereignty's promise of democracy. He pointed out that he opposed Lecompton because it violated those principles and the English Compromise because it set a new population standard that had not been uniformly applied to the territories. Those positions had exacted a political cost, Douglas reminded his audience, in exciting the Buchanan administration's "war" against his reelection. At the Freeport debate, Douglas attempted to reconcile *Dred Scott* with popular sovereignty, offering the innovation that the territorial population could still exclude slavery by refusing to enact the "local police regulations" necessary to slavery's survival.[104] Repeatedly questioned by Lincoln as to whether he would support Kansas statehood, Douglas answered, if Kansas "has population enough to constitute a slave State, she has people enough for a free State."[105] Douglas needed no higher moral authority than majority rule, a position his racism limited to whites only.[106]

Douglas condemned the Republicans as the party of abolition, black equality, and sectional war. While Lincoln had proclaimed that "a house divided against itself cannot stand," Douglas affirmed that the republic could not only continue divided but could rise to further greatness. Still committed to expansion, Douglas spoke eloquently of the country's future growth and power if only agitators such as Lincoln would cease to trouble the nation's peace.[107]

Lincoln's reply was to insist that it was not Republican policies that had disturbed that peace, but popular sovereignty. Lincoln charged— and Douglas vigorously denied—a Democratic conspiracy to nationalize slavery, of which the Kansas-Nebraska Act and *Dred Scott* decision were components.[108] Unlike Douglas, Lincoln insisted that popular sovereignty had not worked. "Is Kansas in the Union? Is not the slavery agitation still an open question in that Territory?" Not only had popular sovereignty not resolved Kansas's fate, the doctrine could not. "If Kansas should sink to-day, and leave a great vacant space in the earth's surface, this vexed question would still be among us."[109] Popular sovereignty had promised to end "slavery agitation," but, Lincoln pointed out, that agitation had only increased since 1854, climaxing with the Lecompton and English crises. More than that, popular sovereignty promised "to clothe the people of the Territories with a superior degree of self-government, beyond what they had ever had before." It had failed. "Have you heard or known of a people any where on earth who had as little to do, as, in the first instance of its use, the people of Kansas had with this same right of 'self-government?'" Popular sovereignty, Lincoln concluded, *"has been nothing but a living, creeping lie*

Abraham Lincoln at the time of his senatorial debates with Douglas in 1858. (Courtesy of the Illinois State Historical Library, Springfield)

from the time of its introduction till to-day."[110] Kansas had demonstrated the bankruptcy of Douglas's beloved "great principle."

Lincoln still faced a profound dilemma. He must point to popular sovereignty's failure to resolve the moral evil of slavery, yet do so without arousing the racism of his audience. Lincoln conceded the constitutional rights of Southerners to slavery but insisted on Congress's power to limit slavery's extension into the territories. This restriction policy, Lincoln maintained, was that favored by the founders who recognized slavery as an evil not readily removable from the Union but not to be expanded. To counter Douglas's race-baiting, Lincoln claimed that he too believed in white supremacy.[111] Despite the danger of being labeled pro-black, Lincoln declared blacks "entitled to all the natural rights enumerated in the Declaration of Independence."[112] Democracy was not an excuse for one race to oppress another, and if racism were accepted as legitimating inequality, might not other types of inequality, hostile to the rights of some whites, be legitimated as well?[113] Popular sovereignty had failed to protect both the black man's right to liberty and the white man's right to abhor slavery. By his sensitivity to slavery as a moral issue, Lincoln distanced himself from Douglas's racist language and insistence that slavery was no different from any other political issue.[114] Lincoln condemned popular sovereignty as meddling with the intent of the republic's founders, who "left [slavery] with many clear marks of disapprobation upon it."[115] The "fathers'" policy had been "to restrict [slavery] forever to the old States," putting it "in the course of ultimate extinction." Douglas would "cease speaking of it as in any way a wrong."[116] But Douglas tarred Lincoln with abolitionism for acknowledging a moral problem with slavery, contending that the morality or immorality of the institution must be left to the private consciences of the slaveowners.[117] As a southern observer put it, Douglas "is *sound on niggers*," while Lincoln is a "crazy fanatic, who openly proclaims the equality of the black and white races."[118] Lincoln thus underscored a central weakness of popular sovereignty—its inability to resolve a fundamentally moral question—as he opened himself to Douglas's race-baiting. Lincoln's solution was to acknowledge slavery as an evil and oppose its expansion; but he framed this position as preserving the territories for white settlers.[119]

The midterm elections were a success for the Republicans and anti-Lecompton Democrats. Every anti-Lecompton Democrat who ran for reelection won, including Douglas. Although the Republicans polled four thousand more votes than the Douglas Democrats in Illinois, the distribution of seats in the state legislature, which would elect the senator, narrowly favored the Democrats. Douglas held onto his Senate seat, a necessary condition to position himself for the 1860 election. Nonetheless, the near defeat of Douglas advanced Lincoln's prestige within the Republican party and indicated that a significant number of Illinoisans found Lincoln's doubts about popular sovereignty's ability to resolve a moral issue such as slavery compelling.[120]

Seemingly unaware that the Democratic policy of popular sovereignty was under attack from both southern adherents of *Dred Scott* and Republican assertions of a moral stigma upon slavery, the administration congratulated itself on a successful policy.[121] The president wrote his niece, "We will present a record of success at the meeting of Congress which has rarely been equalled. We have hitherto succeeded in all our undertakings. Poor bleeding Kansas is quiet & is behaving herself in a orderly manner." Indeed, the president made much of that boast in his annual message.[122] This happy forecast was misleading. Lincoln had been more right than he knew when he told Douglas that agitation would continue even if Kansas disappeared from the globe. Kansas had bled because both sides made the territory the focus of their demands for political rights: the proslavery party for their constitutional right to own slaves and the free staters for the right of self-government. Kansas was the "concrete embodiment of the choices facing the nation's future."[123] The struggle had radicalized both parties. Southerners now increasingly demanded express protection of slavery in the territories. Only a few free-state Kansans had felt committed to the struggle for black liberty, but the Leavenworth Constitution revealed that some white Kansans had come to favor black rights. A free-state movement increasingly radicalized on the issue of race now fought for black liberty, a battle some free staters would wage not only on the plains of the territory but also in the hills of a slave state.

A Fruit of the Kansas Tree
The Harpers Ferry Raid

By 1858, the Kansas struggle had entered a new and distinct phase. What had begun as a quarrel over the political rights of white men to exclude or possess slaves in the territory had become increasingly radicalized. With free-state control of the territorial legislature and the death of the Lecompton Constitution, there was no longer a credible possibility of making Kansas a slave territory or state. Yet fighting continued in Kansas, and the Kansas guerrilla John Brown brought territorial-style violence to Virginia, panicking slaveowners all through the South with the possibility of a bloody slave revolt. Why did violence not cease in Kansas with the political triumph of the free-state forces? Why did it spread beyond the territory?

Some Kansans certainly fought for revenge. Some, like Brown, had long been convinced of the moral rightness of using violence to overthrow slavery. But for many others, such as Brown's ally, James Montgomery, and the young men who followed Brown and Montgomery, experiences in Kansas radicalized them to the point of realizing the link between enslaving blacks and undermining the liberty of whites. Territorial Kansans debated more openly the possibility of black rights as the Leavenworth Constitution revealed. In 1855, fearful of their own rights, residents of Lawrence had returned a runaway slave woman. By 1858, Kansans debated the best way to aid runaways and turned more and more openly to what proslavery partisans condemned as "kidnapping," helping slaves gain their freedom. Bleeding

Kansas taught many Kansans violence and made its use respectable. Experiences in Kansas inspired a small number to take the war home to the heart of slave country. The violence of 1856 had been rooted in the struggle for control of the territorial government, the struggle to implement popular sovereignty for a largely free-state territorial population in the face of proslavery control of territorial offices. By 1858, free staters controlled much of the territorial government, causing the party to officially repudiate violence. But previous sufferings at proslavery hands rendered many free staters reluctant to repudiate those such as Montgomery and Brown who used violence. In fact, many Northerners, reflecting on what they thought to be Brown's personal history, would be unable to condemn him fully when he struck outside the territory.

Although Kansas politics seemed relatively calm by late 1858, southern Kansas remained in turmoil. The unseasonably warm late winter months of 1858 made guerrilla action possible. Large bodies of men, armed with cannon and rifles, menaced Fort Scott. They wanted redress for the robbery of a free-state man. On Valentine's Day, a force marched on the town before daylight, but Judge J. Williams, the Buchanan administration official there, and other leading men were able to placate them. Meanwhile, Williams also suppressed the efforts of townsmen to call on Missouri for help. There were "violent men" with grudges to settle on both sides, Williams concluded, all of whom were a threat to peace. Governor Denver sent troops to Fort Scott to maintain order.[1] A Mound City man wrote that "the free state men are collecting in considerable numbers, with canon."[2] Judge Williams estimated their numbers at between 250 and 300 men.[3]

The free staters were led by James Montgomery. The Kansas Civil War had radicalized Montgomery's views on race and slavery. Montgomery, who was born in Ohio, moved to Kentucky in his youth. He married into a slaveowning family and migrated to Missouri in 1854, and then to Kansas the following year. Despite hard work as a carpenter and miller, he was unsuccessful and blamed slave labor in Kentucky for his failure to prosper there. In Kansas, he became a free stater because he did not want his children to grow up in a slave state. But he became the victim of proslavery attacks when he settled in Linn

County, Kansas. His family was burned out in the summer of 1856. His dislike of slavery caused Montgomery to resist the kidnapping of Arkansas free blacks and runaway Missouri slaves who had settled in southeastern Kansas. By late 1857, Montgomery had formed his own band which set about evicting proslavery men who had taken free-state claims. If he and his men used violence, their defenders excused it on the grounds that they had been "deeply wronged."[4]

Forced away from Fort Scott by the presence of the troops, Montgomery's men committed atrocities in the hinterlands, where they stole horses and attacked outlying houses. Williams claimed that the free-state men had held burning swatches of prairie grass to the faces of two boys, badly burning one, interrogating them as to the location of the federal troops. Five men were killed on their claims and proslavery settlers were in a "stampede" out of Kansas.[5]

In late April, U.S. troops clashed with a party of the free-state guerrillas they were pursuing. Caught grazing their horses, the free-state men fled but were pursued by the troops and forced to turn and fight, taking position in the timber past a small creek. When the soldiers failed to obey a command to halt, the free staters opened fire. The soldiers wounded one of the free-state men, but one soldier was killed and two or three were wounded. While the troops waited for reinforcements, the free staters made their escape from what locals called the Battle of the Yellow Paint.[6] The troops had failed to relieve the problems around Fort Scott. Judge Williams reported that Montgomery's "murderers, & robbers" operated in daylight within sight of town. Horses were stolen by the hundreds in what the free-state guerrillas called "pressing."[7]

The proslavery side retaliated in mid-May. The leader of a proslavery band, Georgian Charles A. Hamilton, had come to Kansas in 1855. A veteran of guerrilla fighting, Hamilton had stolen horses and threatened free-state settlers as well as having been the victim of free-state harassment. That May he had been ordered out after depredations against settlers along the Osage River. He had apparently left, although some claimed to have seen him near his old fort. On May 19, Hamilton proposed a war of extermination against free staters to a gathering of proslavery men. Twenty-five chose to follow him.[8]

James Montgomery, free-state military leader.
(Kansas State Historical Society, Topeka)

Hamilton and his men rode into Chouteau's trading post that morning. They took several prisoners, robbing and releasing others. The band marched northeast for two miles, taking more prisoners along the way. The only resistance came from Eli Snyder, a blacksmith, who fired on Hamilton's men and fled with his son. Snyder was wounded in the back and leg, but he escaped. The eleven prisoners marched three more miles to a narrow ravine, where Hamilton repeatedly gave the order to present arms. Some of his men refused to obey. One turned his horse away, saying "he would have nothing to do with such business." Hamilton was "swearing terribly," but when he ordered "fire," others of the band complied. Some even went down into the ravine, where the victims fell, to finish them off and rifle their pockets for loot.[9] William Hairgrove, as he lay in the ravine, heard one of Hamilton's men say, "We have got eleven of the dammed Abolitionists biting the dust, and will return in a few days and sweep the entire Valley." Hairgrove was not the only survivor. Five of the eleven were killed,

five were wounded, and another, not hit by the volley, had feigned
death.[10]

An initial proslavery account of what was called the Marais des
Cygnes massacre described the victims as prisoners taken in Hamilton's
ongoing war with Montgomery. Hamilton had released them on the
promise they would return home, but they had armed themselves and
fired on Hamilton and his men. In self-defense, Hamilton's company
had returned fire, killing ten.[11] But proslavery propaganda quickly lost
ground to its free-state counterpart. John Greenleaf Whittier again
immortalized victims of Kansas violence:

> A blush as of roses
>   Where rose never grew!
> Great drops on the bunch-grass,
>   But not of the dew!
> A taint in the sweet air
>   For wild bees to shun!
> A stain that shall never
>   Bleach out in the sun!

Condemning the proslavery raiders, Whittier concluded:

> The foul human vultures
>   Have feasted and fled;
> The wolves of the Border
>   Have crept from the dead.[12]

The Marais des Cygnes massacre further enflamed the border. Judge
Williams reported both sides prepared to invade the other. A free-
state force marched on West Point, to which the murderers were
believed to have fled. They took only one prisoner but released him
when they discovered he was only the brother of one of the murderers. In the week after the killings, Montgomery extended his reach
into Missouri itself, warning out residents there.[13] Missourians formed
companies and asked the governor to arm them for self-defense.
Worried, Missouri governor Robert M. Stewart ordered organization
of a volunteer force to counter any invasion from Kansas.[14]

In southern Kansas, Montgomery and Hamilton were at war. Montgomery's band had attacked Hamilton's men at a log house, wounding

Marais des Cygnes Massacre (Kansas State Historical Society, Topeka)

two of them. Montgomery lost eleven men and five more were wounded. When Hamilton's men retreated into Missouri, Montgomery followed with 150 men and two cannon. They attacked West Point, Missouri. At Barnesville, Missouri, Montgomery arrested several men and seized writs of arrest for himself and his men, as well as Governor Denver's mail. Many free-state men blamed Montgomery for the violence but refused to act against him, feeling Montgomery and his men acted in the spirit of "retaliation for 1856." Sheriff Walker of Douglas County even cooperated with Montgomery to arrest three men, including the proslavery land officer for the Fort Scott district, George W. Clarke, for the Marais des Cygnes murders.[15]

In late June, Denver made an inspection tour of southern Kansas, including a visit to the Marais des Cygnes site. He found the countryside depopulated and heard tales of theft and violence. Because the people did not trust the local authorities, they had formed their own organizations. Denver sought to replace these with patrols under the command of territorial officials and proposed electing new officials in Bourbon County. He thought stationing troops on the Missouri border and suspending action on old writs until their legitimacy was proven would cause Montgomery and other guerrillas to disband. At a meeting at Fort Scott, Denver gave a conciliatory address and expected the other speaker, Epaphroditus Ransom, a former Michigan governor, to reciprocate. Denver's wandering attention was brought back to the speaker when he heard Ransom denouncing the free staters. Another man interrupted and an argument appeared likely. Denver placed himself between the two men and ordered Ransom back to his seat. As the crowd of almost one thousand was well-armed—in fact, some guns were drawn—he wanted to forestall violence.[16]

Despite the near disaster, early reports were encouraging as to the success of Denver's trip. Robinson endorsed Denver's plan and Montgomery even promised to submit to it. Denver himself urged the volunteer patrols to cooperate with the Missouri authorities.[17] Still, Denver was uneasy. At the end of June, he protested the rotation of U.S. troops at Fort Scott because "any new and unexpected movements of the troops among a public greatly alarmed and very suspicious cannot but be very prejuidicial, and for the results of which I will not be answerable." That latter phrase was fast becoming one of his favorites.[18]

Denver's lack of assurance was well-founded. Horse theft and other depredations continued, now complicated as perpetrators claimed immunity under the governor's peace resolutions.[19] By the end of July, John Brown, who was traveling under the alias Shubel Morgan, found "deserted houses & farms . . . in all directions" in the area around the Marais des Cygnes.[20] The governor of Missouri stationed military forces along the border. Yet by this time, the Kansas governor was concluding that troops were no longer necessary along the border.[21]

Perhaps Denver just wished for an end to the violence so as to ease his own departure. On September 1, he submitted his resignation, assuring the administration that peace existed in Kansas, that U.S. troops had been withdrawn, and that "there will be no more 'Kansas troubles.'"[22] At a farewell dinner for Governor Denver, the diners toasted "'Bleeding Kansas'—The country may rest in quiet, her wounds are healed. The great question is now at rest. None but demagogues will ever attempt to revive it."[23] Settlers in western Kansas bestowed the governor's name on a gold rush settlement in Colorado. Denver went back to his job as commissioner of Indian Affairs and returned to

California in 1859. He served in the Union Army, resuming his law practice after the war, and died in 1892.[24] Denver possessed the dubious distinction of being the first Kansas governor not forced from office, perhaps indeed an indication of the territory's relative calm.

But Denver was not being blindly optimistic when he praised Kansas's quiet. Significantly, the fighting in southern Kansas failed to reignite free-state resistance to the territorial government, for free staters now controlled the territorial legislature and had more to gain from good relations with the governor. After repudiating Montgomery, Charles Robinson had endorsed the Denver administration. And Jim Lane was too preoccupied with his trial for killing Gaius Jenkins to take advantage of the turmoil. Ironically, the final defeat of Lecompton brought comparative peace to Kansas, which not even Montgomery's maraudings could disturb.

In Montgomery, "Old John Brown" finally found an ally who shared his radical vision of a war against slavery and slaveowners. While Montgomery continued the free-state war against proslavery men, John Brown used his Kansas credentials to expand the antislavery campaign. Traveling in the east during 1857, he used his fame as "Captain Brown" of Kansas to raise money from credulous easterners, including the National Kansas committee. Brown's immediate backers—a collection of eastern philanthropists, intellectuals, and businessmen known as the Secret Six—believed that Brown intended to return to Kansas. In February 1858, Brown announced his target was Virginia. But Hugh Forbes, a mercenary soldier whom Brown had hired to help train his men but failed to pay, threatened to reveal Brown's plan. The Secret Six, nervous at Forbes's blackmail attempt, made Brown postpone his Virginia project and return to the territory. The Secret Six preferred not to "burden" the National Kansas committee with "inconvenient" information about Brown's plans in Virginia. Ill much of the time, Brown spent the last half of 1858 in Kansas.[25]

As late fall settled over the prairies, Brown joined Montgomery in committing depredations throughout southern Kansas. Together Brown and Montgomery erected a "stockade fort" on Little Sugar Creek. From this fortification, which was rumored to have one or possibly two brass howitzers, they sallied forth to rob and warn out settlers. Their victims feared to swear out complaints because local law officers were often friendly with the free-state bandits. When southern Kansans held public meetings to reaffirm Denver's peace resolutions, Montgomery's supporters voted their move down.[26] The sheriff of Linn County reported, "Our county is now in a desperate state of excitement."[27] Wary of prejudicing the policy of the new governor, Acting Governor Hugh B. Walsh was reluctant to act. He complained that he had no troops to send and that deep snow made pursuit impossible.[28]

On the morning of December 16, Montgomery and a band of fifty to one hundred men attacked Fort Scott while residents were still in their beds. They freed one of their men, who was being held in chains at the town hotel. Arresting and disarming townsmen as they emerged from their houses, Montgomery's men forced them into a circle of prisoners. When J. H. Little and his son attempted to defend their store, the younger man was shot through the head and killed. Montgomery later said the death was warranted, as the father had been a member of the Lecompton constitutional convention. After firing several houses, the raiders departed with five thousand dollars worth of property. Montgomery was rumored to have said "that he had whipped Uncle Sam, and could do it again."[29] After Montgomery issued this defiant speech, one of his men cried out, "See what Freeman can do."[30]

The new governor, Samuel Medary, an Ohio politician and a Douglas supporter, was unsure what to do about the turmoil Montgomery and Brown caused.[31] Others were equally unsure about Medary. When the new governor asked to pay his barber bill monthly, the black barber replied, "If you please, mass'r, I prefer to have you pay by de shave; dese new gub'ners goes away so mighty sudden!"[32] Moving as cautiously as his barber, Medary gathered information, asked for power to institute martial law in southern Kansas, and requested troops and arms. Missouri governor Robert M. Stewart wanted to cooperate with the Kansas authorities if they would only tell him what they planned to do.[33]

At the beginning of January, Montgomery offered to cease fighting provided that Medary would guarantee an amnesty for his men, let him choose the local sheriffs, and not allow refugees in Missouri to return. Although these terms could hardly have been acceptable, Medary's correspondents warned that Montgomery could muster forces of from two hundred to one thousand men. Besides, thick snow in southern Kansas would hamper troop movements. One man awoke to a blanket of three inches that had blown in over his bed at night.[34] Nonetheless, when he reported to Missouri governor Stewart, Medary sounded optimistic about the chances of trapping Montgomery and Brown. Asking the governor to help block any escape into Missouri, he wrote, "I hope to make so complete a work of it, that it will not want doing over again in that region."[35]

Medary benefited from free-state cooperation. Newspapers, including one in Lawrence, denounced Montgomery. All but one member of the territorial legislature disapproved of Montgomery, although the legislature balked at Medary's request that $250 rewards be offered for Montgomery and Brown. Grudgingly, President Buchanan gave Medary the authority to use troops. With less reluctance, Congress soon provided the territorial government with $30,000 to suppress the border difficulties.[36]

Perhaps recognizing the forces building against him, in mid-January, Montgomery turned himself in for the crime of robbing the mails. Although Medary possessed little faith in Montgomery's pledges of good behavior, he hoped that the court would restore order. Within days, Montgomery had brought in six of his men for trial. But the territorial legislature intervened, passing an amnesty bill for southern Kansas. The bill provided that no criminal offense arising out of a political dispute would be prosecuted, and that such prosecutions now in process would be dismissed.[37] A Mound City settler congratulated the legislature for determining that "the times have come that Kansas is at peace no more trouble will be here now."[38] Missourians were less enthusiastic, however, and viewed the amnesty law as an admission that "nothing can . . . be done toward establishing Law and order in the Teritory."[39] But the echoes of law and order were now faint. That cry no longer had the power to bring large numbers of Missourians across the border. St. Louis Germans published a broadside that satirized Stewart's preoccupation with "the army of rascals from a free state,/wading up to their knees in blood,/closely encircling Missouri./ They took Fort Scott for breakfast,/Fort Leavenworth for lunch, by God!/Then St. Joseph as Supper." The Germans made light of their governor as "Stewart, who invented the war,/the war in the deepest peace."[40]

Even on the border, Missourians seemed ready to give up. A Kansas City newspaper sought Kansas correspondents who would talk about climate, soil, crops, and trade—anything but politics, the consuming passion of Kansans.[41] The editor wrote, "We are tired of this eternal wrangle over the territories and the niggers. . . . It was *the* question of Kansas; and although that Territory bled profusely, and Missouri bled much more, practically, yet we are today where we were when the Kansas-Nebraska Bill was passed."[42]

The only one who attempted to make political capital out of the amnesty act was Jim Lane, who badly needed to stage a political come-back. When the deputy marshal of Bourbon County was en route to Lawrence, he learned of the amnesty and ordered his prisoners re-leased, but they refused to have their chains taken off until they reached town. Lane made a show of the men, saying it was shameful to see free-state men in chains. Throwing bricks, stones, and mud, a crowd attacked posse members and drove them out of town.[43] As Lane's successful theatrics demonstrated, free staters had not abandoned their belief that their cause was the cause of liberty. A Mound City settler penned the couplet, "Montgomery and freedom/Brown and Liberty."[44]

Free-state principles still brought conflict between the territorial legislature and governor, but none that threatened to revive the internecine struggles of earlier years. The free-state legislators ad-journed to Lawrence after a bitter fight with Governor Medary, who opposed the move. The legislature preferred that town to Lecompton not only out of "prejudice" against the old seat of the proslavery ter-ritorial government but also because Lawrence provided more and better accommodations—an indication that free-state settlements had flourished while proslavery ones had not. Medary reluctantly acqui-esced to the change.[45]

The legislature then got down to work, debating three versions of a bill to end slavery in the territory. One version simply abolished slav-ery and repealed the territorial slave code, another added penalties, making it a felony to own or bring slaves to Kansas, and a third vari-ant also asserted "the legal rights of blacks."[46] Despite the *Dred Scott* decision, territorial house members felt confident that they had the right to abolish slavery. But the bill stalled in the council, a body of more "conservative" men elected before the general free-state sweep of the legislature. The council substituted a bill "merely repealing slavery," which the House accepted at the last minute. Legislators then took the bill to the governor at midnight. Medary persuaded a sympathetic council member to return with it the next day, when the session was officially over, and when, by not signing it, he could pocket veto the measure. The governor claimed never to have seen the slavery bill, which some thought a transparent piece of "treachery." Apparently to appease free staters whom he had angered over the slavery bill, Medary signed the constitutional convention bill that he had earlier stonewalled.[47]

Kansas voters decided 5,306 to 1,425 in favor of a constitutional convention. Nonetheless, H. Miles Moore detected much apathy about the vote, noting that "we have been Constitutioned to death."[48] The vote was low because of a late March snowstorm, but still a solid majority had registered their support for the free-state party.[49]

The constitutional movement also marked the final days of the Free State party as an organization separate from the Republican party. After the defeat of Lecompton, S. N. Wood resigned as chairman of the Free-State Central Committee, saying that their work was done. Others were more reluctant to give up the old Free State party, mocking "Republicanism" as the "Bastard Free State Convention."[50] In order to "revive" the Free State party, a convention met on May 12, at Big Springs, where the original party had been organized in 1855. That did not stop others from meeting a week later at Osawatomie, where, declaring that the Free State party had done its work, they began to organize the Republican party.[51] Despite heavy rains, about seventy delegates and five hundred spectators gathered at Osawatomie to hear Horace Greeley condemn Democrats as "the bitter foe of the people of Kansas and the enemy of popular rights everywhere." Endorsing nonintervention, the Kansas Republican party specifically denied that the U.S. Constitution carried slavery into the territory.[52] One observer contemptuously dismissed Osawatomie Republicans as endorsers of "Sophistry Sovereignty," for they did not embrace the national Republican position that

Congress could exclude slavery from the territory.[53] Perhaps the free staters had so accustomed themselves to working within the framework of popular sovereignty, and having finally secured control of the territorial legislature through the ballot box, that they could not conceive of rejecting popular sovereignty outright.

The goals of popular sovereignty or slavery exclusion were, however, too limited for many Kansans. Antislavery activity became more prevalent, and despite the legal penalties for aiding runaways, more open. Montgomery's war had subverted property rights in men. In 1856, Lane fought for white rights, not black. In 1858, Montgomery fought for both. In 1858, a traveler recorded his conversation with a slave in western Missouri. Asked whether he would like his freedom, the black man enthusiastically agreed, "Yes, sah, deed I would! Dinah and me has versed togeder about if de war went on, mebbe Massa Montgomery would come over wid his men and set all de niggars free, but day say dat peace is making up and dar's no furder hope for de liberation ob poor Julius."[54]

Like Montgomery, John Brown helped the fugitive. Brown's final sojourn in Kansas was drawing to a close in December when Jim Daniels, a Missouri slave, sought him out. Daniels reported that he and four members of his family were to be sold by their Missouri master. Given a Sunday off to sell his own wares, Daniels went looking for help. He looked in the right place. Soon after learning of Daniels's plight, Brown led fifteen men to the farm of Harvey C. Hicklan, Daniels's master. Brown freed Daniels and his family and then went to the home of John B. Larue, a neighbor who lived a mile from Hicklan, where he took another five slaves. Larue and a guest were taken hostages and freed a week later. Another group of Brown's men took a slave woman from the home of David Cruise, killing Cruise when he made a sudden move as if to draw a gun. Having helped themselves to horses, food, and supplies, the two groups reunited at daybreak.[55]

The eleven slaves—three men, five women, and three children—hid for a month along Pottawatomie Creek. A child was born to the Daniels during the escape. On January 20, the party started east. By mid-February they had reached Grinnell, Iowa, where they received an "enthusiastic" welcome from the New England settlers of the town.

The town's founder, Josiah B. Grinnell, hired a boxcar to take the party to Chicago, failing to specify the nature of the freight. The party reached Detroit in mid-March, and from there took a ferry to Windsor, Ontario.[56] An administration informant found Brown unashamed of the raid: "He is an earnest fanatic who thinks himself, and declares himself, called of God to make war on slavery and to kill whoever comes in the way of his mission."[57] Brown himself remained proud that he had "liberated" the blacks from Missouri.[58]

On January 25, 1859, Dr. John W. Doy and his son, Charles, were caught traveling with thirteen runaway slaves. Doy was a physician from Rochester, New York, and had emigrated in 1854 with the first New England Emigrant Aid party. On the day of their capture, Doy's party had left Lawrence in two wagons, bound for Iowa or Nebraska, when they were overtaken by twenty armed men who escorted them to Weston, Missouri. Two members of Doy's party had been cooks at a Lawrence hotel, but they lacked free papers. All the blacks were returned to their masters. Charged with kidnapping slaves from Missouri, the Doys were held for a hearing at Platte City.[59]

Dr. Doy and his son were to be tried in March. By then the territorial legislature of Kansas had raised one thousand dollars for their defense. Leading the defense team was ex-governor Wilson Shannon who asked for a change of venue, given the hostility of local Missourians to the defendants. The trial was moved to St. Joseph, Missouri, and lasted three days. While Shannon gently suggested that slaves had been known to run away on their own initiative, the prosecution pressed home the theme that the Doys were "negro stealers." When the jury could not reach a verdict, prosecutors dropped charges against Charles Doy and decided to retry his father in June. At that trial, John Doy was found guilty on the one count of kidnapping a slave claimed by the mayor of Weston, Missouri. Doy was sentenced to five years hard labor, while he still awaited trial on the twelve other counts. In late July, five days before the Supreme Court was to sentence him, a party of five men, including Charles Doy, rescued the elder Doy from prison. Although the men were from Lawrence, they deliberately avoided carrying Sharps rifles, which would have betrayed them as Kansas abolitionists. Entering the jail on the pretext of bringing in a horse thief, they forced the jailer to free Doy, who had been warned by an earlier visitor to expect an attempt that night. The men successfully escaped town, crossed the river in boats, and arrived in Lawrence by evening of the next day.[60]

Like the Doy party, fugitive slaves made Lawrence their destination because it was "the best advertised anti-slavery town in the world."[61] Sometimes such antislavery scruples did not aid the runaway. A slave named Peter worked at a Lawrence hotel. He had saved a third of the nine hundred dollars he needed to buy his freedom, and a local newspaper ran a letter asking for donations toward the balance. One reader responded that since property in man was illegitimate, a true "Republican" would not contribute, as Peter owed his master nothing. This "Republican" would, however, help Peter escape.[62]

Fugitives could find help in other parts of Kansas, not just Lawrence. In January, two men kidnapped a black man named Charles Fisher, a barber at the Planter's Hotel in Leavenworth. The men climbed into Fisher's shop by a ladder, handcuffed him, and took him to an island in the river. In the early morning, when his captors fell asleep, Fisher escaped and rowed himself back to town, where he found someone to file the cuffs off. Some friends moved Fisher to an undisclosed location. Of a divided mind, Leavenworth citizens held meetings both to celebrate and to denounce the rescue.[63] A runaway slave from West Point, Missouri, escaped to Kansas Territory but was pursued by his owner, a Mr. Bell. Bell and two friends traveled to Osawatomie, where they stayed at a cabin. At 1 A.M., they were awakened by thirty to forty armed men who had heard of the Missourians' mission. The men agreed to give Bell the black man if he were indeed the missing slave. When they brought in the alleged fugitive, he swore, unsurprisingly, to be a free black from Virginia. To the three Missourians' dismay, they were forced to return home without him.[64]

Just as Missouri whites had feared, a free Kansas endangered slavery, permitting blacks to exploit the unsettled nature of slavery and race relations on the border. On a March morning, an Irishman attacked a black employee who was bringing water into Daniel Read Anthony's Leavenworth office. Another black grabbed the Irishman by the throat and threw him to the ground. When another Irishman threatened to join the fight, the second black grabbed a gun from Anthony's office and threatened him with it. Paraphrasing the *Dred Scott* decision, Anthony remarked that "a white man has no rights which a nigger is bound to respect."[65] In 1855 and 1856, Kansans had occasionally returned slaves to Missouri claimants. The free-state movement had avowed that it did not want blacks—free or slave—in Kansas. Now many white Kansans looked the other way as runaways came to the territory, and some openly aided their flight.

Indeed the Fourth of July brought reflections on freedom and slavery—themes that Charles Robinson had addressed four years earlier. In the day's oration, Reverend D. Foster emphasized "all men are created equal," describing the minister's black Dartmouth College classmate. Several slaveowners in the audience walked away, but Julia Lovejoy praised the speech for its "strength and vitality." Lovejoy reflected that a slave man, carrying the child of the white woman whom he followed through the crowd, seemed to look at the flags and bunting as if to say, "'What is all this show to me? The 'stripes' on the flag, I know how to decypher—would that I had never been born—this galling servitude, must it last *forever?'*"[66] Foster and Lovejoy's Fourth differed from Robinson's in that the emphasis on liberty had shifted from political liberty for whites to human liberty for all.

When Kansans again met in constitutional convention that July, this time at Wyandotte, the delegates brought expanded ideas about liberty to their deliberations. One correspondent found the debates dull by the standards of earlier Kansas constitutional conventions, with much discussion of banking. Early in their proceedings, the delegates abandoned the Topeka Constitution as a model for their deliberations and favored instead the constitutions of western states such as Ohio and Indiana. Democrats repeatedly resurrected the issue of black rights, apparently to embarrass Republicans who still smarted from the Leavenworth debacle. Indeed, the constitution contained too many "negro-equality features" to suit some. Wyandotte prohibited slavery, gave both black men and women the right to vote in school elections, and left to the legislature the decision whether to provide black suffrage. One commentator found the old issues of freedom and slavery defunct, having been replaced by competition over locating the capital, which would be moved to Topeka.[67] But Wyandotte really indicated the extent to which the free-state movement had widened its conception of liberty.

Democrats disliked the constitution's failure to prohibit black immigration. Some feared that Wyandotte would encourage further black migration to the territory.[68] One man concluded that its pro-black features effectively ceded the rights of white men, as if blacks could only gain freedom and rights at the expense of whites. He warned Kansans, "You will not easily regain the freedom you have lost."[69]

On October 4, Kansans voted 10,421 to 5,530 in favor of the Wyandotte Constitution. Most of the opposition came from the old proslavery areas of the territory.[70] When Julia Lovejoy "heard the booming of cannon along the river" on election day, she knew "that free principles were triumphing, and pro-slavery subserviency was breathing its last gasp in Kansas."[71] A Missouri editorialist advocated admission, claiming that Kansas now had a constitution Congress could accept. Men on the border were ready to let bygones be bygones and cultivate friendly relations between Missouri and Kansas. Congress should do likewise.[72]

As border residents moved toward a peaceful resolution of the slavery issue, those who advocated violence went elsewhere. In 1858, John Brown had dallied on the border waiting for the opportunity to bring his master plan to fruition. For many years, Brown had believed that a small guerrilla force operating out of the Appalachian Mountains could fatally undermine slavery. This force would encourage slaves to run away, whereupon they would be armed and incorporated into maroon bands in the mountains. According to one of Brown's supporters, Brown met objections with the riposte, "If God be for us, who can be against us?"[73]

Brown persuaded the Secret Six to support his plan not just by his unwavering confidence. These eastern abolitionists turned to violence because they feared abolitionism had failed to destroy slavery, which they considered morally abominable, by peaceful means. More than that, these white men saw violence as a way of redeeming the slave from his innate docility and instilling manliness in him. The Secret Six believed that just as the revolutionary violence of their ancestors had established American society, so would black insurrectionary violence earn the slave a place in that society.[74]

The young white men who followed Brown also believed violence the only way to end slavery. For most, their experiences in Kansas had prepared them to accept Brown's ideas. Over half of Brown's white followers had been Kansas settlers, many of them having served in free-state military companies. John Henry Kagi had seen the U.S. troops disperse the Topeka legislature in July 1856 and had fought in a free-state company.[75] Jeremiah G. Anderson's brother wrote that the young man had been "a target in Kansas for the Border Ruffians and all, for what? Why because he purchased a claim & wished to settle on it & live by the sweat of his *own* brow."[76] Another of his acquaintances recalled that Anderson had been made "*a Sworn Enemy to Slavery*" by imprisonment at Fort Scott. "[I] was surprised at Brown's foolish raid into Virginia," the former Kansas friend recalled, "but I expected to find Anderson with him, where ever he turned to *Strike*."[77] John Cook was at the side of a New York man shot down by a Border Ruffian in the winter of 1856. The Missourian had escaped when Cook's pistol misfired, so Cook spent his days target shooting. "He appeared to us like a young man of good morals, and one who has been accustomed to good society," wrote Lovejoy of Cook, whose brother-in-law was the governor of Indiana.[78] Certainly, the letters written by Brown's recruits bespoke a youthful idealism and a happiness in enduring hardships for "the good of humanity."[79] William H. Leeman, another veteran of the Kansas struggle, wrote his mother explaining, "I have been engaged in a *good Cause. A Noble Cause* for the last year I have been engaged in the Cause of *Freedom* and ere long it will be shown to the world and if we succeed in our undertaking it would well pay me for years of toil."[80]

Some of Brown's men had no need for an education in Kansas to sharpen their desire to end slavery. The runaway slave Shields Green had joined Brown in defiance of Frederick Douglass's better judgment. Dangerfield Newby had been born into slavery in Virginia, but although freed by his white father, his wife and six children still remained slaves. Osborn P. Anderson was a northern free black, skilled as a printer, who had moved to Canada after 1850. Lewis Leary and John A. Copeland, uncle and nephew, were free blacks long resident in the abolitionist town of Oberlin, Ohio.[81] For different reasons, these men, like Brown's white recruits, followed the hero of Osawatomie. Whether Brown's men had experienced fighting in Kansas or not, the territorial struggle over popular sovereignty made Brown's eastern plans possible. Without his fame as a guerrilla captain in Kansas, Brown would not have gotten the money or the men to undertake his raid in Virginia.

In the summer of 1859, Brown and his men moved to a farm in Maryland a few miles from the federal arsenal in Harpers Ferry, Virginia. A couple of the Brown women had been brought in to make the camp look more homelike. The size of his force numbered only a couple dozen men. While he waited for more white abolitionist and free black volunteers, Brown presented himself as a farmer named Isaac Smith. In September, pikes arrived that Brown had ordered from a Connecticut blacksmith ostensibly for Kansas settlers. Yet pikes were unsuitable weapons for the guerrilla fighters of Kansas, who carried state-of-the-art Sharps rifles. And Kansas was no longer bleeding. Brown had all along intended the pikes—simple, cheap, and crude weapons—for use by untrained warriors. Pikes would serve quite well as a means of quickly arming a slave population. The arrival of the pikes, along with other portents, signaled to Brown that the time to act had come.[82]

Brown moved on the night of October 16. Leaving a few men at the farmhouse, he led the main force into Harpers Ferry. They took possession of the armory, arsenal, and rifle works and cut the telegraph wire. Brown sent several men to seize as hostages Colonel Lewis Washington, who was the great-grandnephew of the first president, and two others, a local planter named John Allstadt and his son. Rousing Washington from his bed, Aaron D. Stevens, one of his captors, asked if he had heard of Osawatomie Brown. Washington said no. "Then," said Stevens, "you have paid very little attention to Kansas matters." Washington said he had grown "so much disgusted with Kansas" that he refused to read any more about it. But Washington could not evade the agitation over Kansas for Kansans had brought the problems of the border home to the east.[83] To the watchman at the armory gate, Brown announced his presence by saying, "I came here from Kansas, and this is a slave State; I want to free all the negroes in this State."[84] Meanwhile Brown's men at the Ferry barricaded the railroad tracks, stopping the train from Wheeling. Around 1 A.M., Brown's men fired on a watchman at the railroad station and then on the baggage master, a free black named Hayward Shepherd. Fatally injured, Shepherd was the first to die during Brown's raid. Strangely, Brown allowed the train to continue its journey after several hours' delay. Passengers spread the alarm, but in the town few realized there was a problem at the armory. In the morning, armory workers arrived to begin their day's labor and joined the growing number of hostages, which Washington estimated as thirty or forty men.[85]

By dawn, the townsmen were thoroughly alarmed. Local men poured into Harpers Ferry, trapping Brown in the arsenal. As the forces arrayed against him grew, Brown made no attempt to escape, but exchanged fire with militia and the enraged citizenry. Although local whites rallied to suppress the insurrection, no slaves came to Brown's rescue. While local slaves may have had little idea of Brown's intentions or capabilities, they possessed a very good knowledge of the retaliatory capacity of white society. Brown's plan to ignite a massive slave insurrection had failed. Outnumbered and outgunned, he and his men were trapped. As one of Brown's sons lay dying on the armory floor, Brown hushed his cries, saying, "No, my son, have patience; I think you will get well; if you die, you die in a glorious cause, fighting for liberty."[86]

The initial reports from Harpers Ferry reflected the panic of local residents rather than the reality of Brown's desperate plight. With a headline announcing "THE NEGRO INSURRECTION," the New York Times claimed that six hundred fugitives had joined the hundred or so white insurrectionists.[87] Reports of hundreds of "rioters," black and white, capturing the federal arsenal spurred the mobilization of troops. Volunteer companies offered their service, as did Maryland officials, who reported their militia ready to aid the Virginians. The president of the Baltimore and Ohio Railroad requested federal soldiers.[88]

U.S. Marines, commanded by Colonel Robert E. Lee, arrived on October 18. Lt. J. E. B. Stuart, approaching the engine house in order

Capture of John Brown at the arsenal in Harpers Ferry, 1859.
(Kansas State Historical Society, Topeka)

to demand a surrender, recognized the elderly man at the door as
Osawatomie Brown, "who had given us so much trouble in Kansas."
When Brown refused Lee's terms of unconditional surrender, the
Marines stormed the building, breaking the door with a battering ram.
Brown's men fired back but were quickly overrun. Lt. Israel Green,
having Brown pointed out to him by Washington, stabbed Brown with
his dress sword and clubbed him into unconsciousness with its hilt. So
ended Brown's last effort to resolve slavery through violence.[89]

By the end of that day, President Buchanan received the report,
"Everything is quiet." The troops had taken five prisoners, three of
whom were wounded, at the cost of six dead Virginians and a wounded
Marine. The hundreds of insurrectionists were in fact only nineteen
conspirators; their slave allies, only five free blacks. At the Maryland
farmhouse that had been Brown's headquarters, hundreds of guns and
fifteen hundred pikes were discovered, as were flints, axes, blankets,
and clothing. The investigators also found papers, some on the body
of J. G. Anderson, that purported to be constitutions and documents

of a provisional government.[90] Here was another residue of Brown's Kansas experience—the continual writing of extralegal, revolutionary governments.

Democrats immediately traced Brown's treason to its free-state roots. William Bigler remarked in a letter to the president, "What an inglorious end for the great Kansas Shrieker! Brown was a shining light in Kansas and it was for traitors like he that you were asked to permit the laws to be trampled underfoot."[91] But even those who condemned Brown could not help but admire him. Edward Bates spoke of the "wild & mad project to abolish slavery by a general servile insurrection," and of its "wickedness" and "utter futility." Bates also commented on Brown's "cool intrepidity &, apparently, courious rectitude."[92]

As the first news of the raid became public, Northerners began to construct their rationale for Brown's actions. "Of him, we might say with truth, his wrongs have made him mad," a Kansas paper concluded.[93] An editorial in the *New York Times* recorded that Brown had "suffered severely" at Missouri hands in the loss of property and his sons, whose deaths had driven him mad. Revenge had motivated his war on Missouri and prompted his "uneasy spirit" to look elsewhere, continuing the war on slaveowners even after Kansas no longer bled.[94] Author Lydia Maria Child asked permission to nurse Brown. A Minnesota man even offered to die in Brown's place. And a ten-year-old Massachusetts girl begged, "Oh! do not have him hung."[95] Child told Governor Wise that "because slaveholders so recklessly sowed the wind in Kansas, they reaped a whirlwind at Harper's Ferry."[96] This rationale for Brown's actions became the stated explanation of the northern members of the congressional investigating committee on Harpers Ferry. Although proclaiming that lawlessness was "without excuse," the Northerners promptly found one for Brown: "The lawless armed invasions of our own people in our own weak Territory of Kansas, not only unpunished, but justified, sustained, and even rewarded, all, it is believed, to extend and sustain slavery, tended strongly to suggest acts of lawless violence to destroy it, especially in those who had witnessed and suffered by these collisions."[97]

Such constructions attempted to reassure Southerners that Brown had acted alone. There was no large northern conspiracy, but only "the crazy freak of Ossawatomie Brown." This reassurance failed because it placed the blame for Brown's madness in southern hands. "Goaded to insanity by wrongs inflicted on him by Pro-Slavery ruffians in Kansas," Brown had embarked on "certain self-destruction in quest of revenge."[98] Who was to blame, the madman who sought vengeance or those who drove him to it? John A. Andrew, a Boston lawyer hired for Brown's defense, told southern senators investigating Harpers Ferry that Brown had invaded Virginia in retaliation for Missouri's invasion of Kansas: "And I think that his foray into Virginia was a fruit of the Kansas tree."[99]

Blacks needed no rationalizations to honor Brown. The Boston minister J. Sella Martin said that the only difference between Brown's effort and the American Revolution was that Brown wanted to help blacks. Whereas the Patriots fought for the liberties of white men, Brown fought for the liberty of blacks. The spring after Harpers Ferry, John S. Rock spoke on the occasion of Boston's Massacre Day. He compared Brown to Crispus Attucks, explaining that blacks excused Brown's violence because they saw it in its context: "The whole pattern of black-white relations in antebellum America was to blacks a form of violence."[100] Recent historians have suggested that black knowledge of and support for Brown's raid was wider than usually acknowledged. Brown had discussed the raid with black leaders such as Frederick Douglass and may have communicated with free blacks in the Harpers Ferry region. But Brown was unable to give his supporters firm dates, first because he was still raising money, then because of Hugh Forbes. Even after his band collected in Maryland, Brown moved up the date of the attack when local women became suspicious of the black men at the farmhouse.[101] Whether Brown's plans to raise a large black army in western Virginia were realistic or not, after his capture, northern blacks understood his motives better than any other group.

Missourians had a different explanation for Brown's actions. He was simply a "professional murderer." He had not been driven mad by the wrongs done him in Kansas. In fact, it was Brown who had committed the first murders there, and who had even "forced his children to participate in the bloody deed." One of Brown's sons had consequently become "a real maniac."[102] Throughout the slaveowning states, Brown's plan to initiate "race war" horrified southern whites.[103] Fire-eater

Edmund Ruffin acquired some of Brown's pikes and sent one to the governor of each slave state with the warning, "SAMPLE OF THE FAVORS DESIGNED FOR US BY OUR NORTHERN BRETHREN."[104]

The raid further estranged the South from the Union. The southern-dominated congressional committee which investigated Harpers Ferry concluded that the willingness of prominent Northerners to support Brown proved "the utter insecurity of the peace and safety of some of the States of this Union."[105] Southerners found it difficult to distinguish between the abolitionism of a John Brown and the Republican party's opposition to slavery's extension.[106] Southerners distrusted the Republicans as the "Brown-Helper" party, despite Republican denials of a party connection to the raid or the party's endorsement of violent abolition.[107] The *Richmond Enquirer* suggested that Northerners must learn from the Harpers Ferry affair "that the only settlement of the disturbing and dangerous question of slavery is in the acknowledgment of its constitutional rights and their protection."[108]

Only a few acknowledged the real issues posed by the Harpers Ferry raid. How was a moral evil to be eradicated from a democratic society that tolerated it? Brown had decided on violence. After all, slavery was a state of war between master and slave, so the use of force to free slaves was justified.[109] James Redpath felt that in pursuing this cause, Brown had emulated his revolutionary ancestors: "I would as soon think of vindicating Washington for resisting the British Government to the death, as to apologize for John Brown assailing the Slave Power with the only weapons that it fears."[110] David Davis thought Brown wrong to conclude that democratic processes could not work. "What a dreadful affair the Harper's Ferry insurrection had been," Davis moaned to his son. "These wild fanatics will be taught a lesson—that it is only through the peaceful mode of the ballot box, that slavery can be reached."[111] With his close friend, Abraham Lincoln, Davis shared that preference for political action over violence. Lincoln admired Brown's courage and abhorrence of slavery, but would go no further than that. On the day after Brown's execution, acknowledging "even though [Brown] agreed with us in thinking slavery wrong," Lincoln told a Leavenworth audience, "that cannot excuse violence, bloodshed, and treason."[112] As Redpath's and Davis's reactions reveal, the raid had polarized the sections: Northerners increasingly defended the use of violence in the cause of antislavery reform, putting moderates such as Davis and Lincoln on the defensive, but Southerners insisted all Northerners were violent abolitionists.[113]

Brown's papers, found in the Maryland farmhouse, provided considerable grist for southern fears. Following the raid, Virginia governor Henry A. Wise received numerous requests for information from all parts of the South. His correspondents sought confirmation that a local minister or teacher or politician had links to Brown and was named in the captured documents. Although Wise ignored most of these requests, Brown's arrest panicked the Secret Six.[114] Gerrit Smith retreated to an insane asylum and George L. Stearns, Franklin B. Sanborn, and Samuel Gridley Howe to Canada. Thaddeus Hyatt spent three months in a Washington, D.C., jail in mid-1860 for refusing to testify before the Senate committee investigating Brown's raid. Howe eventually testified as well—having conveniently lost or destroyed those of his papers concerning Brown.[115] Only Brown and the men caught with him in Virginia faced prosecution.

Northerners criticized Virginia's unseemly speed in pushing the trial, which lasted only five days, forward. Even more unusual, although provoking less comment, was Virginia's charge of treason. The constitutional convention of 1787 had left states a concurrent power to punish treason, opening Brown to prosecution for treason in Virginia. Yet prosecutions of treason were rarely undertaken, even by the federal government, because they were not usually considered necessary for maintaining a state's security, and there was also fear of suppressing legitimate political dissent. There had never been an execution for treason. The only treason prosecutions completed by a state were those of Brown and the leader of Rhode Island's 1842 Dorr Rebellion, Thomas W. Dorr. Brown's biographer attributes the treason charge, which was accompanied by indictments for murder and conspiring to bring about a slave rebellion, to the court's haste. Brown's counsel argued that Brown was not a citizen of Virginia, owed it no allegiance, and hence could not be guilty of treason against it. The arguments failed. After a short deliberation, the jury returned a guilty verdict. Two days later, Judge Richard Parker sentenced Brown to hang.[116]

Virginia authorities feared Brown's northern supporters would rescue him before the sentence could be carried out.[117] Montgomery recruited one of Brown's men, who had wandered to the gold fields of Pike's Peak instead of to Harpers Ferry, but deep snow in Virginia thwarted their efforts. Brown himself opposed such an attempt.[118] The real deterrence may have been Brown's jailers, who responded to reports of potential rescuers with a curt, "We are ready for them. If an attack be made the Prisoners will be Shot, by the Inside Guards."[119] The Virginians were also on guard because of a spate of fires, believed set by slaves. One of the jurors who had convicted Brown had his haystack burned. There were numerous rumors of other slave insurrections. Because of security concerns, Virginians made elaborate preparations for Brown's execution. Railroad officials limited passenger cars and provided an extra train for troops.[120]

"Captain Brown was as cheerful on the morning of his execution as I ever saw him," one of the Harpers Ferry raiders reported.[121] Dressed as a "typical Western farmer," Brown passed out of the jail into a mass of soldiers. A wagon conveyed him to the scaffold. When Brown ascended the platform, he asked not to be kept waiting. Nonetheless, over a quarter of an hour passed while the troops filed into their places. Then a hush fell over the crowd. The fire-eater Edmund Ruffin, who had joined the cadets of the Virginia Military Institute in order to be present, grudgingly conceded Brown's "physical or animal courage" as the old man silently waited, hood over his head, until the sheriff's hatchet severed the rope, plummeting Brown to his death.[122] As Brown swung from the gallows, a Virginia Military Institute colonel called out, "So perish all such enemies of Virginia! All such enemies of the Union! All such foes of the human race!"[123]

From Charlestown, a soldier reported, "Brown has been Executed. Everything passed off quietly. He was not permitted to say a word."[124] But Brown had written his last testament and passed it to a jailor: "I John Brown am now quite certain that the crimes of this *guilty land will never* be purged *away,* but with Blood. I had as I *think vainly* flattered myself that without *very much* bloodshed; it might be done."[125] Perhaps Brown merely possessed, as Stephen Vincent Benét wrote, a "certain minor-prophet air,/That fooled the world to thinking him half-great/When all he did consistently was fail."[126] But what Brown saw more clearly than any other white man was the role violence would play in ending slavery. He had first realized in Kansas that violent means would be required, and after Harpers Ferry, he understood the scope of that violence.

Brown's actions forced others to link the causes of white and black freedom and to contemplate how much force liberty required for its preservation. On the day of Brown's execution, an antislavery convention in Lawrence saluted their "old comrade in arms," praising his work in Kansas. He and his men "will swell the noble column of those who have fallen in the great battle for Freedom."[127] When Virginia senator James M. Mason distinguished between the cause of white voting rights in Kansas and black liberty, Samuel Gridley Howe, one of the Secret Six replied, "I know no distinction of color in freedom. I know no distinction of color in men."[128] In Brown's old neighborhood of Osawatomie, a free-state settler pondered the narrowly averted kidnapping of a local free black into slavery. He condemned the federal law that ruled in Kansas territory, "the law that pursues such as John Brown—mistaken and erring but noble in his objects—with most deadly and unrelenting hatred, but never has punished a kidnapper—never has punished one of those traitors who tried to steal the liberties of the whole people of Kansas."[129] Speaking on the theme "Courage," Ralph Waldo Emerson endorsed Brown's methods: "One heard much cant of peace-parties long ago in Kansas and elsewhere, that their strength lay in the greatness of their wrongs, and dissuading all resistance, as if to make this strength greater. But were their wrongs greater than the negro's? And what kind of strength did they ever give him? It was always invitation to the tyrant, and bred disgust in those who would protect the victim."[130] Emerson and others concluded that violence, Brown's solution, was morally and tactically superior to the free-state party's use of nonresistance.

So it seemed with good reason that some feared that execution would confer martyrdom on Brown, encouraging imitation of his deeds. A southern doctor requested Brown's body for dissection, intending to prevent Northerners from giving Brown's body a triumphal procession to an eastern grave. Humanely, Wise saw that Brown's widow received

the body.[131] Some Northerners did treasure relicts of Brown's execution as if they were holy. In his desk drawer, James Redpath kept a
small piece of wood labeled "A bit of the true Cross,—a chip from the
Scaffold of John Brown."[132] Emerson and Henry David Thoreau would
both compare Brown to Christ.[133] While a Boston newspaper repudiated Brown's actions, the editorialist hoped that the raid would reveal
to Southerners "how deep and real a thing the conscientious opposition to slavery is."[134]

A deep moral objection to slavery never animated the free-state
movement. When Charles Robinson testified at the congressional hear-
ings which followed the Harpers Ferry raid, he emphasized the difference between Brown's purpose "to create difficulties and disturbances"
in Kansas that would cause the country to abolish slavery and his own
purpose. Robinson wanted only "to establish a free-State government
in Kansas," a goal in which Brown had no interest. Clearly Robinson
was protecting himself and the free-state cause. In the hysteria that
followed Harpers Ferry, many in the antislavery cause, including Senators Henry Wilson and William H. Seward, sought to distance themselves from Brown's extremism. But Robinson was also right. Brown
had never championed the free-state cause except as the platform to
bring about the greater liberty of blacks.[135]

Despite Brown's divergence from the free-state party's goal of political rights for white men, Captain Brown became in 1859, and has
remained ever since, the archetypal character of Bleeding Kansas.
Brown's martyrdom overshadowed the labors of Charles Robinson and
Jim Lane, and other free staters, who did more to make Kansas a free
state than did Brown. But Kansans accepted Brown as their symbol
because the free-state movement increasingly embraced the cause of
black rights as its own. Brown did not need his experience in Kansas
to radicalize him on the issue of race, but Kansans needed those like
Brown and Jim Daniels, the abolitionist and the runaway slave, to force
them into an expanded definition of liberty. Unfortunately for Kansas,
the rest of the country was not yet prepared to accept such radicalism. Congress tabled the Wyandotte Constitution in December 1859.
Although the debate centered not on slavery but on the boundary and
the lack of sufficient population, the effect was the same: Kansas was

denied statehood.[136] Perhaps the delay had something to do with Governor Medary's lament that, if Kansas were admitted, "we [would] have to submit to the eternal disgrace of having it go forth as a Black Old John Brown state."[137] Not until civil war engulfed the entire nation would violent abolitionism and the name of John Brown seem prophetic rather than insane.

I Am Here for Revenge
The National Civil War

The national civil war engulfed the border once again in violence. Both Kansans and Missourians seized the opportunity to revenge old grievances. The argument over liberty often became lost in opportunism, greed, and sadism. Without the earlier struggle over freedom in Kansas, though, neither side would have felt the need for revenge. Yet issues of liberty remained at the war's core. White Kansans who had once resisted the federal government as tyrannous now joined other Northerners to defend the Union as the bulwark of freedom. They were willing to tolerate a wide range of violations of individual liberty, especially the rights of slaveowners, for freedom.[1] Meanwhile, Missourians, even those loyal to the Union, feared the war's threat to slavery. Some Missourians thought such rights could only be protected by secession; others hoped that armed invasion would liberate Missouri from Union rule. The most lasting element of the war, however, was that its upheaval finally executed the promise that liberty would encompass blacks. Kansans welcomed the runaways who fled Missouri, and they were at the forefront of pushing for black rights during the war, much to the horror of Missourians who saw the war fulfill their worst fears about the revolutionary implications of freedom.

When Thomas Ewing, Jr., wrote a Missouri uncle in 1860 to wish him a happy New Year, he lightheartedly asked if his relative planned to go North or South if the Union fell apart.

Yet it was a serious question, for a "strong secession party" existed in Missouri.[2] While Missourians considered whether to leave the Union, Kansans still sought admission. On February 14, 1860, the Wyandotte Constitution went before Congress. Ewing felt sure Kansas met the population requirement, but he still followed the bill's progress with anxiety. Admission passed the House easily, 134 to 73.[3] But in the Senate, Charles Sumner's strong speech in favor "rekindl[ed]" old animosities. Southern opposition quickly gathered.[4] Senator Louis T. Wigfall of Texas denounced the territory as a den of "outlaws and traitors."[5] With all the Republicans and two Democrats opposing, the Senate voted 33 to 27 to postpone the bill.[6] Once again, Congress had thwarted Kansans' hopes for self-government.

Nevertheless, some thought the free-state movement had triumphed. "The battle of Freedom has been fought on the plains of Kansas and won," a Lawrence man wrote.[7] In September, Charles Robinson welcomed William Henry Seward to Kansas. Noting that Seward had challenged Southerners in 1854 to settle the territory, Robinson declared, "Six years have elapsed, & today we present you Kansas *Free* to grace your triumph, with a Constitution adopted by her people without a stain of slavery to mar its beauty."[8] Even Missourians agreed. An editorialist "deplore[d]" the "bad spirit" of the Senate debate and the "lugging in of the old questions no longer at issue in Kansas."[9]

A drought caused Kansans more concern than did the failure to gain admission. With no rain, and temperatures in the 90s, all hopes of a crop were gone by early June. The prairie grass was stunted and brown. By September, the Wakarusa ran dry but for occasional pools. As wells and springs failed, farmers trekked miles to fetch water for their cattle.[10]

Admission would have brought federal resources for drought-stricken Kansas. Thaddeus Hyatt peppered the president with pleas describing the "deplorable and starving condition of that scorched and famine-stricken land" of Kansas. Hyatt asked for a postponement of the land sales as many Kansans had left the territory; those who remained lacked clothes and food for the winter.[11] President Buchanan made a one hundred dollar donation and, in his annual message, recommended the suffering Kansas settlers to Congress's attention.[12]

Some Kansans deemed admission irrelevant to the freedom for which they fought. In an attack on Ball's Mill that November, James Montgomery "stole a number of negroes and murdered six or eight men."[13] A suspicious Judge Williams reported that Montgomery had used the drought as a pretext to import arms "in boxes marked as donations for Kansas sufferers."[14] John Brown's martyrdom may have inspired Montgomery to renew the war against slavery. Residents of western Missouri reported that Montgomery was once again making war on them, "kidnapping and freeing slaves, murdering slave owners, and destroying property." A runaway slave from Bates County led one of his detachments.[15]

One of Montgomery's victims was Russell Hindes, a young Missourian who was visiting his mother in Kansas Territory. A black man had stopped by the house of Lewis B. Reece and asked for the road to Kansas. Although the man had a pass, Reece was suspicious. When the man saw that Reece did not believe him and was going to take him into custody, he confessed that the pass was a forgery and that he had run away from his master in Bates County, Missouri. Hindes happened to pass by at this time and agreed to help Reece, who split the reward with him. Upon learning of Hindes's aid in recovering the fugitive, Montgomery's men lynched him and left a note in his pocket declaring he had been executed for "kidnapping negroes."[16] As the fate of Russell Hindes indicated, Montgomery was one Kansan whose conception of liberty had broadened to include blacks. Montgomery had sworn to aid fugitives and kill anyone enforcing the Fugitive Slave Act, a position too extreme even for some southern Kansans who accepted Montgomery's killing Missourians but balked at his liberating, or "kidnapping," as white Southerners called it, blacks.[17]

Even those Kansans most sympathetic to black rights, however, could not guarantee the safety of blacks from kidnapping. Both sides kidnapped, as the term was used by blacks and their white allies to mean forcing blacks into slavery, as well as by those whose slaves were being freed. Near Lawrence, five men abducted a free black man from the field he had been plowing. A Lawrence posse rescued him. In another incident, a black woman fled her Kansas home at night when she heard noises. Neighbors, including other blacks, caught one of the would-be kidnappers. As long as slavery was legal and the Fugitive Slave Law protected owners' right to recover runaways, free blacks in Kansas would face such attacks and Montgomery would be considered a "nigger thief," not a liberator.[18]

Although the law favored their property rights in slaves, Southerners drew other lessons from Montgomery's actions. The *Richmond Enquirer* complained that it had expected Northerners to repudiate abolition fanaticism after Harpers Ferry. That had not happened. Instead, "armed bands of traitors, in all the panoply of war, are openly invading the State of Missouri, murdering the people, burning the towns, and proclaiming the purpose to *'free every slave in Southwestern Missouri.'* How long—in God's name!—how long are we to suffer the humiliation of such insulting outrage?"[19] Montgomery, like John Brown before him, confirmed the worst fears of what northern dominance might mean for the South.[20]

Because Southerners increasingly distrusted the North's commitment to uphold southern rights, some Southerners demanded federal protection of slavery. When the Kansas territorial legislature prohibited slavery and then passed a personal liberty law, Albert Gallatin Brown of Mississippi felt that the time for federal intervention had arrived. Jefferson Davis proposed a set of resolutions, in early February, for congressional intervention if a territory acted against slavery. Although he claimed it was not a slave code, it was not much different.[21]

Northern Democrats refused to agree to congressional protection of slaveholding in territories that had no slaves and probably never would. Instead, northern Democrats united behind the candidacy of Stephen A. Douglas, the standard bearer of popular sovereignty. In 1856, Douglas had been the favorite candidate of the Lower South. By 1860, those same states walked out of the Democratic convention rather than accept him. This reverse occurred because of Douglas's opposition to the Lecompton Constitution and the English Compromise, and his continued adherence to popular sovereignty despite the *Dred Scott* decision. Anathema to Southerners, these positions were a matter of principle for Douglas and necessary for his political survival in the North.[22]

The legacy of Kansas disputes haunted the 1860 campaign. Douglas's enemies sought evidence that he betrayed his principles in the Lecompton controversy. Republicans hoped to discredit Douglas in the North by proving he had engineered the Lecompton "swindle." Both Republicans and southern Democrats approached John Calhoun's widow in order to buy Calhoun's correspondence with Douglas. An administration official offered her two thousand dollars for Douglas's letters to her husband. She refused.[23]

Republicans also sought to embarrass the Democrats by investigating how the Buchanan administration had handled the Lecompton Constitution. Republicans touted the findings of the Covode committee, which came out just before the Charleston Democratic convention, as evidence of Democratic party corruption and circulated thousands of copies of the report. That document, the report of a congressional investigation, concluded that the Buchanan administration had bought votes and betrayed Governor Walker.[24] The administration had "attempt[ed] to convert Kansas into a slave State by means of forgeries, frauds, and force."[25] It was a powerful attack but a largely irrelevant one, for Buchanan was not up for reelection. In fact, by describing the administration's "proscription of democrats of high standing" who had refused to back the Lecompton and English bills, the Republican report reminded voters of Douglas's sacrifices for popular sovereignty.[26] But popular sovereignty's appeal failed to bring Douglas the northern electoral votes necessary for victory.

The Republican candidate, Abraham Lincoln, won narrowly on a platform of no slavery extension, a platform that condemned popular sovereignty as "a deception and a fraud." The election of 1860 marked the emergence of the Republicans as the majority party in the North; Lincoln received not a single southern electoral vote. Southerners viewed Lincoln's election as fundamentally illegitimate. Despite Republican avowals not to interfere with slavery where it already existed, Southerners dismissed the party and its standard bearer as another John Brown. Speculating on the possibility Lincoln's election would incite slave rebellions, a Texas newspaperman wrote that it would not occur because slaves were unhappy but because "Kansas ruffians" would incite them to violence.[27] Rejecting the legitimacy of the president-elect, and seeking to protect whites' liberty to own slaves and to maintain white supremacy, southern states began to leave the Union.[28]

"We are waiting anxiously to get into the 'Union' before it *Busts,*" a Kansan lamented.[29] Actually secession aided Kansas's efforts to become a state. With the Southerners absent, Kansas "so long the Congressional firebrand, was settled tamely enough."[30] On January 29, 1861, Kansas gained admission. The *New York Times* called it an "offset for *one* of the seceding States."[31] H. Miles Moore reflected, "*So the agony is over & Kansas is a State.* . . . So K.T. is played out."[32] In Wyandotte, people celebrated "being delivered from federal tyranny" with bonfires, illuminations, and cannon fire.[33]

Ironically, Kansans would soon be asked to fight for the same federal government they had long resisted. On April 14, Isaac Goodnow recorded in his diary, "Exciting news from Ft. Sumpter—fighting."[34] For most Northerners, the Union was inseparable from liberty. An attack on the Union was not just a threat to a particular form of political organization but to the very ideal of liberty. That made the attack on Fort Sumter an attack on white liberty, the sacred institution of self-government.[35]

The border soon felt the impact of the Civil War's outbreak. Secession flags flew in Missouri.[36] Missouri Governor Claiborne Jackson refused to respond to Lincoln's call for troops. War Department officials concluded that "the State authorities in Missouri are too far committed to Secession to admit of any confidence."[37] In fact, Jackson had urged Missourians to join the South, and he had also asked Confederate President Jefferson Davis for help in seizing the St. Louis arsenal. Jackson's plans were foiled, however. The convention elected to consider secession instead voted to remain in the Union. Cleverly, Captain Nathaniel Lyon of the U.S. Army successfully spirited the arsenal's munitions to the Illinois side of the Mississippi River—a feat accomplished under the noses of proslavery Missourians. Then Lyon surrounded and forced the surrender of secessionist militia at Camp Jackson in St. Louis. Shouting insults and throwing bricks, an angry pro-southern mob harassed the captured militiamen and their Union guards. When a man fired a revolver at the troops, they opened fire on the crowd. Two soldiers and twenty-eight civilians died. When a conference including Jackson and Lyon failed to resolve the divisions within the state, Lyon occupied Jefferson City and drove Confederate forces under Sterling Price into the southwest corner of Missouri.[38] A southern newspaper reported that abolitionists had surrounded a small Missouri town on Lyon's march, "thrusting the oath of allegiance to LINCOLN down everybody's throat."[39] In late July 1861, Jackson and the pro-southern state legislature fled, whereupon the Unionist state convention declared itself the provisional government of Missouri.[40]

Southerners welcomed Jackson's government-in-exile, rejoicing that "the noble State of Missouri is now formally a member of the Confederacy—the twelfth state in the Southern Constellation."[41] But their celebration was premature. Even Price's victory over Lyon at Wilson's Creek, where Lyon was killed in August, and Price's successful push northward in Missouri during September, proved only temporary gains for the Confederacy. By the end of September, Price lacked the manpower to maintain his possession of the state and retreated again to its southwest corner.[42]

John C. Frémont, the politically well-connected explorer and first presidential candidate of the Republican party, was appointed by Lincoln to be the Union commander in Missouri. To an unsympathetic observer, Frémont was "a huge humbug" and an embarrassment to the government; disliked by Missouri Unionists, he surrounded himself with foreigners, Californians, and fancy imported European weaponry. Desperate to repel Price's invasion, Frémont issued a proclamation on August 30 that freed the slaves of Missouri Confederates. Conservative Missourians worried that the proclamation would endanger Union sentiment in Border South states. But some concluded that the war would free the slaves in time, provided Frémont stopped playing "grand monarch" and got to work.[43] Charles Robinson put it bluntly: "If it is true that the continued existence of slavery requires the destruction of the Union, it is time to ask if the existence of the Union does not require the destruction of slavery."[44] Opposed to any alteration of race relations, many Missourians wanted Frémont's removal. Lincoln gratified them by forcing Frémont to rescind the proclamation, and then by exiling Frémont to West Virginia.[45] Frémont's abortive career in Missouri notwithstanding, the "hard war" against slavery was to appear early along the border, the path to it having been paved by the previous territorial struggle.[46]

Many feared that war would bring renewed violence between Kansas and Missouri. A minister recalled riding in western Missouri with a young man of good family. As they discussed the possibility of war, the young Missourian said "with evident bitterness, *'I am glad war is coming; we want a chance at Kansas.'*" His companion answered, "'Does it not occur to you that it would also *give Kansas a chance at Missouri?*'"[47] Even the normally restrained Robinson, now governor of the new state of Kansas, commented at the beginning of the war, "Missouri must be taught a lesson & I should be glad of an opportunity to give it."[48] Some Missouri Unionists expected Kansans to threaten their property rights. A nephew of provisional Governor Hamilton R. Gamble predicted the abolitionists would use the war to accomplish "their hellish purposes."[49] His fears would be confirmed. Both Jim Lane and James Montgomery were organizing regiments.[50] No wonder one Missourian noted, "Many don't like the U.S. arming the Kanzas militia; I think myself it is rather ominous & . . . no good to Missouri."[51]

Lane's military ambitions brought him friendship with the new president. In the war's first weeks, when Washington, D.C., seemed isolated from the rest of the North, Lane, newly elected as senator, formed a "Frontier Guard" of Kansas men to protect the White House. The Kansans camped in the East Room. Lincoln, perhaps feeling a kinship with a fellow westerner whose humble origins and rough-hewn demeanor closely resembled his own, became a strong supporter of the Kansan. Lane exploited the president's favor to get his own command and interfere with Governor Robinson's military prerogatives. Others could only despair of the president's bad judgment. If Lincoln gave Lane a command "*after having seen the man,*" then he was "beyond the reach of sensible counsel."[52] Robinson fumed that "the War department chooses . . . to ignore the state government of Kansas & even insult it by authorizing an insane fanatic to run riot independent of all authority."[53] Secretary of War Edwin M. Stanton gave Lane power to raise troops in Kansas, violating Robinson's right as governor to control the state's military patronage. Lane's enemies hoped his military ambitions would force his resignation as senator, but Lane turned down a commission as brigadier general to keep his Senate seat. With typical dexterity, declining the commission did not prevent Lane from actively interfering in military affairs, recruiting troops, and planning expeditions.[54]

Revenge motivated many Kansans who took up arms against Missouri secessionists. One observer described the spirit of the war's first year as "that joyous time of springtide when, with flags and banner's flapping, the jayhawkers had swooped across the state line to crush the rebellion for God and the Union and in the process pluck old Missouri clean for God and themselves."[55] Jayhawkers, a term of obscure origin, referred to the Kansas counterparts of the Border Ruffians. In his description of a Kansas raid, which was undertaken to capture the secession flag a Missouri town had put up, H. Miles Moore deplored that spirit: "We have no more business to interfere with Mo than she has with us." Nevertheless, Moore joined Lane's brigade.[56]

On a late September night, Kansas Jayhawkers marched into Osceola, Missouri, and drove off a small company with artillery. The Kansans loaded wagons with store goods and set the town on fire before leaving.[57] "Lane said he meant to make the secessionists of Missouri feel the difference between being loyal and disloyal citizens and he is doing it," one of Montgomery's men reported.[58] One Kansan thought the Jayhawkers did as much damage to Union property as to rebel: "Old Jem Lanes brig keps op steling as mich as aver. It is Cold the jayhakers where aver we go thay confiscat Union property very ner as mich as rabols."[59] According to their victims in Missouri, Jayhawkers stole thousands of dollars of property in slaves, livestock, clothing, and household valuables. A Missouri woman recalled the difficulty of bathing when Jayhawkers might descend at any moment; one woman bathed while another kept watch.[60]

Charles Jennison, a veteran of Montgomery's guerrilla band, raised the "Independent Mounted Kansas Jayhawkers." More formally known as the Seventh Kansas, it had a company commanded by John Brown, Jr. In November, Jennison crossed into Missouri, burning houses en route.[61] Jennison was said to boast that "Missouri mothers hush their children to sleep by whispering the name of 'Doc Jennison.'"[62] By early 1862, Missourian and artist George Caleb Bingham predicted, "If Jennison were brought to trial and punished as he deserves to be, it would do more for the Union Cause in the Western portion of our State than the presence of a Union Army. . . . If he were *hung*, Price would lose thereby the best recruiting officer he has ever had."[63] For years after the war, western men described the pedigree of a horse of doubtful legal title as "out of Missouri by Jennison."[64]

Pillaging by Kansas troops had become so widespread by the end of January 1862 that they were removed from Missouri and forbidden to return unless ordered by the departmental commander. Relieved of command, Jennison was soon reinstated because of Lane's political influence.[65] No longer an official policy, jayhawking persisted informally among regular troops. A Missouri Union soldier told his fiancée that for amusement the men played cards, or games such as football, and did "a very little quiet jayhawking" when patrols ventured into Missouri. Finding the countryside abandoned, with livestock and farm produce unguarded, "we reconcile our consciences, that nobody loses by us & *Uncle Sam*—& his boys are the gainers."[66] An Iowa soldier in Missouri noted that bored soldiers "went out jay hawking," although the officers later ordered the return of stolen property.[67] Still, a Warren County, Missouri, woman claimed to notice the absence of the Kansas troops: "We are getting along first rate now since the negro stealers are all gone to *Dixie, to whip* the southern boys."[68]

Missourians correctly recognized that jayhawking subverted slavery. Many blacks accompanied the Union soldiers. Kansas troops engaged in none of the soul-searching about whether to return runaway slaves to rebel masters that occurred in the eastern theater. Lane argued that traitors should lose their property. Lane even allowed his chaplain, H. D. Fisher, to escort a band of fugitives to Kansas, a far cry from his 1856 claim that he fought only to free white men.[69] Among Montgomery's force were sixteen contraband teamsters, and Union troops now had black servants.[70] Many blacks sought refuge in Kansas towns. Two hundred runaway slaves were thought to be in Leavenworth, four hundred in Lawrence. "It is true that where the Kansas men march Slavery disappears."[71] The migration occurred because blacks saw their opportunity and the Union army no longer chose to uphold slavery. H. C. Bruce remembered earnest discussions among Missouri slaves about battles and politics because they understood the war's potential to bring emancipation.[72] One colonel "permitted *several hundred* [slaves] to pass his lines *without molesting them* on their way to *Kansas*."[73]

As these accounts make clear, many Missouri blacks eagerly embraced the opportunity to gain freedom. Bruce and his fiancée ran away to Leavenworth.[74] A Missouri woman gave one of her house servants permission to visit a sister, and even lent a horse and buggy as it was raining. Having dressed her children in their best clothes, the slave mother brought them in for the mistress to inspect. "They were really pretty, and she was quite proud of them," the white woman recalled. "I never saw them again." After leaving the horse and buggy on the Missouri side, the mother and children crossed over into Kansas, never to return.[75] Andrew Williams was an eight-year-old child when Kansas soldiers came to his master's house in Mount Vernon, Missouri. As the troops prepared to leave, "one of the oficers Said to my mothr don't you want to go to Kans and Be free my mother Said yess Sir get your childern in this wagon . . . . wee bid the colored famly that did not want to leave good By and all so the white foalks."[76] Williams's family traveled to Lawrence, toward which, a Kansas woman recalled, "a veritable army of slaves drifted . . . as if by instinct, to a sort of haven."[77] A Fort Scott man observed, "Contrabands are increasing beyond the most extravagant abolition expectations throughout the entire Kansas border. Some estimates place the daily emigration from Missouri at from fifty to one hundred. . . . Kansas men are pleased with every escape."[78]

Unthinkable only a few years earlier, Kansans now accepted the new population. During their own civil war, Kansans had gradually broadened their definition of liberty to include more rights for blacks. At Osawatomie, a minister started a school for contrabands. A similar school in Lawrence had eighty pupils, adults and children.[79] The Kansas Emancipation League, organized in March 1862, provided aid and schools for the contrabands. It formed land clubs and savings funds and tried to settle the refugees in rural areas as farm laborers.[80] The runaways usually arrived destitute, with their clothes in tatters, but some residents of Lawrence praised their eagerness to work and regarded the black community as "self-sustaining almost from the start."[81] According to Bruce, he and other ex-slaves were frequently cheated by white Kansans pretending sympathy for his former enslavement. But Bruce worked hard and prospered nonetheless, giving credence to Thomas Ewing's boast "there is not a negro pauper in the State."[82] By the end of the war, blacks made up 8.8 percent of Kansas's population, as compared to 0.6 percent in 1860. In 1865, a greater proportion of Kansas's population was black than ever before or since.[83]

Lane recruited the new Kansans as soldiers. As blacks passed through jayhawk units, many contrabands did more than act as laborers or personal servants. Jennison's regiment was said to be filled with blacks who were "*armed, uniformed and mounted as Soldiers of the United States.*"[84] D. R. Anthony wrote his sister that "In our march we free every slave, *every man* of all nations . . . and arm or use them in such manner as will best aid us in putting down rebels—We hope to stir up an insurrection among the negroes."[85] Although Lane's recruiting has been criticized as "impressment,"[86] Kansans pioneered in the use of black soldiers. In the summer of 1862, Lane moved from the informal use of contrabands to enrolling runaways into the First Kansas Colored Volunteers. He also opened a recruiting office in Leavenworth that accepted blacks as well as whites. Despite reprimands from the Secretary of War, Lane persisted. In August, Lane was officially told not to raise black troops, but he circumvented that order by enrolling them as "laborers." In late October 1862, these troops fought against guerrillas in Bates County, Missouri—the first use of black troops in combat and the first black combat casualties of the Civil War.[87]

As usual, Lane's motivations were complex and not entirely admirable. James Montgomery, who went on to become colonel of the black Second South Carolina Volunteers, acted from a sincere conversion to abolitionism. Lane's motivations were more pragmatic and not yet devoid of that racism that had earlier marked his pronouncements on slavery. Lane invoked military necessity: liberating slaves would undermine the Confederate military effort and arming them would help "crush the rebellion."[88] In a June 1862 speech at Cooper Union, Lane said, "I would like to see every traitor who has to die, die by the hand of his own slave."[89] At a Leavenworth meeting two months later, General James G. Blunt and Lane spoke in favor of enrolling black troops in the U.S. Army. "What about the nigger?" a voice called out as Lane spoke. Lane answered that a white man was as good as a "nigger." Why should blacks stay at home while whites died for them? In fact, blacks should be compelled to fight if they would not volunteer. Opposition to black troops was "sickly sentimentality"—a "nice logic" that preferred to see whites killed. For all that Lane appealed to whites' self-interest in persuading them that blacks should be allowed in the army, Lane did say that blacks should be given the opportunity to prove themselves, and he cited the courage of blacks who fought in the War of 1812.[90] Although the use of black troops became routine, their acceptance was based on motives both enlightened and racist.[91] Regardless of Lane's ambivalence, black troops' combat performance impressed even racist Northerners. "It is useless to talk any more about negro courage," the *Chicago Tribune* reported after Lane's troops skirmished in Missouri. "The men fought like tigers."[92]

Governor Gamble, a Unionist, protested to the president that "organizations of negroes are forming in Kansas armed and equipped as soldiers of the United States for the purpose of entering this state and committing depredations here."[93] Perhaps because of Gamble's objections, Lincoln refused to accept black regiments from Kansas. At the same time, he turned down regiments from Louisiana and South Carolina. After the Emancipation Proclamation, the troops were formally mustered into the Union army, officially making the First Kansas the fourth black regiment to enter the army. Unofficially, however, Kansas had been the first to use black troops.[94] In their most famous engagement, the First Kansas held the Union center at Honey Springs in the Cherokee Nation against a Confederate force of Texans and Native Americans. The black troops exchanged fire at close range for twenty minutes until the Confederates broke and ran. The Kansas troops captured a Texas regiment's flag and earned the praise of General Blunt, commanding the federal troops.[95]

Soldiers in Kansas's black regiments suffered from the same disabilities plaguing other black units. Although Lane commissioned several black men as officers, the War Department insisted officers of black regiments had to be white. Eventually a battery of light artillery raised at Leavenworth would prove unusual for having three black officers when only an estimated one hundred blacks received commissions during the entire Civil War. Lane had promised his troops equal pay, but as with other black regiments, the War Department refused to honor that promise. In fact, because they had been raised in an irregular fashion, they received no pay at all for almost a year. The black soldiers in Kansas regiments also expected to see combat, but instead were often used as laborers despite testimony to their competence and readiness for battle.[96]

Black troops threatened white supremacy by their very existence. Unionist slaveowners disliked their presence and often petitioned for their removal, even when the troops had committed no overt offense. Oftentimes whites testified that black soldiers used their new power to threaten their old masters and challenge their authority. Sam Bowmen ordered his former master to inform his wife that "a Soldiers wife is free" and promised to "punish" the owner if the message was not delivered.[97] Missourians protested that Kansans' arming of blacks threatened "the most serious difficulties" between Missouri and Kansas and alienated loyal Missourians. Even after Lincoln authorized the use of black troops, Missouri officials initially refused to arm black regiments until they were out of the state. Contrabands had already become a target of Confederate guerrillas so that General Schofield had authorized the use of military escorts to protect Missouri slaves running away to Kansas.[98] Now black troops earned their hostility. The Confederate government had officially proscribed the Union's use of black troops, threatening to execute their white officers and send black soldiers into slavery. Confederate guerrilla T. R. Livingston captured several white and black Union soldiers. He offered to exchange the whites but refused to recognize the blacks as "solgers." Colonel James Williams of the First Kansas wanted the blacks treated as prisoners of war and executed a Confederate prisoner when he learned Livingston's men had killed one of the black prisoners.[99]

As Williams's dealings with Livingston revealed, the war along the border was an irregular one. Once Price's army pulled out of Missouri, bushwhackers, as Confederate guerrillas were called, carried on the Confederate cause. On September 6, 1862, Confederate partisans under William Clarke Quantrill struck Olathe, Kansas, and on September 17, Shawneetown. At Olathe, they robbed stores and homes, killed three men, and tore down the Union flag over the recruiting office, trampling it into the dust. Quantrill's men carried six-shot Colt revolvers—sometimes as many as eight apiece. The Union troops still had only single-shot carbines and were completely outgunned.[100]

William Quantrill, who had emerged by 1862 as the foremost Missouri bushwhacker, was a Northerner who had gone over to the South. The slender, boyish Quantrill "did not look more formidable or ferocious than many a man I have met at other times and passed without fear," a Lawrence man recalled.[101] To explain himself to Missourians, Quantrill concocted a story that Montgomery's free-state Kansans had murdered his brother. He told credulous Missourians that after infiltrating Montgomery's band under the name Charley Hart, he had killed them one by one.[102] An insecure, ambitious youth, Quantrill held a grudge against Kansans because he did poorly when he migrated to the territory in 1857. He quarreled with the fellow Ohioans who brought him west and compiled a record of petty theft. In November 1860, Quantrill participated in a free-state raid on a Missouri farm near Blue Springs, but he switched sides and alerted the Missouri family of the raid beforehand. He invented the murdered brother to justify to Missourians his betrayal of the free staters.[103]

Deemed a thief by free-state settlers, Quantrill was attracted to the law and order rhetoric of the proslavery party. In a letter to his mother, dated two months after John Brown's execution for the Harpers Ferry raid, Quantrill wrote,

You have undoubtedly heard of the wrongs committed in this territory by the southern people, or proslavery party, but when one once knows the facts they can easily see that it has been the opposite party that have been the main movers in the troubles & by far the most lawless set of people in the country. They all sympathize for old J. Brown, who should have been hung years ago, indeed hanging was too good for him. May I never see a more contemptible people than those who sympathize for him. A murderer and a robber, made a martyr of; just think of it.[104]

Ironically, Quantrill was writing his own biography.

Quantrill's men, Missourians insisted, came from the "very best families of Missouri," and many became "honored citizens" after the war.[105]

Coleman Younger was one. His father had been a prominent and prosperous citizen of western Missouri who became the target of Jayhawker raids. After the son joined Quantrill's band, the father was killed and the mother, a consumptive, was burned out during winter and suffered from exposure. Frank James, a Confederate soldier, was paroled after being captured at the Battle of Wilson's Creek. Once home, he boasted of southern success in that fight until angry Unionists threw him in jail. Unable to fit in locally, and unable to rejoin Confederate regular forces because of his parole, he joined Quantrill. Local militia retaliated against his family, harassing his younger brother Jesse, hanging and leaving his stepfather for dead, and jailing his mother and sister. Jesse then joined Quantrill, too.[106] Younger and the James brothers fit the pattern of Missouri bushwhackers: they came from respectable families which had suffered at the hands of Unionists, driving them to become Confederate guerrillas.

Quantrill sought respectability by formalizing his ties to the Confederacy. His men fought with Confederate forces in the winter of 1862–1863, while Quantrill went to Richmond, where he sought a commission as colonel in the Confederate Partisan Rangers. He claimed to have received the commission, although historians are uncertain if he did. Confederate General Thomas C. Hindman wanted to recruit men under the provisions of the Partisan Ranger Act, which had been passed by the Confederate congress in April 1862. The act permitted the Confederacy to make use of irregular forces such as Quantrill's. Jefferson Davis disliked the idea of relying on guerrillas, but Hindman still used the act to legalize bands such as Quantrill's.[107] Guerrillas sought legitimacy by claiming and using official titles. Quantrill's lieutenant, Bill Anderson, signed himself "W. Anderson, Commanding Kansas First Guerrillas."[108]

Relying on Confederate guerrillas, however, provoked a harsh Union reaction. The Union frequently took arbitrary measures to deal with the guerrilla threat. Union General John M. Schofield insisted on an "extermination policy."[109] After a brief legal examination, a twenty-two-year-old man, who had been caught in Henry County, Missouri, was ordered to stand to be measured for his coffin. A half hour later, he rode in the coffin to the place of his execution. An observer was shocked to find that the executioners ignored the tradition of including a blank among the ammunition given to the firing squad, which ordinarily permitted none to know who had killed the prisoner. "The Missouri State Militia had but little *squeamishness* about shooting a *bushwhacker*." The blindfolded guerrilla was quickly dispatched.[110]

The task of protecting the border fell to Thomas Ewing, Jr., who commanded a section of the Kansas-Missouri region.[111] Over his wife's objections, Ewing had resigned his judicial post and joined the army. "During the war," he wrote his father, "the Chief Justice of Kansas should be an old man or a cripple."[112] By the summer of 1862, as commander of the District of the Border, he had inherited a "hornet's nest of a District."[113] Ewing used Kansas troops against Missouri guerrillas, declared martial law in Leavenworth, and jailed the guerrillas' womenfolk.[114] Although Ewing was accused of heartlessness for cracking down on civilians, a Union man in Missouri noted that after killing five bushwhackers "in their pockets was [found] a letter from a woman that we had been protect[ing]."[115] Union soldiers recognized that the women provided crucial support, including food and hiding places, to the Confederate bushwhackers. The women were held at Kansas City in an unsound, three-story brick building. An inspection on August 13, 1863 had revealed structural problems, but no effort was made to move the prisoners. Later that day, the building collapsed. Five women were killed, including a sister of bushwhacker Bill Anderson and a cousin of Coleman Younger. Another of Anderson's sisters was permanently crippled.[116]

Even before the prison collapse, Quantrill had decided to raid Lawrence. The town was a notorious abolitionist stronghold and repository of Missouri property, including runaway slaves. William Gregg reported Quantrill as having said, "We can get more revenge, and more money there than anywhere else in the state."[117] The raid on Lawrence brought together the border war's motives of retribution and black rights. Lawrence was noted both for its liberal attitudes on race and as the home of Kansans who had victimized Missourians. Riding into Lawrence, the raiders passed a shanty town where runaway slaves lived. Gregg recognized one woman as the slave of a Missouri acquaintance.[118] Jayhawking outrages prompted one bushwhacker to say of the Lawrence raid, "I am here for revenge—and I have got it."[119]

On the night of August 20, Quantrill's band crossed the border into Kansas, passing south of the army post at Aubry without detection. A nearby farmer estimated their force at over seven hundred men.[120] The raiders swept into town at daybreak as many in Lawrence were just rising. They captured Sallie Young, out for an early morning ride outside town. Ordered to identify the homes of certain townsfolk, she pleaded for the lives of the occupants until Quantrill's men let her go.[121] E. D. Thompson, a guest at the Eldridge House hotel, decided not to risk surrender when he saw a man shot down while kneeling in the street, begging for his life. Thompson escaped out the back of the hotel, evaded guerrilla fire as he crossed the street, and hid in the brush of a ravine. From his hiding place, he saw the guerrillas kill another fugitive, a woman crying over the body of her dead husband, and a black man carrying a wounded child, taking refuge from a burning building by dashing into the brush. Thompson spent over four hours in the ravine before finally emerging, scratched, barefoot, tired, but alive.[122]

Edward Fitch had just been getting his family dressed when the Missourians broke into the house. The Fitches had migrated from Hopkinton, Massachusetts, with NEEAC in 1854. Edward Fitch later served as an emigrant aid company conductor. As the Missourians quarreled about whether Edward's wife Sarah and the children could leave the house, one of them turned and emptied his revolver into Edward. The bushwhackers would not even let Sarah remove his body when they fired the house. Sarah was left to comfort herself that her husband had not suffered, as others had. The raiders left wounded men in buildings that had been set on fire. One who managed to crawl out of his burning business was thrown back in by the Missourians.[123]

Unlike Edward Fitch, H. D. Fisher, the chaplain of Lane's unit, survived the raid with his wife's help. Fisher hid in his cellar. When the Missourians fired the house, Fisher's wife begged to save the carpet, claiming it was a last gift from her father. While one of the raiders held the baby, she dragged the carpet over the trap door to the cellar, permitting her husband to emerge unseen. With her husband rolled up in the carpet, she was then able to smuggle him out to the woodpile where he remained until the danger passed.[124]

For all the chaotic violence of that morning, victims recalled a method to the bushwhackers' attack. It quickly became apparent that women would be spared, a fact the women of Lawrence used, albeit often unsuccessfully, to try to protect their men and homes. Many victims, such as Sarah Fitch, recalled that the bushwhackers had a list of names. She thought they knew of her husband's involvement in a local military company.[125] The use of Sallie Young as a guide also indicated the raiders had decided their victims in advance. Fifteen-year-old William Speer escaped death by giving a false name. Raiders checked a list on which the Speer name doubtless figured, as William's father John Speer was a newspaper editor and Lane ally. William's older brothers, John Jr. and Robert, did not survive the raid. Robert's body was never found, but his pocketbook was on the body of Larkin Skaggs, the only bushwhacker to die in the raid, killed at the end of the day, ironically, by young William Speer and a Delaware Indian, White Turkey.[126] Although Lane successfully escaped the raiders by fleeing into a cornfield, Quantrill specifically asked for Lane's house, showing the raiders had well-defined political targets.[127]

Blacks also were targets of the violence. Although women and children were largely spared, Quantrill's men burned one house though told there was a black baby in it. Numerous observers saw blacks being pursued by the raiders. One Lawrence man was accused of being a "nigger thief" when the raiders found him hiding in a cellar with several blacks. After the raid, Lawrence blacks dragged Skaggs's body through the streets and burned it.[128]

Symbols of the Union also earned the bushwhackers' vengeance. Sarah Fitch thought the raiders were enraged by the U.S. flag her children had attached to the woodshed.[129] The bushwhackers made the army encampment one of their first targets. Entering town, they attacked southern Massachusetts Street, where black and white recruits for the army were camped. As one bushwhacker remembered, the new troops "were just beginning to get up when we struck them. We made short work of them but some of them escaped by swimming in the river."

Surprise and massacre at Lawrence, August 20, 1863, from John W. Barber and Henry Howe, The Loyal West in the Times of the Rebellion *(Cincinnati, 1865)*

Another bushwhacker recalled that the soldiers' camp was leveled in three minutes. From an upstairs window, William L. Bullene saw nine men shot down.[130]

"We left the town in ashes at ten o'clock," recalled one of Quantrill's men. They left just in time. Four miles from the town, the raiders found that "the whole prairie was black with soldiers." In another couple miles, the raiders began to take fire. They scattered into smaller bands to evade pursuit.[131] The bushwhackers lost more men in the retreat, an estimated one hundred, than in Lawrence. Once in Missouri, the guerrillas abandoned their worn-out horses and took to the timber. Their pursuers were equally exhausted. In three days, a Union company rode almost 150 miles and "gained not one thing."[132]

In Lawrence, women and children searched for their menfolk. As many as two hundred men and boys were dead. Some of the victims were burned so badly they were mistaken for blacks. Pieces of flesh came off when the corpses were handled.[133] An eyewitness who arrived in town at nightfall saw "Massachusetts-street one mass of smouldering ruins and crumbling walls, the light from which cast a sickening glare upon the little knots of excited men and distracted women, gazing upon the ruins of their once happy homes and prosperous business."[134] After the raid, a request for doctors was one of the first messages to reach Leavenworth from Lawrence. Aid poured into Lawrence and refugees poured out. So many Lawrence residents went east that the town's population fell by half.[135]

In the days after the raid, all parts of Kansas panicked. A Topeka family slept in their clothes, and the children were given bags of valuables to rescue if the house were set afire.[136] Residents of Manhattan reacted to the "Horrid particulars from Lawrence. . . . People arming for defence."[137] Rumors about Quantrill continued into 1864. A black man near Baldwin City carried a loaded six-shooter because he feared bushwhackers and expected to receive no mercy at their hands.[138] A year after Quantrill's raid, a Kansas man noted, "Found Lawrence under arms watching for an attack from Quantrell. Rather a big scare!!"[139] Military and civilian authorities in Lawrence planned extensive fortifications to protect the town.[140] Although such an attack never recurred, Kansans would not soon recover from the gruesome events of Quantrill's raid.

Quantrill's raid, of course, threatened to renew the cycle of violence of the border war and expand the antislavery war. Feeling was "intense" after "this fearful, fiendish raid," Governor Thomas Carney noted, and Kansans blamed Missourians for their complicity with the raiders.[141] Jim Lane, emerging from the cornfield into which he had fled, proposed to lead Kansans on a military expedition.[142] Lane's critics feared that such an expedition would cause the "indiscriminate murder of all border Missourians."[143] But at the beginning of September, Schofield agreed to discuss with Lane a possible expedition into Missouri. That night, Lane spoke at Leavenworth, telling the audience that military commanders had approved a raid to lay waste the border counties. A cynical Governor Carney told Schofield that Lane probably had no intention of such a raid, but merely wanted credit for willingness to respond forcibly to Quantrill. Blame for any failure would be borne by the military, which would either conduct the raid itself or prevent it from being carried out. Despite advice to give Lane enough rope to hang himself, Schofield issued a proclamation on September 4 forbidding Lane's raid.[144]

Despite Schofield's order, an estimated 3,500 men met at Paola four days later. Lane restrained them from invading Missouri, but used the opportunity to attack the military's caution. Lane advocated an offensive policy that would bring the war home to the slaveowner and give blacks opportunities to escape. Thwarted from attacking Missouri, Kansans still sought a scapegoat. Like Lane, many Kansans called for Schofield's removal.[145] But as commander of the District of the Border, Thomas Ewing, Jr., bore the brunt of responsibility for the disaster. Publicly, Lane defended Ewing, but in private, Lane threatened to push for Ewing's removal unless he retaliated against Missourians.[146]

On August 25, Ewing issued Order No. 11, evicting all persons from selected counties in Missouri, those being Jackson, Cass, Bates, and the northern half of Vernon. The order made refugees of an estimated twenty thousand people.[147] Ewing reacted to the urgency of the moment and the need to prevent reprisals against border Missourians. With "the horrors of the massacre distressing me," Ewing reflected that he did not trust his own judgment.[148] But Schofield had considered removing civilian supporters of the guerrillas from the border counties, and he had drafted an order to that effect even before Quantrill's raid. Some Union officers had been burning out the bushwhackers' families months before Ewing's order.[149] In an unsuccessful effort to restore order, the Union had already imposed loyalty oaths, confiscated property, assessed fines on the disloyal, implemented passport and trade permit regulations, suppressed newspapers, and assassinated suspected guerrillas. Banishment was perhaps the most desperate part of this effort to end the guerrilla fighting, and it stripped away the remaining civilian civil liberties. Order No. 11 was the answer to a number of different problems: depopulating the border counties helped the military effort to end bushwhacking; harsh retribution after Quantrill's raid quieted the panic in Kansas and prevented retaliation against Missouri.[150]

The order caused real hardship to civilians. A Missouri woman remembered, "The road from Independence to Lexington was crowded with women and children, women walking with their babies in their

Order No. 11, *painting by George Caleb Bingham. (Used by permission, State Historical Society of Missouri, Columbia)*

arms, packs on their backs, and four or five children following after them—some crying for bread, some crying to be taken back to their homes."[151] The Missouri painter George Caleb Bingham immortalized the order in a painting finished after the war. Bingham depicted Union soldiers evacuating a family at bayonet point. While the gray-headed patriarch defies Union soldiers over the body of his son, his daughter begs for mercy on her knees, and a faithful slave cradles her swooning mistress. Bingham's artistry clung to white southern faith that the war, although disrupting their lives, had not disrupted southern race relations. Bingham's comforting slave woman is far removed from the many Missouri slaves who used the war to resist, not reinforce, their subordination.[152] Despite Bingham's sentimentalized and misleading imagery, Order No. 11 was the most drastic action against civilians until Sherman's march through Georgia. Unlike Georgia, however, Missouri was still in the Union, and the evacuated included Union families as well as Confederate sympathizers. Controversy over Order No. 11

prompted the Lincoln administration to suspend it in November. Even before then, under pressure not to victimize Unionists along with Confederates, Schofield had backed away from a total destruction of the countryside. Some evicted families returned by the spring.[153]

Order No. 11 left the guerrillas in the field. In early October, Quantrill attacked a Union camp at Baxter Springs. A black unit that Confederate sympathizers found offensive was stationed there. Although the camp was lightly defended, its commander, Lieutenant James B. Pond, managed to fight his way to a howitzer and open fire on the guerrillas who had penetrated the fortifications, driving them back. Pond gave credit to the black troops, saying, "The darkies fought like devils." Pulling back from the camp, Quantrill's party discovered that General Blunt, with an escort of about a hundred men, was nearby. Blunt, at first confused as Pond's men had been by the stolen federal uniforms Quantrill's men wore, soon realized they were forming to attack. Blunt ordered his escort to form a battle line, but the men broke and ran. Blunt rallied fifteen men, drove off the attack, but lost his baggage, including his sword and official papers. Seventy soldiers and ten civilians were killed. Quantrill reported nineteen of his men dead. An officer in Blunt's escort thought only Quantrill's attack on Lawrence surpassed the horror of Baxter Springs.[154]

After successfully humiliating Blunt, Quantrill retreated into Confederate-held territory. In the winter of 1864, Quantrill left for Kentucky, having lost control of the band to Bloody Bill Anderson and Archie Clements. In a skirmish in May 1865, federal forces mortally wounded Quantrill. He died at age 27. Raids such as Quantrill's had little military impact beyond pinning down Union troops that might have been used in other theaters of the war, but they fed off of the long accumulated animosities along the border, animosities created not only by the continual cycle of revenge and violence but also by the political quarrels over Union and secession, black rights and white supremacy.[155]

Although still active in western Missouri, by the spring of 1864, bushwhackers were not the only threat. Sterling Price, a former Missouri governor who now commanded Confederate troops, hoped to reclaim his native state. Confederates in Missouri begged Price to liberate the state from "outrages unparalleled in this, and unprecedented in any other, war," such as the use of black troops.[156] Crossing into Missouri in mid-September, Price appealed to Missourians to rise against the Union, throw off their "shackles," and join his army.[157] Although Price was a "respectable mediocrity" as a military leader, Kansans had a healthy fear of his army of twelve thousand men. Unsure of Price's intended target, General William S. Rosecrans ordered Ewing to stall the Confederates while Union forces organized.[158]

Commanding a thousand men, Ewing took up a position at Pilot Knob, in the path of Price's invasion force. The Confederates surrounded Ewing's small post, cutting off the railroad to the rear. When Ewing refused to surrender, Price miscalculated and ordered a frontal assault without artillery support. It began at 2 P.M. on September 27 and lasted twenty minutes. Price lost a thousand men yet was unable to take the little fort. During the night, Ewing's small force escaped through Confederate lines to avoid the artillery attack expected the next day.[159]

While Price battered his force against Pilot Knob, Bloody Bill Anderson entered Centralia, Missouri, at midmorning on September 27, 1864. Accompanied by thirty to eighty-five guerrillas, Anderson stopped the stage and then the train, robbed the passengers, and executed two dozen unarmed Union soldiers who were on leave.[160]

Union troops caught up with the guerrillas a few miles from town. Believing that the guerrilla force was small, the Union officer, Major A. V. E. Johnson, was shocked to find that Anderson had been reinforced and now had about two hundred men. Johnson's men were untried in battle but had trained as infantry. He ordered them to dismount. Watching the soldiers form their line, one of the guerrillas said, "The fools are going to fight us on foot. God help 'em." When the bushwhackers charged, the soldiers' volley went high, hitting only three guerrillas. As some soldiers desperately attempted to reload, others threw down their guns and surrendered. The guerrillas shot them down. Dead were 114 soldiers and two officers, one of whom was Johnson. The bodies were stripped and some were mutilated by scalping and cutting off ears, noses, and genitals.[161] Anderson was killed a month later when his force was attacked by Missouri militia. His dead body was displayed and photographed.[162]

Price moved on to Jefferson City, where he bypassed the Union defenses, and then headed west to the Kansas border. Military authorities requested help from the Kansas militia, but Governor Carney stalled, fearing the call for militia was a "political scheme" of Lane's. Militia in the field would miss the upcoming election in which, if Carney's slate defeated Lane's, Carney would gain Lane's senate seat. Not until October 9, when Price neared Leavenworth, did Carney issue the call for the militia, which had been requested almost three weeks earlier. Still Price did not appear. Much to the frustration of regular army officers, some militia regiments deserted or refused to cross into Missouri. Carney was ready to send the militia home. Then Price attacked Samuel R. Curtis's force at the Big Blue at midday October 22.[163]

S. J. Reader of the Kansas Second State Militia had only a gun he considered of poor quality and thirteen cartridges that day. The Kansans broke and ran. Reader ran too, but not fast enough, and was captured. When his captors asked if he had ever been in a fight before, Reader did not mention his participation in the 1856 battle of Hickory Point. He suspected being a Kansas free-state Yankee would be worse than just being a Yankee. When the Southerners asked what he was fighting for, Reader said, "Union." *"Nigger equality,"* his captors translated. Reader escaped after the Battle of Westport, but the interchange revealed that grudges from the earlier border war remained as well as that Confederates recognized the radical meaning that the war had for race relations. Despite Reader's flight, General Blunt credited the militia with having "behaved splendidly" in the battle.[164]

Curtis fell back to Westport, where the fighting continued the next day. While Confederate forces attacked, Union reinforcements closed in from the rear. Nearly surrounded, the Confederate army fled. The next day, the Union army pursued the retreating Price to Mine Creek, where his baggage train became stuck in the ford. The Union army attacked, capturing five hundred men. The pursuit continued until Price's demoralized army was driven back into Arkansas by November.[165]

Price's raid was the last Confederate military effort to take Missouri, but it ended in failure. Although Price believed he had accomplished the destruction of much militarily useful property—railroads, bridges, and depots—he lost about two-thirds of his force. Many of those left were too exhausted and dispirited to fight. Despite tying up some nine thousand Union troops, the raid did not significantly impede the Union war effort. Moreover, Price failed to accomplish any of his objectives: he did not take St. Louis; he did not take Jefferson City or install the Confederate state government; he did not damage the Union posts in Kansas; and, although thousands of men rallied to his army, he did not provoke the anticipated popular uprising in Missouri for the Confederacy.[166] Price failed to liberate Missouri from the Union.

Price's retreat caused Charles Robinson to gloat, "*Kansas is saved,*"[167] while Carney's mishandling of the raid lost him the election. Lane's slate won despite widespread charges of corruption. Carney's reluctance to believe in Price's threat had contributed to that result. A newspaper editor remarked that if Kansans "cannot have an honest man in the Senate they prefer that the rascal who represents them, should be a man of brains."[168] Lane, who had once boasted he would as soon buy a slave as a mule, had become a foremost champion of that black equality Missourians feared. During the Civil War, he had pioneered in the recruitment of black troops and advocated greater racial equality. Other Kansas politicians bitterly resented Lane's close ties to the president. In part, the alliance between the Kansas senator and the president stemmed from their mutual recognition that the war had fundamentally altered race relations. Some of Lane's supporters felt that Lincoln was moving too slowly on racial equality, but Lane reassured them that the president would endorse more radical positions.[169]

Kansans' war for white liberty had paved the way for this reordering of social relations. When the Missouri constitutional convention passed an emancipation provision in January 1865, both houses of the Missouri legislature convened in special session to commemorate the event. A motion was made "and enthusiastically carried" that one of the members sing "John Brown." The audience "joined in the swelling chorus, and thus was celebrated, in the Hall of the States Capitol, the new-born story of 'Free Missouri.'"[170] Some months later, Missouri freedmen also sang "John Brown" to lament the death of President Lincoln.[171] A Kansas abolitionist had thus become the symbol of emancipation. Just as proslavery Missourians had always feared, free Kansas created a free Missouri and a free nation.

The end of the Civil War allowed the joyous reunion of families. A Kansas girl recalled, "The war closed and Father with some of the others returned home. I well remember when the news was brought to Mother, how she rejoiced, and we children ran around trying to work at something to let out some of our excess of joy, for Father was to be home that night, and so he came back to Mother and his children."[1] But some families would never be reunited. With 8,498 casualties, Kansas suffered a higher mortality rate than any other Union state.[2]

Communities numbered among the casualties, for the war had pitted neighbor against neighbor. A Missouri man serving in a Kansas army company worried about returning home. A friend had warned that "as a general thing the old neighborhood seems friendly and invited each other to come back and live together again but there was a few exceptions and *you* was mentioned as one that could never live in Mo again because there was men there that would kill you for old grudges."[3] In Waverly, Kansas, a southern settler left during the war and remained away until local passions cooled. On his return, he found that a neighbor, who cursed the "damned rebels," had openly stolen firewood left for his wife. Thinking it unlikely that the situation would improve, the husband and wife sold their goods and left.[4] A Missourian recalled the fate of the Maddox family of Jackson County. Larkin Maddox, the patriarch, owned over two thousand acres and about sixty slaves. During 1855 and 1856, he and his four sons had been "violent 'pro-slavery' men" in Kansas. When the national civil war broke out, jayhawkers burned the plantation and liberated the slaves. Two sons became bushwhackers, including George, who joined Quantrill's band. Not until the early 1870s, did George return to live quietly on the family farm. "He was attending strictly to his own business, and never alluded to the incidents of his past life, and never spoke of the war."[5]

Most guerrillas surrendered to Union authorities in the spring of 1865. Treated as prisoners of war, they were eventually released. Many left the border and many others were able to return to useful lives. Some of the more notorious, however, never successfully made the transition to civilian life. Archie Clements, Bloody Bill Anderson's scalping lieutenant, was killed in a shoot-out with Missouri militiamen who tried to arrest him in 1866. Coleman Younger and Frank and Jesse James, formally of Quantrill's band, embarked on careers as criminals.[6]

Jim Lane did not long survive the war. The Civil War had brought him much success: influence with President Lincoln, pioneering work in recruiting black regiments, and the successful eclipse of his old rival, Charles Robinson. Then Lane abruptly lost his political finesse. In the summer of 1866, he was suddenly despondent. Kansans criticized his failure to oppose President Andrew Johnson's veto of the Civil Rights Bill. He was under investigation for profiting from war contracts and suffering from illness. On July 1, 1866, he committed suicide.[7]

Charles Robinson survived Lane by almost thirty years. He worked with the Greenback and Populist parties, and advocated movements for black and women's rights. He became involved with education, supporting plans for a state university and serving as director of the Haskell Institute for Indians. No longer at the center of Kansas politics, Robinson tried to shape the memory of the Kansas Civil War both through publication of his memoirs and as director of the state historical society.[8]

Robinson was not the only one who sought to shape the meaning of the long sectional conflict on the border. At the end of the century, the surviving members of Quantrill's band began holding reunions. Their rhetoric emphasized Union cruelties, especially Order No. 11, which had driven these good boys to violent retaliation. Kansans held their own reunions, both to commemorate Quantrill's raid and to remember the territorial period.[9]

And what did they remember?

When J. P. Usher, the mayor of Lawrence, spoke at an old settlers' meeting in 1879 on the legacy of the Kansas Civil War, he drew this lesson: "We simply claim to be free men, made so through noble sacrifice of these pioneers gathered here today; and you see in us what free men, such free men, are. . . . That is the condition which we have reached under the Kansas-Nebraska Act."[10] Usher took his hearers back to first principles: popular sovereignty and its promise of expanded political rights for white men.

So did Charles Robinson in his memoirs of territorial Kansans' "resistance" to government oppression.[11] Although Robinson now understated the violence inherent in free-state "resistance," he saw clearly why the free-state movement had won. Kansas had been made a free state by emphasizing the liberties of white men, by avoiding open defiance of a hostile national government, and by insisting that that government honor its avowed principles. Robinson recognized that the success of the movement depended on its promise of political liberty for whites, liberty which would then permit them to reject black slavery.

Unlike Usher and Robinson, Kansas senator Edmund G. Ross recognized that the Kansas conflict had broadened into a wider one: "The outcome and the verdict of the Kansas struggle, [was] signed and sealed at Appomattox a few years later."[12] In giving meaning to Bleeding Kansas, Ross thus gave primacy to the antislavery struggle: he demonstrated how the struggle for white liberty had bred a conflict that brought greater liberty to blacks.

C. K. Holliday, speaking at a Lawrence pioneer reunion, best joined the themes of white and black liberty. With forgivable hyperbole he predicted,

The historian will assign to Kansas, and to the brave sons and daughters of her early territorial days, the honor of having turned the current of human affairs and human government into the channel of universal liberty; that the defeat of slavery—the slave power—of the slave spirit—upon the plains of Kansas was the defeat of the same power and the same spirit in our own and all other nations; and that the triumph of freedom upon the plains of Kansas was the triumph of freedom throughout the circuit of the globe.[13]

Holliday spoke in 1879, the year of the Exodusters, as black migrants to Kansas were called. Missouri slaves had long viewed Kansas as the land of freedom. After the Civil War, a white Missouri woman marveled at the determination of Missouri blacks to move to Kansas: "Nothing would do but to Kansas they must go."[14] The black population of Kansas soared from 627 in 1860 to 17,108 in 1870. The migrants of the 1860s had been poor but had benefited from labor shortages created by the war and the continued availability of land. Although H. C. Bruce remembered friction between Irish workers and contrabands competing for employment, Bruce became a businessman in Leavenworth, ran for state office, and achieved the position of doorkeeper of the state senate before receiving federal patronage jobs secured by his brother, a Mississippi U.S. senator.[15] During the war, Kansas blacks had petitioned for the vote. The legislature provided for a referendum on suffrage for blacks and women in 1867. After an ugly campaign in which Republicans refused to endorse woman suffrage, insisting that the women must defer to black men, and woman suffrage leaders criticized blacks in often racist language, both measures were defeated, and woman suffrage more decisively than black. The antagonism of woman suffrage and black suffrage proponents helps explain the failure of black suffrage to triumph in Kansas. Only two northern states gave blacks the vote before the Fifteenth Amendment made black suffrage universal in 1870. But black suffrage received almost thirty-five percent of the vote, despite the nastiness of the campaign, and was endorsed by the Kansas Republican party.[16]

Nonetheless the memory of Kansas as sanctified to black liberty persisted among southern blacks. The Exoduster migration arose in part from that memory and called on white Kansans to acknowledge that their revolution for white liberty had come to have special meaning for blacks.

At the end of Reconstruction, when southern blacks despaired of a better life in the South, many of them now embarked for new homes in Kansas, bringing the black population to 43,107 in 1880. Attracted not only by the hope of fertile land, which also drew white settlers, blacks remembered Kansas as the land where men such as John Brown had fought for freedom. "I am anxious to reach your state," G. R. M. Newman wrote Kansas governor John P. St. John from Louisiana in 1879, "not because of the great race now made for it but because of the sacredness of her soil washed by the blood of humanitarians for the cause of freedom."[17] An elderly black woman, stepping off a steamboat in Kansas in 1880, exclaimed, "Bress God, I'se reached de land of freedom at las."[18] Some accused Republicans of encouraging blacks to "go west, young black man where John Brown's soul is doing perpetual guard duty."[19] Some recognized the Exoduster movement as being a Kansas tradition. The *New York Tribune* pointed out that "emigration societies had made Kansas what it was."[20] John Brown, Jr., even called for a new NEEAC to aid the Exodusters. St. John, a Republican and Union veteran, initially supported the Exodusters, but white Kansans' fears of a flood of impoverished blacks tempered his enthusiasm and cost him reelection.[21]

Kansas did not always fulfill the expectations of black migrants. Kansans welcomed the Exodusters but, as the migration swelled, quickly lost their enthusiasm. They feared that the state could not absorb so many desperately poor people. Kansas officials tried to move the migrants on to Colorado or Nebraska. A St. Louis newspaper sarcastically pointed out that by rejecting black migrants, Kansans were not living up to the principles of Bleeding Kansas. Economic prosperity, as well as full political and civil rights, eluded many black migrants. A black schoolteacher who expected social equality in Kansas was disappointed to find race prejudice existed there. Many black farmers, accustomed to cotton agriculture, could not adapt to the crops and tools demanded by the arid West. Many were able to get farms of only a few acres, woefully insufficient to sustain themselves on the Great Plains. They failed, as did many white farmers on the Plains, and returned east.[22] Still, as Nell Irvin Painter writes, "Kansas was no Canaan, but it was a far cry from Mississippi and Louisiana."[23] A well-to-do Louisiana black agreed: "They do not kill Negroes here for voting."[24]

In January 1880, the cover of *Harper's Weekly* showed an Exoduster arriving at a depot whose sign proclaimed it "(Free Soil) Kansas." An Irishman challenged the black's right "to be afther laving your native place an' coming here?" But the Irishman's very presence endorsed the freedom of African Americans to migrate. More than that, however, the illustration recognized Kansas's special place as a symbol of freedom. Why should Kansas be labeled "free soil" when, by 1880, all the United States was such? Was not the black migrant's presumed southern "native place" not also free?

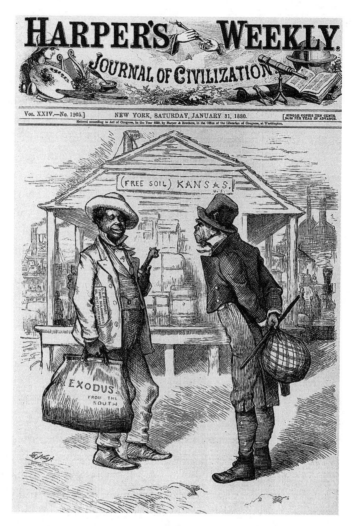

Exoduster meets Irishman in Kansas, from Harper's
Weekly, *January 31, 1880. (Kansas State Historical
Society, Topeka)*

By the 1880s, many Americans had abandoned the "emancipation-ist legacy" of the Civil War in favor of honoring the soldiers' bravery. Such an emphasis hastened reconciliation between white Unionists and Confederates but denied the importance of the black experience to the war's meaning.[25] The tension between white and black rights had been present all during the Kansas Civil War. In the 1850s, free-state Kansans had struggled to make Kansas free for white settlers to exercise the political rights popular sovereignty promised. In so doing, Kansas settlers increasingly asserted the right of blacks to their liberty. White Kansans, Exodusters, and the *Harper's Weekly* illustrator recognized that Kansas had a unique claim to be called "free." The Kansas Civil War had contributed to a more universal, though still imperfect, liberty for whites and blacks.

NOTES

INTRODUCTION

1. *(Lawrence) Herald of Freedom,* July 7, 1855.
2. Alice Nichols, *Bleeding Kansas* (New York, 1954), which emphasized the quarrel over slavery, has long been the standard account of events in Kansas. James A. Rawley, *Race and Politics: "Bleeding Kansas" and the Coming of the Civil War* (Lincoln, Nebr., 1969), made race the central issue in the debates over Kansas, arguing that blacks were not wanted in territorial Kansas whether they were slave or free. Paul Wallace Gates insisted that quarrels over land, rather than slavery or race, were central to the problems in Kansas in his *Fifty Million Acres: Conflicts over Kansas Land Policy, 1854–1900* (Ithaca, N.Y., 1954). More recently, Gunja SenGupta has sought to balance the economic preoccupations of Kansans with their political and moral concerns over slavery in *For God and Mammon: Evangelicals and Entrepreneurs, Masters and Slaves in Territorial Kansas, 1854–1860* (Athens, Ga., 1996). For an overview of Bleeding Kansas historiography, see Gunja SenGupta, "Bleeding Kansas," *Kansas History* 24 (winter 2001–2002): 318–41.

   The political difficulties of the Democratic party in Kansas have been the focus of Kenneth M. Stampp, *America in 1857: A Nation on the Brink* (New York, 1990), and David M. Potter, *The Impending Crisis, 1848–1861* (New York, 1976). Much of the work tracing the disintegration of the Union has emphasized the breakdown in the second party system and the rise of the third. Roy Nichols, *The Disruption of American Democracy* (New York, 1948); Michael F. Holt, *The Political Crisis of the 1850s* (New York, 1978); and William E. Gienapp, *The Origins of the Republican Party, 1852–1856* (New York, 1987) examine the political realignments of that period.

   Eric Foner, *Free Labor, Free Soil, Free Men: The Ideology of the Republican Party before the Civil War* (New York, 1970), credited northern belief in the superiority of a free labor economy and society with stimulating northern opposition to slavery's extension into the territories. Michael A. Morrison takes seriously the political language of the antebellum period and its emphasis on liberty in his *Slavery and the American West: The Eclipse of Manifest Destiny and the Coming of the Civil War* (Chapel Hill, N.C., 1997).
3. David Thomas Konig, "Introduction," in *Devising Liberty: Preserving and Creating Freedom in the New American Republic,* ed. by David Thomas Konig (Stanford, Calif., 1995), 1–9, esp. 1–2.

   For the ideology of republicanism, see Bernard Bailyn, *The Ideological Origins of the American Revolution* (Cambridge, Mass., 1967); Gordon S. Wood, *The Creation of the American Republic, 1776–1787*

(Chapel Hill, N.C., 1969); J. G. A. Pocock, *Virtue, Commerce, and History: Essays in Political Thought and History, Chiefly in the Eighteenth Century* (Cambridge, Eng., 1985); Drew R. McCoy, *The Elusive Republic: Political Economy in Jeffersonian America* (Chapel Hill, N.C., 1980), 67–69; and Joyce Appleby, *Liberalism and Republicanism in the Historical Imagination* (Cambridge, Mass., 1992).

On freedom, see Eric Foner, *The Story of American Freedom* (New York, 1998), xiii–xv; David M. Potter, *Freedom and Its Limitations in American Life,* ed. by Don E. Fehrenbacher (Stanford, Calif., 1976), 41; Robert H. Wiebe, *Self-Rule: A Cultural History of American Democracy* (Chicago, 1995); Michael Kammen, *Spheres of Liberty: Changing Perceptions of Liberty in American Culture* (Madison, Wisc., 1986), 5–9; and Major L. Wilson, *Space, Time, and Freedom: The Quest for Nationality and the Irrepressible Conflict, 1815–1861* (Westport, Conn., 1974), vii–viii, 4–21.

4. Wilson, *Space, Time, and Freedom,* 4–21; Stephen A. Douglas, "The Dividing Line between Federal and Local Authority: Popular Sovereignty in the Territories," *Harper's Magazine,* Sept. 1859, 519–37; Kammen, *Spheres of Liberty,* 80–81, 96–101; James Brewer Stewart, *Holy Warriors: The Abolitionists and American Slavery* (New York, 1997), 74, 104; and James Oakes, *Slavery and Freedom: An Interpretation of the Old South* (New York, 1990), 173.

5. Bruce Levine, *Half Slave and Half Free: The Roots of Civil War* (New York, 1992), 143; Larry E. Tise, *Proslavery: A History of the Defense of Slavery in America, 1701–1840* (Athens, Ga., 1987), 110–11, 24–40, 51–52, 347–62; Stewart, *Holy Warriors,* 6–7; Brian Holden Reid, *The Origins of the American Civil War* (London, 1996), 41; Bertram Wyatt-Brown, *The Shaping of Southern Culture: Honor, Grace, and War, 1760s–1890s* (Chapel Hill, N.C., 2001), 199–200, 209, 217, 135–53; William J. Cooper, Jr., *Liberty and Slavery: Southern Politics to 1860* (New York, 1983), vi; Kammen, *Spheres of Liberty,* 51; Jan Lewis, "The Problem of Slavery in Southern Political Discourse," in *Devising Liberty: Preserving and Creating Freedom in the New American Republic,* ed. by David Thomas Konig (Stanford, Calif., 1995), 265–97; Oakes, *Slavery and Freedom,* 72–73, 132; James Oakes, *The Ruling Race: A History of American Slaveholders* (New York, 1982), 30–31, 141; and David F. Ericson, *The Debate over Slavery: Antislavery and Proslavery Liberalism in Antebellum America* (New York, 2000), 19–25.

6. Harry V. Jaffa, *Equality and Liberty: Theory and Practice in American Politics* (New York, 1965), 47; John Hope Franklin, "The North, the South, and the American Revolution," *Journal of American History* 62 (June 1975): 5–23; Tise, *Proslavery,* 116; and Drew Gilpin Faust, *The Creation of Confederate Nationalism: Ideology and Identity in the Civil War South* (Baton Rouge, 1988), 14.

7. David R. Roediger, *The Wages of Whiteness: Race and the Making of the American Working Class* (London, 1991), 12–13; Noel Ignatiev, *How the Irish Became White* (New York, 1995), 183; and George M. Frederickson, *The Black Image in the White Mind: The Debate on Afro-American Character and Destiny, 1817–1914* (New York, 1971), 94–96. See Peter Kolchin, "Whiteness Studies: The New History of Race in America," *Journal of American History* 89 (June 2002): 154–73 for a penetrating analysis of the current state of whiteness studies.

8. E. J. Hobsbawm, *Nations and Nationalism since 1780: Programme, Myth, Reality,* 2d ed. (Cambridge, Eng., 1990), 9–13, 78; David Waldstreicher, *In the Midst of Perpetual Fetes: The Making of American Nationalism, 1776–1820* (Chapel Hill, N.C., 1997), 3, 8; David Lowenthal, *The Past Is a Foreign Country* (Cambridge, Eng., 1985), 105–24; and Bert James Loewenberg, *American History in American Thought: Christopher Columbus to Henry Adams* (New York, 1972), 15, 50–56. George B. Forgie argues that the Revolutionary legacy was so important to the Civil War generation that they pushed the nation into conflict in order to give themselves the role of defenders of that legacy. George B. Forgie, *Patricide in the House Divided: A Psychological Interpretation of Lincoln and His Age* (New York, 1979), 280–84.

9. Benedict Anderson, *Imagined Communities: Reflections on the Origin and Spread of Nationalism* (London, 1991), 6–7.

10. Morrison, *Slavery and the American West,* 159. On the Slave Power conspiracy, see Leonard L. Richards, *The Slave Power: The Free North and Southern Domination, 1780–1860* (Baton Rouge, 2000) and David Brion Davis, *The Slave Power Conspiracy and the Paranoid Style* (Baton Rouge, 1969), 18, 40.

11. Daniel J. McInerney, *The Fortunate Heirs of Freedom: Abolition and Republican Thought* (Lincoln, Nebr., 1994), 1–2, 128; Dwight Lowell Dumond, *Antislavery: The Crusade for Freedom in America* (Ann Arbor, 1961), 175; Lewis Perry, *Radical Abolitionism: Anarchy and the Government of God in Antislavery Thought* (Ithaca, N.Y., 1973), 188; Louis Filler, *The Crusade against Slavery, 1830–1860* (New York, 1960), 93; Stewart, *Holy Warriors,* 12–13; Aileen S. Kraditor, *Means and Ends in American Abolitionism: Garrison and His Critics on Strategy and Tactics, 1834–1850* (New York, 1969), 102–3; Stanley Harrold, *American Abolitionists* (Harlow, Eng., 2001), 25; and Edward Magdol, *The Antislavery Rank and File: A Social Profile of the Abolitionists' Constituency* (Westport, Conn., 1986), 137–79.

12. John Patrick Diggins, *The Lost Soul of American Politics: Virtue, Self-Interest, and the Foundations of Liberalism* (New York, 1984), 319–20; and James L. Huston, "Democracy by Scripture versus Democracy by Process: A Reflection on Stephen A. Douglas and Popular Sovereignty," *Civil War History* 43 (Sept. 1997): 189–200.

1. THE TRIUMPH OF SQUATTER SOVEREIGNTY

1. [Carl Schurz], *The Reminiscences of Carl Schurz*, vol. 2 (New York, 1907), 30–31.
2. Robert W. Johannsen, *Stephen A. Douglas* (New York, 1973), vii.
3. Stephen A. Douglas to J. H. Crane, D. M. Johnson, and L. J. Eastin, Dec. 17, 1853, in Robert W. Johannsen, ed., *The Letters of Stephen A. Douglas* (Urbana, Ill., 1961), 268–71, esp. 270.
4. *New York Times*, March 4, 1854; James C. Malin, *The Nebraska Question, 1852–1854* (Lawrence, Kans., 1953), 1–23; Johannsen, *Stephen A. Douglas*, 390–400; Allan Nevins, *Ordeal of the Union*, vol. 2 (New York, 1947), 100–109; Don E. Fehrenbacher, *The Dred Scott Case: Its Significance in American Law and Politics* (New York, 1978), 179–81. Douglas also advocated constructing a Pacific railroad. Such a transcontinental railroad would not only benefit his constituents, and possibly his own Chicago real estate interests, but would also promote westward development. Frank Heywood Hodder, "The Railroad Background of the Kansas-Nebraska Act," *Mississippi Valley Historical Review* 12 (June 1925): 3–22.
5. [A. T. Andreas], *History of the State of Kansas* (Chicago, 1883), 82–83; William E. Connelley, *History of Kansas State and People,* vol. 1 (Chicago, 1928), 276–88; William Elsey Connelley, *James Henry Lane: The 'Grim Chieftain' of Kansas* (Topeka, 1899), 13–15; Harry V. Jaffa, *Crisis of the House Divided: An Interpretation of the Lincoln-Douglas Debates* (Seattle, 1973), 149–51; Morton M. Rosenberg, "The Kansas-Nebraska Act in Iowa: A Case Study," *Annals of Iowa* 26 (1964): 436–57; and Robert R. Russel, "The Issues in the Congressional Struggle over the Kansas-Nebraska Bill, 1854," *Journal of Southern History* 29 (May 1963): 187–210.
6. Perry McCandless, *A History of Missouri,* vol. 2, *1820–1860* (Columbia, Mo., 1972), 227–88.
7. John S. Brickey to Little Toby, July 4, 1852, John S. Brickey Papers, Missouri Historical Society, St. Louis.
8. James A. Rawley, *Race and Politics: "Bleeding Kansas" and the Coming of the Civil War* (Lincoln, Nebr., 1969), 28; and Gerald W. Wolff, "Party and Section: The Senate and the Kansas-Nebraska Bill," *Civil War History* 18 (Dec. 1972): 293–311.
9. *(St. Louis) Missouri Democrat,* Jan. 11, 1854.
10. C. F. Jackson to [D. R. Atchison], Jan. 18, 1854, David Rice Atchison Papers, Western Historical Manuscript Collection, Columbia, Mo.
11. Rawley, *Race and Politics,* 28; and William E. Parrish, *David Rice Atchison of Missouri: Border Politician* (Columbia, Mo., 1961).
12. Michael A. Morrison, *Slavery and the American West: The Eclipse of Manifest Destiny and the Coming of the Civil War* (Chapel Hill, N.C., 1997); Anders Stephanson, *Manifest Destiny: American Expansion and the Empire of Right* (New York, 1995), 28–65; Holman Hamilton, *Pro-*

logue to Conflict: The Crisis and Compromise of 1850 (New York, 1964); and David M. Potter, *The Impending Crisis, 1848-1861* (New York, 1976), 1-120.

13. Roy F. Nichols, "The Kansas-Nebraska Act: A Century of Historiography," *Mississippi Valley Historical Review* 43 (Sept. 1956): 187-212; Johannsen, *Stephen A. Douglas,* 405-18; and Russel, "Congressional Struggle," 187-210. The bill only repealed the Missouri Compromise in Kansas and Nebraska territories. It remained in effect for Minnesota Territory. Fehrenbacher, *Dred Scott Case,* 186.

14. *New York Times,* Jan. 6, 1854.

15. Parrish, *David Rice Atchison,* 142-51; and Jaffa, *Crisis of the House Divided,* 170-77.

16. N. P. Banks to Whiting Griswold, Jan. 20, 1854, Whiting Griswold Papers, Library of Congress.

17. Roy F. Nichols, *Franklin Pierce: Young Hickory of the Granite Hills* (Philadelphia, 1958), 83-86, 224-26, 319-24, 542.

18. Russel, "Congressional Struggle," 187-210.

19. *Boston Daily Advertiser,* Jan. 31, 1854.

20. Russel, "Congressional Struggle," 206-7; Rosenberg, "Kansas-Nebraska Act in Iowa," 436-57; and Hamilton, *Prologue to Conflict.*

21. Willard Carl Klunder, *Lewis Cass and the Politics of Moderation* (Kent, Ohio, 1996), xiv; and Allen Johnson, "Genesis of Popular Sovereignty," *Iowa Journal of History and Politics* 3 (1905): 3-19; Potter, *Impending Crisis,* 115-16; Robert W. Johannsen, "Stephen A. Douglas, Popular Sovereignty and the Territories," *Historian* 22 (1960): 378-95; Jean H. Baker, *Affairs of Party: The Political Culture of Northern Democrats in the Mid-Nineteenth Century* (Ithaca, N.Y., 1983), 177-96; Milo Milton Quaife, *The Doctrine of Non-Intervention with Slavery in the Territories* (Chicago, 1910), 20, 130-31; and Peter B. Knupfer, *The Union as It Is: Constitutional Unionism and Sectional Compromise, 1787-1861* (Chapel Hill, N.C., 1991), 174.

22. Alexander H. Stephens to W. W. Burwell, May 7, 1854, Ulrich Bonnell Phillips, ed., *The Correspondence of Robert Toombs, Alexander H. Stephens, and Howell Cobb* (New York, 1970), 343-44.

23. Robert Toombs to W. W. Burwell, Feb. 3, 1854, ibid., *Correspondence of Toombs, Stephens, and Cobb,* 342-43.

24. Quaife, *Doctrine of Non-Intervention,* 26-28; and William J. Cooper, Jr., *The South and the Politics of Slavery, 1828-1856* (Baton Rouge, 1978), 347-48.

25. *Missouri Democrat,* Jan. 22, 1854; and *New York Times,* Feb. 24, 27, 1854.

26. *New York Times,* March 7, 1854.

27. *Richmond Enquirer,* May 2, 1854; Rawley, *Race and Politics,* 143; Eric Foner, *Politics and Ideology in the Age of the Civil War* (New York, 1980), 44; Russel, "Congressional Struggle," 187-210; and Don E.

Fehrenbacher, *The South and Three Sectional Crises* (Baton Rouge, 1980), 49–52.

28. Frederick J. Blue, *Salmon P. Chase: A Life in Politics* (Kent, Ohio, 1987), 79–94.

29. "Appeal of the Independent Democrats in Congress to the People of the United States," *Congressional Globe,* 33d Cong., 1st sess., 1854, 281–82.

30. *New York Times,* Feb. 4, 7, 1854.

31. Ibid., Feb. 22, 1854.

32. Ibid., April 24, March 15, 1854.

33. Ibid., April 13, 1854.

34. James L. Huston, "Democracy by Scripture versus Democracy by Process: A Reflection on Stephen A. Douglas and Popular Sovereignty," *Civil War History* 43 (Sept. 1997): 189–200.

35. *New York Times,* Feb. 16, 1854.

36. John Thomson Mason to James Buchanan, Feb. 20, 1854, James Buchanan Papers, Historical Society of Pennsylvania, Philadelphia. Douglas had tried tinkering with the bill's wording, introducing yet another version of the bill on February 7. Reworded, it now read that the Missouri Compromise was "inconsistent" with the popular sovereignty principle upon which the Compromise of 1850 had been based. Douglas convinced few. Even a Democrat pointed out that the new language repealed the Missouri Compromise, but just did not admit it so clearly. Russel, "Congressional Struggle," 187–210; *New York Times,* Feb. 8, 1854; and James B. Bowlin to James Buchanan, April 21, 1854, Buchanan Papers (HSPenn).

37. Franklin Pierce to James Buchanan, Feb. 22, 1854, Buchanan Papers (HSPenn). *New York Times,* Feb. 20, 1854; Russel, "Congressional Struggle," 207–8; Johannsen, *Stephen A. Douglas,* 424–34; and James B. Bowlin to James Buchanan, April 21, 1854, Buchanan Papers (HSPenn).

38. Russel, "Congressional Struggle," 208; James Ford Rhodes, *History of the United States from the Compromise of 1850,* vol. 1, *1850–1854* (1890; reprint, New York, 1901), 384–506; and *New York Times,* March 2, 3, 7, 1854.

39. *New York Times,* March 6, 1854.

40. Ibid., March 1, 1854.

41. *Richmond Examiner,* March 24, 1854, in *New York Times,* March 27, 1854.

42. *New York Times,* March 22, 1854; and Johannsen, *Stephen A. Douglas,* 424–34.

43. *New York Times,* March 28, 29, 30, April 1, 1854. President Pierce also received an anti-Kansas-Nebraska petition from the ministers of his hometown, Concord, New Hampshire. [May 1854], Franklin Pierce Papers, Library of Congress.

44. *New York Times,* April 19, 24, 25, May 3, 1854.

45. Johannsen, *Stephen A. Douglas,* 424–34; and *New York Times,* May 8, 9, 12, 13, 16, 1854.

46. *New York Times,* May 23, 25, 26, 1854; Johannsen, *Stephen A. Douglas,* 424–34; and Gerald W. Wolff, *The Kansas-Nebraska Bill: Party, Section, and the Coming of the Civil War* (New York, 1977), 37–46.

47. Russel, "Congressional Struggle," 208–9; and Wolff, *Kansas-Nebraska Bill,* 77, 156–58.

48. Johannsen, *Stephen A. Douglas,* 424–34; Robert W. Johannsen, "The Kansas-Nebraska Act and Territorial Government in the United States," in *Territorial Kansas: Studies Commemorating the Centennial* (Lawrence, 1954), 17–32; *New York Times,* March 1, 3, 24, 1854; and Wolff, *Kansas-Nebraska Bill,* 37–46.

49. Johannsen, *Stephen A. Douglas,* 240, 283–303; Johannsen, "Kansas-Nebraska Act," 28–30; and Morrison, *Slavery and the American West,* 142–56.

50. John Ashworth, *"Agrarians" and "Aristocrats": Party Political Ideology in the United States, 1837–1846* (London, 1987); Michael F. Holt, *The Rise and Fall of the American Whig Party: Jacksonian Politics and the Onset of the Civil War* (New York, 1999); Baker, *Affairs of Party;* Michael F. Holt, *The Political Crisis of the 1850s* (New York, 1978), 1–38, 101–38; William E. Gienapp, *The Origins of the Republican Party, 1852–1856* (New York, 1987), 13–67; and Potter, *Impending Crisis,* 141–44, 225–65.

51. I. Toucey to Horace Sabin, Oct. 28, 1854, Isaac Toucey Manuscript, Connecticut Historical Society, Hartford.

52. Rhodes, *History,* vol. 1, 384–506; *New York Times,* March 15, Feb. 21, 1854; and Wolff, *Kansas-Nebraska Bill,* 1–24.

53. *New York Times,* March 24, 1854.

54. John F. Wright to T. Ewing, Feb. 10, 1854, Thomas Ewing Family Papers, Library of Congress.

55. *New York Times,* Jan. 24, 1854; E. J. Palmer to J. M. Palmer, June 22, 1854, John M. Palmer Papers II, Illinois State Historical Library, Springfield; B. B. Hamilton to Yates, April 17, 1854, Richard Yates Papers, Illinois State Historical Library, Springfield; and Johannsen, *Stephen A. Douglas,* 439–64. Alas, the delightful story that Douglas ended his attempts by informing the audience "It is now Sunday morning; I'll go to church, and you may go to hell" appears to be a myth. Douglas actually finished speaking before midnight on a Friday evening. Rawley, *Race and Politics,* 72.

56. Quoted in Rawley, *Race and Politics,* 72. According to Yonatan Eyal, Douglas knew the bill would be controversial, but underestimated how lasting the controversy would prove to be. Yonatan Eyal, "With His Eyes Open: Stephen A. Douglas and the Kansas-Nebraska Disaster of 1854," *Journal of the Illinois State Historical Society* 91 (winter 1998): 175–217.

57. *New York Times,* Feb. 24, March 2, 4, 15, 1854; Rawley, *Race and Politics,* 78; and Gienapp, *Origins of the Republican Party.*

58. *New York Times,* Feb. 18, May 15, Jan. 31, 1854.

59. Ibid., Jan. 31, 1854.
60. Ibid., Feb. 24, March 4, 6, 15, 23, 1854.
61. William Henry Seward in ibid., Jan. 31, 1854.
62. Ibid., Feb. 15, March 23, 1854.
63. Ibid., May 15, 1854.
64. Ibid., Feb. 7, 1854.
65. Ibid., Feb. 20, 1854.
66. Ibid., May 15, 1854.
67. D. Davis to Rockwell, July 15, 1854, David Davis Family Papers, Illinois State Historical Library, Springfield.
68. *New York Times,* Jan. 31, 1854.
69. Ibid., Feb. 11, 1854.
70. Ibid., Feb. 24, 1854.
71. Tyler Anbinder, *Nativism and Slavery: The Northern Know Nothings and the Politics of the 1850s* (New York, 1992), 52–74, 94–102, 246–47.
72. Charles A. Dana quoted in Anbinder, *Nativism and Slavery,* 277–78.
73. Dwight Lowell Dumond, *Antislavery: The Crusade for Freedom in America* (Ann Arbor, 1961).
74. Joel H. Silbey, "The Surge of Republican Power: Partisan Antipathy, American Social Conflict, and the Coming of the Civil War," in *Essays on American Antebellum Politics, 1840–1860,* ed. by Stephen E. Maizlish and John J. Kushma (College Station, Tex., 1982), 199–229; Louis Filler, *The Crusade against Slavery, 1830–1860* (New York, 1960), 233; and Major L. Wilson, *Space, Time, and Freedom: The Quest for Nationality and the Irrepressible Conflict, 1815–1861* (Westport, Conn., 1974), 197–98.
75. Speech at Peoria, Oct. 16, 1854, Roy P. Basler, ed., *The Collected Works of Abraham Lincoln,* vol. 2 (New Brunswick, N.J., 1953), 247–83; and Kenneth J. Winkle, *The Young Eagle: The Rise of Abraham Lincoln* (Dallas, 2001), 291–97.
76. *New York Times,* Feb. 24, March 4, 6, 15, 23, 1854.
77. Ibid., Feb. 23, 1854.
78. *Richmond Enquirer,* Feb. 3, 1854.
79. Alexander Stephens to T. W. Thomas, May 23, 1854, roll 2, Alexander H. Stephens Papers, Library of Congress; and Alexander H. Stephens to J. W. Duncan, May 26, 1854, Phillips, *Correspondence of Toombs, Stephens, and Cobb,* 345.
80. Alexander H. Stephens to W.W. Burwell, May 7, 1854, Phillips, *Correspondence of Toombs, Stephens, and Cobb,* 343–44.
81. *Savannah Morning News* in *New York Times,* March 27, 1854.
82. Christopher Phillips, *Missouri's Confederate: Claiborne Fox Jackson and the Creation of Southern Identity in the Border West* (Columbia, Mo., 2000), 198.
83. *(St. Louis) Missouri Republican,* Feb. 2, 1854.
84. Ibid., June 7, 1854.

85. *New York Times,* May 27, 1854; and [Schurz], *Reminiscences of Carl Schurz,* 33–34.
86. Morrison, *Slavery and the American West,* 121–23.
87. U.S. House, *Howard Report,* 34th Cong., 1st sess., 1856, Rept. 200, serial 869, 938.

2. FREEDOM IN THE SCALE

1. [John McNamara], *Three Years on the Kansas Border by a Clergyman of the Episcopal Church* (New York, 1856), 22–24.
2. Frederick to Father, Aug. 1, 1854, Frederick Starr, Jr., Papers, Western Historical Manuscript Collection, Columbia, Mo.
3. Missourians were 46.5 percent of the population. The remainder of the population came from foreign countries or claimed nativity in Kansas Territory. Territory of Kansas Census of 1855, Kansas State Historical Society, Topeka.
4. *New York Times,* June 27, 1854.
5. Ibid.
6. James Oakes, *The Ruling Race: A History of American Slaveholders* (New York, 1982), 69–87, 95.
7. *(St. Louis) Missouri Democrat,* April 24, 1855.
8. *(Atchison, Kans.) Squatter Sovereign,* Feb. 3, 1855.
9. Gunja SenGupta, *For God and Mammon: Evangelicals and Entrepreneurs, Masters and Slaves in Territorial Kansas, 1854–1860* (Athens, Ga., 1996), 119–21; and James A. Rawley, *Race and Politics: "Bleeding Kansas" and the Coming of the Civil War* (Lincoln, Nebr., 1969), 80.
10. Kansas Census of 1855; and SenGupta, *For God and Mammon,* 119–20.
11. James C. Malin, *The Nebraska Question, 1852–1854* (Lawrence, Kans., 1953), 361–406; Donald B. Dodd, comp., *Historical Statistics of the States of the United States: Two Centuries of the Census, 1790–1900* (Westport, Conn., 1993), 51, 43; and *New York Times,* Aug. 16, 1854.
12. *New York Times,* June 29, 1854.
13. Rawley, *Race and Politics,* 81–82.
14. W. A. Phillips, "Kansas History," vol. 4, *Transactions of the Kansas State Historical Society* (Topeka, 1890), 351–59, esp. 357.
15. Samuel N. Wood to Editor of the *National Era,* Aug. 20, 1854, Robert W. Richmond, "A Free-Stater's 'Letters to the Editor': Samuel N. Wood's Letters to Eastern Newspapers, 1854," *Kansas Historical Quarterly* 23 (summer 1957): 181–90, esp. 188–89.
16. Albert D. Richardson, *Beyond the Mississippi: From the Great River to the Great Ocean: Life and Adventure on the Prairies, Mountains, and Pacific Coast, 1857–1867* (Hartford, Conn., 1867), 132. Another account claims it was an 1827 Galena lead mine rush that caused Illinoisans to claim Missouri had taken a "puke." George Earlie Shankle, *State Names, Flags, Seals, Songs, Birds, Flowers, and Other Symbols* (New York, 1934), 128.

17. G. Douglas Brewerton, *The War in Kansas: A Rough Trip to the Border* (New York, 1856), 72–74.

18. William Phillips, *The Conquest of Kansas by Missouri and Her Allies* (Boston, 1856), 29; and Rawley, *Race and Politics*, 85.

19. Alice Nichols, *Bleeding Kansas* (New York, 1954), 9–11, 24, 26.

20. William E. Parrish, *David Rice Atchison of Missouri: Border Politician* (Columbia, Mo., 1961), 162–63; *(Atchison, Kans.) Squatter Sovereign,* Feb. 3, 1855; and Oakes, *Ruling Race*, 147–49.

21. *New York Times*, July 1, 1857.

22. Frederick to Father, Aug. 21, 1854, Starr Papers; and Frederick to Father, Sept. 19, 1854, ibid.; July 23–24, 1854 entries, Henry Miles Moore Journals, Yale University.

23. July 21, 1854 entry, Moore Journals; and Starr to Father and Mother, Oct. 18, 1854, Starr Papers.

24. —— to Father, Oct. 30, 1854, Starr Papers.

25. [McNamara], *Three Years on the Kansas Border*, 41–43; —— to Father, Oct. 30, 1854, Starr Papers; July 29, 1854 entry, Moore Journals; and Thomas H. Gladstone, *The Englishman in Kansas or Squatter Life and Border Warfare* (1857; reprint, Lincoln, Nebr., 1971), 18.

26. *Squatter Sovereign*, Feb. 3, 1855.

27. *Missouri Democrat*, Sept. 14, 1854; and *(Lawrence) Herald of Freedom,* Jan. 13, 1855.

28. A. W. Reese, "Recollections of the Civil War," 1870, Western Historical Manuscript Collection, Columbia, Mo.

29. Phillips, *Conquest of Kansas*, 47–48.

30. *(Atchison, Kans.) Squatter Sovereign*, Feb. 3, 1855.

31. Russel B. Nye, *Fettered Freedom: Civil Liberties and the Slavery Controversy: 1830–1860* (East Lansing, Mich., 1949), 139–76.

32. Samuel A. Johnson, *The Battle Cry of Freedom: The New England Emigrant Aid Company in the Kansas Crusade* (Westport, Conn., 1977), 73.

33. House, *Howard Report*, 34th Cong., 1st sess., 1856, serial 869, Rept. 200, 953–54.

34. W. H. T. Wakefield, "Squatter Courts in Kansas," vol. 5, *Transactions of the Kansas State Historical Society* (Topeka, 1896), 71–74; and *(St. Louis) Missouri Republican*, Aug. 25, 1854.

35. Sept. 9, 1854 entry, Moore Journals.

36. Johnson, *Battle Cry of Freedom*, 7–10, 16–27, 65–71; Eli Thayer, *A History of the Kansas Crusade, Its Friends and Its Foes* (New York, 1889), 18–27; and *New York Times*, Oct. 13, 1854. Frederick Douglass's "strangely naive" idea for a free black colony is discussed in David W. Blight, *Frederick Douglass' Civil War: Keeping Faith in Jubilee* (Baton Rouge, 1989), 48–49.

37. Johnson, *Battle Cry of Freedom*, 111–17, 31, 14–15, 47–50; William Lawrence, *Life of Amos A. Lawrence* (Boston, 1888); Thomas H. O'Connor, "Cotton Whigs in Kansas," *Kansas Historical Quarterly* 26

(spring 1960): 34–58; and Richard H. Abbott, *Cotton and Capital: Boston Businessmen and Antislavery Reform, 1854–1868* (Amherst, Mass., 1991), 10–27.

38. Thayer, *Kansas Crusade*, 1–2.
39. Rawley, *Race and Politics*, 84–85; House, *Howard Report*, 834–35; Johnson, *Battle Cry of Freedom*, 75–77, 117–18.
40. Kansas Census of 1855; and *Eighth Census of the United States*, Washington, D.C., 1860, 166.
41. S. C. Pomeroy to Mr. Lawrence, Sept. 22, 1854, Samuel Clarke Pomeroy Collection, Kansas State Historical Society, Topeka; Johnson, *Battle Cry of Freedom*, 169–72; Thayer, *Kansas Crusade*, 108; Edward Everett Hale, "New England in the Colonization of Kansas," in *The New England States*, ed. by D. H. Hurd (Boston, 1897), 79–90, esp. 86; and Thomas H. Webb, *Information for Kanzas Immigrants* (Boston, 1855), 3–24.
42. Charles Robinson, *The Kansas Conflict* (Lawrence, Kans., 1898), 77–90.
43. "Lawrence" in *New York Times*, Oct. 30, 1854.
44. Robinson, *Kansas Conflict*, 77–90.
45. Johnson, *Battle Cry of Freedom*, 123–33.
46. Brewerton, *The War in Kansas;* and Don W. Wilson, *Governor Charles Robinson of Kansas* (Lawrence, Kans., 1975), 1–16.
47. Johnson, *Battle Cry of Freedom*, 123–33; and Accounts of the New York State Kansas Committee, Williams Family Papers, Albany Institute of History and Art, Albany, N.Y.
48. *New York Times*, Aug. 4, 1854.
49. W. J. Bassett, "Personal Recollections of the Kansas Episode from 1856 to 1860," 1896, W. J. Bassett Collection, Kansas State Historical Society, Topeka.
50. *Herald of Freedom*, Feb. 17, 1855; and House, *Howard Report*, 838–40.
51. Leonard L. Richards, *The Slave Power: The Free North and Southern Domination, 1780–1860* (Baton Rouge, 2000).
52. *Herald of Freedom*, April 19, 1856.
53. "Personal Reminiscences," Isaac Tichenor Goodnow Collection, Kansas State Historical Society, Topeka. Rawley, *Race and Politics*, 84–85, estimates that one-third of the settlers returned home.
54. Julia Louisa Lovejoy to Editor, April 13, 1855, Julia Louisa Lovejoy, "Letters from Kanzas," *Kansas Historical Quarterly* 11 (Feb. 1942): 29–44, esp. 36; Johnson, *Battle Cry of Freedom*, 119–21; and *(Lawrence) Herald of Freedom*, Feb. 3, 1855.
55. "Personal Reminiscences," Goodnow Collection.
56. *Boston Daily Advertiser*, Nov. 24, 1854.
57. Louise Barry, "The New England Emigrant Aid Company Parties of 1855," *Kansas Historical Quarterly* 12 (Aug. 1943): 227–68, esp. 254–55.
58. *Missouri Republican*, March 24, 1855.

59. Geo. W. Spivey to William Spivey, Jan. 22, 1855, George W. Spivey Letter, Western Historical Manuscript Collection, Columbia, Mo.
60. C. D. Dowse to Goodnow, March 29, Nov. 28, 1855, Goodnow Collection.
61. "Personal Reminiscences," Goodnow Collection.
62. Ibid.; and Johnson, *Battle Cry of Freedom,* 62–63.
63. John Greenleaf Whittier, *The Complete Poetical Works of John Greenleaf Whittier* (Boston, 1894), 391–92; Miriam Davis Colt, *Went to Kansas; Being a Thrilling Account of an Ill-Fated Expedition to That Fairy Land, and Its Sad Results* (Watertown, [N.Y.], 1862), 32–33; Charles and Sara T. D. Robinson Papers (microfilm), Kansas State Historical Society, Topeka; *Herald of Freedom,* Oct. 21, 1854.
64. Wm. E. Goodnow to wife, June 10, 1855, Goodnow Collection.
65. Wm. to wife, June 17, 1855, Goodnow Collection. Paul Gates's seminal work asserted the primacy of land over politics in developing early Kansas. Paul Wallace Gates, *Fifty Million Acres: Conflicts over Kansas Land Policy, 1854–1890* (Ithaca, N.Y., 1954), 1–10, 58–59.
66. Thayer, *History of the Kansas Crusade,* 88.
67. Walter L. Fleming, "The Buford Expedition to Kansas," *American Historical Review* 6 (Oct. 1900), 38–48; and Elmer Leroy Craik, "Southern Interest in Territorial Kansas, 1854–1858," vol. 15, *Transactions of the Kansas State Historical Society* (Topeka, 1919), 334–450, esp. 349.
68. *Richmond Enquirer,* April 22, 1856.
69. Leverett W. Spring, *Kansas: The Prelude to the War for the Union* (Boston, 1885), 44.
70. Fleming, "Buford Expedition," 38–48. Buford spent $24,625.06 and received contributions of only $13,967.90. *Missouri Republican,* Dec. 24, 1856.
71. Clement Eaton, *The Growth of Southern Civilization, 1790–1860* (New York, 1961), 25–48; Joan E. Cashin, *A Family Venture: Men and Women on the Southern Frontier* (New York, 1991); and Donald B. Dodd, comp., *Historical Statistics of the States of the United States: Two Centuries of the Census, 1790–1990* (Westport, Conn., 1993), 2–87.
72. Johnson, *Battle Cry of Freedom,* 73–74; James R. Shortridge, *Peopling of the Plains: Who Settled Where in Frontier Kansas* (Lawrence, Kans., 1995), 1–14, 20; Kansas Census of 1855; and *Eighth Census,* 166. The remainder came from New England (4%), Missouri (11%), other parts of the South (15%) and North (12%), foreign countries (12%), or had been born in Kansas (10%).
73. Wendell Holmes Stephenson, *The Political Career of General James H. Lane* (Topeka, 1930), 43; Robinson, *Kansas Conflict,* 143–44; Richardson, *Beyond the Mississippi,* 44–47; *Lecompton (Kans.) Union,* Aug. 30, 1856; and G. W. Brown to Wm. E. Connelley, Jan. 4, 1911, George W. Brown Papers, Illinois State Historical Library, Springfield. Rumors abounded that Lane refused his wife financial support and that he had once so "shamefully abused" her that she had fled the house in her nightgown. Lane, Robinson claimed, joined the free-state movement only when

the proslavery Kansas territorial legislature refused to grant him a divorce. The Lanes apparently reconciled, for Mary Lane later joined her husband in the territory. For attitudes of the western settlers on race, see Eugene H. Berwanger, *The Frontier against Slavery: Western Anti-Negro Prejudice and the Slavery Extension Controversy* (Urbana, Ill., 1967) and Nicole Etcheson, *The Emerging Midwest: Upland Southerners and the Political Culture of the Old Northwest* (Bloomington, Ind., 1996), 94–102.

74. Stephenson, *James H. Lane,* 36–37; and Etcheson, *Emerging Midwest.*

75. Brewerton, *War in Kansas,* 84.

76. John Speer, *Life of Gen. James H. Lane, "The Liberator of Kansas" with Corrobative Incidents of Pioneer History* (Garden City, Kans., 1897), 18–19.

77. Thomas H. Gladstone, *Kansas; or, Squatter Life and Border Warfare in the Far West* (London, 1886), 109.

78. Eli Thayer, *The New England Emigrant Aid Company: And Its Influence, through the Kansas Contest, upon National History* (Worcester, Mass., 1887), 29n.

79. *New York Times,* Sept. 1, 1854.

80. Ed. M. Dobson to Brother, Sept. 9, 1854 in *New York Times,* Oct. 25, 1854.

81. *Richmond Enquirer,* Oct. 10, 1854.

82. Speech at Peoria, Oct. 16, 1854, Roy P. Basler, ed., *The Collected Works of Abraham Lincoln,* vol. 2 (New Brunswick, N.J., 1953), 271.

83. Thayer, *History of the Kansas Crusade,* 187.

84. House, *Howard Report,* 937–30.

85. Gladstone, *Kansas,* 110–12.

86. *Boston Daily Advertiser,* May 5, 1855.

87. *Missouri Democrat,* July 18, 1854.

88. *New York Times,* Nov. 8, 1855.

89. *Herald of Freedom,* Aug. 4, 1855.

90. *Squatter Sovereign,* Feb. 3, 1855.

91. James C. Malin, "The Proslavery Background of the Kansas Struggle," *Mississippi Valley Historical Review* 10 (Dec. 1923): 285–305.

92. Mary J. Klem, "Missouri in the Kansas Struggle," *Mississippi Valley Historical Association Proceedings* 9, pt. 3 (1917–1918), 393–413.

93. *New York Times,* Dec. 1, 1854.

94. S. C. Pomeroy to Mr. Lawrence, Sept. 22, 1854, Pomeroy Collection.

3. ALL RIGHT ON THE HEMP

1. *New York Times,* Dec. 26, 1854.

2. A. H. Reeder to F. Gwinner, D. A. N. Grover, Robert C. Miller, William F. Dyer, and Alfred Jones, Nov. 21, 1854, in *New York Times,* Dec. 22, 1854.

3. Alexander Keyssar, *The Right to Vote: The Contested History of Democracy in the United States* (New York, 2000), 28, table A.9,

63–65; Chilton Williamson, *American Suffrage: From Property to Democracy, 1760–1860* (Princeton, 1960), 272–78; Kenneth J. Winkle, "Ohio's Informal Polling Place: Nineteenth-Century Suffrage in Theory and Practice," in *The Pursuit of Public Power: Political Culture in Ohio, 1787–1861*, ed. by Jeffrey P. Brown and Andrew R. L. Cayton (Kent, Ohio, 1994), 169–84; Kenneth J. Winkle, *The Politics of Community: Migration and Politics in Antebellum Ohio* (Cambridge, Eng., 1988), 63; and "Executive Minutes," vol. 3, *Transactions of the Kansas State Historical Society* (Topeka, 1886), 226–78, esp. 251–59.

4. William Elsey Connelley, *Kansas Territorial Governors* (Topeka, 1900), 18–36; and James A. Rawley, *Race and Politics: "Bleeding Kansas" and the Coming of the Civil War* (Lincoln, Nebr., 1969), 86.

5. Oct. 7, 1854 entry, Henry Miles Moore Journals, Yale University Library.

6. "Executive Minutes," vol. 3, *Transactions,* 226–78, esp. 232–33, 235.

7. Danl. Woodson to wife, [Dec. 1854], Daniel Woodson Papers (Kansas State Historical Society, Topeka).

8. ——— to Father, March 19, 1855, Frederick Starr, Jr., Papers, Western Historical Manuscript Collection, Columbia, Mo.

9. *New York Times,* Jan. 8, 1855.

10. Frederick to ———, Dec. 1, 1854, Starr Papers.

11. House, *Howard Report,* 34th Cong., 1st sess., 1856, Serial 869, Rept. 200, 23–24.

12. Ibid., 9.

13. Ibid., 36–38, 10.

14. Ibid., 1–2.

15. Ibid., 3–4.

16. "Executive Minutes," vol. 3, *Transactions,* 240; Russell K. Hickman, "The Reeder Administration Inaugurated: Part I—The Delegate Election of November, 1854," *Kansas Historical Quarterly* 36 (autumn 1970), 305–40, esp. 322–23, 334–35; and House, *Howard Report,* 8.

17. Alice Nichols, *Bleeding Kansas* (New York, 1954), 22; House, *Howard Report,* 1–2.

18. Danl. Woodson to wife, [Dec. 1854], Woodson Papers.

19. Connelley, *Kansas Territorial Governors,* 18–36.

20. D. R. Atchison to Col. O. Anderson, Jan. 11, 1855, James Blythe Anderson Papers, University of Kentucky.

21. D. R. Atchison to Col. O. Anderson, Jan. 30, 1855, Anderson Papers.

22. *(Lawrence) Herald of Freedom,* April 28, 1855.

23. J. W. Reid to Col. Anderson, March 26, 1855, Anderson Papers.

24. Feb. 20, March 5, 15, 1855, Moore Journals.

25. [Frederick Starr] to Father, March 31, 1855, Starr Papers.

26. House, *Howard Report,* 389–92.

27. House, *Howard Report,* 308–11, 192–99; *Herald of Freedom,* March 31, 1855.

28. *New York Times,* April 10, 1855; House, *Howard Report,* 114–20, 123–26; Thomas H. Gladstone, *The Englishman in Kansas or Squatter Life and Border Warfare* (1857; reprint, Lincoln, Nebr., 1971), 255–56.
29. House, *Howard Report,* 148–49.
30. Ibid., 114–20, 149–50, 154–55.
31. Ibid., 168–72, 174–76.
32. March 30, 1855 entry, Moore Journals.
33. House, *Howard Report,* 351–53.
34. *New York Times,* May 9, 1857.
35. *(Atchison, Kans.) Squatter Sovereign,* March 27, 1855.
36. House, *Howard Report,* 123–26.
37. Locke Hardeman to Genl. G. R. Smith, June 10, 1855, General George R. Smith Collection, Missouri Historical Society, St. Louis.
38. *New York Times,* May 4, 1855; David Grimsted, *American Mobbing, 1828–1861: Toward Civil War* (New York, 1998), 246–65, esp. 249.
39. April 17, 1855 entry, William B. Napton Diary, Missouri Historical Society, St. Louis.
40. Locke Hardeman to Gen. G. R. Smith, June 10, 1855, Smith Collection.
41. *Herald of Freedom,* April 21, May 5, 1855; [Frederick Starr to Father, April 1855], Starr Papers; *New York Times,* May 19, 1855; and Samuel C. Pomeroy to Geo. S. Parks [April 24, 1855], Samuel C. Pomeroy Collection, Kansas State Historical Society, Topeka.
42. Pardee Butler to Editor, Aug. 28, 1855 in *Herald of Freedom,* Sept. 8, 1855; House, *Howard Report,* 960–63; and *Squatter Sovereign,* Aug. 21, 1855.
43. [John McNamara], *Three Years on the Kansas Border by a Clergyman of the Episcopal Church* (New York, 1856), 50–54; *New York Times,* June 7, 1855; and May 17, 1855 entry, Moore Journals.
44. House, *Howard Report,* 925–27.
45. Ibid., 127–28.
46. Ibid., 159–65.
47. Ibid., 27–32.
48. Ibid., 199–201, 168–72, 174–76. On election fraud, see Mark W. Summers, *The Plundering Generation: Corruption and the Crisis of the Union, 1849–1861* (New York, 1987), xii–xiii, 52–53, 58, and n63. Most studies of elections concentrate on suffrage requirements and voting procedures, reserving issues of fraud for the Gilded Age. Keyssar, *Right to Vote;* Williamson, *American Suffrage;* and Kirk H. Porter, *A History of Suffrage in the United States* (New York, 1969).
49. *Daily Pennsylvanian* quoted in *New York Times,* May 21, 1855.
50. "Executive Minutes," vol. 3, *Transactions,* 250–51; *New York Times,* April 18, 1855; and Rawley, *Race and Politics,* 87–89.
51. "Memorial from Citizens of Kansas Territory to Congress," *New York Times,* May 11, 1855.

52. *Herald of Freedom,* April 28, 1855.
53. C. F. Brennan to J. S. Rollins, May 10, 1855, James S. Rollins Papers, Western Historical Manuscript Collection, Columbia, Mo.
54. Andrew Wylie to Rollins, May 17, 1855, Rollins Papers.
55. Smith quoted in Elmer Leroy Craik, "Southern Interest in Territorial Kansas, 1854–1858," vol. 15, *Transactions of the Kansas State Historical Society* (Topeka, 1919), 334–450, esp. 387.
56. House, *Howard Report,* 652–57.
57. D. R. Atchison to Col. O. Anderson, March [April?] 5, 1855, Anderson Papers. Although the letter is dated March 5, Atchison was clearly writing after, not before, the election, probably the correct date is April 5.
58. D. R. Atchison to Col. O. Anderson, March [April?] 5, 1855, Anderson Papers; *Squatter Sovereign,* April 17, 1855; "Executive Minutes," vol. 3, *Transactions,* 260–71; Nichols, *Bleeding Kansas,* 28; and House, *Howard Report,* 30.
59. "Executive Minutes," vol. 3, *Transactions,* 271–73; C. I. H. Nichols to Samuel Woodward, April 7, 1855, in Joseph G. Gambone, "The Forgotten Feminist of Kansas: The Papers of Clarina I.H. Nichols, 1854–1885," *Kansas Historical Quarterly* 39 (spring 1973), 12–57, esp. 56–57; Rawley, *Race and Politics,* 87–89; and House, *Howard Report,* 30.
60. *Herald of Freedom,* June 30, 1855; and House, *Howard Report,* 36.
61. *New York Times,* April 18, 1855; and *Squatter Sovereign,* April 3, 1855.
62. Rawley, *Race and Politics,* 90–91; *New York Times,* April 26, May 4, 12, 1855; J. W. Forney to James Buchanan, May 12, 1855, James Buchanan Papers, Historical Society of Pennsylvania, Philadelphia; Roy F. Nichols, *Franklin Pierce: Young Hickory of the Granite Hills* (Philadelphia, 1958), 407–18; n.d. [1855], Franklin Pierce Papers, Library of Congress; and House, *Howard Report,* 933–49.
63. *Herald of Freedom,* Sept. 8, 1855.
64. Ibid., June 30, 1855.
65. Sara T. L. Robinson, *Kansas; Its Interior and Exterior Life,* 7th ed. (Boston, 1857), 65.
66. "Governor Reeder's Administration," vol. 5, *Transactions of the Kansas State Historical Society* (Topeka, 1896), 163–234, esp. 180–90.
67. M. F. Conway to A. H. Reeder, June 30, 1855, in *Herald of Freedom,* July 14, 1855.
68. Samuel D. Houston to A. H. Reeder, July 20, 1855, in "Governor Reeder's Administration," vol. 5, *Transactions,* 198–99; and *Herald of Freedom,* July 28, 1855.
69. Charles Robinson, *The Kansas Conflict* (Lawrence, Kans., 1898), 153–56; and *Herald of Freedom,* July 21, 14, 1855.
70. C. K. Holliday to wife, July 24, 1855, Lela Barnes, ed., "Letters of Cyrus Kurtz Holliday, 1854–1859," *Kansas Historical Quarterly* 6 (Aug. 1937), 241–94, esp. 260–61.

71. *New York Times,* Aug. 17, 1855.
72. Daniel W. Wilder, *The Annals of Kansas* (Topeka, 1875), 56.
73. "Governor Reeder's Message," July 3, 1855, in *New York Times,* July 21, 1855.
74. *New York Times,* Aug. 18, 20, 30, Sept. 7, 1855; Rawley, *Race and Politics,* 91; and *The Border Ruffian Code in Kansas* [1856], 1-4.
75. Nichols, *Bleeding Kansas,* 38-39.
76. *(St. Louis) Missouri Republican,* Aug. 29, 1855.
77. Ibid., Aug. 16, 1855.
78. Robert S. Kelley to G. W. Brown, Sept. 7, 1855, in *Herald of Freedom,* Sept. 22, 1855.
79. *New York Times,* Dec. 8, 1855.
80. *Squatter Sovereign,* Dec. 9, 1856.
81. *Squatter Sovereign,* Dec. 4, 1855.
82. A. A. L. to ———, March 31, 1855, in William Lawrence, *Life of Amos A. Lawrence* (Boston, 1888), 89-92.
83. Robinson, *Kansas,* 69.
84. *Herald of Freedom,* July 7, 14, 1855; and Robinson, *Kansas,* 69-77.
85. Robinson, *Kansas Conflict,* 144.
86. Ibid., 111-12.
87. House, *Howard Report,* 652-57.
88. *Herald of Freedom,* July 7, 1855.
89. Summers, *Plundering Generation,* 154-55. Reeder's speculations were unique in that he speculated in government-owned land. Reeder's land partner, an army officer, was later court-martialed and found guilty of irregularities in purchasing Indian land. *New York Times,* April 30, 1855; and Nichols, *Bleeding Kansas,* 33-36.
90. *New York Times,* April 30, 1855; and Nichols, *Bleeding Kansas,* 33-36.
91. House, *Howard Report,* 264-66, 274-78, 933-49, 1186-87; *Herald of Freedom,* July 14, 1855; *New York Times,* July 20, 19, 1855; Samuel D. Houston to A. H. Reeder, July 20, 1855, in "Governor Reeder's Administration," vol. 5, *Transactions,* 198-99; and Nichols, *Bleeding Kansas,* 35.
92. *New York Times,* July 26, 31, 1855.
93. C. K. Holliday to Wife, July 29, 1855, Barnes, "Letters of Cyrus Kurtz Holliday," 261-62.
94. *Herald of Freedom,* June 30, 1855; *New York Times,* July 7, 9, 1855; John Tappan to Mrs. Goodnow, June 29, 1855, Isaac Tichenor Collection, Kansas State Historical Society, Topeka; and *Boston Daily Advertiser,* July 9, 1855.
95. "Memorial from the Legislature of Kansas to the President of the United States," *Herald of Freedom,* Aug. 18, 1855; and *New York Times,* Aug. 4, 1855.
96. William E. Parrish, *David Rice Atchison of Missouri: Border Politician* (Columbia, Mo., 1961), 172; and Allan Nevins, *Ordeal of the Union,* vol. 2 (New York, 1947), 389; and House, *Howard Report,* 933-49.

97. A. H. Reeder to W. L. Marcy, Aug. 15, 1855, "Governor Reeder's Administration," vol. 5, *Transactions,* 234; *New York Times,* July 31, Aug. 1, 1855; and Nichols, *Franklin Pierce,* 407–18.

98. *New York Times,* Oct. 22, Aug. 22, 1855.

99. R. Monaghan to James Buchanan, Dec. 3, 1855, Buchanan Papers (HSPenn).

100. *(St. Louis) Missouri Democrat,* Oct. 26, 1855.

4. WE ARE BUT SLAVES

1. [Hannah Anderson Ropes], *Six Months in Kansas* (Boston, 1856), 54.

2. See Sam W. Haynes, *Soldiers of Misfortune: The Somervell and Mier Expeditions* (Austin, 1990) for a description of Shannon's career in Mexico; and William Elsey Connelley, *Kansas Territorial Governors* (Topeka, 1900).

3. Nov. 12, 1855 entry, Henry Miles Moore Journals, Yale University Library, New Haven.

4. G. Douglas Brewerton, *The War in Kansas: A Rough Trip to the Border* (New York, 1856), 135–36.

5. *New York Times,* Sept. 13, 14, 29, Nov. 8, 1855; Wilson Shannon to G. W. Brown, Oct. 6, 1855, *(Lawrence) Herald of Freedom,* Oct. 27, 1855.

6. *Herald of Freedom,* Aug. 18, 1855; *New York Times,* Aug. 24, Oct. 22, 1855; April 24, 1878, W. I. R. Blackman Miscellaneous Collections, Kansas State Historical Society, Topeka; and Charles Robinson, *The Kansas Conflict* (Lawrence, Kans., 1898), 169–71.

7. *Herald of Freedom,* Sept. 8, 1855; Alice Nichols, *Bleeding Kansas* (New York, 1954), 41–45; James A. Rawley, *Race and Politics: "Bleeding Kansas" and the Coming of the Civil War* (Lincoln, Nebr., 1969), 94; April 24, 1878, Blackman Miscellaneous Collections; Daniel W. Wilder, *The Annals of Kansas* (Topeka, 1875), 60–62; R. G. Elliott, "The Big Springs Convention," vol. 8, *Transactions of the Kansas State Historical Society* (Topeka, 1903–1904), 362–77; and James C. Malin, "The Topeka Statehood Movement Reconsidered: Origins," in *Territorial Kansas: Studies Commemorating the Centennial* (Lawrence, Kans., 1954), 33–69, esp. 34, 40–44.

8. *Herald of Freedom,* June 30, 1855; Wendell Holmes Stephenson, *The Political Career of General James H. Lane* (Topeka, 1930), 43–48; and Robinson, *Kansas Conflict,* 143–44.

9. Thomas Brower Peacock, "The Rhyme of the Border War," in *Poems of the Plains and Songs of the Solitudes* (New York, 1889), 207–305, esp. 216.

10. *Herald of Freedom,* Aug. 18, 1855; *New York Times,* Aug. 24, Oct. 22, 1855; April 24, 1878, Blackman Miscellaneous Collections; and Robinson, *Kansas Conflict,* 169–71.

11. House, *Howard Report,* 34th Cong., 1st sess., 1856, Serial 869, Rept. 200, 658–70.

12. John Speer, *Life of Gen. James H. Lane, "The Liberator of Kansas" with Corrobative Incidents of Pioneer History* (Garden City, Kans., 1897), 45.

13. *Herald of Freedom,* Sept. 8, 1855; Nichols, *Bleeding Kansas,* 41–45; Rawley, *Race and Politics,* 94; April 24, 1878, Blackman Miscellaneous Collections; and Wilder, *Annals of Kansas,* 60–62.

14. *Herald of Freedom,* Sept. 8, 1855; Nichols, *Bleeding Kansas,* 41–45; Rawley, *Race and Politics,* 94; April 24, 1878, Blackman Miscellaneous Collections; and Wilder, *Annals of Kansas,* 60–62.

15. *Herald of Freedom,* Sept. 8, 1855; Rawley, *Race and Politics,* 94; and Wilder, *The Annals of Kansas,* 60–62.

16. House, *Howard Report,* 603–4; A. H. Reeder to Halderman, Oct. 6, 1855, John Adams Halderman Collection, Kansas State Historical Society, Topeka. Reeder's continued speculation in Kansas real estate after his dismissal from office indicates he still felt an interest in the territory.

17. C. K. Holliday to Wife, Sept. 10, 1855, Lela Barnes, ed., "Letters of Cyrus Kurtz Holliday, 1854–1859," *Kansas Historical Quarterly* 6 (Aug. 1937): 241–94, esp. 266–67.

18. Rawley, *Race and Politics,* 94; and Wilder, *Annals of Kansas,* 60–62.

19. House, *Howard Report,* 608–12.

20. Stephenson, *General James H. Lane,* 50–51; J. H. Lane to Legal Voters of Kansas, *Herald of Freedom,* Sept. 29, 1855; and House, *Howard Report,* 612–16.

21. C. Stearns to Editor, Sept. 1, 1855, *Herald of Freedom,* Sept. 22, 15, 1855.

22. Sept. 18, 20, 1855 entries, Moore Journals; and *Herald of Freedom,* Sept. 22, 1855.

23. E. P. Fitch to Father, Sept. 19, 1855, John M. Peterson, ed., "Letters of Edward and Sarah Fitch, Lawrence, Kansas, 1855–1863," *Kansas History* 12 (spring 1989): 48–70, esp. 56.

24. *(St. Louis) Missouri Democrat,* Oct. 22, 1855.

25. *Boston Daily Advertiser,* Nov. 17, 1855.

26. *(St. Louis) Republican,* Sept. 18, 1855 in *New York Times,* Sept. 22, 1855. Historian Samuel A. Johnson agreed that the Big Springs delegates had a "proclamation of revolution." Samuel A. Johnson, *The Battle Cry of Freedom: The New England Emigrant Aid Company in the Kansas Crusade* (Westport, Conn., 1977), 107–8.

27. *Herald of Freedom,* Sept. 8, 15, 1855; and *New York Times,* Oct. 15, 1855.

28. A. A. L. to ———, Aug. 10, 1855, William Lawrence, *Life of Amos A. Lawrence* (Boston, 1888), 100–101.

29. *New York Times,* Sept. 18, 1855; and *Herald of Freedom,* Sept. 22, 1855.

30. Sept. 12, 14, 1855 entries, Moore Journals.

31. *Boston Daily Advertiser,* Oct. 8, 1855.

32. Edward P. Fitch to Parents, Sept. 30, [1855], Peterson, "Letters of Edward and Sarah Fitch," 56–57.

33. *New York Times,* Oct. 16, 1855; Oct. 1, 1855 entry, Moore Journals; and House, *Howard Report,* 549.

34. Edward P. Fitch to Parents, Sept. 30, [1855], Peterson, "Letters of Edward and Sarah Fitch," 56–57.

35. *New York Times,* Oct. 22, Nov. 3, 8, 16, Dec. 4, 1855; House, *Howard Report,* Executive Documents, 34th Cong., 3d sess., 1856, serial 893, no. 1, 51; and *Kansas City (Mo.) Enterprise,* Dec. 22, 1855.

36. *Washington Union,* Nov. 6, 1855 in *New York Times,* Nov. 8, 1855.

37. Edward P. Fitch to Parents, Sept. 30, [1855], Peterson, "Letters of Edward and Sarah Fitch," 56–57.

38. Rawley, *Race and Politics,* 95; and Wilder, *Annals of Kansas,* 68–70.

39. House, *Howard Report,* 617–32.

40. *New York Times,* Nov. 5, 20, 26, 1855; Robinson, *Kansas Conflict,* 175–80; Rawley, *Race and Politics,* 95; and *Herald of Freedom,* Nov. 24, 1855. The Topeka Constitution also prohibited indentures made by blacks before they were brought into the state. In many western states, such indentures had been used to circumvent the Northwest Ordinance's prohibition of slavery.

41. Robinson, *Kansas Conflict,* 169.

42. Henry P. Waters to Charles Sumner, Nov. 5, 1855, Edward Lillis Pierce Collection, Kansas State Historical Society, Topeka.

43. Rawley, *Race and Politics,* 95; Dec. 15, 1855 entry, Moore Journals; and House, *Howard Report,* 797.

44. *Herald of Freedom,* Jan. 12, 1856; and *New York Times,* Jan. 21, Feb. 2, 1856.

45. *Herald of Freedom,* Nov. 17, Dec. 29, 1855.

46. A. A. L. to———, July 20, 1855, Lawrence, *Life of Amos A. Lawrence.*

47. Senate, Report No. 34, 34th Cong., 1st sess., 1856, serial 836, 27–30.

48. John H. Gihon, *Geary and Kansas: Governor Geary's Administration in Kansas: With a Complete History of the Territory until July 1857* (Philadelphia, 1857), 47–48; House, *Howard Report,* 905–21, 975–78; William Hutchinson Papers, Kansas State Historical Society, Topeka; and Brewerton, *War in Kansas,* 59–60.

49. W. H. Isely, "The Sharps Rifle Episode in Kansas History," *American Historical Review* 12 (April 1907): 546–66.

50. Eli Thayer to Howard, Aug. 1, 1855, Mark Howard Papers, Connecticut Historical Society, Hartford.

51. Robinson, *Kansas Conflict,* 123–28; Nichols, *Bleeding Kansas,* 37; and Isely, "Sharps Rifle Episode," 546–66.

52. Amos A. Lawrence to Wm. W. Stone, Aug. 11, 1855, Howard Papers; and Frederick Law Olmsted to F. G. Adams, Dec. 24, 1883, History Cannon, Kansas State Historical Society, Topeka.

53. Jas. B. Abbott to Mark Howard, Nov. 1855, Howard Papers.

54. Amos A. Lawrence to Giles Richards, Dec. 10, 1855, Amos A. Lawrence Miscellaneous Collections, Kansas State Historical Society, Topeka;

C. Robinson to Thayer, July 26, 1855, Charles and Sara T. D. Robinson Papers (microfilm), Kansas State Historical Society, Topeka; and C. Robinson to Thayer, July 26, 1855, Howard Papers.

55. Edward P. Fitch to Parents, Sept. 8, 1855, Peterson, "Letters of Edward and Sarah Fitch," 55.
56. Johnson, *Battle Cry of Freedom,* 141.
57. *(Atchison) Squatter Sovereign,* Oct. 23, 1855.
58. Wilder, *Annals of Kansas,* 70; *New York Times,* Nov. 26, 1855; and Nichols, *Bleeding Kansas,* 47–49.
59. *Missouri Democrat,* Nov. 26, 1855.
60. Brewerton, *War in Kansas,* 223–32; O. N. Merrill, *A True History of the Kansas Wars, and Their Origin, Progress and Incidents* (1856; reprint, Tarrytown, N.Y., 1932), 15–23; and House, *Howard Report,* 1060–65.
61. *Herald of Freedom,* Nov. 24, 1855; J. S. E. in *New York Times,* Dec. 8, 1855; Nichols, *Bleeding Kansas,* 49–52; House, *Howard Report,* 1060–65, 1042–44; Brewerton, *War in Kansas,* 223–32; Merrill, *True History,* 15–23; Thomas H. Gladstone, *The Englishman in Kansas or Squatter Life and Border Warfare* (1857; reprint, Lincoln, Nebr., 1971), 283–87; and Sara T. L. Robinson, *Kansas; Its Interior and Exterior Life* (Boston, 1857), 104.
62. *Herald of Freedom,* July 28, 1855; Merrill, *True History,* 15–23; and House, *Howard Report,* 1056–60.
63. House, *Howard Report,* 102–4, 1060–65; *New York Times,* Dec. 11, 1855; *Herald of Freedom,* Dec. 1, 1855; and Robinson, *Kansas Conflict,* 184–86.
64. *Organization of the Free State Government in Kansas, with the Inaugural Speech and Message of Governor Robinson* (Washington, D.C., 1856), 4.
65. J. R. Kennedy in Charles S. Gleed, ed., *The Kansas Memorial, A Report of the Old Settlers' Meeting Held at Bismarck Grove, Kansas, September 15th and 16th, 1879* (Kansas City, Mo., 1880), 207–9; *New York Times,* Dec. 11, 1855; *Herald of Freedom,* Dec. 1, 1855; Nichols, *Bleeding Kansas,* 52–59; and House, *Howard Report,* 103–4.
66. J. R. Kennedy in Gleed, ed., *Kansas Memorial,* 183–88, 207–9; and Robinson, *Kansas Conflict,* 184–86. Although Jones refused to show it, he did have a warrant from Justice of the Peace Hugh Cameron. Free-state leaders were later forced to concede that fact, but they protested that soliciting Cameron to issue the warrant was a deliberate affront to them, for Cameron not only possessed his office by appointment from the territorial legislature, but had also been a judge of the election on March 30.
67. *New York Times,* Feb. 20, 1856.
68. Ibid., Dec. 11, 1855; House, *Howard Report,* 1069–74; Wilson Shannon to General H. J. Strickler, Nov. 27, 1855, "Executive Minutes," vol. 3, *Transactions of the Kansas State Historical Society* (Topeka, 1886), 283–337, esp. 292; and Wilson Shannon to Major Gen. Wm. P. Richardson, Nov. 27, 1855, ibid., 291–92.

69. Wilson Shannon to Franklin Pierce, Nov. 28, 1855, "Executive Minutes," vol. 3, *Transactions*, 292–94; Wilson Shannon to President, Nov. 28, 1855, House, Executive Documents, 34th Cong., 3d sess., 1856, serial 893, no. 1; and Wilson Shannon to Col. Sumner, Dec. 1, 1855, Daniel Woodson Papers, Kansas State Historical Society, Topeka. Uncertain of his place in the growing crisis, Sumner first informed the governor he would provide the troops but then reneged. E. V. Sumner to Wilson Shannon, Dec. 5, 1855, "Executive Minutes," vol. 3, *Transactions*, 296; Wilson Shannon to Col. Sumner, Dec. 6, 1855, ibid., 296–97; and E. V. Sumner to Wilson Shannon, Dec. 7, 1855, ibid., 299.

70. Wilson Shannon to Franklin Pierce, Nov. 28, 1855, "Executive Minutes," vol. 3, *Transactions*, 292–94.

71. Proclamation of Gov. Shannon, Nov. 29, 1855, "Executive Minutes," vol. 3, *Transactions*, 294–95.

72. *(Louisville) Courier* in *New York Times*, Dec. 7, 1855; *New York Times*, Dec. 13, 1855; and Wm. T. Davis to Catharine, Dec. 5, 1855, Davis-Hughes Correspondence, Western Historical Manuscript Collection, Columbia, Mo.

73. Dec. 1, 1855 entry, Moore Journals.

74. Brewerton, *War in Kansas*, 168.

75. C. K. Holliday to Wife, Dec. 13, 1855, Lela Barnes, ed., "Letters of Cyrus Kurtz Holliday," 275–76; and C. K. Holliday to Wife, Dec. 6, 1855, ibid., 275.

76. Edward to Parents, [Dec. 8, 1855], Peterson, "Letters of Edward and Sarah Fitch," 57–58.

77. William Phillips, *The Conquest of Kansas by Missouri and Her Allies* (Boston, 1856), 203, 205–6; Gladstone, *Englishman in Kansas*, 22–23; *Herald of Freedom*, Nov. 24, Dec. 1–3, Dec. 15, 1855; and Robinson, *Kansas*, 128–59.

78. *Herald of Freedom*, Dec. 2, 1855; *New York Times*, Dec. 17, 18, 20, 1855; and Phillips, *Conquest of Kansas*, 203.

79. B. Hornsby to Genl. G. R. Smith, Dec. 11, 1855, General George R. Smith Collection, Missouri Historical Society, St. Louis.

80. Dec. 6, 1855 entry, Moore Journals.

81. Brewerton, *War in Kansas*, 303–10; and Nichols, *Bleeding Kansas*, 66–68.

82. Robinson, *Kansas*, 141–59; Lois H. Walker, "Reminiscences of Early Times in Kansas," vol. 5, *Transactions of the Kansas State Historical Society* (Topeka, 1896), 74–76; and Brewerton, *War in Kansas*, 268–75.

83. *New York Times*, Dec. 17, 1855.

84. Brewerton, *War in Kansas*, 319–22; Merrill, *True History*, 24–28; Gladstone, *Englishman in Kansas*, 288–92; and House, *Howard Report*, 1128, 1121–26.

85. Phillips, *Conquest of Kansas*, 214; and Robinson, *Kansas Conflict*, 216–18.

86. Wilson Shannon to President, Dec. 11, 1855, *New York Times*, Feb. 20, 1856; and Wilson Shannon to Franklin Pierce, Dec. 11, 1855, "Executive Minutes," vol. 3, *Transactions*, 299–301.

87. Nichols, *Bleeding Kansas*, 59–65; Brewerton, *War in Kansas*, 171–89; and *Herald of Freedom*, Dec. 15, 1855.

88. Phillips, *Conquest of Kansas*, 219.

89. *New York Times*, Dec. 24, 1855; and Brewerton, *War in Kansas*, 171–89.

90. Wilson Shannon to President, Dec. 11, 1855, *New York Times*, Feb. 20, 1856; and *New York Times*, Dec. 28, 1855. For the settlement's text, see *Herald of Freedom*, Jan. 12, 1856.

91. Wilson Shannon to Franklin Pierce, Dec. 11 1855, "Executive Minutes," vol. 3, *Transactions*, 299–301; *Herald of Freedom*, Dec. 15, 1855.

92. D. R. Atchison to A. R. Corbin, Dec. 14, 1855, Rutgers College Collection, Missouri Historical Society, St. Louis.

93. William E. Parrish, *David Rice Atchison of Missouri: Border Politician* (Columbia, Mo., 1961), 182; Wilson Shannon to Franklin Pierce, Dec. 11, 1855, "Executive Minutes," vol. 3, *Transactions*, 299–301; and *Herald of Freedom*, Dec. 15, 1855.

94. Wilson Shannon to Franklin Pierce, Dec. 11, 1855, "Executive Minutes," vol. 3, *Transactions*, 299–301; Wilson Shannon to S. J. Jones, Dec. 8, 1855, ibid., 298; Wilson Shannon to General Strickler, Dec. 8, 1855, ibid.; and Wilson Shannon to General Richardson, Dec. 8, 1855, ibid.

95. *Herald of Freedom*, Jan. 12, 1856; Speer, *Gen. James H. Lane*, 64–65; and *New York Times*, Dec. 28, 1855.

96. House, *Howard Report*, 1102–10; Brewerton, *War in Kansas*, 191–202; and Nichols, *Bleeding Kansas*, 72–79.

97. Speer, *Gen. James H. Lane*, 64–65; John Brown to Wife and Children, Dec. 16, 1855, John Brown Jr. Papers (microfilm), Ohio Historical Society, Columbus; and Oswald Garrison Villard, *John Brown, 1800–1859: A Biography Fifty Years After* (Boston, 1911), 125–26.

98. Villard, *John Brown*, 121–24.

99. Edward F. to Parents, Dec. 12, [1855], Peterson, "Letters of Edward and Sarah Fitch," 58.

100. Wilson Shannon to Franklin Pierce, Dec. 11, 1855, "Executive Minutes," vol. 3, *Transactions*, 299–301; and Annual Message, Dec. 31, 1855, James D. Richardson, *A Compilation of the Messages and Papers of the Presidents, 1789–1908*, vol. 5 (Washington, D.C., 1908), 340.

101. Robinson, *Kansas*, 141–59; *New York Times*, Dec. 28, 29, 1855; and Brewerton, *War in Kansas*, 124–26.

102. *Missouri Republican*, Dec. 25, 1855.

103. Isaac T. Goodnow Diary, Dec. 21, 1855, Isaac Tichenor Goodnow Collection, Kansas State Historical Society, Topeka.

104. D. L. Child to N. P. Banks, Jan. 3, 1856, Nathaniel P. Banks Papers, Library of Congress.

105. J. Gillespie to [Lyman Trumbull], Jan. 3, 1856, Lyman Trumbull Family Papers, Illinois State Historical Library, Springfield.

106. H. A. Wilcox to Rice, Jan. 8, 1856, Salmon P. Chase Papers, Ohio Historical Society, Columbus.

107. J. H. Lane for Committee of Safety to N. P. Banks, Jan. 20, 1856, Banks Papers; J. H. Lane, Ch. Robinson, and G. W. Deitzler to Governor of Ohio, Jan. 21, 1856, in *Herald of Freedom,* Feb. 23, 1856. Ohio Governor Salmon P. Chase referred the letter to the General Assembly. J. H. Lane and C. Robinson to Governor of Minnesota, Jan. 22, 1856, Robinson Papers; and Lydia Pittall to Charles Sumner, Jan. 27, 1856, Pierce Collection.

108. Thomas H. Shelby to N. P. Banks, Jan. 29, 1856, Banks Papers; and S. C. Pomeroy to [Banks], Feb. 2, 1856, ibid.

109. John H[arland] to Phil, Jan. 20, 1856, Bulkley Family Papers, Missouri Historical Society, St. Louis.

110. C. M. Clay to Jas. S. Rollins, Jan. 5, 1856, James S. Rollins Papers, Western Historical Manuscript Collection, Columbia, Mo.

111. *Missouri Democrat,* Nov. 28, 1855; and *Squatter Sovereign,* Dec. 4, 1855.

112. D. R. Atchison to A. R. Corbin, Dec. 14, 1855, Rutgers College Collection.

113. *Herald of Freedom,* Dec. 22, 1855.

114. Wilder, *Annals of Kansas,* 92.

5. THE WAR COMMENCES IN EARNEST

1. Isaac Tichenor Goodnow Diary, Jan. 26, 1856, Isaac Tichenor Goodnow Collection, Kansas State Historical Society, Topeka.

2. Sara T. L. Robinson, *Kansas; Its Interior and Exterior Life,* 7th ed. (Boston, 1857), 177; *New York Times,* Feb. 25, 16, 1856; and Lydia Pittall to Charles Sumner, Jan. 27, 1856, Edward Lillis Pierce Collection, Kansas State Historical Society, Topeka.

3. *New York Times,* Jan. 29, Feb. 2, 1856; and *(Lawrence) Herald of Freedom,* Jan. 19, 1856.

4. *Herald of Freedom,* Jan. 26, Feb. 2, 16, March 29, 1856; *New York Times,* Jan. 29, Feb. 2, 4, 1856; House, *Howard Report,* 34th Cong., 1st sess., 1856, serial 869, rept. 200, 981–1002, 1006–15, 1018–20, 1026–35; Alice Nichols, *Bleeding Kansas* (New York, 1954), 82–83; and T. H. Gladstone, *The Englishman in Kansas or Squatter Life and Border Warfare* (1857; reprint, Lincoln, Nebr., 1971), 294–95. Sam F. Tappan wrote to Charles Sumner that Missourians had demanded the polls at Easton and fired on the free-state men when these were not delivered. Four men, two from each side, had been killed. Sam F. Tappan to [Charles Sumner], Jan. 18, 1856, Pierce Collection.

5. *New York Times,* Jan. 29, Feb. 2, 1856; *Herald of Freedom,* Jan. 19, 1856; and House, *Howard Report,* 650.

6. President's special message, Jan. 24, 1856, *New York Times,* Jan. 26, 1856; and James A. Rawley, *Race and Politics: "Bleeding Kansas" and the Coming of the Civil War* (Lincoln, Nebr., 1969), 117–18.

7. *New York Times,* Jan. 28, 1856.
8. Pierce's biographer says the message had a very narrow purpose: to persuade the Southern Know-Nothings to support the Democrats in organizing the House leadership. If so, it failed. Republicans won the balloting. Roy Franklin Nichols, *Franklin Pierce: Young Hickory of the Granite Hills* (Philadelphia, 1958), 441–45; and Allan Nevins, *Ordeal of the Union,* vol. 2 (New York, 1947), 416–18.
9. E. P. Fitch to Parents, Feb. 24, 1856, John M. Peterson, "Letters of Edward and Sarah Fitch, Lawrence, Kansas, 1855–1863," *Kansas History* 12 (spring 1989): 48–70, 62.
10. Nichols, *Franklin Pierce,* 441–45; Jefferson Davis to Cols. Sumner and Cooke, Feb. 15, 1856, and W. L. Marcy to Wilson Shannon, Feb. 16, 1856, in *New York Times,* Feb. 20, 1856; Rawley, *Race and Politics,* 119; Nichols, *Bleeding Kansas,* 93–94, 86; James D. Richardson, *A Compilation of the Messages and Papers of the Presidents, 1789–1908,* vol. 5 (Washington, D.C., 1908), 390–91; and President's Proclamation, Feb. 11, 1856, in *Herald of Freedom,* March 8, 1856.
11. *Kansas City (Mo.) Enterprise,* March 22, 1856.
12. *Richmond Enquirer,* March 23, 1856.
13. *Organization of the Free State Government in Kansas, with the Inaugural Speech and Message of Governor Robinson* (Washington, D.C., 1856), 3–5; and Governor's Message, March 4, 1856, in *Herald of Freedom,* March 8, 1856.
14. *Free State Government,* 4–13.
15. March 4, 1856 entry, Henry Miles Moore Journals, Yale University Library.
16. March 5, 1856 entry, Moore Journals.
17. April 11, 30, 1856 entries, Goodnow Diary, Goodnow Collection; and *Herald of Freedom,* May 10, 1856.
18. David R. Atchison to Amos A. Lawrence, April 15, 1856, *Kansas City Enterprise,* June 28, 1856.
19. *Herald of Freedom,* Feb. 9, 1856.
20. *New York Times,* Jan. 21, April 4, March 25, 1856; John [Everett] to Father, April 11, 1856, "Letters of John and Sarah Everett, 1854–1864," *Kansas Historical Quarterly* 8 (Feb. 1939), 3–34, esp. 27–28; W. A. Russell and others to J. Riddlebarger and Co., March 21, 1856, William Hutchinson Papers, Kansas State Historical Society, Topeka; David S. Hoyt Statement, New England Emigrant Aid Company Records, Boston University Special Collections.
21. *New York Times,* Feb. 27, 1856.
22. *Herald of Freedom,* March 1, 1856. Italics added by *Herald of Freedom.*
23. Axalla to Sister, Aug. 3, 1856, William Stanley Hoole, "A Southerner's Viewpoint of the Kansas Situation, 1856–1857: The Letters of Lieut. Col. A. J. Hoole, C.S.A.," *Kansas Historical Quarterly* 3 (Feb. 1934): 43–68, esp. 61.

24. W. H. Russell and others to the People of the Southern States, March 25, 1856, William Barnes Collection, Kansas State Historical Society, Topeka.
25. A. P. Butler to D. R. Atchison, Feb. 28, 1856, David Rice Atchison Papers, Western Historical Manuscript Collection, Columbia, Mo.
26. A. P. Butler to Atchison, March 10, 1856, Atchison Papers.
27. Mary J. Klem, "Missouri in the Kansas Struggle," pt. 3 of *Mississippi Valley Historical Association Proceedings* 9 (1917–1918), 393–413, esp. 407–8.
28. Klem, "Missouri in the Kansas Struggle," 407–8.
29. D. F. Jamison to D. R. Atchison, March 26, 1856, Atchison Papers.
30. Peter to Sister, Feb. 14, 1856, Kennerly Family Papers, Missouri Historical Society, St. Louis.
31. *Herald of Freedom,* March 29, 1856; April 6, 17, 18 entries, Moore Journals.
32. W. T. Davis to Mother, March 8, 1856, Davis-Hughes Correspondence, Western Historical Manuscript Collection, Columbia, Mo.
33. *New York Times,* March 22, 1856.
34. James J. Brooks to Barnes, April 10, 1856, Barnes Collection.
35. [John Brown, Jr.] to Louisa, March 29, 1856, John Brown Papers, Boyd B. Stutler Collection, Ohio Historical Society, Columbus.
36. D. A. Clayton, Jr., to Barnes, April 7, 1856, Barnes Collection.
37. Joseph R. Hearst to ———, April 22, 1856, Barnes Collection.
38. Wilson Shannon to William L. Marcy, April 11, 1856, House, Executive Documents, 34th Cong., 3d sess., 1856, serial 893, no. 1, 66–67.
39. James Ford Rhodes, *History of the United States from the Compromise of 1850,* vol. 2, *1854–1860* (New York, 1900), 122–27; Robert W. Johannsen, *Stephen A. Douglas* (New York, 1973), 491–505; Senate, Report No. 34, 34th Cong., 1st sess., 1856, serial 836; Report from the Senate Committee on Territories by Mr. Collamer, in *New York Times,* March 14, 1856; and Rawley, *Race and Politics,* 120–21.
40. Senate, Report No. 34, p. 61.
41. Rhodes, *History of the United States,* 122–27; and Rawley, *Race and Politics,* 119–20.
42. Report from the Senate Committee on Territories by Mr. Collamer, in *New York Times,* March 14, 1856; Rawley, *Race and Politics,* 120–21; Johannsen, *Stephen A. Douglas,* 491–505; I. Washburn to J. S. Stevens, April 4, 1856, Israel Washburn Papers, Library of Congress; Wm. M. Chace, James Wickham, Wingate Hayes to N. P. Banks, May 1, 1856, Nathaniel P. Banks Papers, Library of Congress; and O. R. Matteson to H. H. Hawley, May 2, 1856, Orsamus Benajah Matteson Miscellaneous Papers, New-York Historical Society.
43. *New York Times,* April 10, 1856.
44. Nichols, *Bleeding Kansas,* 94–95; Rawley, *Race and Politics,* 124–25; Johannsen, *Stephen A. Douglas,* 491–505; and *New York Times,* April 16, 1856.

45. *New York Times,* April 28, 1856; Johannsen, *Stephen A. Douglas,* 491–505; *Herald of Freedom,* May 10, 1856; Nichols, *Bleeding Kansas,* 94–95; Rawley, *Race and Politics,* 124–25; and Leverett W. Spring, *Kansas: The Prelude to the War for the Union* (Boston, 1885), 74–77.

46. *New York Times,* April 10, 1856.

47. Ibid., May 24, 1856.

48. [Carl Schurz], *The Reminiscences of Carl Schurz,* vol. 2 (New York, 1907), 35–36.

49. David M. Potter, *The Impending Crisis, 1848–1861* (New York, 1976), 210.

50. *Congressional Globe Appendix,* 34th Cong., 1st sess., 1856, 544–47.

51. Ibid., 545.

52. Ibid., 544–47.

53. Potter, *Impending Crisis,* 209–11; and James M. McPherson, *Ordeal by Fire: The Civil War and Reconstruction* (New York, 1982), 93–94.

54. *Boston Daily Advertiser,* May 26, 1856; and Richard H. Sewell, *A House Divided: Sectionalism and Civil War, 1848–1865* (Baltimore, 1988), 51.

55. June 13, 1856 entry, Goodnow Journal, Goodnow Collection.

56. *Richmond Enquirer,* June 6, 1856.

57. Bertram Wyatt-Brown, *The Shaping of Southern Culture: Honor, Grace, and War, 1760s–1890s* (Chapel Hill, N.C., 2001), 195–98; and Bertram Wyatt-Brown, *Southern Honor: Ethics and Behavior in the Old South* (New York, 1982), 369.

58. Axalla to Mother, April 14, 1856, Hoole, "Southerner's Viewpoint," 45–46; John H. Gihon, *Geary and Kansas: Governor Geary's Administration in Kansas: With a Complete History of the Territory until July 1857* (Philadelphia, 1857), 51; Samuel J. Jones to Wilson Shannon, April 20, 1856, Senate, Executive Documents, 35th Cong., 1st sess., 1858, serial 923, no. 17; John Speer, *Life of Gen. James H. Lane, "The Liberator of Kansas" with Corrobative Incidents of Pioneer History* (Garden City, Kans., 1897), 76–78; Nichols, *Bleeding Kansas,* 97–101; *New York Times,* May 2, 1856; and Edward P. Fitch to Father, April 21, 1856, Peterson, "Letters of Edward and Sarah Fitch," 63.

59. Samuel J. Jones to Wilson Shannon, April 20, 1856, Senate, Executive Documents, 6; Wm. J. Preston, J. C. Anderson, W. F. Donaldson, April 28, 1856, ibid., 7–8; Nichols, *Bleeding Kansas,* 97–101; Edward P. Fitch to Father, April 21, 1856, Peterson, "Letters of Edward and Sarah Fitch," 63.

60. Wilson Shannon to Col. Sumner, April 20, 1856, Senate, Executive Documents, 6–7; E. V. Sumner to Wilson Shannon, April 21, 1856, ibid., 7; Nichols, *Bleeding Kansas,* 97–101; Lt. James McIntosh to Wilson Shannon, April 30, 1856, Senate, Executive Documents, 19–20; *Herald of Freedom,* April 26, 19, 1856; and *New York Times,* May 3, 1856.

61. Wilson Shannon to Sec. of State Marcy, April 27, 1856, Senate, Executive Documents, 2–5; *Herald of Freedom,* April 26, 1856; Lt. James McIntosh

to Wilson Shannon, April 30, 1856, Senate, Executive Documents, 19–20; and O. N. Merrill, *A True History of the Kansas Wars, and Their Origin, Progress and Incidents* (1856; reprint, Tarrytown, N.Y., 1932), 46–47.

62. *(Atchison) Squatter Sovereign,* April 29, 1856.

63. *Lecompton (Kans.) Union,* n.d. 1856.

64. L. P. Hanscom to N. P. Banks, April 26, 1856, Banks Papers. See also Nelson Rusk to Barnes, April 26, 1856, Barnes Collection.

65. Axalla to Brother, April 27, 1856, in Hoole, "A Southerner's Viewpoint," 47–48.

66. *Herald of Freedom,* April 26, 1856.

67. L. P. Hanscom to N. P. Banks, April 26, 1856, box 10, Banks Papers; and John Sherman, *Recollections of Forty Years in the House, Senate and Cabinet* (Chicago, 1896), 96–105.

68. Wm. O. Howard to N. P. Banks, Jr., April 30, 1856, box 10, Banks Papers; and Wm. O. Howard to N. P. Banks, May 4, 1856, ibid.

69. Rawley, *Race and Politics,* 130–32; *New York Times,* May 13, June 14, 1856; Nichols, *Bleeding Kansas,* 101–3; and April 5, 1856 entry, Moore Journal.

70. Speer, *Gen. James H. Lane,* 22–23.

71. [Andrew H. Reeder], "Governor Reeder's Escape from Kansas," vol. 3, *Transactions of the Kansas State Historical Society* (Topeka, 1886), 205–23, esp. 205–8; Charles Robinson, *The Kansas Conflict* (Lawrence, 1898), 234–38; Charles S. Gleed, ed., *The Kansas Memorial, A Report of the Old Settlers' Meeting Held at Bismarck Grove, Kansas, September 15th and 16th, 1879* (Kansas City, Mo., 1880), 62–63; James F. Legate to Charles Sumner, May 20, 1856, Pierce Collection; House, *Howard Report,* 65–67; and Sherman, *Recollections of Forty Years,* 96–105.

72. [Reeder], "Governor Reeder's Escape from Kansas," 208–10, 213–16.

73. Jno. Sherman to [N. P. Banks], May 9, 1856, Banks Papers.

74. Robinson, *Kansas Conflict,* 134–38; *New York Times,* May 13, 1856; Robinson, *Kansas,* 267–72; Gladstone, *Englishman in Kansas,* 56, 61–63; Wm. Phillips to [Sara Robinson], May 26, 1856, Charles Robinson Papers, University of Kansas Library, Lawrence; and Margaret Sarah Cecilia Sherman to Sara Robinson, May 25, 1856, Charles and Sara T. D. Robinson Papers, Kansas State Historical Society, Topeka.

75. Robinson, *Kansas,* 267–72; and Robinson, *Kansas Conflict,* 281–83.

76. *Boston Daily Advertiser,* May 14, 1856; and Sherman, *Recollections of Forty Years,* 97.

77. C. W. Topliff, W. G. Roberts, and John Hutchinson to Col. E. V. Sumner, May 11, 1856, in *New York Times,* Aug. 8, 1856; and *New York Times,* May 23, 1856.

78. Col. E. V. Sumner to S. Cooper, May 19, 1856, in *New York Times,* Aug. 8, 1856; and James McIntosh to Col. E. V. Sumner, May 21, 1856, House, Executive Documents, 39–40.

79. Axalla to Sister, May 18, 1856, Hoole, "Kansas Situation," 52.

80. Edward to Parents, May 18, 1856, in Peterson, "Letters of Edward and Sarah Fitch," 64.
81. Memorial to the President from Inhabitants of Kansas, May 22, 1856, House, Executive Documents, 73–85.
82. Gladstone, *Englishman in Kansas*, 30–38; *New York Times*, May 30, 1856; and Memorial to the President from Inhabitants of Kansas, May 22, 1856, House, Executive Documents, 73–85. On the motives for destroying the hotel, see Richard Cordley, *A History of Lawrence, Kansas from the First Settlement to the Close of the Rebellion* (Lawrence, Kans., 1895), 92. According to a later account, Lecompte refused to issue an order for the destruction of the hotel but Jones lied to his men and told them he had such an order. James C. Malin, "Judge Lecompte and the 'Sack of Lawrence,' May 21, 1856: Part Two: The Historical Phase," *Kansas Historical Quarterly* 20 (Nov. 1953): 553–97; A. W. Reese, "Recollections of the Civil War," 1870 (microfilm), Western Historical Manuscript Collection, Columbia, Missouri; and Nichols, *Bleeding Kansas*, 105–9.
83. Nichols, *Bleeding Kansas*, 116; Nevins, *Ordeal of the Union*, vol. 2, 436–37.
84. David R. Atchison Speech, May 21, 1856, box 1, Richard Hinton Papers, Kansas State Historical Society, Topeka; and William E. Parrish, *David Rice Atchison of Missouri: Border Politician* (Columbia, Mo., 1961), 200–202.
85. C. K. Holliday et al. [May 22, 1856], Salmon P. Chase Papers (microfilm), Ohio Historical Society, Columbus.
86. *New York Times*, May 26, 1856.
87. [Reeder], "Governor Reeder's Escape from Kansas," 216–21; and [George C. Brackett], "Statement of Hon. George C. Brackett," vol. 3, *Transactions of the Kansas State Historical Society* (Topeka, 1886), 223–25.
88. [Reeder], "Governor Reeder's Escape from Kansas," 221–23.
89. *New York Times*, June 13, 1856.
90. William Elsey Connelley, *John Brown* (Topeka, 1900), 163–68, 189–206.
91. Oliver Brown to Mother, Brother, and Sisters, Jan. 6 [1856], Oliver Brown Papers, Ohio Historical Society, Columbus.
92. Stephen B. Oates, *To Purge This Land with Blood: A Biography of John Brown* (New York, 1970).
93. James Brewer Stuart, *Holy Warriors: The Abolitionists and American Slavery* (New York, 1997), 155–62, 167–70, 175; Lewis Perry, *Radical Abolitionism: Anarchy and the Government of God in Antislavery Thought* (Ithaca, N.Y., 1973), 232–67; John Stauffer, *The Black Hearts of Men: Radical Abolitionists and the Transformation of Race* (Cambridge, Mass., 2002), 27, 121–23; and Stanley Harrold, *American Abolitionists* (Harlow, Eng., 2001), 81–83.
94. John Brown to Wife and Children, June 28, 1855, in F. B. Sanborn, *The Life and Letters of John Brown, Liberator of Kansas, and Martyr of Virginia* (1885; reprint, New York, 1969), 193–94.

95. Oates, *Purge This Land with Blood,* 160.

96. *Herald of Freedom,* May 10, 17, 1856; and Oates, *Purge This Land with Blood,* 113, 117–21.

97. Oates, *Purge This Land with Blood,* 102, 113, 117–21, 257; John Brown to Father, Oct. 19, 1855, Louis Ruchames, ed., *John Brown: The Making of a Revolutionary* (New York, 1969), 95–96; John Brown to Editor, Dec. 20, 1855, ibid., 96–101; Sept. 6, 1856 entry, Journal of Richard Hinton, Hinton Papers; and W. A. Phillips, Ruchames, ed., *John Brown,* 220.

98. House, *Howard Report,* 1193–95.

99. Ibid., 1194–95; and Connelley, *John Brown,* 189–206.

100. House, *Howard Report,* 1197–99.

101. Ibid., 1195–97.

102. Richard J. Hinton, *John Brown and His Men* (1894; reprint, New York, 1968), 82n1.

103. D. G. Watt, "Reminiscences of Pottawatomie Creek and Vicinity, 1856," Kansas State Historical Society, Topeka; E. A. Coleman, in Gleed, *Kansas Memorial,* 196–97; Oswald Garrison Villard, *John Brown, 1800–1859: A Biography Fifty Years After* (Boston, 1911), 164–88; Connelley, *John Brown,* 160–68; ch. 3, p. 2, August Bondi Collection, Kansas State Historical Society, Topeka; William W. Caine to F. G. Adams, Feb. 28, 1889, William W. Caine Miscellaneous Collections, Kansas State Historical Society, Topeka; and Robinson, *Kansas Conflict,* 265, 273–79.

104. Coleman, in Gleed, *Kansas Memorial,* 196–97.

105. Connelley, *John Brown,* 239.

106. Robinson, *Kansas Conflict,* 265, 273–79.

107. Lacey Baldwin Smith, *Fools, Martyrs, Traitors: The Story of Martyrdom in the Western World* (New York, 1997), 245.

108. Stauffer, *Black Hearts of Men,* 6, 121–23.

109. E. to S. E. Bridgman, postscript dated May 27 to a May 25, 1856 letter, Edward Bridgman Papers, State Historical Society of Wisconsin, Madison.

110. William Barber to Wilson Shannon, May 26, 1856, Senate, Executive Documents, 22; Wm. A. Heiskell to Wilson Shannon, May 26, 1856, ibid., 22–23; and Lt. Jno. R. Church to Capt. T. J. Wood, May 26, 1856, ibid., 23.

111. Wm. Phillips to [Sara Robinson], May 26, 1856, Robinson Papers; and Margaret Sarah Cecilia Sherman to Sara Robinson, May 25, 1856, Robinson Papers.

112. Margaret Sarah Cecilia Sherman to Sara Robinson, May 25, 1856, Robinson Papers; and Gladstone, *Englishman in Kansas,* 63–64.

6. WE FIGHT TO FREE WHITE MEN

1. D. R. Anthony to Wm. Barnes, June 6, 1856, William Barnes Collection, Kansas State Historical Society, Topeka.

2. John H[arland] to Phil [Bulkley], June 7, 1856, Bulkley Family Papers, Missouri Historical Society, St. Louis.

3. William Phillips, *The Conquest of Kansas, by Missouri and Her Allies* (Boston, 1856), 367–69.
4. *Kansas City (Mo.) Enterprise,* June 21, 1856.
5. Alice Nichols, *Bleeding Kansas* (New York, 1954), 120–24; John Brown to Messrs. Whitman and Eldridge, John Brown Papers, VFM 1393, Ohio Historical Society, Columbus, Ohio; and Jules Abels, *Man on Fire: John Brown and the Cause of Liberty* (New York, 1971), 83–87.
6. Wilson Shannon to Col. Sumner, June 4, 1856, "Executive Minutes," vol. 3, *Transactions of the Kansas State Historical Society* (Topeka, 1886), 311–12; and Proclamation by Gov. Shannon, June 4, 1856, ibid., 312–13.
7. Wilson Shannon to Col. Sumner, May 27, 1856, "Executive Minutes," vol. 3, *Transactions,* 283–337, esp. 310; Capt. J. J. Woods to Wilson Shannon, May 28, 1856, House, Executive Documents, 34th Cong., 3d sess., 1856, serial 893, no. 1, 71; Wilson Shannon to Franklin Pierce, June 17, 1856, ibid., 67–70; and Capt. E. W. B. Newby to Wilson Shannon, May 31, 1856, ibid., 71.
8. Nichols, *Bleeding Kansas,* 120–24; and Richard J. Hinton, *John Brown and His Men* (1894; reprint, 1968), 97. Sumner did not arrest Brown because he lacked a warrant. *New York Times,* June 19, 1856; E. V. Sumner to Col. S. Cooper, June 8, 1856, House, Executive Documents, 44–45.
9. "Personal Reminiscences," ch. 2, August Bondi Collection, Kansas State Historical Society, Topeka, 30.
10. George Ela Diary, June 3, [1856], William Elsey Connelley Collection, Western History Collections, University of Oklahoma Libraries.
11. Gov. Shannon to Col. Sumner, June 4, 1856, "Executive Minutes," vol. 3, *Transactions,* 313–14.
12. *New York Times,* June 14, 19, 1856; and George Ela Diary, June 3, [1856], Connelley Collection.
13. Sara T. L. Robinson, *Kansas; Its Interior and Exterior Life* (Boston, 1857), 292.
14. Wilson Shannon to Franklin Pierce, June 27, 1856, "Executive Minutes," vol. 3, *Transactions,* 317–18.
15. James A. Rawley, *Race and Politics: "Bleeding Kansas" and the Coming of the Civil War* (Lincoln, Nebr., 1969), 158; and John H[arland] to Phil [Bulkley], June 7, 1856, Bulkley Family Papers.
16. Nichols, *Bleeding Kansas,* 140–44; William Elsey Connelley, *Kansas Territorial Governors* (Topeka, 1900), 91–93; Wilson Shannon to Col. Sumner, June 23, 1856, House, Executive Documents, 51–53; E. V. Sumner to D. Woodson, June 28, 1856, ibid., 53–54; and Danl. Woodson to Col. Sumner, June 30, 1856, "Executive Minutes," vol. 3, *Transactions,* 318–19.
17. *New York Times,* July 17, 1856; and Geo. W. Smith et al., "To the Friends of 'Law and Order' Convened at Topeka," July 1, 1856, James Blood Papers, Kansas State Historical Society, Topeka.

18. C. K. Holliday to Wife, July 2, 1856, Lela Barnes, ed., "Letters of Cyrus Kurtz Holliday, 1854–1859," *Kansas Historical Quarterly* 6 (Aug. 1937): 241–94, esp. 285.

19. E. V. Sumner to Col. S. Cooper, July 7, 1856, House, Executive Documents, 56–58; and Journal of the House of Representatives of Kansas in Wendell Holmes Stephenson, *The Political Career of General James H. Lane* (Topeka, 1930), 67n51.

20. *New York Times,* July 18, 1856.

21. Nelson Rusk to Wm. Barnes, July 13, 1856, Barnes Collection.

22. July 2, 4, 1856 entries, Henry Miles Moore Journals, Yale University.

23. S. Cooper to E. V. Sumner, July 21, 1856, House, Executive Documents, 60; S. Cooper to Col. E. V. Sumner, Aug. 28, 1856, ibid., 32–33; and *New York Times,* Aug. 13, 1856.

24. Col. E. V. Sumner to Col. S. Cooper, Aug. 31, 1856, House, Executive Documents, 61.

25. John H. Gihon, *Geary and Kansas: Governor Geary's Administration in Kansas: With a Complete History of the Territory until July 1857* (Philadelphia, 1857), 92; and Roy Franklin Nichols, *Franklin Pierce: Young Hickory of the Granite Hills* (Philadelphia, 1958), 473–80.

26. John Sherman, *Recollections of Forty Years in the House, Senate and Cabinet* (Chicago, 1896), 99–102; and James Ford Rhodes, *History of the United States from the Compromise of 1850,* vol. 2, *1854–1860* (New York, 1900), 201–2.

27. *New York Times,* Aug. 20, 1856; and Nichols, *Bleeding Kansas,* 131.

28. Axalla to Sister, June 8, 1856, in William Stanley Hoole, "A Southerner's Viewpoint of the Kansas Situation, 1856–1857: The Letters of Lieut. Col. A. J. Hoole, C.S.A.," *Kansas Historical Quarterly* 3 (Feb. 1934): 43–68.

29. Thomas H. Gladstone, *The Englishman in Kansas or Squatter Life and Border Warfare* (1857; reprint, Lincoln, Nebr., 1971), 296–30; D. R. Anthony to Wm. Barnes, June 6, 1856, Barnes Collection; and *Boston Daily Advertiser,* Sept. 16, 1856.

30. George Ela Diary, June 11, 1856, Connelley Collection.

31. James McIntosh to Daniel Woodson, June 13, 1856, House, Executive Documents, 72–73.

32. C. K. Holliday to Wife, July 2, 1856, in Barnes, "Letters of Cyrus Kurtz Holliday," 286.

33. *Boston Daily Advertiser,* July 9, 1856.

34. *New York Times,* Sept. 9, 19, Oct. 14, 1856; and T. W. Higginson to ———, [July] 21, 1856, William Chase Crosby Collection, University of Maine Library.

35. Nelson Rusk to Wm. Barnes, July 13, 1856, Barnes Collection.

36. Horace White to Wm. Barnes, Aug. 25, 1856, Barnes Collection.

37. Danl. Woodson to Col. P. St. George Cooke, June 29, 1856, "Executive Minutes," vol. 3, *Transactions,* 317; Danl. Woodson to Col. Sumner, June 30, 1856, ibid., 318–19; Persifor F. Smith to S. Cooper, July 14, 1855

[1856], House, Executive Documents, 65–66; and *New York Times,* Aug. 13, 1856.

38. F. B. Sanborn, *The Life and Letters of John Brown, Liberator of Kansas, and Martyr of Virginia* (1885; reprint, New York, 1969), 338. In early September, Lane came close to capture when U.S. troops under Col. P. St. George Cooke intercepted his army near Lecompton. Lane quickly stepped into the ranks, took a gun, and pretended to be a common soldier. Although evidently suspicious, Cooke did not perceive the deception. Sept. 4, Aug. 30–31, 1856 entries, Moore Journals; and Albert D. Richardson, *Beyond the Mississippi: From the Great River to the Great Ocean: Life and Adventure on the Prairies, Mountains, and Pacific Coast, 1857–1867* (Hartford, Conn., 1867), 44–47.

39. Sept. 4, 1856 entry, Moore Journals.

40. Julia Louisa Lovejoy to Editor, Sept. 22, 1856, "Letters of Julia Louisa Lovejoy, 1856–1864," *Kansas Historical Quarterly* 15 (May, 1947), 127–42, esp. 137.

41. Axalla to Sister, Oct. 12, 1856, Hoole, "A Southerner's Viewpoint," 43–68.

42. Atchison suggested a rotating settlement, with each county sending fifty men to make claims in Kansas. Missourians would take turns, lasting thirty days, after which they would be relieved by another fifty. Each rotation would continue to maintain the claims until the October elections, when "all handy will be there to vote or fight as the case requires." D. R. Atchison to Col. Anderson, May 31, 1856, James Blyth Anderson Papers, University of Kentucky.

43. J. M. Mason to Atchison, Sept. 5, 1856, David Rice Atchison Papers, Western Historical Manuscript Collection, Columbia, Mo.

44. *New York Times,* Sept. 18, 1856.

45. William W. Caine to F. G. Adams, Feb. 28, 1889, William W. Caine Miscellaneous Collections, Kansas State Historical Society, Topeka.

46. D. R. Atchison et al., in *(Independence) Western Dispatch,* Aug. 17, 1856, Broadsides 1856, Missouri Historical Society, St. Louis; and "War in Kansas!," Aug. 20, [1856], ibid.

47. D. R. Atchison et al., in *(Independence) Western Dispatch,* Aug. 17, 1856, Broadsides 1856; "War in Kansas!," Aug. 20, [1856], ibid.; Edward Payson Bridgman and Luke Fisher Parsons, *With John Brown in Kansas: The Battle of Osawatomie* (Madison, Wisc., 1915), 15–17; and *New York Times,* Aug. 23, 1856.

48. D. R. Atchison et al., in *(Independence) Western Dispatch,* Aug. 17, 1856, Broadsides 1856; "War in Kansas!," Aug. 20, [1856], ibid.; and *(St. Louis) Missouri Democrat,* Aug. 21, 1856.

49. Bridgman and Parsons, *With John Brown in Kansas,* 15–17.

50. *New York Times,* Aug. 29, 1856.

51. Bridgman and Parsons, *With John Brown in Kansas,* 4–7, 17–21; John Brown, Sept. 7, 1856, Brinton Webb Woodward Collection, Kansas State Historical Society, Topeka; and *New York Times,* Sept. 16, 1856.

52. John Everett, n.d., "Letters of John and Sarah Everett, 1854–1864," *Kansas Historical Quarterly* 8 (May 1939): 143–74, esp. 147–48.

53. Nichols, *Bleeding Kansas*, 140–44; and Connelley, *Kansas Territorial Governors*, 91–93.

54. Mary J. Klem, "Missouri in the Kansas Struggle," pt. 3, *Mississippi Valley Historical Association Proceedings* 9 (1917–1918), 393–413, esp. 412–13.

55. Danl. Woodson to Maj. Gen. Wm. P. Richardson, Aug. 21, 1856, "Executive Minutes," vol. 3, *Transactions*, 324; and Danl. Woodson to Major General Coffey, Aug. 21, 1856, ibid., 324–25.

56. Danl. Woodson to Maj. Gen. Wm. P. Richardson, Sept. 1, 1856, "Executive Minutes," vol. 3, *Transactions*, 327; Persifor F. Smith to Col. S. Cooper, Aug. 29, 1856, House, Executive Documents, 77–79; P. St. George Cooke to Daniel Woodson, Sept. 1, 1856, ibid., 92–93; Woodson to Cooke, Sept. 1, 1856, ibid., 93; and Daniel Woodson to Lt. Col. P. St. George Cooke, Sept. 1, 1856, ibid., 90–91.

57. W. W. Updegraff to W. Hutchinson, Aug. 5, 1856, William Hutchinson Papers, Kansas State Historical Society, Topeka.

58. Journal of Richard J. Hinton, Aug. 21, Sept. 3, 1856, Richard Hinton Papers, Kansas State Historical Society, Topeka; "Autobiography," Samuel James Reader Papers, Kansas State Historical Society, Topeka; "Personal Reminiscences," ch. 3, p. 25, Bondi Collection; and A. A. Preston to Brother, Sept. 2, 1856, Civil War Collection, Missouri Historical Society, St. Louis.

59. James Redpath, *The Public Life of Capt. John Brown* (Boston, 1860), 111–14.

60. The others were G. W. Brown, George W. Deitzler, George W. Smith, Samuel N. Wood, and Gauis Jenkins. *New York Times*, June 14, July 4, 5, 1856.

61. Marcus Parrott to John Sherman, July 16, 1856, John Sherman Papers, Library of Congress.

62. *New York Times*, June 28, July 5, 1856.

63. Robinson, *Kansas*, 300–317; and Gihon, *Geary and Kansas*, 145–47.

64. John Greenleaf Whittier, *The Complete Poetical Works of John Greenleaf Whittier* (Boston, 1894), 392.

65. In his memoirs, Robinson speculated that Lane wanted to get the prisoners killed in an escape attempt, for many were his political and personal enemies, including not only Robinson but Gaius Jenkins, with whom Lane had a land claim dispute. Lane marched on Lecompton anyway and was only deterred by U.S. troops. Stephenson, *General James H. Lane*, 76n56; Charles Robinson, *The Kansas Conflict* (Lawrence, Kans., 1898), 302–4; and P. St. George Cooke to Maj. George Deas, Sept. 5, 1856, House, Executive Documents, 101–4.

66. Bradley Chapin, *The American Law of Treason: Revolutionary and Early National Origins* (Seattle, 1964), 7, 82–117; and James Willard Hurst,

The Law of Treason in the United States: Collected Essays (Westport, Conn., 1971), 7, 13n15, 186–98.

67. Thomas P. Slaughter, *Bloody Dawn: The Christiana Riot and Racial Violence in the Antebellum North* (New York, 1991), 112–38; and Paul Finkelman, "The Treason Trial of Castner Hanway," in *American Political Trials,* ed. Michal R. Belknap (Westport, Conn., 1994), 77–95.

68. Michal R. Belknap, "Introduction: Political Trials in the American Past," in Belknap, *American Political Trials,* xiii–xxviii, esp xvi.

69. *New York Times,* July 12, Aug. 5, 1856; *Boston Daily Advertiser,* Aug. 8, 1856; and Nichols, *Franklin Pierce,* 473–80.

70. *New York Times,* Aug. 15, Sept. 20, 1856. Some of the pressure on the president came from closer to home. The First Lady's aunt was Amos Lawrence's stepmother who forwarded a personal plea from Sara Robinson for her husband's freedom to Mrs. Pierce who read it to her husband. Leverett W. Spring, *Kansas: The Prelude to the War for the Union* (Boston, 1885), 196; William Lawrence, *Life of Amos A. Lawrence* (Boston, 1888), 111; Nichols, *Franklin Pierce,* 481–83, 473–80; and *New York Times,* Sept. 20, 1856.

71. *New York Times,* Sept. 20, 1856.

72. Robert W. Johannsen, *Stephen A. Douglas* (New York, 1973), 524–28; *New York Times,* June 24, 1856; Kenneth M. Stampp, *America in 1857: A Nation on the Brink* (New York, 1990), 147; Rhodes, *History of the United States from the Compromise of 1850,* vol. 2, 189–96; *New York Times,* July 3, 1856; and Michael F. Holt, "Another Look at the Election of 1856," in *James Buchanan and the Political Crisis of the 1850s,* ed. by Michael J. Birkner (Selinsgrove, Pa., 1996), 37–67, esp. 55–56.

73. *New York Times,* July 2, 1856.

74. House, *Howard Report,* 34th Cong., 1st sess., 1856, serial 869, Rept. 200, 1–2, 42, 57.

75. House, *Howard Report,* p. 67. A minority report, written by the Missouri congressman on the committee, disputed these findings. According to Oliver, those disturbances which had marred the Kansas elections were normal in U.S. politics. Oliver cited NEEAC interference and free-state military preparation as spurs to Missouri intervention in the territory. While the two Republicans had skipped testimony on the Pottawatomie murders, Oliver included it, identifying Captain John Brown as the probable assailant. House, *Howard Report,* 68–109; and Spring, *Kansas,* 145–46.

76. Rawley, *Race and Politics,* 153–56; Johannsen, *Stephen A. Douglas,* 524–28; and Nichols, *Franklin Pierce,* 475–77.

77. *Border Ruffian Code in Kansas,* 7–8.

78. O. S. Deming to Banks, June 10, 1856, Nathaniel P. Banks Papers, Library of Congress; Rev. Asa Prescott to N. P. Banks, June 17, 1856, ibid.; and Morris L. Hallowell to N. P. Banks, Jr., July 22, 1856, ibid.

79. John to ———, July 24, [1856], "Letters of John and Sarah Everett," 145; H. B. Hurt to William Barnes, Aug. 5, 1856, Barnes Collection; Stampp,

America in 1857, 147; Wm. Bigler to James Buchanan, July 15, 1856, James Buchanan Papers, Historical Society of Pennsylvania, Philadelphia; Denton J. Snider, *The American Ten Years' War, 1855–1865* (St. Louis, 1906), 120–24; and Rawley, *Race and Politics,* 157.

80. Eric H. Walther, *The Fire-Eaters* (Baton Rouge, 1992), 178.

81. Wm. Bigler to James Buchanan, June 23, 1856, Buchanan Papers; John Pettit to James Buchanan, June 27, 1856, ibid.; and Wm. Hale to James Buchanan, June 28, 1856, ibid.

82. J. W. Bradbury to James Buchanan, Sept. 11, 1856, roll 28, ibid.

83. Howell Cobb to James Buchanan, Dec. 5, 1854, Ulrich Bonnell Phillips, ed., *The Correspondence of Robert Toombs, Alexander H. Stephens, and Howell Cobb* (New York, 1970), 348; and J. Glancy Jones to James Buchanan, Feb. 4, 1856, Buchanan Papers.

84. J. Glancy Jones to James Buchanan, March 22, 1856, Buchanan Papers; Benj. Parke to James Buchanan, Aug. 7, 1856, ibid.; and James Buchanan to Democratic party, June 15, 1856 in *Border Ruffian Code in Kansas.*

85. Rawley, *Race and Politics,* 157; Robinson, *Kansas Conflict,* 230; and *New York Times,* Aug. 6, 1856.

86. *Lecompton Union,* Aug. 30, 1856.

87. W. H. Hutter to James Buchanan, June 9, 1856, Buchanan Papers; *New York Times,* June 25, 1856; *United States* v. *Andrew H. Reeder,* Daniel Woodson Papers, Kansas State Historical Society, Topeka; and *Boston Daily Advertiser,* June 19, 1856.

88. S. N. Wood to G. W. Brown, Feb. 25, 1856, *Herald of Freedom,* March 15, 1856.

89. *Border Ruffian Code in Kansas,* 11–12.

90. John Graham to James Buchanan, Oct. 17, 1856, Buchanan Papers.

91. S. C. Harrington to Amasa Walker and others, Oct. 19, 1856, S. C. Harrington Papers, Duke University Special Collections Library.

92. *New York Times,* Oct. 23, 1856.

93. Thomas A. Emmet to Christie, Aug. 14, 1856, Alexander Christie Papers, Missouri Historical Society, St. Louis.

94. Sarah M. C. Everett to Cynthia, Aug. 1, 1856, "Letters of John and Sarah Everett," 146–47.

95. *Border Ruffian Code in Kansas,* 10–11.

96. R. M. T. Hunter speech, Oct. 1, 1856, R. M. T. Hunter Papers, University of Virginia.

97. Daniel Dana to James Buchanan, Oct. 18, 1856, Buchanan Papers.

98. Nichols, *Bleeding Kansas,* 139.

99. Rawley, *Race and Politics,* 159; D. Strong to John W. Geary, July 30, 1856, John White Geary Papers, Yale University.

100. Gihon, *Geary and Kansas,* iv.

101. W. L. Marcy to John W. Geary, Aug. 26, 1856, Geary Papers.

102. Gihon, *Geary and Kansas,* 104–6, 115–19. Shannon did not dislike the territory enough to shun it permanently. He later returned to Kansas to

practice law and was well-liked by former free-state men. He died in Lawrence in 1877. Connelley, *Kansas Territorial Governors,* 37–60.

103. Nichols, *Bleeding Kansas,* 152–57.

104. John W. Geary Letters and Executive Minutes, Kansas State Historical Society, Topeka.

105. Jno. W. Geary to Maj. Genl. P. F. Smith, Sept. 19, 1856, Geary Papers.

106. Persifor F. Smith to S. Cooper, Aug. 11, 1856, House, Executive Documents, 68; Danl. Woodson to Wm. Hutchinson and H. Miles Moore, Sept. 3, 1856, W. I. R. Blackman Miscellaneous Collections, Kansas State Historical Society, Topeka; George Deas to Lt. Col. P. St. George Cooke, Sept. 3, 1856, House, Executive Documents, 95–97; Persifor F. Smith to Col. Samuel Cooper, Sept. 10, 1856, ibid., 80–83; and Persifor F. Smith to S. Cooper, Aug. 6, 1856, ibid., 67–68.

107. P. St. Geo. Cooke to Maj. George Deas, Sept. 10, 1856, House, Executive Documents, 115–16.

108. Sterling Price to John W. Geary, Sept. 9, 1856, Geary Letters and Executive Minutes; and Jno. W. Geary to Sterling Price, Sept. 20, 1856, ibid.

109. Robinson, *Kansas Conflict,* 317–23.

110. Sept. 14, 1856 entry, Moore Journals; and Sept. 6, 1856 entry, Journal of Richard J. Hinton, Hinton Papers.

111. J. H. Kagi to Father, Sept. 4, 1856, Hinton Papers.

112. P. St. Geo. Cooke to Maj. F. J. Porter, Sept. 13, 1856, House, Executive Documents, 113–14; Sept. 14, 15, 16, 1856 entries, Moore Journals; P. St. Geo. Cooke to Maj. F. J. Porter, Sept. 13, 1856, House, Executive Documents, 113–14; Persifor F. Smith to Col. Samuel Cooper, Sept. 15, 1856, ibid., 112; and Secretary's Note, Geary Letters and Executive Minutes.

113. Julia Louisa Lovejoy to Editor, Sept. 19, 1856, "Letters of Julia Louisa Lovejoy," 127–42.

114. Sept. 14, 15, 16, 1856 entries, Moore Journals; P. St. Geo. Cooke to F. J. Porter, Sept. 13, 1856, House, Executive Documents, 113–14; Persifor F. Smith to Col. Samuel Cooper, Sept. 15, 1856, ibid., 112; and Secretary's Note, Geary Letters and Executive Minutes.

115. Sept. 14, 15, 16, 1856 entries, Moore Journals; P. St. Geo. Cooke to Maj. F. J. Porter, Sept. 13, 1856, House, Executive Documents, 113–14; Persifor F. Smith to Col. Samuel Cooper, Sept. 15, 1856, ibid., 112; Secretary's Note, Geary Letters and Executive Minutes; Louise Barry, "The Emigrant Aid Company Parties of 1854," *Kansas Historical Quarterly* 12 (May 1943): 115–55, esp. 124; and Gihon, *Geary and Kansas,* 166–81.

116. Robinson, *Kansas Conflict,* 323–24.

117. J. H. Lane to Gov. Charles Robinson, Sept. 13, 1856, Hinton Papers; "Autobiography," Jan. 25, 1896, Reader Papers; George A. Root, ed., "The First Day's Battle at Hickory Point," *Kansas Historical Quarterly* 1

(Nov. 1931): 28–49, esp. 38–49; Thomas J. Wood to Lt. Col. P. St. George Cooke, Sept. 15, 1856, House, Executive Documents, 123–26; Stephenson, *General James H. Lane*, 76, 78–81; and *Herald of Freedom*, Nov. 15, 1856.

118. *Herald of Freedom*, Nov. 15, 1856; and *Missouri Democrat*, Oct. 30, 1856.
119. *New York Times*, Nov. 17, 1856; and John Speer, *Life of Gen. James H. Lane*, *"The Liberator of Kansas" with Corrobative Incidents of Pioneer History* (Garden City, Kans., 1897), 110–26.
120. *New York Times*, Sept. 22, 1856; Julia Louisa Lovejoy to Editor, Sept. 22, 1856, "Letters of Julia Louisa Lovejoy," 136–37; George D. Bayard to father, Sept. 24, 1856, Samuel J. Bayard, *Life of George Dashiell Bayard* (New York, 1874), 96–98; and Persifor F. Smith to Samuel Cooper, Nov. 11, 1856, House, Executive Documents, 144–45.
121. Sat to Cynthia, July 22, 1856, "Letters of John and Sarah Everett," 144–45.
122. W. J. Newton to T. J. Wright, Sept. 10, 1856, House, Executive Documents, 114–15; *New York Times*, Oct. 20, 1856; W. F. M. Arny to W. Barnes, Oct. 23, 1856, Barnes Collection; L. W. Hoover to ———, Oct. 24, 1856, Blood Papers; Oct. 27, 1856 entry, George Ela Diary, Connelley Collection; Rawley, *Race and Politics*, 160. Traditional estimates of those who died in territorial Kansas have ranged as high as 200. Dale Watts, however, counts only 157 deaths from 1855 to 1860, with only 56 having political causes. The rest resulted from land disputes and personal grudges that led to violence. Many of these, however, such as the Dow-Coleman feud took on political importance after the death of one of the parties. Dale E. Watts, "How Bloody Was Bleeding Kansas?: Political Killings in Kansas Territory, 1854–1861," *Kansas History* 18 (summer 1995): 116–29.
123. Circular Letter, Dec. 2, 1856, Miscellaneous Manuscripts, New York Historical Society, New York.
124. *Herald of Freedom*, Dec. 13, 1856, Jan. 3, 10, 1857; A. Curtis to Wm. Hutchinson, Dec. 21, 1856, Hutchinson Papers; and Nichols, *Bleeding Kansas*, 134.
125. *Boston Daily Advertiser*, Nov. 12, 1856.
126. "Yeoman," *New York Times*, July 10, 1856; and *Herald of Freedom*, Dec. 20, 1856.
127. Edward J. Renehan, Jr., *The Secret Six: The True Tale of the Men Who Conspired with John Brown* (New York, 1995), 93.
128. Renehan, *Secret Six*, 92–93.
129. J. H. Perkins to W. C. Crosby, Oct. 27, 1856, Crosby Collection.
130. S. Cabot Jr. to James Blood, Dec. 28, 1856, Blood Papers.
131. Richard H. Sewell, *Ballots for Freedom: Antislavery Politics in the United States, 1837–1860* (New York, 1976), 290, 292.
132. David M. Potter, *The Impending Crisis, 1848–1861* (New York, 1976), 259–65; and Tyler Anbinder, *Nativism and Slavery: The Northern Know Nothings and the Politics of the 1850s* (New York, 1992), 243–44.

133. C. B. Haddock to James Buchanan, Nov. 25, 1856, Buchanan Papers.
134. George Booker to R. M. T. Hunter, Nov. 16, 1856, in Charles Henry Ambler, *Correspondence of Robert M. T. Hunter, 1826–1876* (New York, 1971), 200–201.
135. *New York Times*, Oct. 11, 28, 1856.
136. *Herald of Freedom*, Nov. 1, 1856; Jno. W. Geary to William L. Marcy, Oct. 7, 1856, Geary Letters and Executive Minutes; Stampp, *America in 1857*, 147–48; and A. H. Reeder to ——, Dec. 2, 1856, Hutchinson Papers.
137. Jno. W. Geary to Franklin Pierce, Sept. 16, 1856, Geary Letters and Executive Minutes; Jno. W. Geary to [Franklin Pierce], Sept. 19, 1856, ibid.; Gihon, *Geary and Kansas*, 113–14, 157–66; Samuel D. Lecompte to J. W. Geary, Oct. 6, 1856, Geary Letters and Executive Minutes; and Jno. W. Geary to Franklin Pierce, Nov. 14, 1856, ibid.
138. Gihon, *Geary and Kansas*, 166–81; Nichols, *Bleeding Kansas*, 159; *New York Times*, Dec. 5, 1856; and Jn. M. Geary to Franklin Pierce, Dec. 22, 1856, Franklin Pierce Papers, Library of Congress. The list of suggested removals included Donaldson, Woodson, and especially Calhoun.
139. Nichols, *Franklin Pierce*, 495–501.
140. P. St. George Cooke to Maj. F. J. Porter, Oct. 7, 1856, House, Executive Documents, 139–40; A. J. H. to Jack, Dec. 21, 1856, in Hoole, "Kansas Situation," 150–51; and *New York Times*, Dec. 5, 1856.
141. *Missouri Democrat*, Dec. 6, 1856.
142. Nov. 17, 1856 entry, George Ela Diary, Connelley Collection.

7. IMPOSING A CONSTITUTION AGAINST THEIR WILL

1. Jno. M. Geary to Franklin Pierce, Jan. 12, 1857, Franklin Pierce Papers, Library of Congress.
2. *(Atchison, Kans.) Squatter Sovereign*, Jan. 27, 1857.
3. *Squatter Sovereign*, Feb. 3, 17, 1857; and *Lecompton (Kans.) Union*, Feb. 7, 1857.
4. *Lecompton Union*, Jan. 7, 1857.
5. Axalla to Sister, Jan. 4, 1857, William Stanley Hoole, ed., "A Southerner's Viewpoint of the Kansas Situation, 1856–1857: The Letters of Lieut. Col. A. J. Hoole, C.S.A." *Kansas Historical Quarterly* 3 (May 1934): 145–71, esp. 154–55.
6. Report of the Judiciary Committee, House of Representatives, Kansas Territory, "Governor Geary's Administration," vol. 5, *Transactions of the Kansas State Historical Society* (Topeka, 1896), 277–83; W. T. Sherrard to Judiciary Committee, House of Representatives, Kansas Territory, Jan. 21, 1857, ibid., 283–85; *Lecompton Union*, Jan. 27, Feb. 21, 1857; *(Lawrence) Herald of Freedom*, Feb. 21, 1857; Jno. W. Geary to James Buchanan, Feb. 10, 1857, John W. Geary Letters and Executive Minutes, Kansas State Historical Society, Topeka; A. J. H. to Mother, Feb. 22, 1857, in Hoole, "A Southerner's Viewpoint," 145–71; and John

H. Gihon, *Geary and Kansas: Governor Geary's Administration in Kansas: With a Complete History of the Territory until July 1857* (Philadelphia, 1857), 227–44.

7. Gihon, *Geary and Kansas*, 218–27; Alice Nichols, *Bleeding Kansas* (New York, 1954), 176–78; *(St. Louis) Missouri Republican*, Feb. 8, 1857; *Herald of Freedom*, Jan. 10, 1857; and House Journal, Feb. 13, 1857, "Governor Geary's Administration," vol. 5, *Transactions*, 264–89; *Lecompton Union*, Feb. 13, 1857.

8. Kenneth M. Stampp, *America in 1857: A Nation on the Brink* (New York, 1990), 155; and *New York Times*, Feb. 19, 1857.

9. *Herald of Freedom*, Jan. 17, 1857; *New York Times*, Jan. 24, 1857; and Jno. W. Geary to Franklin Pierce, Jan. 12, 1857, Geary Letters and Executive Minutes.

10. Gihon, *Geary and Kansas,*, 214–16; Axalla to Sister, Jan. 4, 1857, Hoole, ed., "A Southerner's Viewpoint," 154–55; Jno. W. Geary to Franklin Pierce, Jan. 12, 1857, Geary Letters and Executive Minutes; Charles Robinson, *The Kansas Conflict* (Lawrence, 1898), 339–41; and *New York Times*, Jan. 17, 1857. The cases were never brought to trial.

11. Jno. W. Geary to Brother Edwards, Jan. 21, 1857, John W. Geary Collection, Kansas State Historical Society, Topeka.

12. *Missouri Republican*, Jan. 27, 1857; Stampp, *America in 1857*, 153; and *Herald of Freedom*, Jan. 24, 1857.

13. Jno. W. Geary to James Buchanan, Jan. 16, 1857, James Buchanan Papers, Historical Society of Pennsylvania, Philadelphia.

14. Veto Message, *Herald of Freedom*, March 14, 1857; Gihon, *Geary and Kansas*, 260–70; and Allan Nevins, *The Emergence of Lincoln*, vol. 1, *Douglas, Buchanan, and Party Chaos, 1857–1859* (New York, 1950), 137–39.

15. John [Everett] to Father, Jan. 28, 1857, "Letters of John and Sarah Everett, 1854–1864," *Kansas Historical Quarterly* 8 (May 1939): 143–74.

16. *Herald of Freedom*, Feb. 28, 1857; Gihon, *Geary and Kansas*, 21–22; and W. F. M. Arny to [Gov. Robert J. Walker], Aug. 20, 1857, Miscellaneous Manuscripts, New-York Historical Society, New York.

17. *Lecompton Union*, April 1, 1857.

18. Jno. W. Geary to brother, Feb. 25, 1857, Geary Collection. Geary went on to a distinguished career as a Union general and governor of Pennsylvania. He died in 1873. William Elsey Connelley, *Kansas Territorial Governors* (Topeka, 1900), 61–90.

19. *Herald of Freedom*, April 18, 1857; and Inaugural Address in James D. Richardson, *A Compilation of the Messages and Papers of the President, 1789–1908*, vol. 5 (Washington, 1908), 431–33.

20. Nevins, *Emergence of Lincoln*, 95.

21. *Richmond Enquirer*, March 21, 1857.

22. David M. Potter, *The Impending Crisis, 1848–1861* (New York, 1976), 283–91.

23. *New York Times,* March 27, 1857; Wm. Bigler to James Buchanan, Feb. 12, 1857, Buchanan Papers (HSPenn); James P. Shenton, *Robert John Walker: A Politician from Jackson to Lincoln* (New York, 1961), 124-38, 146-49; James A. Rawley, *Race and Politics: "Bleeding Kansas" and the Coming of the Civil War* (Lincoln, 1969), 204-6; Nevins, *Emergence of Lincoln,* 145; Connelley, *Kansas Territorial Governors,* 94-110; House, *Covode Report,* 36th Cong., 1st sess., 1860, rept. 648, serial 1071, 105-6; and Stampp, *America in 1857,* 159.

24. R. J. Walker to James Buchanan, March 26, 1857, in *New York Times,* April 18, 1857.

25. D. L. Yulee to R. J. Walker, April 4, 1857, Robert J. Walker Papers, New-York Historical Society, New York; and R. J. Walker to Sister, April 6, 1857, Robert J. Walker Collection, Library of Congress.

26. Rawley, *Race and Politics,* 204-6; and *New York Times,* June 6, 1857.

27. House, *Covode Report,* 93-119.

28. Lewis Cass to Robert J. Walker, March 30, 1857, "Governor Walker's Administration," vol. 5, *Transactions of the Kansas State Historical Society* (Topeka, 1896), 290-464, esp. 322-23.

29. Fred. P. Stanton to Lewis Cass, April 17, 1857, "Governor Walker's Administration," vol. 5, *Transactions,* 324; Stampp, *America in 1857,* 161-64, 167; C. Robinson et al. to F. Stanton, April 25, 1857, "Governor Walker's Administration," vol. 5, *Transactions,* 433-35; *New York Times,* May 5, 1857; Fred'k P. Stanton to C. Robinson et al., April 30, 1857, ibid., 435-36; and Nichols, *Bleeding Kansas,* 190, 194.

30. G. W. Brown to Ewing, April 9, 1857, Thomas Ewing Family Papers, Library of Congress.

31. *Herald of Freedom,* March 14, 1857; and Robinson, *Kansas Conflict,* 339-41.

32. Schuyler Colfax to Gov. Chas. Robinson, April 8, 1857, Walker Collection. On immigration, see *New York Times,* April 24, 1857.

33. *New York Times,* May 4, 1857.

34. Ibid., June 4, 1857.

35. Inaugural Address, May 27, 1857, "Governor Walker's Administration," vol. 5, *Transactions,* 328-41; and *Herald of Freedom,* June 16, 1857.

36. Robert Toombs to W. W. Burwell, July 11, 1857, in Ulrich Bonnell Phillips, ed., *The Correspondence of Robert Toombs, Alexander H. Stephens, and Howell Cobb* (New York, 1970), 403-4.

37. Shenton, *Robert John Walker,* 150-84.

38. R. J. Walker to Lewis Cass, June 2, 1857, "Governor Walker's Administration," vol. 5, *Transactions,* 326-27; *Herald of Freedom,* June 20, 1857; Stampp, *America in 1857,* 166-67; and Albert D. Richardson, *Beyond the Mississippi: From the Great River to the Great Ocean: Life and Adventure on the Prairies, Mountains, and Pacific Coast, 1857-1867* (Hartford, Conn., 1867), 40-41.

39. R. J. Walker to James Buchanan, June 28, 1857, House, *Covode Report,*

115–19; R. J. Walker to Lewis Cass, July 15, 1857, "Governor Walker's Administration," vol. 5, *Transactions,* 341–48; Robinson, *Kansas Conflict,* 352–55; and *(St. Louis) Missouri Democrat,* June 15, 1857.

40. Stampp, *America in 1857,* 167; and *Herald of Freedom,* June 27, 1857.
41. John to Mother, June 23, 1857, "Letters of John and Sarah Everett," 279–310.
42. James Buchanan to Robert J. Walker, July 12, 1857, House, *Covode Report,* 112–13.
43. [1857], p. 208, William B. Napton Diary, Missouri Historical Society, St. Louis.
44. [1857], pp. 216–17, Napton Diary.
45. Alexander H. Stephens to the Voters of the Eighth Congressional District of Georgia, Aug. 14, 1857, in Phillips, *Toombs, Stephens, and Cobb,* 409–20; Thomas R. R. Cobb to Howell Cobb, July 15, 1857, ibid., 404–5; William O. Goode to R. M. T. Hunter, July 21, 1857, in Charles Henry Ambler, *Correspondence of Robert M. T. Hunter, 1826–1876* (New York, 1971), 210; Thomas S. Bocock to R. M. T. Hunter, July 23, 1857, ibid., 210–11; and A. D. Banks to R. M. T. Hunter, July 24, 1857, ibid., 211–12.
46. Howell Cobb to Lucius, July 27, 1857, Walker Papers.
47. Richardson, *Beyond the Mississippi,* 37.
48. *New York Times,* July 25, Aug. 8, 12, 1857; *Herald of Freedom,* July 25, 1857; Stampp, *America in 1857,* 177–79; Col. Wm. S. Harney to Gov. Robert J. Walker, July 15, 1857, Walker Papers; Geo. W. Brown, *Reminiscences of Gov. R. J. Walker; With the True Story of the Rescue of Kansas from Slavery* (1881; reprint, Rockford, Ill., 1902), 56–58; R. J. Walker to Lewis Cass, July 20, 1857, "Governor Walker's Administration," vol. 5, *Transactions,* 358–60; and *Missouri Democrat,* Aug. 1, 1857.
49. John B. Floyd to James Buchanan, July 31, 1857, Buchanan Papers (HSPenn); Lewis Cass to James Buchanan, July 31, 1857, ibid.; and John Appleton to James Buchanan, Aug. 6, 1857, ibid.
50. *Herald of Freedom,* July 18, 11, Aug. 1, 1857.
51. Ibid., Aug. 8, 1857.
52. Tom to Father, Aug. 5, 1857, Ewing Family Papers.
53. T. Ewing to Tom, July 23, 1857, Ewing Family Papers; and T. Ewing to Tom, July 23, 1857, Hist. Constitutions, Kansas State Historical Society, Topeka.
54. *New York Times,* Sept. 3, 1857; *Herald of Freedom,* Sept. 5, 1857; and Stampp, *America in 1857,* 259–60.
55. *Herald of Freedom,* July 25, 1857; and Wendell Holmes Stephenson, *The Political Career of General James H. Lane* (Topeka, 1930), 87–89.
56. G. W. Smith, Jr., to Kansas State Central Committee, July 17, 1857, James Blood Papers, Kansas State Historical Society, Topeka.
57. R. J. Walker to Lewis Cass, July 27, 1857, "Governor Walker's Administration," vol. 5, *Transactions,* 362–64; and R. J. Walker to Lewis Cass, Aug. 18, 1857, ibid., 372–74.

58. *New York Times,* Aug. 28, 1857.
59. J. S. Black to Robert J. Walker, Aug. 1, 1857, Jeremiah S. Black Papers, Library of Congress; Brown, *Gov. R. J. Walker,* 22–23; and Lewis Cass to Robert J. Walker, Aug. 23, 1857, "Governor Walker's Administration," vol. 5, *Transactions,* 378–82.
60. *New York Times,* Aug. 19, 1857; and John and Sarah to Father, Aug. 14, 1857, "Letters of John and Sarah Everett," 282–83.
61. *New York Times,* Sept. 3, 1857; Richardson, *Beyond the Mississippi,* 82; Stampp, *America in 1857,* 181; and *Missouri Democrat,* Aug. 26, 1857.
62. Robert W. Johannsen, "The Lecompton Constitutional Convention: An Analysis of Its Membership," *Kansas Historical Quarterly* 23 (autumn 1957): 225–43.
63. Wm. Bigler to J. S. Black, Aug. 26, 1857, Black Papers; Johannsen, "Lecompton Constitutional Convention," 237; *New York Times,* Sept. 16, 1857; and Robert W. Johannsen, *Stephen A. Douglas* (New York, 1973), 468.
64. *New York Times,* Sept. 17, 19, 1857; and Howell Cobb to Alexander H. Stephens, Sept. 19, 1857, in Phillips, *Correspondence of Toombs, Stephens, and Cobb,* 423–24.
65. *New York Times,* Sept. 22, 20 1857; and Stampp, *America in 1857,* 266–68.
66. John to Sister Cynthia, Oct. 5, 1857, "Letters of John and Sarah Everett," 285; *New York Times,* Oct. 15, 1857; Brown, *Gov. R. J. Walker,* 75–77; *(Kansas City, Mo.) Western Journal of Commerce,* Oct. 24, 1857; and R. J. Walker to Lewis Cass, Oct. 10, 1857, "Governor Walker's Administration," vol. 5, *Transactions,* 400–401.
67. *Herald of Freedom,* Oct. 10, 17, 24, 1857; Rawley, *Race and Politics,* 213–14; John to Father, Oct. 26, 1857, "Letters of John and Sarah Everett," 286–88; and *New York Times,* Feb. 10, 1858.
68. R. J. Walker and Fred. P. Stanton, "Proclamation to the People of Kansas," *Herald of Freedom,* Oct. 24, 31, 1857; and Nichols, *Bleeding Kansas,* 197–99.
69. Robinson, *Kansas Conflict,* 362–65.
70. D. R. Anthony to Father, Nov. 2, 1857, Edgar Langsdorf and R. W. Richmond, eds., "Letters of Daniel R. Anthony, 1857–1862: Part One, 1857," *Kansas Historical Quarterly* 24 (spring 1958): 6–30, esp. 26–27.
71. R. J. Walker to Lewis Cass, Nov. 3, 1857, "Governor Walker's Administration," vol. 5, *Transactions,* 402–3; *Herald of Freedom,* Nov. 14, Oct. 24, 1857; Nichols, *Bleeding Kansas,* 197–99; Stampp, *America in 1857,* 260–65, 239–40, 245, 257; John to Father, Oct. 26, 1857, "Letters of John and Sarah Everett," 286–88; Richard McAllister to R. J. Walker, Nov. 7, 1857, Walker Collection; *(Lecompton) Kansas National Democrat,* Nov. 5, 1857; and *Richmond Enquirer,* Nov. 13, 1857.
72. *Herald of Freedom,* Oct. 24, 1857.

73. Howell Cobb to Alexander H. Stephens, Oct. 9, 1857, in Phillips, *Correspondence of Toombs, Stephens, and Cobb,* 424.
74. House, *Covode Report,* 210–14; and *Herald of Freedom,* Sept. 26, 1857.
75. J. S. Black draft of letter to a Philadelphia meeting, Sept. 25, 1857, Black Papers.
76. *Herald of Freedom,* Oct. 17, 1857.
77. Ibid., Nov. 28, 1857; *New York Times,* Dec. 1, 1857; Stampp, *America in 1857,* 272–75; and Daniel W. Wilder, *The Annals of Kansas* (Topeka, 1875), 134–47.
78. Stampp, *America in 1857,* 268–70; O. Jennings Love to James Buchanan, Dec. 17, 1857, Buchanan Papers (HSPenn); House, *Covode Report,* 154–74; *Missouri Republican,* Nov. 12, 1857; and G. A. Wise to [Henry A. Wise], Dec. 11, 1857, Henry Alexander Wise and Family Collection, Library of Congress.
79. C. Robinson to J. Sherman, Nov. 24, 1857, vol. 2, John Sherman Papers, Library of Congress.
80. *Herald of Freedom,* Nov. 21, 1857; and Stampp, *America in 1857,* 317–18.
81. Nov. 13, 1857 entry, Henry Miles Moore Journals, Yale University Library.
82. *Boston Daily Advertiser,* Nov. 19, 1857.
83. Nov. 29, 1857 entry, Moore Journals; Stephenson, *General James H. Lane,* 90–91; and Stampp, *America in 1857,* 317–18.
84. *New York Times,* Dec. 4, 1857.
85. *Herald of Freedom,* Dec. 5, 12, 1857; Nov. 29, 1857 entry, Moore Journals; Stephenson, *General James H. Lane,* 90–91; and Stampp, *America in 1857,* 317–18.
86. Nichols, *Bleeding Kansas,* 204–5; Stampp, *America in 1857,* 318; *Herald of Freedom,* Dec. 12, 1857; and Fred. P. Stanton to House of Representatives, Kansas Territory, Dec. 15, 1857, "Governor Walker's Administration," vol. 5, *Transactions,* 319.
87. Fred. P. Stanton to Lewis Cass, Dec. 9, 1857, "Governor Walker's Administration," vol. 5, *Transactions,* 414.
88. Stampp, *America in 1857,* 318–19; Lewis Cass to James W. Denver, Dec. 11, 1857, "Governor Walker's Administration," vol. 5, *Transactions,* 419–21; G. A. Wise to [Henry A. Wise], Dec. 11, 1857, Wise and Family Collection; and Connelley, *Kansas Territorial Governors,* 120–28.
89. John H. Stringfellow to James Buchanan, Jan. 5, 1858, Buchanan Papers (HSPenn).
90. William J. Cooper, Jr., *Liberty and Slavery: Southern Politics to 1860* (New York, 1983), 259–62.
91. J. W. Park to Dodler, Jan. 1, 1858, Park Brothers Collection, Wichita State University Special Collections.
92. John A. Quitman to Lawrence Keitt, July 23, 1857, quoted in Eric H. Walther, *The Fire-Eaters* (Baton Rouge, 1992), 109–10.

93. Stampp, *America in 1857*, 329–31; and Cooper, *Liberty and Slavery*, 259–62.

94. R. M. T. Hunter to Shelton F. Leake, Oct. 16, 1857, in Ambler, *Correspondence of Hunter*, 237–41; and A. D. Banks to R. M. T. Hunter, Oct. 31, 1857, ibid., 250.

95. James D. Tradewell to James H. Hammond, Feb. 11, 1858, quoted in Don E. Fehrenbacher, *The South and Three Sectional Crises* (Baton Rouge, 1980), 540.

96. David E. Meerse, "Buchanan, the Patronage, and the Lecompton Constitution: A Case Study," *Civil War History* 41 (Dec. 1995): 291–312, esp. 297; Fehrenbacher, *South and Three Sectional Crises*, 53, 65; and Walther, *Fire-Eaters*, 282–83.

97. *Herald of Freedom*, Dec. 19, 1857; and *New York Times*, Dec. 1, 1857.

98. Annual Message, Dec. 8, 1857, Richardson, *Papers of the Presidents*, vol. 5, 449–54.

99. Elbert B. Smith, *The Presidency of James Buchanan* (Lawrence, Kans., 1975); and Jas. C. Van Dyke to James Buchanan, Dec. 1, 1857, Buchanan Papers (HSPenn).

100. Wm. Bigler to ———, Dec. 8, 1857, John Adams Halderman Collection, Kansas State Historical Society, Topeka.

101. R. J. Walker to Lewis Cass, Dec. 15, 1857, "Governor Walker's Administration," vol. 5, *Transactions*, 421–30. In 1860, Walker provided a confidential letter in which Buchanan had pledged himself to stand or fall on the issue of submission to a congressional investigating committee. S. M. Johnson to James Buchanan, Jan. 2, 1858, Buchanan Papers (HSPenn); Nichols, *Disruption of American Democracy*, 150–55; and Shenton, *Robert John Walker*, 150–84.

102. Levi G. Clover to Judge [Black], Feb. 3, 1858, Black Papers; Wm. Hopkins to Judge Black, Feb. 24, 1858, ibid.; *New York Times*, Feb. 11, 10, March 2, 1858; R. J. Walker to Col. John W. Forney, Feb. 6, 1858, Robert J. Walker Papers, Mississippi Department of Archives and History, Jackson; and W. F. Boone to J. S. Black, Feb. 8, 1858, Black Papers.

103. S. A. Douglas to J. A. McClernand, Nov. 23, 1857, John A. McClernand Papers, Illinois State Historical Library, Springfield; and *New York Times*, Dec. 1, 1857.

104. S. M. Johnson to James Buchanan, Aug. 17, 1857, Buchanan Papers (HSPenn); House, *Covode Report*, 269–73; Don E. Fehrenbacher, *Prelude to Greatness: Lincoln in the 1850s* (Stanford, Calif., 1962), 53–57; and Nichols, *Disruption of American Democracy*, 150–55.

105. *New York Times*, March 26, 1858; Stampp, *America in 1857*, 289–93; and Nevins, *Emergence of Lincoln*, 253.

106. Stampp, *America in 1857*, 282–85; Nichols, *Disruption of American Democracy*, 155–58; and Nevins, *Emergence of Lincoln*, 244–49, 255.

107. *Congressional Globe*, 35th Cong., 1st sess., 1858, 5–8, 14–22, 42–52, 113–22, 53–59; and *New York Times*, Dec. 10, 11, 19, 22, 1857.

108. *Congressional Globe,* 1858, 5–8, 14–22; Lyman Trumbull to W. C. Flagg, Jan. 8, 1858, Lyman Trumbull Family Papers, Illinois State Historical Library, Springfield.

109. Charles Heffley to J. S. Black, Dec. 15, 1857, Black Papers (LC).

110. John Stanton Gould to F. P. Blair, Dec. 17, 1857, Blair Family Papers, Library of Congress; and Lyman Trumbull to A. Lincoln, Dec. 25, 1857, Trumbull Family Papers.

111. *New York Times,* Dec. 21, 1857.

112. Stampp, *America in 1857,* 319–20; Richardson, *Beyond the Mississippi,* 101; and *Herald of Freedom,* April 13, 1858.

113. *New York Times,* Dec. 31, 1857.

114. Stampp, *America in 1857,* 301–7; and *New York Times,* Dec. 24, 29, 1857.

115. Joseph H. Trego to Wife, Dec. 21, 1857, Edgar Langsdorf, ed., "The Letters of Joseph H. Trego, 1857–1864, Linn County Pioneer," *Kansas Historical Quarterly* 19 (May 1951): 122–24; Joseph H. Trego to Wife, Jan. 24, 1858, ibid., 113–32; J. Williams to Judge, Dec. 24, 1857, Black Papers; Tho. Ewing Jr. to Father, Dec. 21, 1857, Ewing Family Papers; *Herald of Freedom,* Dec. 26, 1857; Brown, *Gov. R. J. Walker,* 127–39; and Stampp, *America in 1857,* 320–21.

116. Thomas Ewing, Jr. to Hugh Ewing, Jan. 2 [1858], Ewing Family Papers.

117. Tho. Ewing Jr., to Father, Dec. 21, 1857, Ewing Family Papers; *Herald of Freedom,* Dec. 26, 1857; Brown, *Gov. R. J. Walker,* 127–39; and Stampp, *America in 1857,* 320–21.

118. Handbill, Dec. 28, 1857, Ewing Family Papers; and J. H. Lane to ———, Dec. 30, 1857, Charles A. Foster Collection, Kansas State Historical Society, Topeka.

119. Proclamation to the People of Kansas Territory, Dec. 26, 1857, Ewing Family Papers.

120. Denver to wife, Jan. 4, 1858, James William Denver Collection, Kansas State Historical Society, Topeka.

121. Denver to wife, Jan. 4, 1858, Denver Collection.

122. J. W. Denver to E. S. Dennis, Jan. 9, 1858, "Governor Denver's Administration," vol. 5, *Transactions,* 464–561, esp. 472; and J. W. Park to Dodler, Jan. 1, 1858, Park Brothers Collection.

123. J. W. Park to Dodler, Jan. 1 [1858], Park Brothers Collection.

124. Richardson, *Beyond the Mississippi,* 100.

125. Ibid., 100; and *Herald of Freedom,* April 3, 1858.

126. G. Murlin Welch, *Border Warfare in Southeastern Kansas, 1856–1859* (Pleasanton, Kans., 1977), 50–52, 166–68; and *Herald of Freedom,* Jan. 16, 1858.

127. Stampp, *America in 1857,* 321.

128. Fred. P. Stanton to R. J. Walker, Jan. 5, 1858, Walker Papers.

129. *Western Journal of Commerce,* Jan. 30, 1858.

130. *Missouri Republican,* Jan. 18, 1858; Richardson, *Beyond the Mississippi,* 102–3; and *Herald of Freedom,* Jan. 16, 30, 1858.

131. A. Pleasanton to James Buchanan, Jan. 8, 1858, Buchanan Papers (HSPenn); Tho. Ewing Jr. to Father, Jan. 18, 1858, Ewing Family Papers; and *Herald of Freedom,* April 3, 1858.

132. Thomas Ewing Jr. to Hugh, Jan. 18, 1858, Ewing Family Papers.

133. Tho. Ewing Jr. to Father, Jan. 18, 1858, ibid.

134. Tho. Ewing to Ellen, Jan. 12, [1858], ibid.

135. Thomas Ewing, Jr., to Father, Feb. 3, 1858, ibid.; Thomas Ewing, Jr., June 29, 1863, ibid.; —— to Thomas Ewing, Jr., July 1, 1863, ibid.; and Charley Torry to Thomas Ewing, Jr., July 1, 1863, History Constitutions.

136. Hugh Ewing to Father, Feb. 9, 1858, Ewing Family Papers.

137. J. W. Denver to James Buchanan, Jan. 16, 1858, Buchanan Papers (HSPenn).

138. *Missouri Republican,* July 7, 23, 1858; and *Western Journal of Commerce.*

139. "Kansas Quarter-Centennial, 1861–1886," vol. 3, *Transactions of the Kansas State Historical Society* (Topeka, 1886), 367–469, esp. 440; and Fred. P. Stanton to R. J. Walker, Jan. 5, 1858, Walker Papers.

140. House, *Covode Report,* 280–88.

141. *New York Times,* March 3, 5, 1858; and Mark W. Summers, "Dough in the Hands of the Doughface? James Buchanan and the Untameable Press," in *James Buchanan and the Political Crisis of the 1850s,* ed. by Michael J. Birkner (Selinsgrove, Pa., 1996), 68–92.

142. Isaac Hugens to Judge [Black], Feb. 7, 1858, Black Papers.

143. Rush Elmore to J. W. Denver, Jan. 31, 1858, Denver Papers.

8. THE LANGUAGE OF A FREEMAN

1. Kenneth M. Stampp, *America in 1857: A Nation on the Brink* (New York, 1990), 323–25.

2. James Buchanan to Senate and House of Representatives, Feb. 2, 1858 in James D. Richardson, *A Compilation of the Messages and Papers of the Presidents, 1789–1908,* vol. 5 (Washington, D.C., 1908), 471–81.

3. *Congressional Globe,* 35th Cong., 1st sess., 1858, 476–80.

4. James A. Rawley, *Race and Politics: "Bleeding Kansas" and the Coming of the Civil War* (Lincoln, Nebr., 1969), 236–37; and Stampp, *America in 1857,* 321.

5. Roy F. Nichols, *The Disruption of American Democracy* (New York, 1948), 158–64.

6. Nichols, *Disruption of American Democracy,* 158–64; *Congressional Globe,* 1858, 596–606; and *New York Times,* Feb. 6, 8, 1858.

7. Wm. L. Harris to Jno. A. McClernand, Feb. 16, 1858, John A. McClernand Papers, Illinois State Historical Library, Springfield.

8. Nichols, *Disruption of American Democracy,* 158–64; *Congressional Globe,* 1858, 621–23, 679; and *New York Times,* Feb. 3, March 10, 1858.

9. *New York Times,* Feb. 4, 1858; Jere McKibben to J. S. Black, Feb. 20, 1858, Jeremiah S. Black Papers, Library of Congress; David E. Meerse, "Buchanan, the Patronage, and the Lecompton Constitution: A Case Study," *Civil War History* 41 (Dec. 1995), 291–312, esp. 311–12; and House, *Covode Report,* 36th Cong., 1st sess., 1860, serial 1071, 138–50, 184–97, 214–18. The *Covode Report* sought to expose the administration's improper methods in the fight over Lecompton. Although the Republican-dominated committee found many shady dealings, it failed to directly implicate the president. S. A. Douglas to J. A. McClernand, Feb. 21, 1858, McClernand Papers; and Mark W. Summers, *The Plundering Generation: Corruption and the Crisis of the Union, 1849–1861* (New York, 1987), 239–60.

10. *New York Times,* March 4, 11, 22, 1858.

11. *Congressional Globe,* 1858, 521–27.

12. Ibid., 570–79.

13. *Congressional Globe Appendix,* 35th Cong., 1st sess., 1858, 49–53.

14. Ibid., 75–141, 298–315; and *Congressional Globe,* 1858, 1153–65, 1177.

15. *Congressional Globe,* 1858, 841–60.

16. Ibid., 770–82; and *Congressional Globe Appendix,* 1858, 339–42.

17. Joseph E. Brown to Alexander H. Stephens, Feb. 9, 1858, in Ulrich Bonnell Phillips, ed., *The Correspondence of Robert Toombs, Alexander H. Stephens, and Howell Cobb* (New York, 1970), 431.

18. *Congressional Globe,* 1858, 1000.

19. Ibid., 814–27.

20. J. I. Coombs to Thos. Ewing, Jr., Feb. 7, 1858, Thomas Ewing Family Papers, Library of Congress.

21. *Congressional Globe,* 1858, 814–27; and *Congressional Globe Appendix,* 1858, 62–64.

22. *Congressional Globe,* 1858, 1025–35; and *Congressional Globe Appendix,* 1858, 153–204.

23. *Congressional Globe Appendix,* 1858, 68–71.

24. *Congressional Globe,* 1858, 1079–84.

25. Ibid., 1087–1101; and *Congressional Globe Appendix,* 1858, 174–204.

26. *Congressional Globe,* 1858, 1111–16, 1120–24.

27. Benj. Benson to John Sherman, April 8, 1858, vol. 4, John Sherman Papers, Library of Congress.

28. *Congressional Globe,* 1858, 1042–59, 608–21.

29. Ibid., 175–77, 428–29, 270–73; Meerse, "Lecompton Constitution," 301–4; and *New York Times,* Jan. 4, 11, 12, 18, 1858.

30. *Congressional Globe,* 1858, 1009–20.

31. *Congressional Globe Appendix,* 1858, 75–124, 174–204.

32. *Congressional Globe,* 1858, 1258–65; *New York Times,* Jan. 15, 1858; and Rawley, *Race and Politics,* 246–50.

33. C. Robinson to Thomas Ewing, Jr., March 24, 1858, Ewing Family Papers.
34. *(Lawrence) Herald of Freedom,* March 20, 1858.
35. E. B. Sadler to John Sherman, March 15, 1858, vol. 4, Sherman Papers.
36. Saml. Walker to John Sherman, March 16, 1858, vol. 4, Sherman Papers.
37. *New York Times,* Feb. 16, 22, 23, 1858; *Herald of Freedom,* March 6, Feb. 20, 1858; and Alice Nichols, *Bleeding Kansas* (New York, 1954), 216–18.
38. *Congressional Globe,* 1858, 1330–66.
39. Ibid., 1371–81.
40. *New York Times,* March 29, 31, 1858.
41. *Congressional Globe Appendix,* 1858, 315–36.
42. Rawley, *Race and Politics,* 246–50; Frank Heywood Hodder, "Some Aspects of the English Bill for the Admission of Kansas," *Annual Report of the American Historical Association for the Year 1906,* vol. 1 (Washington, D.C., 1908), 199–210; *Congressional Globe,* 1858, 1435–38, 1440–45; Meerse, "Lecompton Constitution," 305–6; and Marcus Parrott to Thos. Ewing, Jr., April 2, 1858, Ewing Family Papers.
43. *New York Times,* April 2, 1858; *Congressional Globe,* 1858, 1589–91, 1604; and Nichols, *Disruption of American Democracy,* 164–70.
44. R. S. Stevens to J. W. Denver, April 3, 1858, James William Denver Collection, Kansas State Historical Society, Topeka.
45. *New York Times,* April 21, 1858.
46. F. Patterson to James Buchanan, April 5, 1858, James Buchanan Papers, Historical Society of Pennsylvania, Philadelphia.
47. C. Robinson to Thos. Ewing, April 13, 1858, Historical Constitutions, Kansas State Historical Society, Topeka; and C. Robinson to Thos. Ewing, April 13, 1858, Ewing Family Papers.
48. Jeff Thompson to A. G. Davis, Feb. 12, 1858, Albert G. Davis Papers, Western Historical Manuscript Collection, Columbia, Mo.
49. Denver to wife, Jan. 4, 1858, Denver Collection.
50. *New York Times,* Feb. 16, 22, 23, 1858; *Herald of Freedom,* March 6, Feb. 20, 1858; and Alice Nichols, *Bleeding Kansas,* 216–18.
51. [I. T. Goodnow] to Brother Sherman, April 1, 1858, Isaac Tichenor Goodnow Collection, Kansas State Historical Society, Topeka; and March 24, 1858 entry, Henry Miles Moore Journals, Yale University Library.
52. T. Dwight Thacher, "The Leavenworth Constitutional Convention," vol. 3, *Transactions of the Kansas State Historical Society* (Topeka, 1886), 5–15, esp. 12–13.
53. *(St. Louis) Missouri Republican,* April 8, 1858.
54. Ibid., April 8, 9, 1858.
55. Ibid., April 10, 8, 1858.
56. April 2, 1858 entry, Moore Journals.

57. D. R. Anthony to Sister, Sept. 10, 1858, Daniel Read Anthony Collection, Kansas State Historical Society, Topeka; and D. R. Anthony to Sister, Sept. 10, 1858, Edgar Langsdorf and R. W. Richmond, eds., "Letters of Daniel R. Anthony, 1857–1862—Continued: Part Two, 1858–1861," *Kansas Historical Quarterly* 24 (summer 1958): 198–226.

58. *(Kansas City, Mo.) Western Journal of Commerce,* May 1, 1858.

59. Charles Robinson, *The Kansas Conflict* (Lawrence, 1898), 381–83, 388–90; and Thacher, "Leavenworth Constitutional Convention," vol. 3, *Transactions,* 5–15.

60. S. N. Wood to Tho. Ewing Jr., April 9, 1858, Ewing Family Papers.

61. C. Robinson to T. Ewing, Jr., Aug. 14, 1858, Ewing Family Papers.

62. *New York Times.* April 17, 1858; and *Herald of Freedom,* April 17, 1858.

63. R. Toombs to James Buchanan, April 18, 1858, Buchanan Papers (HSPenn); *New York Times,* April 19, 1858; Rawley, *Race and Politics,* 246–50; Hodder, "English Bill," 201–10; and Nichols, *Disruption of American Democracy,* 164–70.

64. Stampp, *America in 1857,* 327–28; and *Congressional Globe,* 1858, 1758–63, 1786–1805, 1814–28, 1843–55.

65. *Congressional Globe,* 1858, 1868–80.

66. Stampp, *America in 1857,* 327–28; *Congressional Globe,* 1858, 1868–80; *New York Times,* April 22, 1858; and Nichols, *Disruption of American Democracy,* 170–75.

67. John to Father, April 24, 1858, "Letters of John and Sarah Everett, 1854–1864," *Kansas Historical Quarterly* 8 (Aug. 1939): 279–310.

68. *New York Times,* May 5, 1858; R. S. Stevens to J. W. Denver, April 25, 1858, Denver Collection.

69. *New York Times,* April 24, 1858.

70. *Congressional Globe,* 1858, 1765–70, 1779–81, 1806–10, 1857–67, 1880–90, 1900–1906; and *New York Times,* April 29, 1858.

71. *Congressional Globe,* 1858, 1900–1906; *New York Times,* May 1, 1858; and House, *Covode Report,* 317–23, 224–28, 277–80.

72. *Congressional Globe,* 1858, 1900–1906; and Rawley, *Race and Politics,* 250.

73. *Congressional Globe,* 1858, 1892–99; and Rawley, *Race and Politics,* 250.

74. *New York Times,* May 1, 1858.

75. Ibid., May 3, 1858.

76. Danl. Shatton to John Sherman, June 11, 1858, vol. 5, Sherman Papers.

77. Joseph E. Brown to Alexander H. Stephens, May 7, 1858, in Phillips, *Correspondence of Toombs, Stephens, and Cobb,* 434.

78. *New York Times,* April 24, 1858.

79. J. S. Black to D. Webster, [1858], Black Papers.

80. John F. Schroder to James Buchanan, April 24, 1858, Buchanan Papers (HSPenn); and *New York Times,* May 5, 1858.

81. [T. Ewing] to Hugh Ewing, May 2, 1858, Ewing Family Papers.

82. Gen. Lane's Answer to the President's Message, Feb. 13, 1858, James Henry Lane Papers, University of Kansas Library.

83. John Speer, *Life of Gen. James H. Lane, "The Liberator of Kansas" with Corrobative Incidents of Pioneer History* (Garden City, Kans., 1897), 187–218; Tom to Ellen, June 7, 1858, Ewing Family Papers; *New York Times,* June 14, 24, 25, 26, July 1, 2, 9, 1858; Richardson, *Beyond the Mississippi,* 113; *Herald of Freedom,* June 5, 12, 19, 24, 25, 26, July 1, 2, 9, 1858; and Wendell Holmes Stephenson, *The Political Career of General James H. Lane* (Topeka, 1930), 96–97.

84. Hamilton G. Fant to Tom, May 12, 1858, Ewing Family Papers.

85. J. R. Osborn to John Sherman, May 3, 1858, vol. 4, Sherman Papers.

86. John McLean to Thos. Ewing, Jr., May 6, 1858, Hist. Constitutions.

87. Thomas Ewing, Jr. to James G. Blaine, May 11, 1858, Ewing Family Papers.

88. Jas. B. Abbott to Mark Howard, May 5, 1858, Mark Howard Papers, Connecticut Historical Society, Hartford.

89. *Herald of Freedom,* May 22, 1858.

90. John R. Everett to Sisters, May 20, 1858, "Letters of John and Sarah Everett," 297.

91. Erastus Heath to James Buchanan, June 1, 1858, Black Papers; and Wm. Brindle to James Buchanan, July 26, 1858, Buchanan Papers (HSPenn).

92. Howell Cobb to R. M. T. Hunter, July 26, 1858, in Charles Henry Ambler, *Correspondence of Robert M. T. Hunter, 1826–1876* (New York, 1971), 261–62.

93. *New York Times,* June 3, 1858.

94. Hodder, "English Bill," 201–10; *Herald of Freedom,* Aug. 14, 1858; John R. Everett to Father and Mother, Aug. 12, 1858, "Letters of John and Sarah Everett," 299–301; and Aug. 2–3, 1858 entry, Moore Journals.

95. *(Lecompton) Kansas National Democrat,* June 17, 1858.

96. Eric Foner, *Politics and Ideology in the Age of the Civil War* (New York, 1980), 48.

97. *Congressional Globe Appendix,* 1858, 289–98.

98. Nichols, *Disruption of American Democracy,* 175–76, 214–15; Robert W. Johannsen, *Stephen A. Douglas* (New York, 1973), 602–3; and Meerse, "Lecompton Constitution," 311.

99. James Buchanan to Judge Black, Aug. 4, 1858, Black Papers.

100. Geo. W. Jones to Sidney Breese, Sept. 17, 1858, Sidney Breese Papers, Illinois State Historical Library, Springfield; Stampp, *America in 1857,* 307–10; David Davis to George Davis, Nov. 14, 1858, David Davis Family Papers, Illinois State Historical Library, Springfield; and Johannsen, *Stephen A. Douglas,* 675.

101. Edward Dodd to Washburn, Sept. 10, 1858, Elihu B. Washburne Papers, Library of Congress.

102. Harry V. Jaffa, *Crisis of the House Divided: An Interpretation of the Lincoln-Douglas Debates* (Seattle, 1973), 9.

103. John Patrick Diggins, *The Lost Soul of American Politics: Virtue, Self-Interest, and the Foundations of Liberalism* (New York, 1984), 15–17; Louis Filler, *The Crusade against Slavery, 1830–1860* (New York, 1960), 260; and David Zarefsky, *Lincoln, Douglas, and Slavery: In the Crucible of Public Debate* (Chicago, 1990), 166–97.

104. Robert W. Johannsen, ed., *The Lincoln-Douglas Debates of 1858* (New York, 1965), 206–7, 88; and Harry V. Jaffa, *Equality and Liberty: Theory and Practice in American Politics* (New York, 1965), 95–96, 111–12.

105. Johannsen, *Lincoln-Douglas Debates*, 87.

106. Ibid., 322–29; Jaffa, *Equality and Liberty*, 96; and Zarefsky, *Lincoln, Douglas, and Slavery*, 167–68.

107. Johannsen, *Lincoln-Douglas Debates*, 37–48, 257–77.

108. Ibid., 49–67, 75–107.

109. Ibid., 199–200.

110. Ibid., 300–22.

111. Ibid., 49–54, 131–52, 219–37, 245–57, 277–84.

112. Ibid., 52–53.

113. Jaffa, *Equality and Liberty*, 88–92, 149; and Zarefsky, *Lincoln, Douglas, and Slavery*, 183–84.

114. Jaffa, *Crisis of the House Divided*, 304–5; Johannsen, *Lincoln-Douglas Debates*, 136; and Zarefsky, *Lincoln, Douglas, and Slavery*, 175–77.

115. Johannsen, *Lincoln-Douglas Debates*, 311–12.

116. Ibid., 199–200.

117. Ibid., 157; and Zarefsky, *Lincoln, Douglas, and Slavery*, 197.

118. J. Henry Smith to Alexander H. Stephens, Aug. 3, 1858, Alexander H. Stephens Papers, Library of Congress.

119. Johannsen, *Lincoln-Douglas Debates*, 316; and Zarefsky, *Lincoln, Douglas, and Slavery*, 183–84.

120. Allan Nevins, *The Emergence of Lincoln*, vol. 1, *Douglas, Buchanan, and Party Chaos, 1857–1859* (New York, 1950), 403; David M. Potter, *The Impending Crisis, 1848–1861* (New York, 1976), 354–55, 421; and Zarefsky, *Lincoln, Douglas, and Slavery*, 204–22.

121. Michael A. Morrison, *Slavery and the American West: The Eclipse of Manifest Destiny and the Coming of the Civil War* (Chapel Hill, N.C., 1997), 189n; and Don E. Fehrenbacher, *The South and Three Sectional Crises* (Baton Rouge, 1980), 54–56.

122. James Buchanan to Harriet, Oct. 15, 1858, James Buchanan Papers, Library of Congress; and Annual Message, Dec. 6, 1858, in Richardson, *Papers of the Presidents*, 497–503.

123. Zarefsky, *Lincoln, Douglas, and Slavery*, 220.

9. A FRUIT OF THE KANSAS TREE

1. J. Williams to Judge [Black], Feb. 14, 1858, Jeremiah S. Black Papers, Library of Congress; J. G. Anderson to brother, Feb. 17, 1858, Richard Hinton Papers, Kansas State Historical Society, Topeka; J. W. Denver

to Brev. Col. John Monroe, Feb. 15, 1858, "Governor Denver's Administration," vol. 5, *Transactions of the Kansas State Historical Society* (Topeka, 1896), 478–79; and J. Williams to J. S. Black, Feb. 24, 1858, Black Papers.

2. Joseph H. Trego to Wife, Feb. 28, 1858, in Edgar Langsdorf, ed., "The Letters of Joseph H. Trego, 1857–1864, Linn County Pioneer," *Kansas Historical Quarterly* 19 (May 1951): 113–32, esp. 132.

3. J. Williams to James Buchanan, March 3, 1858, James Buchanan Papers, Historical Society of Pennsylvania, Philadelphia.

4. *Boston Daily Advertiser,* Dec. 4, 1860; and William P. Tomlinson, *Kansas in Eighteen Fifty-Eight* (New York, 1859), 163–204.

5. J. Williams to James Buchanan, March 3, 1858, Buchanan Papers, (HSPenn); J. Williams to J. S. Black, April 7, 1858, Black Papers; and J. Williams to James Buchanan, April 23, 1858, Buchanan Papers (HSPenn).

6. David to Judd, April, 28, 1858, David Glenn Cobb, ed., "Letters of David R. Cobb, 1858–1864," *Kansas Historical Quarterly* 11 (Feb. 1942), 65–71, esp. 67–68; and J. Williams to James Buchanan, April 23, 1858, Buchanan Papers (HSPenn); Tomlinson, *Kansas in Eighteen Fifty-Eight,* 163–204.

7. J. Williams to Gov. Denver, May 16, 1858, James Denver Collection, Kansas State Historical Society, Topeka.

8. Charles Robinson, *The Kansas Conflict* (Lawrence, Kans., 1898), 392–93; and Tomlinson, *Kansas in Eighteen Fifty-Eight,* 62–76.

9. *New York Times,* June 9, 1858; and G. Murlin Welch, *Border Warfare in Southeastern Kansas, 1856–1859* (Pleasanton, Kans., 1977), 96–111.

10. *New York Times,* June 9, 1858; and Welch, *Border Warfare,* 96–111.

11. *(St. Louis) Missouri Republican,* May 27, 1858.

12. John Greenleaf Whittier, *The Complete Poetical Works of John Greenleaf Whittier* (Boston, 1894), 395–96.

13. J. Williams to Crawford, May 22, 1858, George A. Crawford Papers, Wichita State University Special Collections; Tomlinson, *Kansas in Eighteen Fifty-Eight,* 80–84; and J. Williams to J. S. Black, May 26, 1858, Black Papers.

14. S. G. Allen to Gov. R. M. Stewart, May 30, 1858, Robert M. Stewart Papers, Western Historical Manuscript Collection, Columbia, Mo.; Jn. S. Hackney to R. M. Stewart, June 1, 1858, ibid.; and R. M. Stewart to G. A. Parsons, May 31, 1858, ibid.

15. J. P. Jones and Ben. J. Newsom to J. W. Denver, June 3, 1858, "Governor Denver's Administration," vol. 5, *Transactions,* 526–28; Jos. Clymer to [Gov. Stewart], June 5, 1858, Stewart Papers; and Geo. W. Clarke to Sam'l J. Jones, June 2, 1858, Denver Collection.

16. J. W. Denver to Lewis Cass, June 23, 1858, "Governor Denver's Administration," vol. 5, *Transactions,* 531–35; Tomlinson, *Kansas in Eighteen Fifty-Eight,* 228–44; Welch, *Border Warfare,* 143–44; James W.

Denver, "Address," vol. 3, *Transactions of the Kansas State Historical Society* (Topeka, 1886), 359–66; and Albert D. Richardson, *Beyond the Mississippi: From the Great River to the Great Ocean: Life and Adventure on the Prairies, Mountains, and Pacific Coast, 1857–1867* (Hartford, 1867), 128–29.

17. N. Lyon to [Denver], June 25, 1858, "Governor Denver's Administration," vol. 5, *Transactions,* 537; *(Lawrence) Herald of Freedom,* June 26, July 10, 1858; and Orders to Capt. A. J. Weaver, June 26, 1858, Stewart Papers.

18. J. W. Denver to Brevet-Major T. W. Sherman, June 29, 1858, "Governor Denver's Administration," vol. 5, *Transactions,* 538.

19. J. Williams to Gov. Denver, July 1, 1858, "Governor Denver's Administration," vol. 5, *Transactions,* 539–40; and *Herald of Freedom,* July 31, Aug. 14, 21, 1858.

20. John Brown to Wife and Children, July 23, 1858, John Brown, Jr., Papers, Ohio Historical Society, Columbus.

21. Charles W. Graeff to Robert M. Stewart, July 29, 1858, Stewart Papers; Affidavit of George W. Harris, July 12, 1858, ibid.; J. F. Snyder to R. M. Stewart, Aug. 7, 1858, ibid.; R. M. Stewart to J. M. Denver, Aug. 7, 1858, ibid.; and J. W. Denver to Officer Commanding, Aug. 9, [1858], "Governor Denver's Administration," vol. 5, *Transactions,* 505–6.

22. J. W. Denver to Lewis Cass, Sept. 1, 1858, "Governor Denver's Administration," vol. 5, *Transactions,* 543–44.

23. *Herald of Freedom,* Oct. 23, 1858; and William Frank Zornow, *Kansas: A History of the Jayhawk State* (Norman, Okla., 1957), 79.

24. William Elsey Connelley, *Kansas Territorial Governors* (Topeka, 1900), 120–28; and Daniel J. Boorstin, *The Americans: The National Experience* (New York, 1965), 120–21.

25. Senate, *Mason Report,* 36th Cong., 1st sess., 1860, rept. 278, 227, 140–45, 253–54; F. B. Sanborn, *The Life and Letters of John Brown, Liberator of Kansas, and Martyr of Virginia* (1885; reprint, New York, 1969), 348–49, 359, 463–66; and Stephen B. Oates, *To Purge This Land with Blood: A Biography of John Brown* (New York, 1970), 229–50. Forbes may have tried to warn Secretary of War John B. Floyd of Brown's intended attack on Harpers Ferry, but Floyd failed to take the anonymous tip seriously. Senate, *Mason Report,* 250–52.

26. J. W. Weaver to Hugh S. Walsh, Nov. 15, 1858, "Governor Denver's Administration," vol. 5, *Transactions,* 548–49; J. Williams to Hugh S. Walsh, Nov. 20, 1858, ibid., 554–55; John C. Sims et al. to Hugh S. Walsh, Nov. 22, 1858, ibid., 556–57; J. E. Jones, Wm. T. Campbell, Chas. Bull to Saml. Medary, [n.d., Nov. 1858], James William Denver Collection, Kansas State Historical Society, Topeka; Hugh S. Walsh to Lewis Cass, Nov. 19, 1858, "Governor Denver's Administration," vol. 5, *Transactions,* 547–48; A. J. Weaver to Hugh S. Walsh, Nov. 26, 1858, ibid., 551; J. E. Jones to H. S. Walsh, Nov. 30, 1858, ibid., 555; J. E. Jones to

H. S. Walsh, Dec. 4, 1858, ibid., 556; and *Herald of Freedom,* Dec. 18, 1858.

27. C. M. M'Daniel to Hugh S. Walsh, Dec. 3, 1858, "Governor Denver's Administration," vol. 5, *Transactions,* 551–52.

28. Hugh S. Walsh to R. B. Mitchell, Dec. 6, 1858, "Governor Denver's Administration," vol. 5, *Transactions,* 553–54; and Hugh S. Walsh to Lewis Cass, Dec. 9, 1858, ibid., 560–61.

29. J. Williams to J. S. Black, Dec. 16, 1858, Black Papers; J. E. Jones, Wm. T. Campbell, Chas. Bull, Dec. 19, 1858, "Governor Medary's Administration," vol. 5, *Transactions of the Kansas State Historical Society* (Topeka, 1896), 561–633, esp. 562; and *New York Times,* Jan. 8, 1859.

30. [Mary Mason Williams to J. S. Black], Dec. 20, 1858, Black Papers.

31. Robert W. Johannsen, *Stephen A. Douglas* (New York, 1973), 356.

32. Richardson, *Beyond the Mississippi,* 296.

33. S. Medary to James Buchanan, Dec. 18, 1858, Buchanan Papers (HSPenn); Wm. Brindle to Judge Black, Dec. 20, 1858, Black Papers; S. Medary to Commanding Officer, Dec. 28, 1858, "Governor Medary's Administration," vol. 5, *Transactions,* 566; S. Medary to James Buchanan, Dec. 28, 1858, ibid., 565–66; and R. M. Stewart to Samuel Medary, Dec. 31, 1858, ibid., 569.

34. Samuel Walker to Samuel Medary, Jan. 3, 1859, "Governor Medary's Administration," vol. 5, *Transactions,* 577–78; D. T. Colby to President, Jan. 8, 1859, ibid., 584–85; and [Hutchinson] to Helen, Jan. 3, 1859, Hinton Papers.

35. S. Medary to R. M. Stewart, Jan. 3, 1859, Robert M. Stewart Papers, Western Historical Manuscript Collection, Columbia, Mo.; and S. Medary to James Buchanan, Jan. 7, 1859, "Governor Medary's Administration," vol. 5, *Transactions,* 582.

36. George Crawford to James Buchanan, Jan. 4, 1859, "Governor Medary's Administration," vol. 5, *Transactions,* 579–80; "Governor's Message on the Troubles in Linn and Bourbon Counties," Jan. 11, 1859, ibid., 589–95; S. Medary to James Buchanan, Jan. 21, 1859, ibid., 598–99; and *Boston Daily Advertiser,* Jan. 19, 1859.

37. S. Medary to [George A. Crawford], Jan. 20, 1859, Crawford Papers; S. Medary to Crawford, Jan. 20, 1859, ibid.; S. Medary to James Buchanan, Feb. 2, 1859, "Governor Medary's Administration," vol. 5, *Transactions,* 602; Resolution, Feb. 11, 1859, ibid., 603–4; and *Herald of Freedom,* Feb. 19, 1859.

38. Frank Walker to Jane, Feb. 18, 1859, Letters from Mound City, 1859, Wichita State University Library, Special Collections.

39. D. A. W. Morehouse to Robert M. Stewart, Feb. 21, 1859, Stewart Papers.

40. "Terrifying Description of the Astonishing Heroic Deeds that the Brave Soldiers of Our City Did in the War with Kansas!" [1858–1859], Broad-

sides 1856, Missouri Historical Society, St. Louis. Translation from the German by Clayton M. Lehmann.

41. *(Kansas City, Mo.) Western Journal of Commerce,* May 17, 1859.

42. Ibid., May 21, 1859.

43. *Herald of Freedom,* Feb. 19, 1859.

44. Frank Walker to Augusta Walker, May 7, 1859, Letters from Mound City.

45. *(St. Louis) Missouri Democrat,* Jan. 12, 13, 1859; and Richard Cordley, *A History of Lawrence, Kansas from the First Settlement to the Close of the Rebellion* (Lawrence, Kans., 1895), 156–57.

46. *Missouri Democrat,* Jan. 25, 1859.

47. Ibid., Jan. 27, Feb. 14, 16, 19, 1859. In the early 1860s, the territorial legislature again passed a bill prohibiting slavery. Medary vetoed it, but his veto was overridden. The bill became law in February but was not enforced and was ruled unconstitutional by the territorial courts. Gary L. Cheathem, "'Slavery All the Time, Or Not At All': The Wyandotte Constitution Debate, 1859–1861," *Kansas History* 21 (autumn 1998): 168–87, esp. 185–86; and *Missouri Democrat,* March 1, 1859. The 1860 census found only two slaves in Kansas. James A. Rawley, *Race and Politics: "Bleeding Kansas" and the Coming of the Civil War* (Lincoln, Nebr., 1969), 49.

48. Zornow, *Kansas,* 80–81; March 28, 1859 entry, Henry Miles Moore Journals, Yale University Library.

49. *Missouri Democrat,* April 17, 1859.

50. *Herald of Freedom,* Sept. 11, 25, Oct. 2, 1858.

51. A. G. W. Safford to Ewing, April 6, 1859, Thomas Ewing Family Papers, Library of Congress; *Herald of Freedom,* April 16, May 14, 28, 1859; Frank W. Blackmar, *The Life of Charles Robinson, The First State Governor of Kansas* (Topeka, 1902), 247–49; and *Missouri Democrat,* May 18, 1859.

52. *New York Times,* May 30, 1859.

53. *Missouri Democrat,* June 17, 1859; and *New York Times,* June 2, 1859.

54. Tomlinson, *Kansas in Eighteen Fifty-Eight,* 249.

55. *New York Times,* Jan. 18, 1859; J. G. Anderson to brother, Jan. 14, 1859, box 1, Hinton Papers; and Benjamin Quarles, *Allies for Freedom: Blacks and John Brown* (New York, 1974), 53–60.

56. *New York Times,* Jan. 18, 1859; J. G. Anderson to brother, Jan. 14, 1859, Hinton Papers; and Quarles, *Allies for Freedom,* 53–60.

57. Geo. A. Crawford to James Buchanan, Jan. 16, 1859, Buchanan Papers (HSPenn).

58. *New York Times,* Jan. 28, 1859.

59. *Herald of Freedom,* Feb. 5, 1859; Louise Barry, "The Emigrant Aid Company Parties of 1854," *Kansas Historical Quarterly* 12 (May 1943): 115–55, esp. 117; James B. Abbott, "The Rescue of Dr. John W. Doy," vol. 4, *Transactions of the Kansas State Historical Society* (Topeka, 1890),

312–23, esp. 313–14; Julia L. Lovejoy to Bro. Haven, Feb. 3, 1859, "Letters of Julia Louisa Lovejoy, 1856–1864," *Kansas Historical Quarterly* 16 (Feb. 1948): 40–75, esp. 46–47; and C. K. Holliday to Mary, Feb. 6, 1859, Lela Barnes, ed., "Letters of Cyrus Kurtz Holliday, 1854–1859," *Kansas Historical Quarterly* 6 (Aug. 1937): 241–94, esp. 292.

60. Abbott, "Rescue of Dr. John W. Doy," vol. 4, *Transactions,* 313–23; and Richardson, *Beyond the Mississippi,* 153. Doy returned to Rochester before the national Civil War. Barry, "Emigrant Aid Company Parties of 1854," 117.

61. Abbott, "Rescue of Dr. John W. Doy," vol. 4, *Transactions,* 312–13.

62. *Herald of Freedom,* Sept. 4, 18, 1858.

63. Ibid., Jan. 22, Feb. 5, 1859.

64. *Western Journal of Commerce,* Dec. 15, 1859.

65. D. R. Anthony to Sister, March 20, 1859, Daniel Read Anthony Collection, Kansas State Historical Society, Topeka.

66. J. Louisa Lovejoy to Editors, July 5, 1859, "Letters of Julia Louisa Lovejoy," 60–61. It is not known whether Lovejoy was familiar with black abolitionist Frederick Douglass's famous "What to the Slave Is the Fourth of July?" speech of 1852. William L. Andrews, ed., *Frederick Douglass Reader* (New York, 1996), 108–30.

67. Equal property rights were granted to women, as were equal rights to minor children. *Missouri Democrat,* July 16, 22, 1859; *Herald of Freedom,* July 16, Aug. 13, 1859; *New York Times,* July 20, Aug. 1, 6, 1859; and *(Lecompton) Kansas National Democrat,* Sept. 15, 1859.

68. *New York Times,* Aug. 8, 1859; and *Kansas National Democrat,* Sept. 15, 1859.

69. *Kansas National Democrat,* Sept. 15, 1859.

70. Zornow, *Kansas,* 85–86; and Cheatham, "'Slavery All the Time,'" 177, 180.

71. Julia L. Lovejoy to Editor, Oct. 6, 1859, "Letters of Julia Louisa Lovejoy," 71.

72. *Missouri Republican,* Aug. 27, 1859. On February 23, 1860, Senator Albert Gallatin Brown submitted a bill making it illegal to interfere with slavery in Kansas. The bill died in congressional committee, but it represented a last-ditch southern effort to stop Wyandotte. Cheatham, "'Slavery All the Time,'" 185–86.

73. Jules Abels, *Man on Fire: John Brown and the Cause of Liberty* (New York, 1971), 167; Sanborn, *Life and Letters of John Brown,* 438–39; and Senate, *Mason Report,* 96–97.

74. Jeffrey Rossbach, *Ambivalent Conspirators: John Brown, the Secret Six, and a Theory of Slave Violence* (Philadelphia, 1982), 268–69.

75. Richard J. Hinton, *John Brown and His Men* (1894; reprint, New York, 1968), 449–582.

76. John I. Anderson to John Brown, Nov. 23, 1859, Hinton Papers.

77. John McCannon to James Montgomery, Dec. 24, 1859, James Montgomery Collection, Kansas State Historical Society, Topeka.

78. Julia L. Lovejoy to Editor, [Nov. 24, 1859], "Letters of Julia Louisa Lovejoy," 72–73; and J. Lucius Davis to [Henry A. Wise], Nov. 1, 1859, Henry Alexander Wise and Family Collection, Library of Congress.
79. C. Whipple to Jenny, Sept. 9, 1859, Hinton Papers.
80. W. H. Leeman to Fair Cousin, Aug. 25, 1858, Hinton Papers.
81. Quarles, *Allies for Freedom*, 84–88.
82. Senate, *Mason Report*, 121–29.
83. Ibid., 29–32.
84. Ibid., 22.
85. Ibid., 37.
86. Oates, *Purge This Land with Blood*, 274–301; —— to Rudy, Oct. 18, 1859, Wise and Family Collection; David M. Potter, *The Impending Crisis, 1848–1861* (New York, 1976), 369–72; and Senate, *Mason Report*, 19.
87. *New York Times*, Oct. 19, 18, 1859.
88. John W. Garrett to James Buchanan, Oct. 1859, Buchanan Papers (HSPenn); John Ritchie to James Buchanan, Oct. 17, 1859, ibid.; John Morris to James Buchanan, Oct. 17, 1859, ibid.; C. B. McCaffrey to J. Buchanan, Oct. 17, 1859, ibid.; —— to Henry A. Wise, Oct. 17, 1859, Wise and Family Collection; and C. J. M. Gwinn to Jas. Buchanan, Oct. 17, 1859, Buchanan Papers (HSPenn).
89. Oates, *Purge This Land with Blood*, 274–301; —— to Rudy, Oct. 18, 1859, Wise and Family Collection; and Potter, *Impending Crisis*, 369–72.
90. Robt. Ould to President, Oct. 18, 1859, Buchanan Papers (HSPenn); and *New York Times*, Oct. 20, 1859.
91. Wm. Bigler to James Buchanan, Oct. 22, 1859, Buchanan Papers (HSPenn).
92. Edward Bates Journal, vol. 1, Oct. 25, 1859, Bates Family Papers, Missouri Historical Society, St. Louis.
93. *Herald of Freedom*, Oct. 29, 1859.
94. *New York Times*, Oct. 19, 1859.
95. Peter Wallenstein, "Incendiaries All: Southern Politics and the Harpers Ferry Raid," in *His Soul Goes Marching On: Responses to John Brown and the Harpers Ferry Raid*, ed. by Paul Finkelman (Charlottesville, Va., 1995), 149–73; Edward Brown to Henry Wise, Nov. 5, 1859, Wise and Family Collection; Miles Bankam to Gov. Wise, Nov. 4, 1859, ibid.; Henry A. Wise to Dr. Stribling, Nov. 10, 1859, ibid.; L. Maria Child to Henry A. Wise, Oct. 26, 1859, L. Maria Child, *Letters of Lydia Maria Child* (1883; reprint, New York, 1969), 103–5; Geo. L. Lunsden to Gov. Wise, Nov. 12, 1859, Wise and Family Collection; and Edda Augusta Richards to Gov. Wise, Nov. 28, 1859, ibid.
96. Child quoted in Elizabeth R. Varon, *We Mean to Be Counted: White Women and Politics in Antebellum Virginia* (Chapel Hill, N.C., 1998), 141.
97. Senate, *Mason Report*, 23–24.

98. *New York Times,* Oct. 20, 1859.

99. Senate, *Mason Report,* 193.

100. Quarles, *Allies for Freedom,* 35, 125, 153.

101. John Stauffer, *The Black Hearts of Men: Radical Abolitionists and the Transformation of Race* (Cambridge, Mass., 2002), 255-61.

102. *Western Journal of Commerce,* Nov. 10, 1859. Historians disagree as to whether guerrilla warfare in Kansas turned Brown toward violence. Bertram Wyatt-Brown, "'A Volcano beneath a Mountain of Snow': John Brown and the Problem of Interpretation," in *His Soul Goes Marching On: Responses to John Brown and the Harpers Ferry Raid,* ed. Paul Finkelman (Charlottesville, Va., 1995), 10-38; and Daniel C. Littlefield, "Blacks, John Brown, and a Theory of Manhood," in Finkelman, *His Soul Goes Marching On,* 67-97.

103. James Oakes, *The Ruling Race: A History of American Slaveholders* (New York, 1982), 233-34.

104. William J. Cooper, Jr., *Liberty and Slavery: Southern Politics to 1860* (New York, 1983), 270.

105. Senate, *Mason Report,* 13.

106. Wallenstein, "Incendiaries All," in Finkelman, *His Soul Goes Marching On,* 149-73; and *Missouri Republican,* Dec. 13, 1859.

107. *Charleston Mercury,* Oct. 23, 1860; and *Boston Daily Advertiser,* Oct. 24, Nov. 3, 1859.

108. *Richmond Enquirer,* Oct. 25, 28, 1859.

109. William Elsey Connelley, *John Brown* (Topeka, 1900), 336-47.

110. James Redpath, *The Public Life of Capt. John Brown* (Boston, 1860), 16-17, 8.

111. David Davis to George Davis, Oct. 30, 1859, David Davis Family Papers, Illinois State Historical Library, Springfield.

112. David Herbert Donald, *Lincoln* (New York, 1995), 188; quoted in Stephen B. Oates, *With Malice toward None: The Life of Abraham Lincoln* (New York, 1977), 183.

113. C. Vann Woodward, "John Brown's Private War," in *The Burden of Southern History* (Baton Rouge, 1960), 41-68.

114. Chas. W. Helm to Hen. A Wise, Nov. 10, 1859, Wise and Family Collection; and H. M. Davis to Henry A. Wise, Nov. 16, 1859, ibid.

115. J. D. Pettel to [Henry A. Wise], Oct. 22, 1859, Wise and Family Collection; Wise to Pettel, Oct. 24, 1859, ibid.; Bob F. Irving to Gov. Wise, Nov. 29, 1859, ibid.; Edgar Langsdorf, "Thaddeus Hyatt in Washington Jail," *Kansas Historical Quarterly* 9 (Aug. 1940): 227-39; Senate, *Mason Report,* 156-72; and James M. McPherson, *Battle Cry of Freedom: The Civil War Era* (New York, 1988), 207.

116. *Boston Daily Advertiser,* Nov. 1, 1859; Bradley Chapin, *The American Law of Treason: Revolutionary and Early National Origins* (Seattle, 1964), 82-97; James Willard Hurst, *The Law of Treason in the United States: Collected Essays* (Westport, Conn., 1971), 186-98; Oates, *Purge This*

Land with Blood, 309, 325–26, 352; and George E. Caskie, "The Trial of John Brown," *American Law Review* 44 (1910): 405–25.

117. Geo. Washington-Chase to Gov. Wise, Nov. 29, [1859], Wise and Family Collection.

118. Edward Payson Bridgman and Luke Fisher Parsons, *With John Brown in Kansas: The Battle of Osawatomie* (Madison, Wisc., 1915), 28–29; T. W. Higginson to Friends, Nov. 4, 1859, John Brown Papers, Boyd B. Stutler Collection, Ohio Historical Society, Columbus. In February 1860, a drunken Irishman put in jail with the remaining raiders, Aaron D. Stevens and Albert Hazlett, turned out to be part of a conspiracy to break them out of prison. The conspirators later recalled that the two men refused to be rescued. Hinton, *John Brown and His Men,* 501–2. The last of Brown's followers, Stevens and Hazlett, were executed March 16, 1860. Oswald Garrison Villard, *John Brown, 1800–1859: A Biography Fifty Years After* (Boston, 1911), 575–80.

119. J. L. Davis to Col. Munford, Nov. 2, 1859, Wise and Family Collection.

120. J. Lucius Davis to Gov. Wise, Nov. 19, 1859, Wise and Family Collection; Connelley, *John Brown,* 384–93; and J. W. Garrett to Gov. Wise, Nov. 29, 1859, Wise and Family Collection.

121. A. D. Stevens to Mr. and Mrs. Lindsley, Dec. 17, 1859, Hinton Papers.

122. Connelley, *John Brown,* 384–93; and Oates, *Purge This Land with Blood,* 351–52.

123. Oates, *Purge This Land with Blood,* 309, 325–26, 352.

124. Maj. Gen. An. B. Taliaferro to Gov. Wise, Dec. 2, 1859, Wise and Family Collection.

125. Dec. 2, 1859, John Brown, Jr., Papers.

126. Stephen Vincent Benét, *John Brown's Body* (1927; reprint, New York, 1954), 53.

127. *Herald of Freedom,* Dec. 10, 1859.

128. Senate, *Mason Report,* 163.

129. John to Father, Dec. 14, 1859, "Letters of John and Sarah Everett, 1854–1864," *Kansas Historical Quarterly* 8 (Nov. 1939): 350–83, esp. 353–54.

130. Ralph Waldo Emerson, "Courage," in *Society and Solitude,* vol. 7, *Complete Works of Ralph Waldo Emerson* (New York, 1968), 251–80, esp. 260.

131. *Boston Daily Advertiser,* Dec. 2, 1859; Lewis A. Sayre to Henry A. Wise, Nov. 30, 1859, Wise and Family Collection. Wise also received letters from Southerners seeking to know if fellow townsmen suspected of antislavery sympathies had been named in Brown's papers. Wise appears to have filed most of these requests without comment, and presumably without answer. Yet when a Kansas Democrat wrote asking for incriminating information linking Martin Conway to Brown's raid for use in upcoming elections in Kansas, Wise endorsed the letter with a notation that he would look through Brown's captured papers for answers to this

inquiry. H. M. Davis to Henry A. Wise, Nov. 16, 1859, ibid.; and Chas. W. Helm to Hen. A. Wise, Nov. 10, 1859, ibid. If Wise did make the search, it failed to incriminate Conway. The Republicans won the Kansas legislature overwhelmingly and Conway a seat in Congress. Zornow, *Kansas*, 860. Maj. Gen. An. B. Taliaferro to Gov. Wise, Dec. 2, 1859, Wise and Family Collection.

132. Jno. Redpath to James H. Holmes, Feb. 3, 1905, George W. Brown Papers, SC 187, Illinois State Historical Library, Springfield.

133. Robert D. Richardson, Jr., *Emerson: The Mind on Fire* (Berkeley, Calif., 1995), 545; and Henry David Thoreau, "A Plea for Captain John Brown," in *Anti-Slavery and Reform Papers* (Montreal, 1963), 42–65, esp. 63.

134. *Boston Daily Advertiser,* Nov. 9, 1859.

135. Senate, *Mason Report,* 196, 140–45, 253–54.

136. Zornow, *Kansas,* 87–88.

137. S. Medary to Halderman, Dec. 10, 1859, John Adams Halderman Collection, Kansas State Historical Society, Topeka.

10. I AM HERE FOR REVENGE

1. Earl J. Hess, *Liberty, Virtue, and Progress: Northerners and Their War for the Union* (New York, 1997), vii–ix, 84.

2. Tom to Charley, Jan. 1, 1860, Thomas Ewing Family Papers, Library of Congress; and Geo. S. Park to Thomas Ewing, Jr., Jan. 19, 1860, ibid.

3. Resolution of the Legislative Assembly of the Territory of Kansas, Senate, Miscellaneous Documents, 36th Cong., 1st sess., 1860, serial 1038, no. 23, 1–2; *New York Times,* Feb. 16, April 2, 11, 14, 1860; Thomas Ewing, Jr., to Father, March 3, 1860, Ewing Family Papers; Tho. Ewing Jr. to Father, Feb. 2, 1860, ibid.; and Thomas Ewing Jr. to Cump, June 11, 1860, ibid.

4. *(Kansas City, Mo.) Western Journal of Commerce,* June 7, 1860; Resolution of the Legislative Assembly of the Territory of Kansas, Senate, Miscellaneous Documents, 1–2; *New York Times,* Feb. 16, April 2, 11, 1860; Leverett W. Spring, *Kansas: The Prelude to the War for the Union* (Boston, 1885), 265; and *Western Journal of Commerce,* June 7, 1860.

5. John A. Halderman to Eds., June 6, 1860, John Adams Halderman Collection, Kansas State Historical Society, Topeka.

6. *Western Journal of Commerce,* June 7, 1860.

7. Rich. G. Wait to John Benjamin, April 5, 1860, John Benjamin and Family Papers, Minnesota Historical Society, St. Paul.

8. Speech, Sept. 20, 1860, Charles and Sara T. D. Robinson Papers, Kansas State Historical Society, Topeka.

9. *Western Journal of Commerce,* June 7, 1860.

10. *New York Times,* June 7, 16, 1860; and Richard Cordley, *A History of Lawrence, Kansas from the First Settlement to the Close of the Rebellion* (Lawrence, Kans., 1895), 170–71.

11. Smith to Ewing, Sept. 30, 1860, Ewing Family Papers; Thaddeus Hyatt to James Buchanan, Oct. 16, 1860, James Buchanan Papers, Historical Society of Pennsylvania, Philadelphia.

12. *New York Times,* Nov. 23, 1860; Annual Message, Dec. 3, 1860, James D. Richardson, *A Compilation of the Messages and Papers of the Presidents, 1789–1908,* vol. 5 (Washington, D.C., 1908), 653.

13. J. H. Leach to D. C. Stone, Nov. 22, 1860, Civil War Collection, Missouri Historical Society, St. Louis.

14. J. Williams to Gov. Stewart, Nov. 20, 1860, Civil War Collection.

15. Citizens of Vernon County to Gov. Robert M. Stewart, Nov. 18, 1860, Civil War Collection; and J. Montgomery to George L. Stearns, Nov. 20, 1860, John Brown Papers, Boyd B. Stutler Collection, Ohio Historical Society, Columbus.

16. Affidavit of Lewis B. Reece, Dec. 4, 1860, Civil War Collection; Affidavit of George Washington Hindes, Dec. 8, 1860, ibid.; Affidavit of Nancy Hindes, Dec. 10, 1860, ibid.; and Citizens to G. A. Parsons, Dec. 2, 1860, ibid.

17. G. M. Beebe to James Buchanan, Nov. 26, 1860, "Governor Medary's Administration," vol. 5, *Transactions of the Kansas State Historical Society* (Topeka, 1896), 561–633, esp. 632–33; and Convention of citizens of Linn and Bourbon counties, KT, n.d., Civil War Collection.

18. S. S. Soule to Thayer, May 9, 1860, Richard Hinton Papers, Kansas State Historical Society, Topeka; and *New York Times,* Feb. 21, 1860; David M. Fox to [R. M. Stewart], Nov. 27, 1860, Robert M. Stewart Papers, Western Historical Manuscript Collection, Columbia, Mo.

19. *Richmond Enquirer,* Nov. 30, 1860.

20. Peter B. Knupfer, "A Crisis in Conservatism: Northern Unionism and the Harpers Ferry Raid," in *His Soul Goes Marching On: Responses to John Brown and the Harpers Ferry Raid,* ed. by Paul Finkelman (Charlottesville, Va., 1995), 119–48.

21. Don E. Fehrenbacher, *The Dred Scott Case: Its Significance in American Law and Politics* (New York, 1978), 531–32; and *New York Times,* Feb. 10, March 2, 1860.

22. William Watson Hick to R. M. T. Hunter, April 27, 1860, Charles Henry Ambler, *Correspondence of Robert M. T. Hunter, 1826–1876* (New York, 1971), 321–22; David M. Potter, *The Impending Crisis, 1848–1861* (New York, 1976), 408–14; and Don E. Fehrenbacher, *The South and Three Sectional Crises* (Baton Rouge, 1980), 59–60.

23. Robert W. Johannsen, *Stephen A. Douglas* (New York, 1973), 785–86, 745. Calhoun's widow notified Douglas of these attempts and informed him that no letters to her husband concerning the Lecompton controversy existed. *(St. Louis) Missouri Republican,* Oct. 19, 1860.

24. Allan Nevins, *The Emergence of Lincoln,* vol. 2, *Prologue to Civil War, 1859–1861* (New York, 1950), 298–302; and Roy Franklin Nichols, *The Disruption of American Democracy* (New York, 1948), 285–86.

25. House, *Covode Report*, 36th Cong., 1st sess., 1860, serial 1071, Rept. 648, 6–9, 29–33, 48–56.
26. Ibid.
27. John Marshall, Sept. 5, 1860, quoted in Clement Eaton, *Freedom of Thought in the Old South* (New York, 1951), 103–4.
28. Howell Cobb to the People of Georgia, Dec. 6, 1860, Ulrich Bonnell Phillips, ed., *The Correspondence of Robert Toombs, Alexander H. Stephens, and Howell Cobb* (New York, 1970), 512; Michael A. Morrison, *Slavery and the American West: The Eclipse of Manifest Destiny and the Coming of the Civil War* (Chapel Hill, N.C., 1997), 210; Fehrenbacher, *South and Three Sectional Crises*, 64; Brian Holden Reid, *The Origins of the American Civil War* (London, 1996), 218; James Oakes, *The Ruling Race: A History of American Slaveholders* (New York, 1982), 239–42; and Harry V. Jaffa, *Equality and Liberty: Theory and Practice in American Politics* (New York, 1965), 48–49.
29. A. S. Weston to Brother, Jan. 9, 1860 [1861], Weston Family Papers, Mississippi Department of Archives and History, Jackson.
30. Nichols, *Disruption of American Democracy*, 475.
31. Alice Nichols, *Bleeding Kansas* (New York, 1954), 252–53; and *New York Times*, Jan. 29, 1861.
32. Jan. 31, 1861, Henry Miles Moore Journals, Yale University Library.
33. *(St. Louis) Missouri Democrat*, Feb. 9, 1861.
34. April 14, 1861, entry, Isaac T. Goodnow Diary, Isaac Tichenor Goodnow Collection, Kansas State Historical Society, Topeka.
35. Paul C. Nagel, *One Nation Indivisible: The Union in American Thought* (New York, 1964), 21; and Hess, *Liberty, Virtue, and Progress*, 29.
36. Chr. H. Isely to President, May 6, 1861, Isely Family Letters, Papers, and Diaries, Wichita State University Special Collections.
37. War Dept. to General, May 21, 1861, Blair Family Papers, Library of Congress.
38. James M. McPherson, *Battle Cry of Freedom: The Civil War Era* (New York, 1988), 290–92.
39. *Charleston Mercury*, July 11, 1861.
40. McPherson, *Battle Cry of Freedom*, 290–92.
41. *Charleston Mercury*, Dec. 2, 1861.
42. McPherson, *Battle Cry of Freedom*, 350–54.
43. S. S. to Judge [Blair], Sept. 3, 1861, Blair Family Papers; and McPherson, *Battle Cry of Freedom*, 352–54.
44. "Governor's Message," March 30, 1861, Governor's Office Files, Administration of Charles A. Robinson, Kansas State Historical Society, Topeka.
45. S. S. to Judge [Blair], Sept. 3, 1861, Blair Family Papers; and McPherson, *Battle Cry of Freedom*, 352–54.
46. Kenneth W. Noe, "Exterminating Savages: The Union Army and Mountain Guerrillas in Southern West Virginia, 1861–1862," in *The Civil War*

in Appalachia: Collected Essays, ed. by Kenneth W. Noe and Shannon
H. Wilson (Knoxville, 1997), 104–30, esp. 104–6.

47. Rev. George Miller, *Missouri's Memorable Decade, 1860–1870* (Columbia, Mo., 1898), 41.

48. C. to S., June 17, 1861, Robinson Papers.

49. C. Gibson to Gov. Gamble, Aug. 20, 1861, Hamilton R. Gamble Papers,
Missouri Historical Society, St. Louis.

50. D. C. Hunter to Col. Snyder, May 24, 1861, Dr. John F. Snyder Collec-
tion, Missouri Historical Society, St. Louis; C. Robinson to Maj. Gen.
J. C. Fremont, Sept. 1, 1861, Robinson Papers; and J. Montgomery to
Geo. Stearns, May 8, 1861, James Montgomery Collection, Kansas State
Historical Society, Topeka.

51. A. W. Mitchell to J. T. Sweringen, May 29, 1861, James T. Sweringen
Papers, Missouri Historical Society, St. Louis.

52. David Herbert Donald, *Lincoln* (New York, 1995), 298; and J. L. S. to
[Thos. Ewing Jr.], May 18, 1861, Ewing Family Papers. The Senate election pitted Lane and S. C. Pomeroy against Tom Ewing. Smith to Tom,
Feb. 11, 1861, Ewing Family Papers; Smith to Tom, Feb. 10, 1861, ibid.;
and *New York Times,* April 2, 1861. Many details of the politicking in the
senate race can be found in box 65 of the Ewing Papers; and A. M. Saltig
to Thos. Ewing, March 10, 1861, box 69, Ewing Family Papers. A bitter
Tom Ewing blamed the result on Pomeroy's liberal use of money to buy
votes. But it seems that Lane and Pomeroy's lieutenants had simply out-
maneuvered Ewing's. Robinson recalled that the vote-switching was so
complex that the balloting required four hours and completely confused
the tally keepers. William Frank Zornow, *Kansas: A History of the Jayhawk
State* (Norman, Okla., 1957), 120–22; Wendell Holmes Stephenson, *The
Political Career of General James H. Lane* (Topeka, 1930), 102–3; Tom
to Father, April 10, 1861, Ewing Family Papers; and Charles Robinson,
The Kansas Conflict (Lawrence, Kans., 1898), 431–32.

53. C. Robinson to Ewing, May 28, 1861, Ewing Family Papers.

54. Albert Castel, *A Frontier State at War: Kansas, 1861–1865* (Ithaca, N.Y.,
1958), 84–89; Zornow, *Kansas,* 120–22; Stephenson, *General James H.
Lane,* 102–3; Tom to Father, April 10, 1861, Ewing Family Papers; and
Robinson, *Kansas Conflict,* 431–32. Robinson's term as state governor
was a failure, marked not only by his lack of influence with the president
but also marred by scandal. In early 1861, the Kansas legislature voted
two bond issues. The disposition of the bonds involved complicated transactions, from which Robinson's friend and business associate, Robert S.
Stevens, profited. An appearance of impropriety thus attached to Robinson's actions, some of which exceeded his authority in handling the bonds.
In February 1862, with Lane lobbying heavily in favor, the Kansas House
voted to hold impeachment proceedings against Robinson. The secretary
of state, John W. Robinson, and the state auditor, George S. Hillyer, were
also tried. In June, Secretary Robinson and Hillyer were removed from

office. Charles Robinson's trial lasted less than a day and he was easily acquitted on all the charges against him. Although cleared, Robinson retired from the governorship at the beginning of 1863, never again to achieve statewide office. Castel, *Frontier State at War,* 67-77.

55. Thomas Goodrich, *Bloody Dawn: The Story of the Lawrence Massacre* (Kent, Ohio, 1991), 18.

56. June 6, 1861 entry, Moore Journals.

57. United Daughters of the Confederacy, Missouri Division, *Reminiscences of the Women of Missouri during the Sixties* (Jefferson City, Mo., n.d.), 54-55, 61-68.

58. Joseph H. Trego to Wife, Oct. 28, 1861, Edgar Langsdorf, ed., "The Letters of Joseph H. Trego, 1857-1864, Linn County Pioneer," *Kansas Historical Quarterly* 19 (Aug. 1951): 287-309, esp. 298.

59. J. F. O. to Cusin Isely, Nov. 18, 1861, Isely Family Letters, Papers, and Diaries.

60. Margaret J. [Hays] to Mother, Nov. 12, 1861, Civil War Collection; and *Women of Missouri,* 214-19.

61. Castel, *Frontier State at War,* 57-60; and Stephen Z. Starr, *Jennison's Jayhawkers: A Civil War Cavalry Regiment and Its Commander* (Baton Rouge, 1973), 91-92.

62. Hildegarde Rose Herklotz, "Jayhawkers in Missouri, 1858-1863," *Missouri Historical Review* 18 (Oct. 1923): 64-101, esp. 70.

63. G. C. Bingham to J. S. Rollins, Jan. 22, 1862, James S. Rollins Papers, Western Historical Manuscript Collection, Columbia, Mo.

64. Richard S. Brownlee, *Gray Ghosts of the Confederacy: Guerrilla Warfare in the West, 1861-1865* (Baton Rouge, 1958), 40.

65. William E. Parrish, *Turbulent Partnership: Missouri and the Union, 1861-1865* (Columbia, Mo., 1963), 84-86.

66. James E. Love to Molly, April 22, 1862, James E. Love Papers, Missouri Historical Society, St. Louis; and James E. Love to Molly, March 26, 1862, ibid.

67. Diary of an Unknown Soldier [19th Iowa], Nov. 15, 1862, Civil War Collection.

68. Lucy Thurman to Cousin Lark, July 1, 1862, ibid.

69. Benjamin Quarles, *The Negro in the Civil War* (Boston, 1953), 66; Joseph T. Glatthaar, *Forged in Battle: The Civil War Alliance of Black Soldiers and White Officers* (New York, 1990), 4; and Michael P. Johnson, "Out of Egypt: The Migration of Former Slaves to the Midwest during the 1860s in Comparative Perspective," in *Crossing Boundaries: Comparative History of Black People in Diaspora,* ed. by Darlene Clark Hine and Jacqueline McLeod (Bloomington, Ind., 1999), 223-45, esp. 232.

70. John W. Park to ———, Oct. 2, 1861, Park Brothers Collection, Wichita State University Special Collections; and Joseph H. Trego to Wife, Nov. 12, 1861, Langsdorf, ed., "Letters of Joseph H. Trego," 299.

71. *New York Times,* Nov. 11, 1861.
72. H. C. Bruce, *The New Man: Twenty-Nine Years a Slave, Twenty-Nine Years a Free Man* (1895; reprint, New York, 1969), 99–100.
73. March 22, 1862 entry, Robert T. McMahan Diary, Western Historical Manuscript Collection, Columbia, Mo.
74. Bruce, *New Man,* 107–11.
75. *Women of Missouri,* 254–56.
76. William A. Dobak, ed., "Civil War on the Kansas-Missouri Border: The Narrative of Former Slave Andrew Williams," *Kansas History* 6 (autumn 1983): 237–42, esp. 239.
77. Agnes Emery, *Reminiscences of Early Lawrence* (Lawrence, Kans., 1955), 19–20.
78. C. M. C. to ———, Aug. 19, 1863, Lela Barnes, "An Editor Looks at Early-Day Kansas: The Letters of Charles Monroe Chase," *Kansas Historical Quarterly* 26 (summer 1960): 113–51.
79. *New York Times,* Jan. 18, 1862; and Richard Cordley, *Pioneer Days in Kansas* (Boston, 1903), 137–51.
80. Quarles, *Negro in the Civil War,* 126.
81. Cordley, *History of Lawrence,* 182–85.
82. Bruce, *New Man,* 111–15; and Thomas Ewing, Jr., to C. W. Marsh, Aug. 3, 1863, *The Black Military Experience,* 2d ser., *Freedom: A Documentary History of Emancipation, 1861–1867,* ed. by Ira Berlin, Joseph P. Reidy, and Leslie S. Rowland (Cambridge, Eng., 1982), 228–30.
83. Richard B. Sheridan, "From Slavery in Missouri to Freedom in Kansas: The Influx of Black Fugitives and Contrabands into Kansas, 1854–1865," *Kansas History* 12 (spring 1989): 28–47; and James R. Shortridge, *Peopling the Plains: Who Settled Where in Frontier Kansas* (Lawrence, Kans., 1995), 29. In fact, during the war, Missouri's black population decreased by more than 41,000 people. Shortridge, *Peopling the Plains,* 29.
84. G. C. Bingham to Jas. S. Rollins and Wm. A. Hale, Feb. 12, 1862, Rollins Papers.
85. D. R. Anthony to Sister, Feb. 3, 1862, Edgar Langsdorf and R. W. Richmond, eds., "Letters of Daniel R. Anthony, 1857–1862—Continued: Part Three, October 1, 1861–June 7, 1862," *Kansas Historical Quarterly* 24 (autumn 1958): 351–70, 359.
86. Dudley Taylor Cornish, "Kansas Negro Regiments in the Civil War," *Kansas Historical Quarterly* 20 (May 1953): 417–29; Dudley Taylor Cornish, *The Sable Arm: Negro Troops in the Union Army, 1861–1865* (New York, 1966), 75–76; Gabriel Grays et al. to H. Ford Douglas, June 19, 1865, in Berlin, Reidy, and Rowland, *Black Military Experience,* 421–22; and H. Ford Douglas to Jno. Barber, June 20, 1865, ibid., 422–23.
87. John Speer, *Life of Gen. James H. Lane, "The Liberator of Kansas" with Corrobative Incidents of Pioneer History* (Garden City, Kans., 1897), 262; Cornish, "Kansas Negro Regiments," 417–29; McPherson, *Battle*

Cry of Freedom, 563-64; Cornish, *Sable Arm,* 69-78; Glatthaar, *Forged in Battle,* 7; and Quarles, *Negro in the Civil War,* 113-15, 120.

88. Quarles, *Negro in the Civil War,* 226-27; Cornish, *Sable Arm,* xi-xii; and Speer, *Life of Gen. James H. Lane,* 258.

89. *New York Times,* June 6, 1862.

90. *(Leavenworth) Daily Times,* Aug. 6, 1862.

91. Thomas Ewing, Jr. to Lt. Col. C. W. Martin, July 4, 1863, Ewing Family Papers; and Edwin H. Staub to Col. James Montgomery, Aug. 9, 1864, Montgomery Collection.

92. Glatthaar, *Forged in Battle,* 122.

93. [H. R. Gamble] to Abraham Lincoln, Sept. 8, 1862, Gamble Papers.

94. McPherson, *Battle Cry of Freedom,* 563-64; Cornish, "Kansas Negro Regiments," 417-49; and Cornish, *Sable Arm,* 69-78.

95. Cornish, *Sable Arm,* 145-47.

96. Berlin, Reidy, and Rowland, *Black Military Experience,* 19, 44-45, 72-73; Glatthaar, *Forged in Battle,* 176, 182; Cornish, *Sable Arm,* 215-16, 182-83; James M. McPherson, *The Negro's Civil War: How American Negroes Felt and Acted during the War for the Union* (New York, 1965), 238-39; J. M. Williams to H. Q. Loring, April 21, 1863; N. P. Chipman to [Samuel R. Curtis], Oct. 16 [1862], ibid., 70-72.

97. Cornish, *Sable Arm,* 158-63; Berlin, Reidy, and Rowland, *Black Military Experience,* 33-34; A. W. Maupin to James O. Broadhead, Dec. 30, 1863, ibid., 236-37; and Sam Bowmen to Mr. Wilson, May 10, 1864, in *The Destruction of Slavery,* 1 ser., vol. 1, *Freedom: A Documentary History of Emancipation, 1861-1867,* ed. Ira Berlin et al. (Cambridge, Eng., 1985), 483-85.

98. Edward M. Samuel et al. to the President, Sept. 8, 1862, in Berlin et al., *Destruction of Slavery,* 471-72; Testimony of B. Gratz Brown, Nov. 30, 1863, ibid.; and Thomas Ewing, Jr., to C. W. Marsh, Aug. 3, 1863, in Berlin, Reidy, and Rowland, *Black Military Experience,* 188, 223-30.

99. T. R. Livingston to Col. Williams, May 20, 1863, in Berlin, Reidy, and Rowland, *Black Military Experience,* 574; J. M. Williams to T. R. Livingston, May 21, 1863, ibid., 575; J. M. Williams to T. R. Livingston, May 26, 1863, ibid., 576; and Cornish, *Sable Arm,* 145-47.

100. Brownlee, *Gray Ghosts,* 94-109; and *New York Times,* Sept. 10, 15, 1862.

101. Judge L. D. Bailey, *Border Ruffian Troubles in Kansas* (Lyndon, Kans., 1899), 52-72.

102. Thomas Brower Peacock, "The Rhyme of the Border War," in *Poems of the Plains and Songs of the Solitudes* (New York, 1889), 207-305; and William H. Gregg, "A Little Dab of History without Embellishment," Western Historical Manuscript Collection, Columbia, Mo.

103. Statement of Andy J. Walker, May 11, 1888, William Clarke Quantrill Papers, University of Kansas Library; Brownlee, *Gray Ghosts,* 53-75;

Albert Castel, *William Clarke Quantrill: His Life and Times* (New York, 1962); and William Elsey Connelley, *Quantrill and the Border Wars* (New York, 1956).

104. W. C. Quantrill to mother, Jan. 26, 1850, Quantrill Papers.

105. Gregg, "Little Dab of History."

106. Carl W. Breihan, *Quantrill and His Civil War Guerrillas* (Denver, 1959), 52–56.

107. Connelley, *Quantrill and the Border Wars;* Brownlee, *Gray Ghosts,* 76–91.

108. Michael Fellman, *Inside War: The Guerrilla Conflict in Missouri during the American Civil War* (New York, 1989), 136.

109. Brownlee, *Gray Ghosts,* 76–91.

110. A. W. Reese, "Recollections of the Civil War," 1870, pp. 239–46, Western Historical Manuscript Collection, Columbia, Mo.

111. Parrish, *Turbulent Partnership,* 155–60; Tom to Father, June 7, 1863, Ewing Family Papers (LC); and J. M. Schofield to Gov. [Gamble], Feb. 2, 1863, Gamble Papers.

112. Thomas Ewing, Jr., to Father, Sept. 5, 1862, Ewing Family Papers.

113. Thomas Ewing, Jr., to Father, Aug. 15, 1863, ibid.

114. Parrish, *Turbulent Partnership,* 155–60; and Thomas Ewing, Jr., to Father, July 24, 1863, Ewing Family Papers.

115. George Wolz to Brother, June 19, 1863, Civil War Collection.

116. Goodrich, *Bloody Dawn,* 7–8, 12, 15.

117. Gregg, "Little Dab of History"; and Goodrich, *Bloody Dawn,* 34–35, 47.

118. Gregg, "Little Dab of History."

119. John C. Shea, ed., *Reminiscences of Quantrell's Raid upon the City of Lawrence, Kas.* (Kansas City, Mo., 1879), 13–15; and Gregg, "Little Dab of History." In his memoirs, Charles Robinson could not resist taking a jab at Jim Lane even at the expense of complimenting the bushwhackers. Quantrill's men, Robinson noted, had not raped the women of Lawrence as Robinson claimed Lane's men had done in Missouri. Robinson, *Kansas Conflict,* 446–47.

120. J. A. Pike, "Statement Concerning the Quantrill Raid," 1917, Western Historical Manuscript Collection, Columbia, Mo.

121. Shea, ed., *Reminiscences of Quantrell's Raid,* 3–7.

122. "Statement of E. D. Thompson," Aug. 5, 1895, Ewing Family Papers.

123. Sarah to Father and Mother, Sept. 2, 1863, John M. Peterson, ed., "Letters of Edward and Sarah Fitch, Lawrence, Kansas, 1855–1863," *Kansas History* 12 (summer 1989): 78–100, esp. 95–97; Louise Barry, "The Emigrant Aid Company Parties of 1854," *Kansas Historical Quarterly* 12 (May 1943): 115–55, esp. 133; Louise Barry, "The New England Emigrant Aid Company Parties of 1855," *Kansas Historical Quarterly* 12 (Aug. 1943): 227–68, esp. 267; and John W. Barber and Henry Howe, *The Loyal West in the Times of the Rebellion* (Cincinnati, 1865), 643–46.

124. Joanna L. Stratton, *Pioneer Women: Voices from the Kansas Frontier* (New York, 1981), 249–50; and Shea, *Reminiscences of Quantrell's Raid*, 24–27.
125. Sarah to Father and Mother, Sept. 2, 1863, "Letters of Edward and Sarah Fitch," 95–97.
126. Connelley, *Quantrill and the Border Wars*, 355–56, 381; and Duane Schultz, *Quantrill's War: The Life and Times of William Clarke Quantrill, 1837–1865* (New York, 1996), 193–94, 213.
127. Speer, *Life of Gen. James H. Lane*, 265.
128. Barber and Howe, *Loyal West*, 643–44; Statement of E. D. Thompson, Aug. 5, 1895, Ewing Family Papers; and Shea, *Reminiscences of Quantrill's Raid*, 3–13.
129. Sarah to Father and Mother, Sept. 2, 1863, "Letters of Edward and Sarah Fitch," 95–97.
130. Shea, *Reminiscences of Quantrell's Raid*, 13–15; L. C. Miller, "Memoirs of the Life of Lee Caruth Miller, M.D.," 1903, pp. 15–16, Western Historical Manuscript Collection, Columbia, Mo.; and Gregg, "Little Dab of History."
131. Miller, "Memoirs," 15–16.
132. Gregg, "Little Dab of History"; Thomas Ewing, Jr., to C. W. Marsh, Aug. 31, 1863, U.S., War Department, *The War of the Rebellion: Official Records of the Union and Confederate Armies* (Washington, D.C., 1880–1901), vol. 32, 579–85; Hervey Johnson to Folks at home, Aug. 29, 1863, in William E. Unrau, ed., "In Pursuit of Quantrill: An Enlisted Man's Response," *Kansas Historical Quarterly* 39 (autumn 1973): 379–91, esp. 386–89; and Hervey Johnson to Sister Sibil, Sept. 1, 1863, ibid., 390–91.
133. Edward E. Leslie, *The Devil Knows How to Ride: The True Story of William Clarke Quantrill and His Confederate Raiders* (New York, 1996), 237n; and Barber and Howe, *Loyal West*, 646–47.
134. Barber and Howe, *Loyal West*, 643–44.
135. *Missouri Democrat*, Aug. 22, 24, 1863; and Goodrich, *Bloody Dawn*, 162.
136. Stratton, *Pioneer Women*, 251–52.
137. Aug. 21, 22, 1863 entries, Isaac T. Goodnow Diary, Goodnow Collection.
138. Julia L. L. to Father, et al., May 10, 1864, "Letters of Julia Louisa Lovejoy, 1856–1864: Part Five, 1860–1864," *Kansas Historical Quarterly* 16 (May 1948): 175–211, esp. 207–8.
139. I. T. G. to wife, Aug. 3, 1864, Goodnow Collection.
140. Geo. T. Robinson to S. R. Curtis, July 18, 1864, U.S. War Dept., *War of the Rebellion*, vol. 84, 253–55; S. R. Curtis to George T. Robinson, July 19, 1864, ibid., 275; and W. D. McLain to Brig. Gen. McKean, July 22, 1864, ibid., 347.
141. Thomas Carney to Major-General Schofield, Aug. 24, 1863, U.S. War Dept., *War of the Rebellion*, vol. 32, 576.

142. Barber and Howe, *Loyal West*, 646–47; and Goodrich, *Bloody Dawn*, 164–65.

143. C. M. C. to ——, Aug. 29, 1863, Barnes, "Editor Looks at Early-Day Kansas," 113–51.

144. Sept. 2, 3 entries, "Events in the Dept. of the Missouri," John McAllister Schofield Papers, Library of Congress; J. F. Legate to J. M. Schofield, Sept. 3, 1863, ibid.; Sept. 4, 6 entries, "Events in the Dept. of the Missouri," ibid.; J. M. Schofield to E. D. Townsend, Sept. 14, 1863, U.S. War Dept., *War of the Rebellion*, vol. 32, 572–75.

145. Sept. 8 entry, "Events in the Dept. of the Missouri," Schofield Papers; *Missouri Democrat*, Sept. 8, 14, 16, 1863.

146. S. O. Thacher to Gen. Ewing, Sept. 1, 1863, Ewing Family Papers; and Connelley, *Quantrill and the Border Wars*, 417–18.

147. Parrish, *Turbulent Partnership*, 155–60; and Fellman, *Inside War*, 95–96.

148. Thomas Ewing, Jr., to J. M. Schofield, Aug. 25, 1863, Ewing Family Papers; and Thomas Ewing, Jr., to Father, Aug. 28, 1863, ibid.

149. Aug. 26 entry, "Events in the Dept. of the Missouri," Schofield Papers; J. M. Schofield to E. D. Townsend, Dec. 10, 1863, U.S. War Dept., *War of the Rebellion*, vol. 32, 12–17; John M. Schofield, *Forty-Six Years in the Army* (Norman, Okla., 1998), 78; E. Lynde to H. G. Loring, May 11, 1863, U.S. War Dept., *War of the Rebellion*, vol. 32, 318–19; and Brownlee, *Gray Ghosts*, 110–27.

150. Brownlee, *Gray Ghosts*, 142–79; and Castel, *Frontier State at War*, 142–45.

151. *Women of Missouri*, 263–67.

152. Tho. C. Fletcher to Genl. Thomas Ewing, Jr., Dec. 9, 1865, Ewing Family Papers. A novel, *Order No. 11*, dramatized the sufferings of one fictional Missouri family. Caroline Abbot Stanley, *Order No. 11: A Tale of the Border* (New York, 1904).

153. Fellman, *Inside War*, 95–96; Sept. 8 entry, "Events in the Dept. of the Missouri," Schofield Papers; and General Orders No. 20, Nov. 20, 1863, Ewing Family Papers.

154. Jas. G. Blunt to Col. Marsh, Oct. 19, 1863, U.S. War Dept., *War of the Rebellion*, vol. 32, 688–90; Charles W. Blair to Oliver D. Greene, Oct. 15, 1863, ibid., vol. 32, 690–93; Benjamin S. Henning to Oliver D. Greene, Oct. 7, 1863, ibid., vol. 32, 693–98; James S. Pond to C. W. Blair, Oct. 7, 1863, ibid., vol. 32, 698–700; and W. C. Quantrill to Major-General Price, Oct. 13, 1863, ibid., vol. 32, 700–701.

155. Brownlee, *Gray Ghosts*, 128–29, 5; Castel, *William Clarke Quantrill*; and Goodrich, *Bloody Dawn*, 185.

156. T. R. Livingston to Sterling Price, May 28, 1863, U.S. War Dept., *War of the Rebellion*, vol. 33, 849–50.

157. Sterling Price to Friends of the Confederacy, Oct. 15, 1864, ibid., vol. 85, 1012.

158. Albert Castel, *General Sterling Price and the Civil War in the West* (Baton Rouge, 1968), v; Richard S. Brownlee, "The Battle of Pilot Knob, Iron

County, Missouri, September 27, 1864," *Missouri Historical Review* 59 (Oct. 1964): 1–30; Parrish, *Turbulent Partnership*, 193–94; P. B. Plumb to General, Dec. 18, 1864, Ewing Family Papers; Oct. 5, 1864 entry, Edward Bates Journal, vol. 11, Bates Family Papers, Missouri Historical Society, St. Louis; Brownlee, *Gray Ghosts*, 208–31; McPherson, *Battle Cry of Freedom*, 784–88; Albert Castel, "War and Politics: The Price Raid of 1864," *Kansas Historical Quarterly* 24 (summer 1958): 129–43, esp. 130–31; and William S. Rosecrans, Report, Dec. 7, 1864, U.S. War Dept., *War of the Rebellion*, vol. 83, 307–17.

159. Brownlee, "Battle of Pilot Knob," 1–30; Thomas Ewing, Jr., Report, Oct. 20, 1864, U.S. War Dept., *War of the Rebellion*, vol. 83, 445–52; Parrish, *Turbulent Partnership*, 193–94; P. B. Plumb to General, Dec. 18, 1864, Ewing Family Papers; William S. Rosecrans, Report, Dec. 7, 1864, U.S. War Dept., *War of the Rebellion*, vol. 83, 307–17; Oct. 5, 1864 entry, Bates Journal, vol. 11, Bates Family Papers; Brownlee, *Gray Ghosts*, 208–31; and McPherson, *Battle Cry of Freedom*, 784–88.

160. Brownlee, *Gray Ghosts*, 208–31; *Western Journal of Commerce*, Oct. 1, 1864. James Rollins, a Unionist politician, was on the stage. Rollins presented himself as a fervent southern sympathizer and so survived. Perry McCandless, *A History of Missouri*, vol. 2, *1820 to 1860* (Columbia, Mo., 1972), 227–88; and Brownlee, *Gray Ghosts*, 216–20.

161. Dan M. Draper to Brig. Gen. Fisk, Sept. 29, 1864, U.S. War Dept., *War of the Rebellion*, vol. 83, 440–41; Clinton B. Fisk to Maj. Gen. Rosecrans, Sept. 29, 1864, ibid., vol. 85, 488; and Brownlee, *Gray Ghosts*, 216–20.

162. S. P. Cox to General Craig, Oct. 27, 1864, U.S. War Dept., *War of the Rebellion*, vol. 83, 442; and Brownlee, *Gray Ghosts*, 229.

163. Brownlee, "Battle of Pilot Knob," 1–30; Parrish, *Turbulent Partnership*, 193–94; P. B. Plumb to General, Dec. 18, 1864, Ewing Family Papers; Oct. 5, 1864 entry, Bates Journal, vol. 11, Bates Family Papers; Brownlee, *Gray Ghosts*, 208–31; McPherson, *Battle Cry of Freedom*, 784–88; Castel, "War and Politics," 132–33, 135–37; S. R. Curtis to Thomas Carney, Oct. 5, 1864, U.S. War Dept., *War of the Rebellion*, vol. 85, 650; Thos. Carney to Maj. Gen. Rosecrans, Oct. 9, 1864, ibid., vol. 85, 724; W. S. Rosecrans to Thomas Carney, Oct. 9, 1864, ibid., vol. 85, 724; Chas. W. Blair to S. R. Curtis, Oct. 17, 1864, ibid., vol. 86, 57–58; Geo. W. Deitzler to Maj. Gen. Curtis, Oct. 17, 1864, ibid., vol. 86, 59; Chas. W. Blair to S. R. Curtis, Oct. 18, 1864, ibid., vol. 86, 94; Samuel R. Curtis to Maj. Gen. Halleck, Jan. 1865, ibid., vol. 83, 471; and "Autobiography," Samuel James Reader Papers, Kansas State Historical Society, Topeka.

164. "Autobiography," Reader Papers; and James G. Blunt to M. H. Insley, Oct. 23, 1864, U.S. War Dept., *War of the Rebellion*, vol. 86, 209.

165. Castel, "War and Politics," 137–42; and Alfred Pleasanton, Report, Dec. 1, 1864, U.S. War Dept., *War of the Rebellion*, vol. 83, 336–39.

166. Brownlee, "Battle of Pilot Knob," 1–30; Sterling Price to W. R. Boggs, Nov. 18, 1864, *War of the Rebellion*, vol. 83, 624–40, esp. 640; Ster-

ling Price to E. K. Smith, July 24, 1864, ibid., vol. 84, 1023–24; W. R. Boggs to S. Price, Aug. 4, 1864, ibid., vol. 84, 1040–41; James R. Shaler testimony, May 2, 1865, ibid., vol. 83, 721–22; Parrish, *Turbulent Partnership*, 193–94; P. B. Plumb to General, Dec. 18, 1864, Ewing Family Papers; Oct. 5, 1864 entry, Bates Journal, vol. 11, Bates Family Papers; Brownlee, *Gray Ghosts*, 208–31; McPherson, *Battle Cry of Freedom*, 784–88; and Castel, *General Sterling Price*, 251–53.

167. C. to S., Oct. 16, 1864, Robinson Papers.

168. Castel, "War and Politics," 142–43.

169. C. to S., Feb. 28, 1864, Robinson Papers; and William Frank Zornow, "The Kansas Senators and the Re-election of Lincoln," *Kansas Historical Quarterly* 19 (May 1951), 133–44.

170. A. W. Reese, "Recollections of the Civil War," 1870, vol. 1, 180–81, Western Historical Manuscript Collection, Columbia, Mo.

171. Reese, "Recollections," vol. 2, 229.

CONCLUSION

1. Joanna L. Stratton, *Pioneer Women: Voices from the Kansas Frontier* (New York, 1981), 252.

2. William Frank Zornow, *Kansas: A History of the Jayhawk State* (Norman, Okla., 1957), 108.

3. James Anderson to [Wm. C. Long], Aug. 22, 1865, William C. Long Papers, Western Historical Manuscript Collection, Columbia, Mo.; and James Anderson to [Wm. C. Long], Oct. 1, 1865, ibid.

4. Eliza Johnston Wiggins, *Impressions of Early Kansas* (Wichita, Kans., 1915), 22–23.

5. A. W. Reese, "Recollections of the Civil War," 1870, 330–36, Western Historical Manuscript Collection, Columbia, Mo.

6. Richard S. Brownlee, *Gray Ghosts of the Confederacy: Guerrilla Warfare in the West, 1861–1865* (Baton Rouge, 1958), 232–46.

7. Samuel J. Crawford, *Kansas in the Sixties* (1911; reprint, Ottawa, Kans., 1994), 235–36.

8. Don W. Wilson, *Governor Charles Robinson of Kansas* (Lawrence, Kans., 1975).

9. Edward E. Leslie, *The Devil Knows How to Ride: The True Story of William Clarke Quantrill and His Confederate Raiders* (New York, 1996), 422–27; and Richard B. Sheridan, "The 1913 Semi-Centennial Memorial Reunion of the Survivors of Quantrill's Raid on Lawrence," *Kansas History* 20 (autumn 1997): 177–91.

10. Charles S. Gleed, ed., *The Kansas Memorial, A Report of the Old Settlers' Meeting Held at Bismarck Grove, Kansas, September 15th and 16th, 1879* (Kansas City, Mo., 1880), 23.

11. Charles Robinson, *The Kansas Conflict* (Lawrence, Kans., 1898), 461.

12. Edmund G. Ross, *The Pilgrim and the Cavalier in Kansas* ([1895]).

13. Gleed, *Kansas Memorial*, 27–28.

14. United Daughters of the Confederacy, Missouri Division, *Reminiscences of the Women of Missouri during the Sixties* (Jefferson City, Mo., n.d.), 254-56.

15. Michael P. Johnson, "Out of Egypt: The Migration of Former Slaves to the Midwest during the 1860s in Comparative Perspective," in *Crossing Boundaries: Comparative History of Black People in Diaspora,* ed. by Darlene Clark Hine and Jacqueline McLeod (Bloomington, Ind., 1999), 223-45; and H. C. Bruce, *The New Man: Twenty-Nine Years a Slave, Twenty-Nine Years a Free Man* (1895; reprint, New York, 1969), 119-20, 155-76.

16. The votes were 19,421 to 10,438 against black suffrage and 19,857 to 10,070 against woman suffrage. James M. McPherson, *The Negro's Civil War: How American Negroes Felt and Acted during the War for the Union* (New York, 1965), 274-75; Quintard Taylor, *In Search of the Racial Frontier; African Americans in the American West, 1528-1990* (New York, 1998), 126-28; Ellen Carol DuBois, *Feminism and Suffrage: The Emergence of an Independent Women's Movement in America, 1848-1869* (Ithaca, N.Y., 1978), 79-104; and Eric Foner, *Reconstruction: America's Unfinished Revolution, 1863-1877* (New York, 1988), 223.

17. W. Sherman Savage, *Blacks in the West* (Westport, Conn., 1976), 201; and Nell Irvin Painter, *Exodusters: Black Migration to Kansas after Reconstruction* (New York, 1977), 159.

18. Robert G. Athearn, *In Search of Canaan: Black Migration to Kansas, 1879-1880* (Lawrence, Kans., 1978), 163.

19. Ibid., 31-78.

20. Ibid., 119.

21. Ibid., 123.

22. Ibid., 51-61, 163, 200, 83, 256; Painter, *Exodusters,* 260; and Taylor, *Racial Frontier,* 136-43.

23. Painter, *Exodusters,* 260.

24. Athearn, *In Search of Canaan,* 205.

25. David W. Blight, *Race and Reunion: The Civil War in American Memory* (Cambridge, Mass., 2001), 1-5, 209.

BIBLIOGRAPHY

MANUSCRIPT COLLECTIONS

Allen Family. Papers. West Virginia and Regional History Collection. West Virginia University, Morgantown.

Anderson, James Blythe. Papers. University of Kentucky, Lexington.

Anthony, Daniel Read. Collection. Kansas State Historical Society, Topeka.

Atchison, David Rice. Papers. Western Historical Manuscript Collection. Columbia, Mo.

Banks, Nathaniel P. Papers. Library of Congress, Washington, D.C.

Barnes, William. Collection. Kansas State Historical Society, Topeka.

Bassett, W. J. Collection. Kansas State Historical Society, Topeka.

Bates, Edward. Papers. Western Historical Manuscript Collection, Columbia, Mo.

Bates Family. Papers. Missouri Historical Society, St. Louis.

Benjamin, John, and Family. Papers. Minnesota Historical Society, St. Paul.

Benton, Thomas Hart. Papers. Missouri Historical Society, St. Louis.

Bissell, Sophia. Letter to Cousin, Sept. 8, 1863. Kansas State Historical Society, Topeka.

Black, Jeremiah S. Papers. Library of Congress, Washington, D.C.

Blackman, W. I. R. Miscellaneous Collections. Kansas State Historical Society, Topeka.

Blair, Frank and Montgomery. Papers. Missouri Historical Society, St. Louis.

Blair Family. Papers. Library of Congress, Washington, D.C.

———. Papers. Western Historical Manuscript Collection, Columbia, Mo.

Blood, James. Papers. Kansas State Historical Society, Topeka.

Bondi, August. Collection. Kansas State Historical Society, Topeka.

Boone, Daniel. Papers. Missouri Historical Society, St. Louis.

Breckinridge, William C. Papers. Western Historical Manuscript Collection, Columbia, Mo.

Breckinridge, William Clark. Papers. Missouri Historical Society, St. Louis.

Breese, Sidney. Papers. Illinois State Historical Library, Springfield.

Brickey, John S. Papers. Missouri Historical Society, St. Louis.

Bridgman, Edward. Papers. State Historical Society of Wisconsin, Madison.

Broadsides 1856. Missouri Historical Society, St. Louis.

Brown, George W. Papers. SC 187. Illinois State Historical Library, Springfield.

Brown, John. Letters. SC 188. Illinois State Historical Library, Springfield.

———. Memorandum Books, 1839–1845, 1857–1859. Kansas State Historical Society, Topeka.

———. Papers. Library of Congress, Washington, D.C.

———. Papers. VFM 1393. Ohio Historical Society, Columbus.

———. Papers. Boyd B. Stutler Collection. Ohio Historical Society, Columbus.

Brown, John, Jr. Collection. Rutherford B. Hayes Presidential Center, Fremont, Ohio.

———. Papers. Ohio Historical Society, Columbus.

Brown, Oliver. Papers. VFM 1435. Ohio Historical Society, Columbus.

Brown, William. "Quantrill Raid Account," 1909. Western Historical Manuscript Collection, Columbia, Mo.

Browning, Orville H. Papers. Illinois State Historical Library, Springfield.

Buchanan, James. Papers. Historical Society of Pennsylvania, Philadelphia.

———. Papers. Library of Congress, Washington, D.C.

Bulkley Family. Papers. Missouri Historical Society, St. Louis.

Burrows, Jerome B. Papers. Western Reserve Historical Society, Cleveland.

Caine, William W. Miscellaneous Collections. Kansas State Historical Society, Topeka.

Cameron, Simon. Papers. Library of Congress, Washington, D.C.

Camp Jackson. Papers. John Knapp Collection. Missouri Historical Society, St. Louis.

Campbell, Hugh. Journal. Missouri Historical Society, St. Louis.

Campbell, James Lyle. Papers. Duke University Special Collections Library, Durham, N.C.

Carr, Benjamin and Harriett. Papers. Colorado Historical Society, Denver, Col.

Case Family. Papers. Missouri Historical Society, St. Louis.

Chapman, John A. J. Day Books. Western Historical Manuscript Collection, Columbia, Mo.

Chase, Salmon P. Papers. Ohio Historical Society, Columbus.

Christie, Alexander. Papers. Missouri Historical Society, St. Louis.

Christy, E. A. Letter. Western Historical Manuscript Collection, Columbia, Mo.

Civil War Collection. Missouri Historical Society, St. Louis.

Clarke, Sylvester H. "Recollections of Territorial Kansas" [1882]. Kansas State Historical Society, Topeka.

Connelley, William Elsey. Collection. Western History Collections. University of Oklahoma Libraries, Norman.

Crawford, George A. Papers. Wichita State University Special Collections, Wichita, Kans.

Crosby, William Chase. Collection. University of Maine Library, Orono.

Croy, Homer. Papers. Western Historical Manuscript Collection, Columbia, Mo.

Davis, Albert G. Papers. Western Historical Manuscript Collection, Columbia, Mo.

Davis, David. Family Papers. Illinois State Historical Library, Springfield.

Davis, Jefferson. Papers. Library of Congress, Washington, D.C.

Davis-Hughes. Correspondence. Western Historical Manuscript Collection, Columbia, Mo.

Denver, James. Collection. Kansas State Historical Society, Topeka.

Denver, James W. Papers. Colorado Historical Society, Denver.

Denver, James William. Collection. Kansas State Historical Society, Topeka.

Dougherty, John. Papers. Missouri Historical Society, St. Louis.

Douglas, Stephen Arnold. Papers. Library of Congress, Washington, D.C.

Duke, John P. Statement. "How the Red Legs Got Their Name." William Elsey Connelley Collection. Western History Collections, University of Oklahoma Libraries, Norman.

Early Kansas Historical Sketches: Turnbo's Regiment. S. C. Turnbo Collection. Western History Collections, University of Oklahoma Libraries, Norman.

Ewing, Philemon B. Papers. University of Notre Dame Archives, South Bend, Ind.

Ewing, Thomas, Family. Papers. Library of Congress, Washington, D.C.

Farley, Alan W. Collection. Western History Collections. University of Oklahoma Libraries, Norman.

Faxon, Frank A. Collection. Kansas State Historical Society, Topeka.

Fort Leavenworth, Kansas, Post Letters, 1861–1863. Western Historical Manuscript Collection, Columbia, Mo.

Foster, Charles A. Collection. Kansas State Historical Society, Topeka.

Gamble, Hamilton B. Papers. Missouri Historical Society, St. Louis.

Ganoe, Lloyd B. Papers. West Virginia and Regional History Collection. West Virginia University, Morgantown.

Geary, John W. Collection. Kansas State Historical Society, Topeka.

———. Letters and Executive Minutes. Kansas State Historical Society, Topeka.

Geary, John White. Papers. Yale University Library, New Haven, Conn.

George, B. James. Collection. Western Historical Manuscript Collection, Columbia, Mo.

———. Papers. Western Historical Manuscript Collection, Columbia, Mo.

Goodnow, Isaac Tichenor. Collection. Kansas State Historical Society, Topeka.

Governor's Office Files. Administration of Charles A. Robinson. Kansas State Historical Society, Topeka.

Greeley, Horace. Miscellaneous Papers. New-York Historical Society, New York.

Gregg, William H., "A Little Dab of History without Embellishment." Western Historical Manuscript Collection, Columbia, Mo.

Griswold, Whiting. Papers. Library of Congress, Washington, D.C.

Guitar, Sarah. Papers. Western Historical Manuscript Collection, Columbia, Mo.

Halderman, John Adams. Collection. Kansas State Historical Society, Topeka.

Hall Family. Papers. Michigan State University Archives, East Lansing.

Hall, Willard P. Papers. Missouri Historical Society, St. Louis.

Hansford, Felix G. Papers. West Virginia and Regional History Collection. West Virginia University, Morgantown.

Harrington, S. C. Papers. Duke University Special Collections Library, Durham, N.C.

Harvey, James M. Collection. Kansas State Historical Society, Topeka.

Hindman, James. "Kansas Travels" [1857]. Kansas State Historical Society, Topeka.

Hinton, Richard. Papers. Kansas State Historical Society, Topeka.
Hist. Constitutions. Kansas State Historical Society, Topeka.
History Cannon. Kansas State Historical Society, Topeka.
Hoffman, Henry C. Collection. Western Historical Manuscript Collection, Columbia, Mo.
Howard, Mark. Papers. Connecticut Historical Society, Hartford.
Howe, Hiram P. Papers. Library of Congress, Washington, D.C.
Hoyt, David S. Statement. New England Emigrant Aid Company Records. Boston University Special Collections, Boston.
Hunter, R. M. T. Papers. University of Virginia, Charlottesville.
Hutchinson, William. Papers. Kansas State Historical Society, Topeka.
Isely Family. Letters, Papers, and Diaries. Wichita State University Special Collections, Wichita, Kans.
Jefferson Barracks. Papers. Missouri Historical Society, St. Louis.
Kansas Civil War Collection. Kansas State Historical Society, Topeka.
Kennerly Family. Papers. Missouri Historical Society, St. Louis.
Kennett Family. Papers. Missouri Historical Society, St. Louis.
Kensinger Family. Papers. Correspondence. Western Historical Manuscript Collection, Columbia, Mo.
Lane, James Henry. Papers. Kansas State Historical Society, Topeka.
———. Papers. University of Kansas Library, Lawrence.
Lawrence, Amos A., Miscellaneous Collections. Kansas State Historical Society, Topeka.
Lecompte, Samuel D. Collection. Kansas State Historical Society, Topeka.
Letters from Mound City, 1859. Wichita State University Library Special Collections, Wichita, Kans.
Long, William C. Papers. Western Historical Manuscript Collection, Columbia, Mo.
Loomis, Daniel H. Letters. Western Historical Manuscript Collection, Columbia, Mo.
Love, James E. Papers. Missouri Historical Society, St. Louis.
Lyman, William A. Diary, 1864–1865. Reminiscence, 1931. Western Historical Manuscript Collection, Columbia, Mo.
Mantor, Rowland S. Letters. Western Historical Manuscript Collection, Columbia, Mo.
Matteson, Orsamus Benajah. Miscellaneous Papers. New-York Historical Society, New York.
McClernand, John A. Papers. Illinois State Historical Library, Springfield.
McMahan, Robert T. Diary. Western Historical Manuscript Collection, Columbia, Mo.
Medary, Samuel. Collection. Ohio Historical Society, Columbus.
Miller, L. C. "Memoirs of the Life of Lee Caruth Miller, M.D.," 1903. Western Historical Manuscript Collection, Columbia, Mo.
Miscellaneous Manuscripts. New-York Historical Society, New York.
Missouri History Collection. Missouri Historical Society, St. Louis.

Missouri Militia. Papers. Missouri Historical Society, St. Louis.

Missouri Volunteer Militia. Papers. Duke University Special Collections Library, Durham, N.C.

Montgomery, James. Collection. Kansas State Historical Society, Topeka.

Moore, Henry Miles. Journals. Yale University Library, New Haven, Conn.

Moore, Thomas Anderson. Collection. Missouri Historical Society, St. Louis.

Morse, Theodore W. "The 'Underground Railroad' in Kansas." Kansas State Historical Society, Topeka.

Napton, William B. Diary. Missouri Historical Society, St. Louis.

Palmer, John M. Papers II. Illinois State Historical Library, Springfield.

Park Brothers. Collection. Wichita State University Special Collections, Wichita, Kans.

Parker-Russell. Papers. Missouri Historical Society, St. Louis.

Paxton, William M. Papers. Western Historical Manuscript Collection, Columbia, Mo.

Pierce, Edward Lillis. Collection. Kansas State Historical Society, Topeka.

Pierce, Franklin. Papers. Library of Congress, Washington, D.C.

Pike, J. A. "Statement Concerning the Quantrill Raid," 1917. Western Historical Manuscript Collection, Columbia, Mo.

Pomeroy, Samuel Clarke. Collection. Kansas State Historical Society, Topeka.

Quantrill, William Clarke. Papers. University of Kansas Library, Lawrence.

Ransom, Epaphroditus. Collection. Kansas State Historical Society, Topeka.

Reader, Samuel James. Papers. Kansas State Historical Society, Topeka.

Reese, A. W. "Recollections of the Civil War," 1870. Western Historical Manuscript Collection, Columbia, Mo.

Reynolds, Thomas C. Papers. Missouri Historical Society, St. Louis.

Richmond, Rollin M. Collection. Kansas State Historical Society, Topeka.

Ricks, Jesse Jay. Collection. Illinois State Historical Library, Springfield.

Robinson, Charles. Papers. University of Kansas Library, Lawrence.

Robinson, Charles and Sara T. D. Papers. Kansas State Historical Society, Topeka.

Rollins, James S. Papers. Western Historical Manuscript Collection, Columbia, Mo.

Rutgers College. Collection. Missouri Historical Society, St. Louis.

Schofield, John McAllister. Papers. Library of Congress, Washington, D.C.

Schrader, William Henry. Reminiscences. Western Historical Manuscript Collection, Columbia, Mo.

Seig, Samuel S. Papers. Duke University Special Collections Library, Durham, N.C.

Seward, William H. Papers. Western Historical Manuscript Collection, Columbia, Mo.

Sherman, John. Papers. Library of Congress, Washington, D.C.

Sherman, William T. Papers. University of Notre Dame Archives, South Bend, Ind.

Shumley, James. Letter. Western Historical Manuscript Collection, Columbia, Mo.

Smith, General George R. Collection. Missouri Historical Society, St. Louis.

Snyder, Dr. John F. Collection. Missouri Historical Society, St. Louis.

Spivey, George W. Letter. Western Historical Manuscript Collection, Columbia, Mo.

Starr, Frederick, Jr. Papers. Western Historical Manuscript Collection, Columbia, Mo.

Stephens, Alexander H. Papers. Library of Congress, Washington, D.C.

Stewart, Robert M. Papers. Western Historical Manuscript Collection, Columbia, Mo.

Stimson, Henry A. Papers. New-York Historical Society, New York.

Stone, Abner. Papers. Missouri Historical Society, St. Louis.

Sweringen, James T. Papers. Missouri Historical Society, St. Louis.

Territory of Kansas Census of 1855. Kansas State Historical Society, Topeka.

Thayer, Eli. Papers. Duke University Special Collections Library, Durham, N.C.

Toucey, Isaac. Manuscript. Connecticut Historical Society, Hartford.

Treat, Samuel. Papers. Missouri Historical Society, St. Louis.

Tredway, David. Papers. Missouri Historical Society, St. Louis.

Trumbull, Lyman, Family. Papers. Illinois State Historical Library, Springfield.

Union League of America. Collection. Kansas State Historical Society, Topeka.

Walker, Frank. Collection. Kansas State Historical Society, Topeka.

Walker, Robert J. Collection. Library of Congress, Washington, D.C.

———. Papers. Mississippi Department of Archives and History, Jackson.

———. Papers. New-York Historical Society, New York.

Washburn, Israel. Papers. Library of Congress, Washington, D.C.

Washburne, Elihu B. Papers. Library of Congress, Washington, D.C.

Watt, D. G. "Reminiscences of Pottawatomie Creek and Vicinity, 1856." Kansas State Historical Society, Topeka.

Webb, James Josiah. Collection. Missouri Historical Society, St. Louis.

Weston Family. Papers. Mississippi Department of Archives and History, Jackson.

Whedon. Miscellaneous Collections. Kansas State Historical Society, Topeka.

Willey, J. W. Recollections. "Capture of Scaggs." Kansas State Historical Society, Topeka.

Williams Family. Papers. Albany Institute of History and Art, Albany, N.Y.

Wilson, Henry. Papers. Library of Congress, Washington, D.C.

Wise, Henry Alexander. Papers. Duke University Special Collections Library, Durham, N.C.

Wise, Henry Alexander, and Family. Collection. Library of Congress, Washington, D.C.

Woodson, Daniel. Papers. Kansas State Historical Society, Topeka.

Woodward, Brinton Webb. Collection. Kansas State Historical Society, Topeka.

Yates, Richard. Papers. Illinois State Historical Library, Springfield.

Young, John F. Civil War Correspondence. Missouri Historical Society, St. Louis.

NEWSPAPERS
(Atchison, Kans.) Squatter Sovereign
Boston Daily Advertiser
Charleston Mercury
Kansas City (Mo.) Enterprise
(Kansas City, Mo.) Western Journal of Commerce
(Lawrence, Kans.) Herald of Freedom
(Leavenworth, Kans.) Daily Times
(Lecompton) Kansas National Democrat
Lecompton (Kans.) Union
(St. Louis) Missouri Democrat
(St. Louis) Missouri Republican
New York Times
New York Tribune
Richmond Enquirer

PUBLISHED PRIMARY SOURCES
Abbott, James B. "The Rescue of Dr. John W. Doy." Vol. 4, *Transactions of the Kansas State Historical Society*. Topeka: 1890, 312–23.
"Administration of Governor Shannon." Vol. 5, *Transactions of the Kansas State Historical Society*. Topeka: 1896, 234–64.
Ambler, Charles Henry. *Correspondence of Robert M. T. Hunter, 1826–1876*. New York: 1971.
Andrews, William L., ed. *Frederick Douglass Reader*. New York: 1996.
"Appeal of the Independent Democrats in Congress to the People of the United States." *Congressional Globe*. 33d Cong., 1st sess. Washington, D.C., 1854.
Bailey, Judge L. D. *Border Ruffian Troubles in Kansas*. Lyndon, Kans.: 1899.
Barber, John W., and Henry Howe. *The Loyal West in the Times of the Rebellion*. Cincinnati: 1865.
Barnes, Lela. "An Editor Looks at Early-Day Kansas: The Letters of Charles Monroe Chase." *Kansas Historical Quarterly* 26 (summer 1960): 113–51.
———, ed. "Letters of Cyrus Kurtz Holliday, 1854–1859." *Kansas Historical Quarterly* 6 (Aug. 1937): 241–94.
Basler, Roy P., ed. *The Collected Works of Abraham Lincoln*. 8 vols. New Brunswick, N.J.: 1953.
Bayard, Samuel J. *Life of George Dashiell Bayard*. New York: 1874.
Benét, Stephen Vincent. *John Brown's Body*. 1927. Reprint, New York: 1954.
Berlin, Ira, et al., eds. *The Destruction of Slavery. Freedom: A Documentary History of Emancipation, 1861–1867*. 1st ser., vol. 1. Cambridge, Eng.: 1985.
———, Joseph P. Reidy, and Leslie S. Rowland, eds. *The Black Military Experience. Freedom: A Documentary History of Emancipation, 1861–1867*. 2d ser. Cambridge, Eng.: 1982.
The Border Ruffian Code in Kansas [1856].
[Brackett, George C.] "Statement of Hon. George C. Brackett." Vol. 3, *Transactions of the Kansas State Historical Society*. Topeka: 1886, 223–25.

Brewerton, G. Douglas. *The War in Kansas: A Rough Trip to the Border.* New York: 1856.

——. *Wars of the Western Border.* New York: 1859.

Bridgman, Edward Payson, and Luke Fisher Parsons. *With John Brown in Kansas: The Battle of Osawatomie.* Madison, Wisc.: 1915.

Brown, Geo. W. *Reminiscences of Gov. R. J. Walker; With the True Story of the Rescue of Kansas from Slavery.* 1881. Reprint, Rockford, Ill.: 1902.

Bruce, H. C. *The New Man: Twenty-Nine Years a Slave, Twenty-Nine Years a Free Man.* 1895. Reprint, New York: 1969.

Child, L. Maria. "The Kansas Emigrants." *New York Tribune,* Oct. 23–25, 28; Nov. 4, 1856.

——. *Letters of Lydia Maria Child.* 1883. Reprint, New York: 1969.

Cobb, David Glenn, ed. "Letters of David R. Cobb, 1858–1864." *Kansas Historical Quarterly* 11 (Feb. 1942): 65–71.

Colt, Miriam Davis. *Went to Kansas; Being a Thrilling Account of an Ill-Fated Expedition to That Fairy Land, and Its Sad Results.* Watertown, N.Y.: 1862.

Congressional Globe. 35th Cong., 1st sess. Washington, D.C., 1858.

Congressional Globe Appendix. 34th Cong., 1st sess. Washington, D.C., 1856.

Congressional Globe Appendix. 35th Cong., 1st sess. Washington, D.C., 1858.

Cordley, Richard. *A History of Lawrence, Kansas from the First Settlement to the Close of the Rebellion.* Lawrence, Kans.: 1895.

——. *Pioneer Days in Kansas.* Boston: 1903.

Crawford, Samuel J. *Kansas in the Sixties.* 1911. Reprint, Ottawa, Kans.: 1994.

Denver, James W. "Address." Vol. 3, *Transactions of the Kansas State Historical Society.* Topeka: 1886, 359–66.

Dickson, C. H. "The 'Boy's' Story: Reminiscences of 1855." Vol. 5, *Transactions of the Kansas State Historical Society.* Topeka: 1896, 76–87.

Dobak, William A., ed. "Civil War on the Kansas-Missouri Border: The Narrative of Former Slave Andrew Williams." *Kansas History* 6 (autumn 1983): 237–42.

Dodd, Donald B., comp. *Historical Statistics of the States of the United States: Two Centuries of the Census, 1790–1900.* Westport, Conn.: 1993.

Douglas, Stephen A. "The Dividing Line between Federal and Local Authority: Popular Sovereignty in the Territories." *Harper's Magazine* 19 (Sept. 1859): 519–37.

Eighth Census of the United States. Washington, D.C.: 1860.

Emerson, Ralph Waldo. "Courage." In *Society and Solitude,* 251–80. Vol. 7, *Complete Works of Ralph Waldo Emerson.* New York: 1968.

Emery, Agnes. *Reminiscences of Early Lawrence.* Lawrence, Kans.: 1955.

Emory, Lt. Col. W. H. *Notes of a Military Reconnoissance, from Fort Leavenworth, in Missouri, to San Diego, in California.* Washington, D.C.: 1848.

"Executive Minutes." Vol. 3, *Transactions of the Kansas State Historical Society.* Topeka: 1886, 226–78, 283–337.

Gambone, Joseph G. "The Forgotten Feminist of Kansas: The Papers of Clarina I. H. Nichols, 1854–1885." *Kansas Historical Quarterly* 39 (spring 1973): 12–57.

Gihon, John H. *Geary and Kansas: Governor Geary's Administration in Kansas: With a Complete History of the Territory until July 1857.* Philadelphia: 1857.

Gladstone, Thomas H. *The Englishman in Kansas or Squatter Life and Border Warfare.* 1857. Lincoln, Nebr.: 1971.

———. *Kansas; or, Squatter Life and Border Warfare in the Far West.* London: 1858.

Gleed, Charles S., ed. *The Kansas Memorial, A Report of the Old Settlers' Meeting Held at Bismarck Grove, Kansas, September 15th and 16th, 1879.* Kansas City, Mo.: 1880.

Goodnow, Isaac T. "Personal Reminiscences and Kansas Emigration, 1855." Vol. 4, *Transactions of the Kansas State Historical Society.* Topeka: 1890, 244–53.

"Governor Denver's Administration." Vol. 5, *Transactions of the Kansas State Historical Society.* Topeka: 1896, 464–561.

"Governor Geary's Administration." Vol. 5, *Transactions of the Kansas State Historical Society.* Topeka: 1896, 264–89.

"Governor Medary's Administration." Vol. 5, *Transactions of the Kansas State Historical Society.* Topeka: 1896, 561–633.

"Governor Reeder's Administration." Vol. 5, *Transactions of the Kansas State Historical Society.* Topeka: 1896, 163–234.

"Governor Walker's Administration." Vol. 5, *Transactions of the Kansas State Historical Society.* Topeka: 1896, 290–464.

Green, C. R. *Early Days in Kansas.* Olathe, Kans.: 1913.

Greene, Albert R. "On the Battle of Wilson Creek." Vol. 5, *Transactions of the Kansas State Historical Society.* Topeka: 1896, 116–27.

Hale, Edward E. *Kanzas and Nebraska: The History, Geographical and Physical Characteristics, and Political Position of Those Territories; An Account of the Emigrant Aid Companies, and Directions to Emigrants.* Boston: 1854.

Hoole, William Stanley. "A Southerner's Viewpoint of the Kansas Situation, 1856–1857: The Letters of Lieut. Col. A. J. Hoole, C.S.A." *Kansas Historical Quarterly* 3 (Feb. 1934): 43–68; 3 (May 1934): 145–71.

Johannsen, Robert W., ed. *The Letters of Stephen A. Douglas.* Urbana, Ill.: 1961.

———, ed. *The Lincoln-Douglas Debates of 1858.* New York: 1965.

"Kansas Quarter-Centennial, 1861–1886." Vol. 3, *Transactions of the Kansas State Historical Society.* Topeka: 1886, 367–469.

Langsdorf, Edgar, ed. "The Letters of Joseph H. Trego, 1857–1864, Linn County Pioneer." *Kansas Historical Quarterly* 19 (May 1951): 113–32; 19 (Aug. 1951): 287–309; 19 (Nov. 1951): 381–400.

———, and R. W. Richmond, eds. "Letters of Daniel R. Anthony, 1857–1862: Part One, 1857." *Kansas Historical Quarterly* 24 (spring 1958): 6–30.

——, eds. "Letters of Daniel R. Anthony, 1857–1862—Continued: Part Two, 1858–1861." *Kansas Historical Quarterly* 24 (summer 1958): 198–226.

——, eds. "Letters of Daniel R. Anthony, 1857–1862—Continued: Part Three, October 1, 1861–June 7, 1862." *Kansas Historical Quarterly* 24 (autumn 1958): 351–70.

——, eds. "Letters of Daniel R. Anthony, 1857–1862—Concluded: Part Four, June 20–September 14, 1862." *Kansas Historical Quarterly* 24 (winter 1958): 458–75.

Leftwich, W. M. *Martyrdom in Missouri*. St. Louis: 1870.

"Letters of John and Sarah Everett, 1854–1864." *Kansas Historical Quarterly* 8 (Feb. 1939): 3–34; 8 (May 1939): 143–74; 8 (Aug. 1939): 279–310; 8 (Nov. 1939): 350–83.

"Letters of Julia Louisa Lovejoy, 1856–1864." *Kansas Historical Quarterly* 15 (May 1947): 127–42; 15 (Aug. 1947): 277–319; 15 (Nov. 1947): 368–403; 16 (Feb. 1948): 40–75; 16 (May 1948): 175–211.

"The Letters of Samuel James Reeder, 1861–1863." *Kansas Historical Quarterly* 9 (Feb. 1940): 26–57; (May 1940): 141–74.

Lovejoy, Julia Louisa. "Letters from Kansas." *Kansas Historical Quarterly* 11 (Feb. 1942): 29–44.

Majors, Alexander. *Seventy Years on the Frontier*. Minneapolis: 1965.

McClure, James R. "Taking the Census and Other Incidents in 1855." Vol. 8, *Transactions of the Kansas State Historical Society*. Topeka: 1903–1904, 227–50.

[McNamara, John]. *Three Years on the Kansas Border by a Clergyman of the Episcopal Church*. New York: 1856.

Meltzer, Milton, and Patricia G. Holland, eds. *Lydia Maria Child: Selected Letters, 1817–1880*. Amherst, Mass.: 1982.

Merrill, O. N. *A True History of the Kansas Wars, and Their Origin, Progress and Incidents*. 1856. Reprint, Tarrytown, N.J.: 1932.

Moffatt, Isaac. "The Kansas Prairie, or, Eight Days on the Plains." *Kansas Historical Quarterly* 6 (May 1937): 147–74.

"Notes on the Proslavery March against Lawrence." *Kansas Historical Quarterly* 11 (Feb. 1942): 45–64.

Oliphant, J. Orin, ed. "The Report of the Wyandot Exploring Delegation, 1831." *Kansas Historical Quarterly* 15 (Aug. 1947): 248–62.

Organization of the Free State Government in Kansas, with the Inaugural Speech and Message of Governor Robinson. Washington, D.C.: 1856.

Peterson, John M., ed. "Letters of Edward and Sarah Fitch, Lawrence, Kansas, 1855–1863." *Kansas History* 12 (spring 1989): 48–70; 12 (summer 1989): 78–100.

Phillips, W. A. "Kansas History." Vol. 4, *Transactions of the Kansas State Historical Society*. Topeka: 1890, 351–59.

Phillips, William. *The Conquest of Kansas by Missouri and Her Allies*. Boston: 1856.

Phillips, Ulrich Bonnell, ed. *The Correspondence of Robert Toombs, Alexander H. Stephens, and Howell Cobb*. New York: 1970.

Redpath, James. *The Public Life of Capt. John Brown*. Boston: 1860.

[Reeder, Andrew H.] "Governor Reeder's Escape from Kansas." Vol. 3, *Transactions of the Kansas State Historical Society*. Topeka: 1886, 205–23.

Richardson, Albert D. *Beyond the Mississippi: From the Great River to the Great Ocean: Life and Adventure on the Prairies, Mountains, and Pacific Coast, 1857–1867*. Hartford, Conn.: 1867.

Richardson, James D. *A Compilation of the Messages and Papers of the Presidents, 1789–1908*. Vol. 5. Washington, D.C.: 1908.

Richmond, Robert W. "A Free-Stater's 'Letters to the Editor': Samuel N. Wood's Letters to Eastern Newspapers, 1854." *Kansas Historical Quarterly* 23 (summer 1957): 181–90.

Robinson, Charles. *The Kansas Conflict*. Lawrence, Kans.: 1898.

Robinson, Sara T. L. *Kansas; Its Interior and Exterior Life*. 7th ed. Boston: 1857.

Root, George A., ed. "The First Day's Battle at Hickory Point." *Kansas Historical Quarterly* 1 (Nov. 1931): 28–49.

[Ropes, Hannah Anderson]. *Six Months in Kansas*. Boston: 1856.

Ross, Edmund G. *The Pilgrim and the Cavalier in Kansas*. N.p.: [1895].

Ruchames, Louis, ed. *John Brown: The Making of a Revolutionary*. New York: 1969.

Schofield, John M. *Forty-Six Years in the Army*. Norman, Okla.: 1998.

[Schurz, Carl]. *The Reminiscences of Carl Schurz*. Vol. 2. New York: 1907.

Shaw, Rev. James. *Early Reminiscences of Pioneer Life in Kansas*. N.p.: 1886.

Shea, John C., ed. *Reminiscences of Quantrell's Raid upon the City of Lawrence, Kas*. Kansas City, Mo.: 1879.

Sherman, John. *Recollections of Forty Years in the House, Senate and Cabinet*. Chicago: 1896.

Speer, John. "Incidents of the Pioneer Days." Vol. 5, *Transactions of the Kansas State Historical Society*. Topeka: 1896, 131–41.

Stanton, Frederick P. "Address." Vol. 3, *Transactions of the Kansas State Historical Society*. Topeka: 1886, 338–58.

Suderow, Bryce A. "McLain's Battery and Price's 1864 Invasion: A Letter from Lt. Caleb S. Burdsal, Jr." *Kansas History* 6 (spring 1983): 29–45.

Thayer, Eli. *The New England Emigrant Aid Company: And Its Influence, through the Kansas Contest, upon National History*. Worcester, Mass.: 1887.

———. *A History of the Kansas Crusade, Its Friends and Its Foes*. New York: 1889.

Thoreau, Henry David. "A Plea for Captain John Brown." In *Anti-Slavery and Reform Papers*. Montreal: 1963, 42–65.

Tomlinson, William P. *Kansas in Eighteen Fifty-Eight*. New York: 1859.

U.S. House. Executive Documents. 34th Cong., 3d sess., 1856. Serial 893, no. 1.

———. 34th Cong., 3d sess., 1856. Serial 894, no. 1.

———. *Howard Report*. 34th Cong., 1st sess., 1856. Rept. 200. Serial 869.

———. *Covode Report*. 36th Cong., 1st sess., 1860. Rept. 648. Serial 1071.

U.S. Senate. Executive Documents. 35th Cong., 1st sess., 1858. Serial 923, no. 17.

——. Miscellaneous Documents. 36th cong., 1st sess., 1860. Serial 1038, no. 23.

——. 34th Cong., 1st sess., 1856. Rept. 34. Serial 836.

——. *Mason Report.* 36th Cong., 1st sess., 1860.

U. S. War Department. *The War of the Rebellion: Official Records of the Union and Confederate Armies.* Washington, D.C.: 1880–1901.

United Daughters of the Confederacy. Missouri Division. *Reminiscences of the Women of Missouri during the Sixties.* Jefferson City, Mo.: n.d.

Unrau, William E., ed. "In Pursuit of Quantrill: An Enlisted Man's Response." *Kansas Historical Quarterly* 39 (autumn 1973): 379–91.

Walker, Lois H. [formerly Mrs. Geo. W. Brown]. "Reminiscences of Early Times in Kansas." Vol. 5, *Transactions of the Kansas State Historical Society.* Topeka: 1896, 74–76.

Walker, William. *The War in Nicaragua.* 1860. Reprint, Tucson: 1985.

Webb, Thomas H. *Information for Kanzas Immigrants.* Boston: 1855.

Wiggins, Eliza Johnston. *Impressions of Early Kansas.* Wichita: 1915.

Wilder, Daniel W. *The Annals of Kansas.* Topeka: 1875.

FICTION AND LITERATURE

Anonymous. *Western Border Life; or, What Fanny Hunter Saw and Heard in Kanzas and Missouri.* New York: 1856.

Peacock, Thomas Brower. "The Rhyme of the Border War." In *Poems of the Plains and Songs of the Solitudes,* 207–305. New York: 1889.

Stanley, Caroline Abbot. *Order No. 11: A Tale of the Border.* New York: 1904.

Swayze, Mrs. J. C. "Ossawatomie Brown; or, a Drama in Three Acts [1859]." *Kansas Historical Quarterly* 6 (Feb. 1937): 37–59.

Whittier, John Greenleaf. *The Complete Poetical Works of John Greenleaf Whittier.* Boston: 1894.

SECONDARY SOURCES

Abbott, Richard H. *Cotton and Capital: Boston Businessmen and Antislavery Reform, 1854–1868.* Amherst, Mass.: 1991.

Abels, Jules. *Man on Fire: John Brown and the Cause of Liberty.* New York: 1971.

Anbinder, Tyler. *Nativism and Slavery: The Northern Know Nothings and the Politics of the 1850s.* New York: 1992.

Anderson, Benedict. *Imagined Communities: Reflections on the Origin and Spread of Nationalism.* London: 1991.

[Andreas, A. T.] *History of the State of Kansas.* Chicago: 1883.

Appleby, Joyce. *Liberalism and Republicanism in the Historical Imagination.* Cambridge, Mass.: 1992.

Ashworth, John. *"Agrarians" and "Aristocrats": Party Political Ideology in the United States, 1837–1846.* London: 1987.

Athearn, Robert G. *In Search of Canaan: Black Migration to Kansas, 1879–1880*. Lawrence, Kans.: 1978.

Bailyn, Bernard. *The Ideological Origins of the American Revolution*. Cambridge, Mass.: 1967.

Baker, Jean H. *Affairs of Party: The Political Culture of Northern Democrats in the Mid-Nineteenth Century*. Ithaca, N.Y.: 1988.

Barry, Louise. "The New England Emigrant Aid Company Parties of 1854." *Kansas Historical Quarterly* 12 (May 1943): 115–55.

———. "The New England Emigrant Aid Company Parties of 1855." *Kansas Historical Quarterly* 12 (Aug. 1943): 227–68.

Belknap, Michal R. "Introduction: Political Trials in the American Past." In *American Political Trials,* edited by Michal R. Belknap, xiii–xxviii. Westport, Conn.: 1994.

Berwanger, Eugene H. *The Frontier against Slavery: Western Anti-Negro Prejudice and the Slavery Extension Controversy*. Urbana, Ill.: 1967.

Blackmar, Frank W. *The Life of Charles Robinson, The First State Governor of Kansas*. Topeka: 1902.

Blight, David W. *Frederick Douglass' Civil War: Keeping Faith in Jubilee*. Baton Rouge: 1989.

———. *Race and Reunion: The Civil War in American Memory*. Cambridge, Mass.: 2001.

Blue, Frederick J. *Salmon P. Chase: A Life in Politics*. Kent, Ohio: 1987.

Boorstin, Daniel J. *The Americans: The National Experience*. New York: 1965.

Breihan, Carl W. *Quantrill and His Civil War Guerrillas*. Denver: 1959.

Brownlee, Richard S. "The Battle of Pilot Knob, Iron County, Missouri, September 27, 1864." *Missouri Historical Review* 59 (Oct. 1964): 1–30.

———. *Gray Ghosts of the Confederacy: Guerrilla Warfare in the West, 1861–1865*. Baton Rouge: 1958.

Cashin, Joan E. *A Family Venture: Men and Women on the Southern Frontier*. New York: 1991.

Caskie, George E. "The Trial of John Brown." *American Law Review* 44 (1910): 405–25.

Castel, Albert. "War and Politics: The Price Raid of 1864." *Kansas Historical Quarterly* 24 (summer 1958): 129–43.

———. "Kansas Jayhawking Raids into Western Missouri in 1861." *Missouri Historical Review* 54 (Oct. 1959): 1–11.

———. *A Frontier State at War: Kansas, 1861–1865*. Ithaca, N.Y.: 1958.

———. *William Clarke Quantrill: His Life and Times*. New York: 1962.

———. *General Sterling Price and the Civil War in the West*. Baton Rouge: 1968.

Chapin, Bradley. *The American Law of Treason: Revolutionary and Early National Origins*. Seattle: 1964.

Cheathem, Gary L. "'Slavery All the Time, or Not At All': The Wyandotte Constitution Debate, 1859–1861." *Kansas History* 21 (autumn 1998): 168–87.

Connelley, William Elsey. *James Henry Lane: The 'Grim Chieftain' of Kansas.* Topeka: 1899.

———. *John Brown.* Topeka: 1900.

———. *Kansas Territorial Governors.* Topeka: 1900.

———. *Quantrill and the Border Wars.* New York: 1956.

Cooper, William J., Jr. *The South and the Politics of Slavery, 1828–1856.* Baton Rouge: 1978.

———. *Liberty and Slavery: Southern Politics to 1860.* New York: 1983.

Cornish, Dudley Taylor. "Kansas Negro Regiments in the Civil War." *Kansas Historical Quarterly* 20 (May 1953): 417–49.

———. *The Sable Arm: Negro Troops in the Union Army, 1861–1865.* New York: 1966.

Craik, Elmer Leroy. "Southern Interest in Territorial Kansas, 1854–1858." Vol. 15, *Transactions of the Kansas State Historical Society.* Topeka: 1919, 334–450.

Davis, David Brion. *The Slave Power Conspiracy and the Paranoid Style.* Baton Rouge: 1969.

Diggins, John Patrick. *The Lost Soul of American Politics: Virtue, Self-Interest, and the Foundations of Liberalism.* New York: 1984.

Donald, David Herbert. *Lincoln.* New York: 1995.

DuBois, Ellen. *Feminism and Suffrage: The Emergence of an Independent Women's Movement in America, 1848–1869.* Ithaca, N.Y.: 1978.

Dumond, Dwight Lowell. *Antislavery: The Crusade for Freedom in America.* Ann Arbor: 1961.

Eaton, Clement. *Freedom of Thought in the Old South.* New York: 1951.

———. *The Growth of Southern Civilization, 1790–1860.* New York: 1961.

Elliott, R. G. "The Big Springs Convention." Vol. 8, *Transactions of the Kansas State Historical Society* (Topeka, 1903–1904), 362–77.

Ericson, David F. *The Debate over Slavery: Antislavery and Proslavery Liberalism in Antebellum America.* New York: 2000.

Etcheson, Nicole. *The Emerging Midwest: Upland Southerners and the Political Culture of the Old Northwest.* Bloomington, Ind.: 1996.

Eyal, Yonatan. "With His Eyes Open: Stephen A. Douglas and the Kansas-Nebraska Disaster of 1854." *Journal of the Illinois State Historical Society* 91 (winter 1998): 175–217.

Faust, Drew Gilpin. *The Creation of Confederate Nationalism: Ideology and Identity in the Civil War South.* Baton Rouge: 1988.

Fehrenbacher, Don E. *Prelude to Greatness: Lincoln in the 1850s.* Stanford, Calif.: 1962.

———. *The Dred Scott Case: Its Significance in American Law and Politics.* New York: 1978.

———. *The South and Three Sectional Crises.* Baton Rouge: 1980.

Fellman, Michael. *Inside War: The Guerrilla Conflict in Missouri during the American Civil War.* New York: 1989.

Filler, Louis. *The Crusade against Slavery, 1830–1860.* New York: 1960.

Finkelman, Paul. "The Treason Trial of Castner Hanway." In *American Political Trials,* edited by Michal R. Belknap, 77–95. Westport, Conn.: 1994.

Fleming, Walter L. "The Buford Expedition to Kansas." *American Historical Review* 6 (Oct. 1900): 38–48.

Foner, Eric. *Free Labor, Free Soil, Free Men: The Ideology of the Republican Party before the Civil War.* New York: 1970.

———. *Politics and Ideology in the Age of the Civil War.* New York: 1980.

———. *Reconstruction: America's Unfinished Revolution, 1863–1877.* New York: 1988.

———. *The Story of American Freedom.* New York: 1998.

Forgie, George B. *Patricide in the House Divided: A Psychological Interpretation of Lincoln and His Age.* New York: 1979.

Franklin, John Hope. "The North, the South, and the American Revolution." *Journal of American History* 62 (June 1975): 5–23.

Fredrickson, George M. *The Black Image in the White Mind: The Debate on Afro-American Character and Destiny, 1817–1914.* New York: 1971.

Gates, Paul Wallace. *Fifty Million Acres: Conflicts over Kansas Land Policy, 1854–1900.* Ithaca, N.Y.: 1954.

Gienapp, William E. *The Origins of the Republican Party, 1852–1856.* New York: 1987.

Glatthaar, Joseph T. *Forged in Battle: The Civil War Alliance of Black Soldiers and White Officers.* New York: 1990.

Goodrich, Thomas. *Bloody Dawn: The Story of the Lawrence Massacre.* Kent, Ohio: 1991.

Grimsted, David. *American Mobbing, 1828–1861: Toward Civil War.* New York: 1998.

Hale, Edward Everett. "New England in the Colonization of Kansas." In *The New England States,* edited by D. H. Hurd, 79–90. Boston: 1897.

Hamilton, Holman. *Prologue to Conflict: The Crisis and Compromise of 1850.* New York: 1964.

Harrold, Stanley. *American Abolitionists.* Harlow, Eng.: 2001.

Haynes, Sam W. *Soldiers of Misfortune: The Somervell and Mier Expeditions.* Austin: 1990.

Herklotz, Hildegarde Rose. "Jayhawkers in Missouri, 1858–1863." *Missouri Historical Review* 18 (Oct. 1923): 64–101.

Hess, Earl J. *Liberty, Virtue, and Progress: Northerners and Their War for the Union.* New York: 1997.

Hickman, Russell K. "The Reeder Administration Inaugurated: Part I—The Delegate Election of November, 1854." *Kansas Historical Quarterly* 36 (autumn 1970): 305–40.

———. "The Reeder Administration Inaugurated: Part II—The Census of Early 1855." *Kansas Historical Quarterly* 36 (winter 1970): 424–55.

Hinton, Richard J. *John Brown and His Men.* 1894. Reprint, New York: 1968.

Hobsbawm, E. J. *Nations and Nationalism since 1780: Programme, Myth, Reality.* 2d ed. Cambridge, Eng.: 1990.

Hodder, Frank Heywood. "Some Aspects of the English Bill for the Admission of Kansas." In *Annual Report of the American Historical Association for the Year 1906.* Vol. 1, 199–210. Washington, D.C.: 1908.

———. "The Railroad Background of the Kansas-Nebraska Act." *Mississippi Valley Historical Review* 12 (June 1925): 3–22.

Holt, Michael F. "Another Look at the Election of 1856." In *James Buchanan and the Political Crisis of the 1850s,* edited by Michael J. Birkner, 37–67. Selinsgrove, Pa.: 1996.

———. *The Political Crisis of the 1850s.* New York: 1978.

———. *The Rise and Fall of the American Whig Party: Jacksonian Politics and the Onset of the Civil War.* New York: 1999.

Hurst, James Willard. *The Law of Treason in the United States: Collected Essays.* Westport, Conn.: 1971.

Huston, James L. "Democracy by Scripture versus Democracy by Process: A Reflection on Stephen A. Douglas and Popular Sovereignty." *Civil War History* 43 (Sept. 1997): 189–200.

Ignatiev, Noel. *How the Irish Became White.* New York: 1995.

Isely, W. H. "The Sharps Rifle Episode in Kansas History." *American Historical Review* 12 (April 1907): 546–66.

Jaffa, Henry V., *Equality and Liberty: Theory and Practice in American Politics.* New York: 1965.

———. *Crisis of the House Divided: An Interpretation of the Lincoln-Douglas Debates.* Seattle: 1973.

Johannsen, Robert W. "The Kansas-Nebraska Act and Territorial Government in the United States." In *Territorial Kansas: Studies Commemorating the Centennial,* 17–32. Lawrence, Kans.: 1954.

———. "The Lecompton Constitutional Convention: An Analysis of Its Membership." *Kansas Historical Quarterly* 23 (autumn 1957): 225–43.

———. "Stephen A. Douglas, Popular Sovereignty and the Territories." *Historian* 22 (1960): 378–95.

———. *Stephen A. Douglas.* New York: 1973.

———, ed. *The Lincoln-Douglas Debates of 1858.* New York: 1965.

Johnson, Allen. "Genesis of Popular Sovereignty." *Iowa Journal of History and Politics* 3 (1905): 3–19.

Johnson, Michael P. "Out of Egypt: The Migration of Former Slaves to the Midwest during the 1860s in Comparative Perspective." In *Crossing Boundaries: Comparative History of Black People in Diaspora,* edited by Darlene Clark Hine and Jacqueline McLeod, 223–45. Bloomington, Ind.: 1999.

Johnson, Samuel A. "The Emigrant Aid Company in the Kansas Conflict." *Kansas Historical Quarterly* 6 (Feb. 1937): 21–33.

———. *The Battle Cry of Freedom: The New England Emigrant Aid Company in the Kansas Crusade.* Westport, Conn.: 1977.

Kammen, Michael. *Spheres of Liberty: Changing Perceptions of Liberty in American Culture.* Madison, Wisc.: 1986.

Keyssar, Alexander. *The Right to Vote: The Contested History of Democracy in the United States.* New York: 2000.

Klem, Mary J. "Missouri in the Kansas Struggle." *Mississippi Valley Historical Association Proceedings* 9, pt. 3. (1917–1918): 393–413.

Klunder, Willard Carl. *Lewis Cass and the Politics of Moderation.* Kent, Ohio: 1996.

Knupfer, Peter B. "A Crisis in Conservatism: Northern Unionsim and the Harpers Ferry Raid." In *His Soul Goes Marching On: Responses to John Brown and the Harpers Ferry Raid,* edited by Paul Finkelman, 119–48. Charlottesville, Va.: 1995.

———. *The Union as It Is: Constitutional Unionism and Sectional Compromise, 1787–1861.* Chapel Hill, N.C.: 1991.

Kolchin, Peter. "Whiteness Studies: The New History of Race in America." *Journal of American History* 89 (June 2002): 154–73.

Konig, David Thomas. "Introduction." In *Devising Liberty: Preserving and Creating Freedom in the New American Republic,* edited by David Thomas Konig, 1–9. Stanford, Calif.: 1995.

Kraditor, Aileen S. *Means and Ends in American Abolitionism: Garrison and His Critics on Strategy and Tactics, 1834–1850.* New York: 1969.

Langsdorf, Edgar. "Thaddeus Hyatt in Washington Jail." *Kansas Historical Quarterly* 9 (Aug. 1940): 227–39.

Lawrence, William. *Life of Amos A. Lawrence.* Boston: 1888.

Leslie, Edward E. *The Devil Knows How to Ride: The True Story of William Clarke Quantrill and His Confederate Raiders.* New York: 1996.

Levine, Bruce. *Half Slave and Half Free: The Roots of Civil War.* New York: 1992.

Lewis, Jan. "The Problem of Slavery in Southern Political Discourse." In *Devising Liberty: Preserving and Creating Freedom in the New American Republic,* edited by David Thomas Konig, 265–97. Stanford, Calif.: 1995.

Littlefield, Daniel C. "Blacks, John Brown, and a Theory of Manhood." In *His Soul Goes Marching On: Responses to John Brown and the Harpers Ferry Raid,* edited by Paul Finkelman, 67–97. Charlottesville, Va.: 1995.

Loewenberg, Bert James. *American History in American Thought: Christopher Columbus to Henry Adams.* New York: 1972.

Lowenthal, David. *The Past Is a Foreign Country.* Cambridge, Eng.: 1985.

Magdol, Edward. *The Antislavery Rank and File: A Social Profile of the Abolitionists' Constituency.* Westport, Conn.: 1986.

Malin, James C. "Judge Lecompte and the 'Sack of Lawrence,' May 21, 1856." *Kansas Historical Quarterly* 20 (Aug. and Nov.): 465–94; 20 (November): 553–97.

———. "The Proslavery Background of the Kansas Struggle." *Mississippi Valley Historical Review* 10 (Dec. 1923): 285–305.

———. "The Topeka Statehood Movement Reconsidered: Origins." In *Territorial Kansas: Studies Commemorating the Centennial,* 33–69. Lawrence, Kans.: 1954.

———. *The Nebraska Question, 1852–1854.* Lawrence, Kans.: 1953.

McCandless, Perry. *A History of Missouri.* Vol. 2, *1820 to 1860.* Columbia, Mo.: 1972.

McCoy, Drew R. *The Elusive Republic: Political Economy in Jeffersonian America.* Chapel Hill, N.C.: 1980.

McInerney, Daniel J. *The Fortunate Heirs of Freedom: Abolition and Republican Thought.* Lincoln, Nebr.: 1994.

McPherson, James M. *The Negro's Civil War: How American Negroes Felt and Acted during the War for the Union.* New York: 1965.

———. *Ordeal by Fire: The Civil War and Reconstruction.* New York: 1982.

———. *Battle Cry of Freedom: The Civil War Era.* New York: 1988.

Meerse, David E. "Buchanan, the Patronage, and the Lecompton Constitution: A Case Study." *Civil War History* 41 (Dec. 1995): 291–312.

Miller, Rev. George. *Missouri's Memorable Decade, 1860–1870.* Columbia, Mo.: 1898.

Morrison, Michael A. *Slavery and the American West: The Eclipse of Manifest Destiny and the Coming of the Civil War.* Chapel Hill, N.C.: 1997.

Nagel, Paul C. *One Nation Indivisible: The Union in American Thought.* New York: 1964.

Nevins, Allan. *The Emergence of Lincoln.* Vol. 1, *Douglas, Buchanan, and Party Chaos, 1857–1859.* New York: 1950.

———. *Ordeal of the Union.* Vol. 2. New York: 1947.

Nichols, Alice. *Bleeding Kansas.* New York: 1954.

Nichols, Roy F. "The Kansas-Nebraska Act: A Century of Historiography." *Mississippi Valley Historical Review* 43 (Sept. 1956): 187–212.

———. *The Disruption of American Democracy.* New York: 1948.

———. *Franklin Pierce: Young Hickory of the Granite Hills.* Philadelphia: 1958.

Noe, Kenneth W. "Exterminating Savages: The Union Army and Mountain Guerrillas in Southern West Virginia, 1861–1862." In *The Civil War in Appalachia: Collected Essays,* edited by Kenneth W. Noe and Shannon H. Wilson, 104–30. Knoxville: 1997.

Nye, Russel B. *Fettered Freedom: Civil Liberties and the Slavery Controversy: 1830–1860.* East Lansing, Mich.: 1949.

O'Connor, Thomas H. "Cotton Whigs in Kansas." *Kansas Historical Quarterly* 26 (spring 1960): 34–58.

Oakes, James. *The Ruling Race: A History of American Slaveholders.* New York: 1982.

———. *Slavery and Freedom: An Interpretation of the Old South.* New York: 1990.

Oates, Stephen B. *To Purge This Land with Blood: A Biography of John Brown.* New York: 1970.

———. *With Malice toward None: The Life of Abraham Lincoln.* New York: 1977.

Painter, Nell Irvin. *Exodusters: Black Migration to Kansas after Reconstruction.* New York: 1977.

Parrish, William E. *David Rice Atchison of Missouri: Border Politician.* Columbia, Mo.: 1961.

———. *Turbulent Partnership: Missouri and the Union, 1861–1865.* Columbia, Mo.: 1963.

Perry, Lewis. *Radical Abolitionism: Anarchy and the Government of God in Antislavery Thought*. Ithaca, N.Y.: 1973.

Phillips, Christopher. *Missouri's Confederate: Claiborne Fox Jackson and the Creation of Southern Identity in the Border West*. Columbia, Mo.: 2000.

Pocock, J. G. A. *Virtue, Commerce, and History: Essays in Political Thought and History, Chiefly in the Eighteenth Century*. Cambridge, Eng.: 1985.

Porter, Kirk H. *A History of Suffrage in the United States*. New York: 1969.

Potter, David M. *Freedom and Its Limitations in American Life*, edited by Don E. Fehrenbacher. Stanford, Calif.: 1976.

———. *The Impending Crisis, 1848–1861*. New York: 1976.

Quaife, Milo Milton. *The Doctrine of Non-Intervention with Slavery in the Territories*. Chicago: 1910.

Quarles, Benjamin. *The Negro in the Civil War*. Boston: 1953.

———. *Allies for Freedom: Blacks and John Brown*. New York: 1974.

Rawley, James A. *Race and Politics: "Bleeding Kansas" and the Coming of the Civil War*. Lincoln, Nebr.: 1969.

Reid, Brian Holden. *The Origins of the American Civil War*. London: 1996.

Renehan, Edward J., Jr. *The Secret Six: The True Tale of the Men Who Conspired with John Brown*. New York: 1995.

Rhodes, James Ford. *History of the United States from the Compromise of 1850*. Vol. 1, *1850–1854*. 1890. Reprint, New York: 1901.

———. *History of the United States from the Compromise of 1850*. Vol. 2, *1854–1860*. New York: 1900.

Richards, Leonard L. *The Slave Power: The Free North and Southern Domination, 1780–1860*. Baton Rouge: 2000.

Richardson, Robert D., Jr. *Emerson: The Mind on Fire*. Berkeley, Calif.: 1995.

Roediger, David R. *The Wages of Whiteness: Race and the Making of the American Working Class*. London: 1991.

Rosenberg, Morton M. "The Kansas-Nebraska Act in Iowa: A Case Study." *Annals of Iowa* 26 (1964): 436–57.

Rossbach, Jeffrey. *Ambivalent Conspirators: John Brown, the Secret Six, and a Theory of Slave Violence*. Philadelphia: 1982.

Russel, Robert R. "The Issues in the Congressional Struggle over the Kansas-Nebraska Bill, 1854." *Journal of Southern History* 29 (May 1963): 187–210.

Sanborn, F. B. *The Life and Letters of John Brown, Liberator of Kansas, and Martyr of Virginia*. 1885. Reprint, New York: 1969.

Savage, W. Sherman. *Blacks in the West*. Westport, Conn.: 1976.

Schultz, Duane. *Quantrill's War: The Life and Times of William Clarke Quantrill, 1837–1865*. New York: 1996.

SenGupta, Gunja. "Bleeding Kansas." *Kansas History* 24 (winter 2001–2002): 318–41.

———. *For God and Mammon: Evangelicals and Entrepreneurs, Masters and Slaves in Territorial Kansas, 1854–1860*. Athens, Ga.: 1996.

Sewell, Richard H. *Ballots for Freedom: Antislavery Politics in the United States, 1837–1860*. New York: 1976.

————. *A House Divided: Sectionalism and Civil War, 1848–1865.* Baltimore: 1988.

Shankle, George Earlie. *State Names, Flags, Seals, Songs, Birds, Flowers, and Other Symbols.* New York: 1934.

Shenton, James P. *Robert John Walker: A Politician from Jackson to Lincoln.* New York: 1961.

Sheridan, Richard B. "From Slavery in Missouri to Freedom in Kansas: The Influx of Black Fugitives and Contrabands into Kansas, 1854–1865." *Kansas History* 12 (spring 1989): 28–47.

————. "The 1913 Semi-Centennial Memorial Reunion of the Survivors of Quantrill's Raid on Lawrence." *Kansas History* 20 (autumn 1997): 176–91.

Shortridge, James R. *Peopling the Plains: Who Settled Where in Frontier Kansas.* Lawrence, Kans.: 1995.

Silbey, Joel H. "The Surge of Republican Power: Partisan Antipathy, American Social Conflict, and the Coming of the Civil War." In *Essays on American Antebellum Politics, 1840–1860,* edited by Stephen E. Maizlish and John J. Kushma, 199–229. College Station, Tex.: 1982.

[Simpson, Benjamin F.] "Biography of Governor Wilson Shannon." Vol. 3, *Transactions of the Kansas State Historical Society.* Topeka: 1886, 279–83.

Slaughter, Thomas P. *Bloody Dawn: The Christiana Riot and Racial Violence in the Antebellum North.* New York: 1991.

Smith, Elbert B. *The Presidency of James Buchanan.* Lawrence, Kans.: 1975.

Smith, Lacey Baldwin. *Fools, Martyrs, Traitors: The Story of Martyrdom in the Western World.* New York: 1997.

Snider, Denton J. *The American Ten Years' War, 1855–1865.* St. Louis: 1906.

Speer, John. *Life of Gen. James H. Lane, "The Liberator of Kansas" with Corrobative Incidents of Pioneer History.* Garden City, Kans.: 1897.

Spring, Leverett W. *Kansas: The Prelude to the War for the Union.* Boston: 1885.

Stampp, Kenneth M. *America in 1857: A Nation on the Brink.* New York: 1990.

Starr, Stephen Z. *Jennison's Jayhawkers: A Civil War Cavalry Regiment and Its Commander.* Baton Rouge: 1973.

Stauffer, John. *The Black Hearts of Men: Radical Abolitionists and the Transformation of Race.* Cambridge, Mass.: 2002.

Stephanson, Anders. *Manifest Destiny: American Expansion and the Empire of Right.* New York: 1995.

Stephenson, Wendell Holmes. *The Political Career of General James H. Lane.* Topeka, 1930.

Stewart, James Brewer. *Holy Warriors: The Abolitionists and American Slavery.* New York: 1997.

Stratton, Joanna L. *Pioneer Women: Voices from the Kansas Frontier.* New York: 1981.

Summers, Mark W. "Dough in the Hands of the Doughface? James Buchanan and the Untameable Press." In *James Buchanan and the Political*

Crisis of the 1850s, edited by Michael J. Birkner, 68–92. Selinsgrove, Pa.: 1996.

———. *The Plundering Generation: Corruption and the Crisis of the Union, 1849–1861.* New York: 1987.

Taylor, Quintard. *In Search of the Racial Frontier: African Americans in the American West, 1528–1990.* New York: 1998.

Thacher, T. Dwight. "The Leavenworth Constitutional Convention." Vol. 3, *Transactions of the Kansas State Historical Society.* Topeka: 1886, 5–15.

Tise, Larry E. *Proslavery: A History of the Defense of Slavery in America, 1701–1840.* Athens, Ga.: 1987.

Varon, Elizabeth R. *We Mean to Be Counted: White Women and Politics in Antebellum Virginia.* Chapel Hill, N.C.: 1998.

Villard, Oswald Garrison. *John Brown, 1800–1859: A Biography Fifty Years After.* Boston, 1911.

Wakefield, W. H. T. "Squatter Courts in Kansas." Vol. 5, *Transactions of the Kansas State Historical Society.* Topeka: 1896, 71–74.

Waldstreicher, David. *In the Midst of Perpetual Fetes: The Making of American Nationalism, 1776–1820.* Chapel Hill, N.C.: 1997.

Wallenstein, Peter. "Incendiaries All: Southern Politics and the Harpers Ferry Raid." In *His Soul Goes Marching On: Responses to John Brown and the Harpers Ferry Raid,* edited by Paul Finkelman, 149–73. Charlottesville, Va.: 1995.

Walther, Eric H. *The Fire-Eaters.* Baton Rouge: 1992.

Watts, Dale E. "How Bloody Was Bleeding Kansas?: Political Killings in Kansas Territory, 1854–1861." *Kansas History* 18 (summer 1995): 116–29.

Welch, G. Murlin. *Border Warfare in Southeastern Kansas, 1856–1859.* Pleasanton, Kans.: 1977.

Wiebe, Robert H. *Self-Rule: A Cultural History of American Democracy.* Chicago: 1995.

Williamson, Chilton. *American Suffrage: From Property to Democracy, 1760–1860.* Princeton: 1960.

Wilson, Don W. *Governor Charles Robinson of Kansas.* Lawrence, Kans.: 1975.

Wilson, Major L. *Space, Time, and Freedom: The Quest for Nationality and the Irrepressible Conflict, 1815–1861.* Westport, Conn.: 1974.

Winkle, Kenneth J. "Ohio's Informal Polling Place: Nineteenth-Century Suffrage in Theory and Practice." In *The Pursuit of Public Power: Political Culture in Ohio, 1787–1861,* edited by Jeffrey P. Brown and Andrew R. L. Cayton, 169–84. Kent, Ohio: 1994.

———. *The Politics of Community: Migration and Politics in Antebellum Ohio.* Cambridge, Eng.: 1988.

———. *The Young Eagle: The Rise of Abraham Lincoln.* Dallas: 2001.

Wolff, Gerald W. "Party and Section: The Senate and the Kansas-Nebraska Bill." *Civil War History* 18 (Dec. 1972): 293–311.

———. *The Kansas-Nebraska Bill: Party, Section, and the Coming of the Civil War*. New York: 1977.

Wood, Gordon S. *The Creation of the American Republic, 1776–1787*. Chapel Hill, N.C.: 1969.

Woodward, C. Vann. "John Brown's Private War." In *The Burden of Southern History*, 41–68. Baton Rouge: 1960.

Wyatt-Brown, Bertram. "'A Volcano Beneath a Mountain of Snow': John Brown and the Problem of Interpretation." In *His Soul Goes Marching On: Responses to John Brown and the Harpers Ferry Raid*, edited by Paul Finkelman, 10–38. Charlottesville, Va.: 1995.

———. *Southern Honor: Ethics and Behavior in the Old South*. New York: 1982.

———. *The Shaping of Southern Culture: Honor, Grace, and War, 1760s–1890s*. Chapel Hill, N.C.: 2001.

Zarefsky, David. *Lincoln, Douglas, and Slavery: In the Crucible of Public Debate*. Chicago: 1990.

Zornow, William Frank. "The Kansas Senators and the Re-election of Lincoln." *Kansas Historical Quarterly* 19 (May 1951): 133–44.

———. *Kansas: A History of the Jayhawk State*. Norman, Okla.: 1957.